NONVERBAL PERCEPTUAL AND COGNITIVE PROCESSES IN CHILDREN WITH LANGUAGE DISORDERS

Toward a New Framework for Clinical Intervention

NONVERBAL PERCEPTUAL AND COGNITIVE PROCESSES IN CHILDREN WITH LANGUAGE DISORDERS

Toward a New Framework for Clinical Intervention

Félicie Affolter
Walter Bischofberger

With Commentary by
Ida J. Stockman

2000

LAWRENCE ERLBAUM ASSOCIATES, PUBLISHERS
Mahwah, New Jersey
London

Lawrence Erlbaum Associates, Inc., Publishers
10 Industrial Avenue
Mahwah, New Jersey 07430

Cover design by Kathryn Houghtaling Lacey

Library of Congress Cataloging-in-Publication Data

Affolter, Félicie.
  Nonverbal perceptual and cognitive processes in children with language disorders :
Toward a new framework for clinical intervention / Félice Affolter, Walter
Bischofberger ; with commentary by Ida J. Stockman.
   p. cm.
 Includes bibliographical references and indexes.
 ISBN 0-8058-3212-2 (cloth : alk. Paper) – ISBN 0-8058-3213-0 (pbk. : alk. Paper)
  1.   Language disorders in children. 2. Cognition in children. 3. Perception in children. 4.
Seriation by children (Psychology) I. Bischofberger, Walter, 1944- II. Stockman, Ida J.
III. Title

RJ496.L35 A38 2000
618.92'855—dc21   00-034122

Books published by Lawrence Erlbaum Associates are printed on acid-free paper,
and their bindings are chosen for strength and durability.

Printed in the United States of America
10   9   8   7   6   5   4   3   2   1

Contents

Acknowledgments

Our thanks—

To Jean Piaget and Bärbel Inhelder, Affolter's teachers in child psychology at the University of Geneva, Switzerland. She learned from them how to observe children—to wonder, to marvel, and to be amazed about how they develop. Jean Piaget shared and stimulated her interest in the question about the relationship between language and cognition; he supported her comparison studies of deaf and hearing children. He followed her interest beyond academic requirements, and offered her a part-time postgraduate research grant at the Centre d'Epistémologie in Geneva.

To James Jenkins, Affolter's teacher when she was on an exchange postgraduate scholarship at the University of Minnesota and to David Palermo who she also met in Minnesota and who later served on her doctoral committee at Pennsylvania State University. Both of them supported her approach to language and thinking within Piaget's framework, appreciated her way of teaching language in contrast to the concepts of verbal behavior and Skinner's theory of behavior modification, aspects that were popular in the years 1960 to 1970, and which are still in use in clinical work.

To Frank Lassman, Hildred Schuell, and Mildred Templin who as teachers and advisors supported Affolter's clinical interests in disabled children and adults with acquired brain damage.

To Robert Brubaker, Affolter's PhD advisor at Pennsylvania State University, Ida Stockman, and William Franklin. They not only supported her research in perceptual development but were open to a wide range of human and cultural problems and differences.

To August Flammer, Bischofberger's PhD advisor at the University of Fribourg, Switzerland, for showing much interest in his approach to developmental aspects in perception and cognition.

To the Center for Cognitive Sciences at the University of Minnesota, founded in 1963 as Center of Human Learning, with James Jenkins as founding director. When shortly afterwards Affolter met James Jenkins on a visit to Minnesota, she acknowledged the foundation of that Center with a smile, expressing her interest in "switching from studying learning in rats to learning in humans." We both owe much to the Center for Cognitive Sciences and its staff. For 20 successive years each spring, the Center offered us refuge to pursue research. In addition, the staff and students provided us with enjoyable interaction and a stimulating atmosphere. We are especially grateful for the intensive collaboration over many years with Ruth Pitt and Maddy Brouwer-Janse in the field of problem solving, with Patricia Broen and Gerald Siegel in the field of communication disorders, with Herb Pick, Jr.

and Ed Reed in the field of child psychology in the areas of spatial development and the Gibsonian approach, and with Al Yonas in the field of visual perception and its development in young children.

To medical persons in the fields of neurology and pediatrics: Wilhelm Zinn, Director of the Medical Center in Bad Ragaz and the Rehabilitation Clinic in Valens, Switzerland,who supported our work and asked us to join the staff at their Postgraduate Study Center; Ernst Stricker and Georg Kuritzkes-Courcet, who for many years showed interest and participated in our research and publications; Edouard Gautier, Director of the pediatric clinic at the University Hospital of Lausanne, Switzerland, chosen from the Swiss National Science Foundation and Gerhard Weber, chosen from the Swiss Academy of Medical Sciences as advisors for our research projects, and also showed great interest and dynamic support throughout the years.

To Alfred Constam and Urs Gessner for their technical engineering assistance for many years.

To the teams of educators, therapists, and psychologists at the Center and at the School for Children with Perceptual Disorders in St. Gallen at the Cité de Genévrier in Vevey and La Castalie in Monthey, Switzerland, as well as at the Rehabilitation Center in Burgau, Germany, with its Postgraduate Study Center. Many thanks for all of them for their intensive collaboration over many years, an interaction that still goes on.

To the children and their parents at the School for Children with Perceptual Disorders and the patients at the Rehabilitation Clinic in Burgau, for their continuing cooperation and interest in our research.

To the persons who helped us with the manuscript, its content and its style, namely, Ruth Pitt, Maddy Brouwer-Janse, Ida Stockman, Blandine Hogan, Anne Seltz, Meredith Manning, Mary Sell, Alice Tuseth, Elizabeth Shelver, and Dorothy Knight.

To the many persons who supported our writing with secretarial help such as the team at the Office of the Center for Cognitive Sciences at the University of Minnesota.

We express our sincere appreciation to our editors Susan Milmoe and Sondra Guideman with Lawrence Erlbaum Associates for their diligent guidance through the process of publishing our work.

Special thanks, last but not least, to the Bischofberger family, Julia, Matthia, and Helen, Walter's wife, for their support of our work during those many years of teaching, doing clinical work, and research.

To the Swiss National Science Foundation (NSF), which made our research possible by supporting it for 10 years (projects 3.237.69; 3.448.70; 3.902.72; 3.2050.73; 3.504.75; 3.711.76; 3.909.078).

Félicie Affolter
Walter Bischofberger

Introduction: From Product to Process in Investigating Problem Solving in Children With Language Disorders

Ida J. Stockman
Michigan State University

Spoken language is complex human behavior requiring coordination of the sensory, motor, perceptual, cognitive, and social systems. It is not surprising that some children in every culture can have difficulty learning it. When they do, there are usually negative consequences. The children may not participate fully in their cultural groups. Communities also must commit long-term resources to their care because developmental delay shows up early in life. It is known now that some children with language disorders[1] never catch up with their same-age peers, and require life-long dependent support. So there is reason to study abnormal language learners and how to clinically treat them. What has been learned from the explosive expansion of research on developmental language disorders across the past 20 years?

The research literature reveals that virtually no aspect of spoken language is spared from potential delay. Children can be delayed in one or more areas of language including its phonologic, morphosyntactic, semantic, and pragmatic aspects (Johnston, 1982; Lahey, 1988; Miller, 1991; Rice, 1991). Moreover, oral language deficits among preschoolers appear to reflect an underlying continuum of difficulty with symbolic learning because some of them have trouble reading, writing, and doing arithmetic once they are school age and diagnosed as learning disabled (LD; Maxwell & Wallach, 1984; Scholl, 1981; Stark & Tallal, 1988).

However, this book is significant because it converges with a growing body of research that also reveals the coexistence of language disorders with nonverbal deficits. Nonverbal research is concerned with performances that do not require explicit knowledge or use of conventional language for social communication.

---

[1]The term *language disorder* is used synonymously with *language delay* and *language impairment* to denote a difference from normal behavior that warrents clinical intervention. The term *developmental language disorder* refers to the difficulty of acquiring language for the first time and is used in contradistinction to an acquired disorder.

Some children with language disorders can have difficulty with even the mundane daily-life activities of self-care (i.e., dressing, eating, bathing), not to mention poor problem-solving performance on standardized psychometric measures.

The coexistence of nonverbal deficits with language disorders has always been obvious in children along the autistic spectrum who exhibit profound developmental delay. In fact, it is their peculiar nonverbal social, cognitive, and perceptual-motor behaviors that identify the clinical syndrome (Bailey, Phillips, & Rutter, 1996; Goodman, 1989). But it is the revelation that nonverbal deficits also exist in children with less debilitating functioning than is typically associated with autism, which has fueled the research on the nonverbal performances of language-disordered children. Such children are diagnosed with developmental aphasia or more recently, specific language impairment (SLI) because they are assumed to have just a spoken language deficit while exhibiting what appear to be intact functions in other domains, including nonverbal mental ability, as measured by standard intelligence tests. Recent research is revealing that children with SLI present a complex pattern of strengths and weaknesses that include perceptual-motor, conceptual, and problem-solving difficulties. See summaries of this work in Bishop, 1992; Johnston, 1982, 1994; Kamhi, 1993. In some studies, differences between children with normal and disordered language have shown up in the patterns of performance on standard nonverbal intelligence tests even when both groups earn the same scores (Swisher, Plante, & Lowell, 1994). Nonverbal perceptual-cognitive delays also have been observed among children with learning disability (LD), namely those who have difficulty with written language (Rourke, 1989; Stark & Tallal, 1988).

The research described in this book expands existing frameworks for investigating the nonverbal performances of language-disordered children on several fronts. Its content is anchored by an intensive study of their nonverbal performances on the classic Piagetian Seriation task. By observing how normal and clinical populations solve the seriation problem at different ages and under different task conditions, this study does more than simply reveal that nonverbal deficits are associated with language disorders. Its outcomes add to the authors' 4 decades of research and clinical observations, which support a new framework for explaining and treating pervasive developmental delay. Hence, this framework has been evolving in Switzerland for a long time. Still, it is not yet well known, particularly to U.S. audiences. The purpose of these introductory remarks is to orient the reader to the book by situating its focus and content within the stream of contemporary research on the nonverbal performance of children with developmental language disorders. First, existing research paradigms are described and evaluated with an eye toward revealing their limitations relative to the research described in this book. This discussion is followed by an overview of the book's content structure and scope.

EXISTING RESEARCH PARADIGMS

Contemporary scholars have found it fruitful to do nonverbal research for both practical and theoretical reasons. From the practical perspective, nonverbal deficits obviously complicate the clinical picture of language disorders and must be respected in determining the type and range of treatment services needed. In clinical evaluations, nonverbal performance has often turned out to be a better estimate of true learning potential than is the typically weaker verbal area.

On a theoretical front, there is the implicit assumption that nonverbal research can provide clues to the cause of the language difficulty. The reason that some children fail to develop normal language is obvious. There is evidence of deafness, blindness, mental, or motor handicaps due to frank chromosomal, metabolic or structural damage to the nervous system before or at birth. But in most cases, the etiology is unknown. The developmental lag is all the more puzzling, particularly in the case of children along the SLI–LD spectrum because they can see, hear, and move the body at will, and even perform within normal limits on some intelligence tests (Stark & Tallal, 1981b). Moreover, their language deficits cannot be blamed on poor environmental stimulation or socioeconomic disadvantage. Scholars have hoped that this puzzling state of affairs can be explained by an underlying dysfunctional mechanism or process that shows up in the nonverbal performance.

Until recently, the search for a nonverbal psychobehavioral cause of language impairment has outpaced the search for competing linguistic and neurobiological explanations. The Chomskian-inspired linguistic explanation holds that language is served by a special biological module. A developmental language disorder is assumed to result from a primary neurobiological deficit that blocks access to the universal grammar. Consequently, researchers have looked for convergent evidence across different languages that the grammatical systems of language-disordered children (those with SLI, specifically) violate principles of a universal grammar that are believed to be hardwired in the brain (Bishop, 1992, Rice, 1994; Rice, Wexler, & Cleave, 1995). The search for an innate biological basis for language disorders has been spurred on by the evidence for familial genetic tendencies in language-impaired populations (Crago & Gopnik, 1994; Tomblin & Buckwalter, 1994), and the possibility that advances in technology may reveal aberrant brain structure and activity (e.g., see Neville, Coffey, Holcomb, & Tallal (1993).

Nevertheless, the search for a nonverbal psychological or perceptual–cognitive cause of language disorders has not been abandoned. The reason not to do so relates not only to the strength of empirical evidence for competing theoretical claims, but also to their intuitive lack of broad theoretical and clinical appeal (Bishop, 1992; Leonard, 1994). A linguistic explanation does not have broad explanatory appeal because it cannot account for any coexisting nonverbal deficits, not to mention the semantic and pragmatic deficits that so often coexist with grammatical ones. The assumption of innateness also does little or nothing to chart a treatment course beyond describing the linguistic deficits to be remediated. Discovering a neurobiological deficit is not useful either, unless it can be directly shown to have negative behavioral consequences, and such consequences can be eliminated by biomedical intervention. Ultimately then we do not escape the need to do nonverbal behavioral research.

Even as scholars have persisted with the search for nonverbal psychobehavioral causes of language disorder, the present book appears at a time when they sense the need to move beyond the goal of revealing differences between normal and disordered speakers on yet another nonverbal task. Across the past 20 years, numerous nonverbal perceptual and cognitive behaviors have been separately explored as the possible critical link to slow or deviant language growth. See literature reviews on children with SLI (Bishop, 1992; Johnston, 1982, 1994; Kamhi, 1993; Leonard, 1987); LD (Rourke, 1989; Scruggs, 1988; Stark & Tallal, 1988), and those along the autistic spectrum (Frith & Baron-Cohen, 1987; Rutter & Schopler, 1987; Sigman, Ungerer, Mundy, & Sherman, 1987). Studies of perception generally have explored auditory and visual attention, discrimination, and recognition of patterns varying in structural complexity, serial order, content, and meaningfulness. Studies of cognition have documented children's responses to classic Piagetian tasks (e.g., object permanence, symbolic play, visual imagery, conservation). More recently, research has focused on different components of the learning process (e.g., memory, hypothesis testing, inferencing, and so on).

The splinter skill approach to investigation may have left us with too many competing hypotheses to make sense of. As Bishop (1992) acknowledged, "The initial impression striking anyone reviewing the literature on underlying processes in specific language impairment is one of total confusion" (p. 52). Stark and Tallal (1988) observed that the many isolated reports of sensory, perceptual or motor disorders in children with developmental communication problems have been" . . . difficult to integrate due to the lack of a cohesive model or theory on which to rely when interpreting the significance of the results" (p.161). This troubled state of theorizing has led some scholars to recommend abandoning the search for a nonverbal causal mechanism altogether.

A more optimistic view is shared by other scholars who argue that it is time to change the framework for doing nonverbal research (Bishop, 1992; Johnston, 1994; Kamhi, 1993). It is recognized that the investigative framework has been too simplistic in its focus on single nonverbal performances as isolated causes of language disorders, and leaving unexplained why the presumed nonverbal causal deficit exists in the first place. According to Johnston (1994), we need to simultaneously examine the relationships among multiple factors while considering the possibility that a more global aberrant mechanism may underlie both depressed verbal and nonverbal performances. In this respect, the information-processing paradigm is emerging as potentially useful for explaining the research data on both the linguistic and nonlinguistic performances of children with SLI (Johnston, 1994; Kamhi, 1993). This paradigm also has been applied to children with LD (e.g., Rosner, 1981; Stark & Tallal, 1988; Wallach & Libergott, 1984) and autism (e.g., Lincoln, Dickstein, Courchesne, Elmasian & Tallal, 1992; Reed, 1994).

The information-processing paradigm has allowed scholars to partly explain the inconsistent performances among developmentally disordered children; namely, why they do not inevitably exhibit poor performance in every study or on every task within a single study. Their failure and success on verbal and nonverbal tasks within and across different studies are being interpreted in terms of the information-processing demands on doing a task. For example, Johnston (1994) concluded from a literature survey that SLI children seem to do poorly whenever the task taxes memory or requires the processing of rapid, brief temporal information or reliance on internal mental representations. The implication of such an information-processing paradigm for treatment seems straightforward. Clinicians need simply to alter or control the amount of information processed during learning tasks. For example, learning ought to be facilitated by talking slower, stressing or altering the hard-to-perceive speech forms in the speech stream (Merzenich et al., 1996).

To be a viable explanatory framework, however, information processing must be more clearly articulated in further research. For one thing, information cannot be described or studied in absolute terms as if it was isolated from perception and cognition. The very notion of *information* needs to be defined and its role in perception and in cognition delineated.

In the discussion that follows, three limitations of existing research are singled out as challenges to making information processing a workable explanatory paradigm for further research. It is argued first that information must be linked to both perception and to cognition. The second challenge is to expand the view of perception so that it includes tactual–kinesthetic sensory information in addition to the more frequently studied auditory and visual senses. The tactual–kinesthetic senses refer here to dynamic or active touch, which combines tactual and proprioceptive sensory information in exploratory interaction with the environment or, in other words, haptic stimulation (Krueger, 1982, p. 19). The third challenge is to expand the view of cognition beyond knowledge as static end-products of learning to include how information processes are used to construct knowledge in online, problem-solving activity. Each of these three issues is considered in turn.

FROM ISOLATION TO INTEGRATION
OF PERCEPTION AND COGNITION

Whenever the word information is used, what comes to mind are the sense impressions of objects and events that frame a verifiable reality outside of the perceiver's body. So information processing is tied intuitively to sensory–

perceptual processes, but not to cognition, at least as it has been historically viewed.[2] In fact, literature surveys of nonverbal research reveal that the expressed focus of one camp of researchers has been perception, whereas another camp has explicitly identified its focus as cognition, as if the two were unrelated to each other. This is the case even though scholars admit that the taking in of information is not entirely a bottom-up process. It also is a top-down process. What we notice and recognize as information is selectively tuned to what is expected from prior stored experiences or knowledge of the world. Kamhi (1993) observed that nonverbal studies of perception were flawed because "the perception and processing of sensory information is viewed as passive and unaffected by situational factors, knowledge states, and previous experiences of the individual" (p. 629).

The potential relationship between perception and cognition becomes evident whenever we study information processing as a function of the child's age, a global index of the amount of stored experience or accumulated knowledge. Older children with language disorders have been shown to outperform their younger language-matched normal peers on nonverbal tasks involving conceptual–logical judgments. All children just know more as they get older, even when development proceeds slowly. They know some things well enough so that their automatic retrieval from stored experience may help to reduce information load in a given situation. Although age is a factor that inherently influences performance in every study, it is seldom explored as a main variable in a single study of language-disordered children. They typically are studied at one age cross-section at a time.

Fortunately, however, age has been recognized as a factor that can account for disparate outcomes across different studies. For example, age was used to explain the earlier erroneous conclusion that children with SLI exhibit auditory, but not visual temporal processing difficulties (Tallal & Piercy, 1973). Apparently, young SLI children (about 5 years) have difficulty on visual, auditory, and tactual temporal tasks, whereas older ones (about 7 years) may no longer show a deficit on visual tasks (Tallal, Stark, Kallman, & Mellits, 1981). Thus, what counts as a critical information-processing variable at one age may not do so at a different age.

Information processing may be influenced not only by the amount of stored experience or prior knowledge; it also may be influenced by the type of prior experience, as indexed by the child's membership in either a normal or particular type of clinical group. For example, the deaf, the blind and physically handicapped experience the world in different ways. These experiential histories potentially influence what becomes relevant information, and possibly the way information is stored and retrieved. We are likely to learn a lot about which information

---

[2]This qualification recognizes the distinction between cognition viewed traditionally as stored knowledge of concepts, relations, and so on, and cognition as knowledge acquisition processes.

processing variables are relevant to language learning by comparing different clinical subgroups, as Kamhi (1993) proposed ought to be done. But research studies seldom are designed to compare different clinical groups. They most often focus on how a single clinical group compares with normal ones. For example, children with SLI seldom are compared with those along the autistic spectrum, who also present obvious language learning difficulties. Such comparisons can be revealing when they are made. Two decades of research on the auditory perception of mostly SLI children have led us to expect abnormal language to be inevitably associated with depressed performance on nonverbal temporal sequential tasks. In one study (Lincoln et al., 1992), it was shown that SLI children performed significantly poorer than children with normal language at comparable ages on a nonverbal temporal sequencing task, but the autistic children did not. Yet the autistic subjects had language deficits. On the other hand, depressed performance has been observed on a serial ordering task among children with an attention deficit disorder, but no language disorder (Ludlow, Cudahy, Bassick, & Brown, 1983). What are we to make of research findings that reveal an auditory sequencing deficit when there is no language disorder, but the absence of such a processing deficit when a language disorder exists? Such disparate outcomes could mean that temporal sequencing is just one of the information-processing variables relevant to learning language.

The present book alerts us to the possibility that the organization of perceptual activity needs to be conceptualized at different levels in order to account for the broad spectrum of deficits, which is associated with abnormal language learning. Much may be learned about how to frame the hypotheses by comparing different clinical groups who presumably bring different experiences to the processing task, as is done in this book.

EXPANDING THE FRAMEWORK OF PERCEPTION: DELINEATING WHAT IS INFORMATION

The viability of an information-processing framework for studying nonverbal perceptual–cognitive performances requires clarification of what is meant by information. Whenever the word information is used, what readily comes to mind are the task demands narrowly construed as the externally presented features of a stimulus array, for example, the number, rate, and order of stimulus presentation, which an investigator manipulates, and typically presents aurally or visually. Such stimulus features are undoubtedly important to perception. Elegant studies have shown that the nonverbal performances of language-disordered children are systematically influenced by the temporal duration, rate, and sequence of stimulus events (Stark & Tallal, 1988; Tallal et al., 1981; Weismer & Hesketh, 1996); the number and complexity of stimulus events (Johnston & Smith, 1989; Montgomery, 1993; Stark & Tallal, 1988); the frequency of stimulus events (Rice, Oetting,

Marquis, Bode, & Pae, 1994); the novelty or familiarity of stimulus events (Weismer & Hesketh,1996), and so on.

The focus on externally presented stimulus variables in isolation of their sensory modality of presentation suggests that information can be passively handed over in a direct way from the outside to the child perceiver. But this book sensitizes us to the view that externally manipulated task demands in a stimulus array translate into information only to the extent that the perceiver actively searches for and senses it via some sensory channel, although the search for information must be constrained by the structure of the external stimulus events. In this view, information is neither entirely in the perceiver nor in the external stimulus events. It is the product of both aspects.

The view that sensory modality and stimulus complexity are separate aspects of task demands is well supported whenever performances are compared on tasks with analogous complexity in different sensory modalities. The same task variables may depress performance in one sensory modality but not another. For example, Tallal and Piercy (1973) observed that older children with SLI exhibited depressed performance on temporal sequences presented in the auditory but not the visual modality. More recently, Montgomery (1993) showed that SLI children exhibited depressed performance relative to normal language learners on a shape discrimination task presented in the tactual modality, but not on the same task presented in a cross-modal, tactual–visual task. In most studies, however, sensory modality and task complexity are confounded in specifying task demand by studying performance in a single modality, typically the visual or auditory one. When this happens, we do not know how much of the performance outcome is due to the sensory modality of presentation or to the stimulus complexity of the task. Presenting a task in different sensory modalities could yield different performance outcomes, as is shown by studies described in this book.

Another reason to study performances in different sensory modalities stems from the assumption that the modalities do not offer equivalent information about the world. If all sensory modalities were biologically equipped to provide identical information about the environment, then we might wonder why so many sensory channels are needed. The differential consequences of blindness or deafness make clear that the senses have different work to do. Deafness clearly denies easy access to a spoken language. It does not prevent acquisition of a conventional nonoral language or adaptive nonverbal cognitive–social intelligence. Some congenitally deaf persons even acquire spoken language. Blindness alone does not deny access to a spoken language code or to adaptive cognitive–social behavior, despite the longer time needed to achieve some skills. On the other hand, most children with developmental language disorders do not experience either auditory or visual sensory deprivation. They can see and hear. Still they fail to develop language adequately or easily in any form. At the same time, they exhibit varying degrees of difficulty on a nonverbal level that can show up in the routine daily-life activities of behaving adaptively at home, school , and play. This common observation, just on its face, suggests intuitively that neither auditory nor visual input alone can be the critical link to normal development.

Alternatively, this book foregrounds the tactual modality as a critical source of information about the world. This hypothesis follows from Affolter and Bischofberger's emphasis on *interaction* as the principal theoretical construct in their developmental model. Interaction involves changes of topological relationships between the body and environment that occur with mutual physical contact, as when one touches and changes the environment in a causative act. Again the information is neither in just the sensory receptors (the body) nor in the structure of the external environment. Affolter and Bischofberger argue that the information source is between the body and the environment at the point of contact. They view such experiences with nonverbal interactions in daily events as the root of development. Interaction experiences presumably lead to knowledge of causes and effects and to more adequate organization of perceptual activity when searching for information. Consequently, Affolter and Bischofberger trace the abnormal development of children with language disorders to inadequate nonverbal interaction experiences. Such interactions are inadequate when a child's search for information is poorly organized, given a deficit in sensing tactual input or integrating it with other sensory input, or sequencing sensory input in time and space.

The role of the tactual sensory system in perceptual–cognitive development is not well understood as it has been less often studied than the auditory and visual senses. Even when studied, the tactual modality is narrowly viewed as the one that provides information about object texture, temperature, pain, and as a complement to more basic visual information about shape, size, space, and so on. In other words, the focus is on the kind of tactual information that could be dismissed as marginal or secondary to visual or auditory information in a developing perceptual–cognitive system. On the contrary, it is argued in this book that the tactual modality is a dynamic sensory system that transforms and shapes the critical information from which cause–effect knowledge of the world is constructed. This important consequence of tactual sensory input is not what usually comes to mind when its role in knowledge acquisition is considered.

EXPANDING THE VIEW OF NONVERBAL COGNITION: FROM PRODUCT TO PROCESS IN PROBLEM SOLVING

An explanatory framework ought not be built around an information-processing paradigm in which the role of cognition is not articulated. Doing so requires that the narrow focus on cognition be expanded to include more than just the already acquired mental representation of experiences. It must include knowledge of acquisition processes, if the goal is to understand how or why people learn and behave as they do. The learning process unites perception and cognition in ways that make information processing particularly relevant to problem solving.

Problem solving often is viewed as the *sine qua non* of the learning process. Problems create the possibility for elaborating existing knowledge. They arise when one has goals to achieve, but is not sure about how to attain them (Holyoak, 1990, p. 118). Problem solving can be characterized as "search" involving activities or operations leading to a resulting end state or solution. Just how information input is used to solve nonverbal problems is an important question to raise. However, it is a question that nonverbal research on developmental language disorders has typically not been designed to answer. Few studies early on were designed to foreground nonverbal problem solving or the learning process in children with language disorders (Miller, 1984). Instead, nonverbal cognitive research documented already acquired knowledge, as measured by success scores on tasks that informed about Piaget's sensorimotor, preoperational, and concrete operational stages of mental function. See studies of children along the SLI–LD continuum. See reviews of children with SLI (Bishop, 1992; Kamhi, 1981), and of children along the autistic spectrum (Sigman et al., 1987). This goal was useful for revealing that nonverbal delays existed among children with language disorders, but it did not move us closer to understanding how or why children performed as they did.

More recent studies have moved closer to problem solving by emphasizing learning mechanisms, such as hypothesis testing, analogical reasoning, and so on (Bishop, 1992; Johnston, 1988; Kamhi, 1993). These "learning" oriented studies have not gone far enough either. They too have focused on the end state of problem solving, as described by success scores on tasks or the type of strategy or solution used to solve the problem. They have not been concerned with the online activities or process used to reach the solutions.

This narrow focus on the static products of problem-solving activity undoubtedly has followed from another limitation of learning-focused research; namely, the failure to study problem solving as an holistic process that involves interrelated activities and processes. Some studies have focused on hypothesis testing (Kamhi, Catts, Koening, & Lewis, 1984; Kamhi, Nelson, Lee, & Gholson, 1985, Weismer, 1991). Others have focused on analogical reasoning (Kamhi, Gentry, Mauer, & Gholson, 1990), planning (Kamhi, Ward, & Mills, 1995), memory (Kirchner & Klatzky, 1985), rule induction (Kiernan, Snow, Swisher, & Vance, 1997), and so on. This fragmented approach is the consequence of failing to foreground the problem-solving process itself. Instead the components of problem-solving process, although in the foreground, have been treated as separate and isolatable nonverbal skills.

This fragmented approach must be abandoned in order to study problem solving as the holistic process that no doubt fits with the reality of everyday life. The problem-solving process in daily-life events is likely to converge multiple perceptual and cognitive subsystems that include the separate skills studied in isolation (Holyoak, 1990; Miller, 1984; Rowe, 1985). In other words, any one problem-solving event considered as a total process involves hypothesis generation, testing, evaluation, inferencing , and so on.

This book orients us to the possibility that the function and type of sensory information used might vary with the particular stage of problem-solving activity. Sensory information must be extracted to judge that there is a problem to be solved or a goal to be achieved; that is, decide whether the situation fits with stored expectancies about the nonverbal event. In ordinary daily-life experiences, one may rely on visual or auditory information to detect that a problem exists. For example, seeing milk or a broken glass on the floor is all that may be required to judge that something is wrong or a problem exists. But visual information about changed object properties—shape, size, and so on is not all that is needed to generate or execute plans for acting on the situation, for example, to remove the broken glass. In order to act and change the situation, one needs to draw on already stored information about causative actions and effects along with the information that is sensed online in the actual situation. In this book, it is argued that the most critical information about causes and effects is of a tactual kind. This input is experienced as changes of resistances that arise from eliciting changes of topological relationships between the body and the environment during nonverbal interactions of daily-life events. Given that problem solving involves so many aspects, it is possible that children may be more adequate on some than others. Failure to solve one or another problem may vary with the kind of information to which they have access. Observing the whole problem-solving process may lead to insight about if and where the information processing breaks down, given the input limitations created by a tactually anchored perceptual deficit.

Understandably, it is difficult to observe the actual online events involved in problem-solving activity. The usual point-and push-button response methods, which have been used to study problem solving so far, do not offer much overt behavior to observe. The subjects do not move. They look and listen. Responses to distant auditory and visual effects created by researchers' interactions are observed. Consequently the problem-solving process must be inferred from covert rather than overt activity. However, nonverbal problem solving in real situations does not involve such passive receptive activity. At the earliest stages of development, in particular, children's nonverbal problem-solving activity is reflected in their overt physical interactions with the environment. Research studies have not been designed to observe what happens during such events. Overcoming this methodological bias requires observation of performance on tasks that permit direct observation of the child's physical engagement with the environment during the problem-solving moment.

Lederman and Klatsky (1987) suggested that haptic tasks provide a window into how the mind works. Such recognition tasks offer an opportunity to observe children's manual activity, as they feel unseen physical forms in a stimulus array and then attempt to match what is felt with a comparison form that is seen or felt. Haptic tasks have been used to study abnormal language learners (Kamhi, 1981; Kamhi et al., 1984; Montgomery, 1993), but their actual manual exploratory activity during the task was not described. This is because researchers have been concerned with success scores or the end goal of solving a problem under one or another task condition and not with the process (the activities) by which children solve the problem. As a result, little is known about the physical exploratory patterns of the language disordered even in a laboratory situation, not to mention natural situations.

However, the research described in this book relies on precedent-setting methodology for coding manual exploratory activity during problem-solving processes. The outcomes of such exploration may provide us with a better vantage point for understanding the nature of nonverbal deficits in language-disordered children with respect to information processes.

THE STRUCTURE AND SCOPE OF THE BOOK

The foregoing analyses of the limitations of existing research leave us with the sense that new studies are needed. In particular, studies are needed that can pave the way for fresh and broader frameworks within which to shape further understanding of the nature of developmental learning disorders and their clinical intervention.

The ideas presented in this book can potentially revitalize the framework for studying the nonverbal performances of children with language disorders. Its focus on information processes in relation to perceptual and cognitive aspects of nonverbal performance coincides with the prior and current research zeitgeist. It converges with prior research by providing additional evidence that language-disordered children present nonverbal perceptual–cognitive differences relative to normal language learners. But it goes beyond this outcome by focusing simultaneously on the performance effects of multiple variables that often have been explored in a piecemeal fashion in other studies, if at all. The overarching aim of the book is to present the evolution and description of a new theoretical framework of perceptual–cognitive development within which language disorders can be understood and a treatment course mapped out. The empirical basis for the framework and its clinical implications are laid out in three chapters.

The first chapter, "The Problem," provides an historical overview of the succession of research studies and clinical observations that led to the principal assumptions of the theoretical framework. The findings from three sets of studies are summarized briefly, as they have been previously described elsewhere. Perceptual performances at different age cross-sections were measured by a

Successive Pattern Recognition task in the first set of studies , and by a Form Recognition or haptic task in the second set. Each task was presented under different sensory modality and stimulus complexity conditions. The performances of normal children were compared at comparable ages to those of children with congenital deafness or blindness (the sensory deprived groups), and to those with language disorders and no hearing or visual impairment. A third research project involved the longitudinal study of language-disordered children in formal and informal, naturalistic observation conditions.

The working hypotheses and assumptions of the theoretical framework that were yielded by the earlier research were formally tested in a fourth study of the Seriation problem-solving task. This is possibly one of the most comprehensive studies of the classic Piagetian Seriation task ever done. This task required children to vertically arrange rectangular bars by physically placing them in order of increasing or decreasing lengths. The study was not motivated by the hypothesis that a seriation deficit per se is a single causal mechanism underlying children's nonverbal or verbal deficits. Instead, the seriation problem was merely the context for examining information processing constraints on nonverbal problem-solving activity. This previously unpublished Seriation study is described at length in the second chapter of this book.

Thus, chapter 2 describes the precedent-setting methodology used to investigate problem solving in the Seriation study. The multidimensional research design reflects the expanded methodological framework called for by many scholars. Age, group membership, sensory modality, and stimulus complexity were explored as independent variables in a complex experimental design. These four causal variables reflect the assumed relevance to performance of the amount of stored experience, as indexed by age, the type of stored experience, as indexed by the child's membership in a normal or particular type of clinical group, the type of sensory information, as indexed by the same child's performance on the Seriation task in the visual, tactual, or tactual-visual modalities, and the complexity of the stimuli, as indexed by the number of the bars arranged in the Seriation task.

The Seriation study also represents a significant methodological precedent. Unlike earlier studies, it focused on more than the end products of performance as measured quantitatively by success scores and/or qualitatively by the types of strategies used to do a task. It also applied a method for observing and coding the children's overt physical activities during the online solving of the seriation problem. A think-aloud verbal protocol which has been used to study the adult problem-solving process was adapted to code children's manual problem-solving activities. The methodological procedure also permitted observation of behaviors to be structured to reflect problem solving as an holistic process, which includes related components such as hypothesis generating, testing, evaluating, as well as planning and inferencing, all of which have been studied as isolated components in prior research.

Consequently, the outcomes of the Seriation study involved many quantitative and qualitative analyses of the data. The analyses were structured to reveal first how the variables of age, group membership, sensory modality, and stimulus complexity differentially influenced success or nonsuccess on the Seriation task (quantitative analysis), and then how they affected the problem-solving activities and solutions used (qualitative analyses). It is the microanalysis of physical behaviors exhibited during the process of trying to solve the seriation problem that makes this study stand out in particular. Here performance is described at the behavioral level of handling the stimulus bars, which involves touching, embracing, displacing, releasing, and comparing them. We leave the chapter with a strong sense that performance on the Seriation task is variable across normal and clinical children. Even the same child's response to the Seriation task varies as a function of sensory information and stimulus complexity.

The results of the empirical observations link information processing to nonverbal perceptual–cognitive deficits in ways that hold strong implications for clinical intervention practices for remediating abnormal nonverbal and verbal behaviors. The theoretical and clinical implications of the findings are discussed in the third chapter. They are integrated with other findings to weave a broad framework within which to view normal development, the diagnosis and treatment of abnormal development, and recovery from acquired brain damage in adults. Within this information-dependent framework, sensory input in the actual situation becomes a critical information variable, which together with prior cognitive knowledge and task complexity, are argued to shape response patterns. The amount and type of all sensory information are viewed as important. But the tactual–kinesthetic system is clearly singled out as playing a critical role in effecting the physical interaction needed to experience causative acts and their effects. Physical causality undergirds the nonverbal problem-solving experiences that support perceptual and cognitive development. Context-dependent variation in the complexity of the stimuli and in the amount and type of sensory information help to account for if and how perceptual–cognitive knowledge or competence is expressed in normal or clinical populations in a given situation.

Affolter and Bischofberger propose a treatment framework that is unmistakably rooted in a Piagetian constructionist view of mind. But their perspective reflects a neopiagetian or contemporary constructionist view. It is reflected in the attempt to model the information processes of nonverbal interaction events in terms of online performance requirements in actual learning situations. This goal has a broad theoretical kinship to dynamic systems view of motor development (Thelen & Smith, 1994), the structure of event representation (Nelson, 1986), and resource dependent models of attention (Bloom, 1996; Kahneman, 1973). One leaves the chapter with specific recommendations for how to take information into account when intervening clinically with disorders in children and in adults with acquired brain injury. The treatment approach challenges the assumption that new learning can be achieved primarily by giving visual–auditory observation and imitating clinician-modeled behavior. The concept of physical or manual guiding is introduced as an alternative strategy for helping a child to become more adequate in the search for information when interacting to solve the problems of daily events.

Finally, the implications chapter summarizes research in progress, which supports the efficacy of intervention framework, as advocated in this book. It also hints at the kind of future research that can be done to further validate the theoretical framework of interaction, as presented in the book.

Given that the nonverbal performances of children with language disorders were emphasized in this book, little discussion was devoted directly to language. Therefore, the final chapter or Epilogue focuses on the implications of Affolter and Bischofberger's framework for understanding the nature of developmental language disorders in children. Nonverbal research has been motivated specifically by the possibility that it may lead to insights about the nature of language disorders in children. It is relevant, if not necessary, to raise the question of whether the theoretical framework of development as put forth in this book can account for the language deficits described in past research or provide new directions for future research. Retrospective and prospective views are taken in responding to this question.

CHAPTER ONE

The Problem

This book describes research on problems we observed during 40 years of working with a variety of clinical populations. Many questions emerged from our observations of children with hearing loss, children with severe difficulties in the acquisition of language, deaf–blind children, adults with acquired brain damage, and elderly adults with degenerative diseases of the nervous system.

Our intervention work began with hearing-impaired children. After a time, hearing children were also referred to our clinical center because of their difficulties in acquiring language. This was not a homogeneous group. For those who came there were many diagnoses: autism, emotional disturbances, behavior disorders, hyperactivity, attention deficit, and so on. We called them children with language disorders because the language acquisition problem was in the foreground for the professionals who referred them to us, and they were classified as "language-disordered" by the Swiss government. This volume focuses on children with language acquisition problems. They became a special concern in our clinical work because their language deficits were puzzling to us. The deficits could not be accounted for by hearing loss. Across time, we also came to realize the extent of the children's additional nonverbal difficulties.

To learn more about these difficulties, we compared children with language disorders to children with congenital deafness and to those with normal hearing and language. Affolter (1954) observed that deaf children did not differ from normally developing children in their nonverbal performances, but children with language disorders did. Although hearing-impaired children's difficulty with acquiring oral language could be accounted for by their hearing loss, this was not the case for children with language disorders. Because most children with language disorders could hear, we asked why they fail to acquire language like other children with no hearing loss.

We observed the behavior of children with language disorders in natural settings. When they walked up the stairs to enter our center, their movements seemed stiff and awkward. This was in contrast to walking up familiar stairs such as those in their own homes. When they shook hands in greeting, they were unable to meet our gaze. Some were clumsy playing with toys; some moved rapidly and superficially from toy to toy; some merely sat motionless in their parents' laps or in a corner of the waiting room.

We also collected, tested, and analyzed data in a more systematic and formal way. In addition to their language problems, these children showed poorer performance than both normal and hearing-impaired children on such nonverbal tasks as: imitation of movements, reconstruction of three-dimensional patterns, and analysis of spatial relationships when reproducing complex figures. Even when they could classify graphic presentations of geometric forms, they were not able to classify pictures that represented events (Affolter, Brubaker, & Bischofberger, 1974). We asked ourselves if there was a relationship between these children's language deficits and their nonverbal difficulties. If the answer was yes, we wondered how the relationship then could be described, and, ultimately, we wanted to determine what kind of treatment would be effective.

To answer such questions, we began our own research in 1970. The first 10 years were financed by the Swiss National Science Foundation. The research became a part of our work at a center for children with hearing impairment and children with severe developmental language delays and nonverbal behavioral problems—the rest of which consisted of clinical evaluation and intervention. The interrelationship between our clinical and research work remained strong over many years—each influencing the other. We drew on the research to answer clinical questions and used the clinical setting to test research hypotheses and findings.

To carry out our research agenda, it was also necessary to investigate normal learning and development so as to have a reference point for abnormal learners. Comparative observations of normal and clinical groups have long been viewed as fruitful for learning more about both normal development and clinical pathology. More than 100 years ago, Jackson (1884) argued that the organization of the brain normally develops in levels during childhood, and that brain damage causes a regression of that acquired organization. The regression appears to affect levels in reverse order of the acquired sequence; the most complex levels are affected before less complex ones. This suggests that developmental data collected on normal children ought to fit observations of persons with acquired brain damage. Conversely, we expected our observations of persons with developmental and acquired language disorders to contribute to knowledge about normal development.

The research program included developmental studies of both cross-sectional and longitudinal types. Cross-sectional studies were structured around a standard set of perceptual–cognitive tasks that could be administered uniformly to a large number of subjects in different populations across a wide age range. In each cross-sectional study, normal subjects were compared, on the same tasks, to subjects from different clinical populations. Successive Pattern Recognition tasks were used in the first cross-sectional perceptual study. Form Recognition tasks were used in the second study, and Seriation tasks were used in the third study. In these studies, tasks were presented, under different complexity and sensory modality conditions, to each child.

Longitudinal studies included observations of children with language disorders. The children were periodically evaluated on a range of verbal and nonverbal skills that represent commonly observed milestones in development such as the emergence of direct imitation or the utterance of first words (see Affolter & Stricker, 1980). All skills had been studied in normal children as well, and many have been described by Piaget in numerous books. The data consisted of naturalistic and test observations.

As the research findings accumulated, it became clear that our data did not support the existing developmental model of hierarchical dependent levels, or for that matter, any other model described in the literature. So we had to find a new model of development. This book presents the evolution of the theoretical and clinical intervention model, that emerged from our research. We take the reader step by step through different stages of the research, with each stage focusing on a new question. The questions for each new study came out of the previous set of studies. They were related to contradicting and supporting data of those studies.

In chapter 1, we summarize the findings of the first two cross-sectional studies and then the longitudinal studies. This research is presented briefly here, as it is described in greater detail in other publications. In chapter 2, we offer a detailed description of the cross-sectional developmental study of seriation performances, as this book provides the first published description of this work. The Seriation study represented a culminating and important point in the research. It was designed to test, empirically, a number of working assumptions that emerged from earlier cross-sectional and longitudinal studies in support of our model.

Throughout the book, we refer to our current research project on babies. The questions being addressed in this latter project followed from the findings of the Seriation study. The Seriation study had been based on normal and language-disordered children in the age range of 3 to 19 years. The findings revealed deviant nonverbal performance profiles for children with language disorders throughout this age range. The profiles suggested that the deviancy may go back to difficulties already observable on a sensorimotor level of development before 18 months of age. Thus, in the new study now in progress (see Section 3.4), 0- to 18-month-old normal babies are being observed and videotaped in natural settings. We refer to some of these observations as needed to clarify claims made in the book.

1.1   THE FRAMEWORK: INITIAL WORKING ASSUMPTIONS

We wanted to answer two fundamental questions, if and how the verbal and nonverbal difficulties were related in children with language disorders. To answer these questions, our earliest research was guided by the assumptions underlying a model of hierarchically dependent levels of development. We set out to reveal how the verbal and nonverbal behavior of the children with language disorders fit into Piaget's hierarchical developmental model in particular. This model was familiar to us and it appeared to fit our clinical experience at that time. Piaget (1936/1952) made two important assumptions.

First, Piaget assumed that skills develop in levels. At a given level of development, skills are interrelated. For example, babies around 18 months typically exhibit several new performances. They begin to understand the meaning of words referring to past or future events, to understand fiction, such as pretending to be asleep by closing the eyes, and to understand actions represented in pictures. Piaget (1945/1962) described such performances as interrelated and part of a general semiotic function. Our own formal and informal observations of children with language disorders supported this expectation. They showed both verbal and nonverbal difficulties in understanding fiction, in pretending and understanding actions represented in pictures, and in understanding past and future events expressed by words. In short, they presented difficulties in all semiotic performances (Affolter, Brubaker, & Bischofberger, 1974).

Second, Piaget assumed that developmental levels were hierarchically dependent, that is, skills at a lower level were considered prerequisites for the emergence of skills at a higher level. We argued: Failure of skills at a higher level could be of a primary or secondary kind of failure. If no skills at lower levels were failed, but only skills at a higher level, they could be considered to be primary. However, if skills at a lower and a higher level were failed, it was concluded that failures at the higher level were secondary, failures at the lower level primary. Treatment had to focus on primary difficulties. Thus, it became important to know at what level primary failures were observable. We reasoned that language is the most complex performance that children acquire (Affolter, 1968; Piaget, 1963). Consequently, language performance is characteristic of the highest level of development. Performances that develop before language acquisition begins belong to less complex levels of development. If language acquisition is disordered, this disorder may be of a primary or secondary kind. To decide, one has to evaluate skills a child begins to develop at lower levels preceding language acquisition. If no skills at lower levels were failed, failures in language acquisition could be considered primary and treated directly. If skills at lower levels were deficient, these deficiencies could be considered primary, with failures in language acquisition as secondary. Treatment had to focus on the primary difficulties.

Among skills developing on lower levels preceding language acquisition, we focused on perceptual skills. Our clinical work with children with hearing impairment corroborated a well-known fact; namely, an early profound hearing loss typically prevents children from perceiving speech well enough to develop an adequate oral language. Other observations fed the hypothesis that perceptual skills may be important prerequisites for language development. These observations came from a pilot study of nonverbal skills of 4- to 10-year-old children with language disorders (Affolter, Brubaker, & Bischofberger, 1974). We analyzed the nonverbal tasks used in terms of their perceptual prerequisites. These analyses revealed that some children with language disorders had particular difficulty with performing tasks, requiring them to rely on tactual information. Such tasks included those that required them to insert puzzle parts into a shape board or to string beads. Other children had difficulty performing tasks such as imitating gestures, which required visual–tactual information or performing tasks that required the integration of sequences, as in the case of constructing building block towers (see Affolter, 1987/1991). Such findings further supported the hypothesis that different perceptual processes may be prerequisites to language acquisition.

With this hypothesis in mind, we turned to Piaget's assumption of hierarchical levels and argued, as follows: Perceptual performances develop to a critical level before language is discovered, and continue to develop throughout the period of language acquisition (Affolter, 1968, 1970). That period appears to last up to 14 years in children (Menyuk, 1971). If developmental levels are hierarchically dependent, then perceptual disorders can be considered to be the primary difficulty, and language disorders the secondary one when both perceptual and language performances are disordered. Thus, we formulated our first research hypothesis: Children with language disorders may fail in verbal and nonverbal performances at higher levels of development because they fail in perceptual performances characteristic of lower levels of development. We tested this basic assumption by investigating improvement of perceptual skills within the age range of 3 to 14 years, the time period spanning the critical stages of language acquisition. We focused first on normal children, then on children with severe congenital hearing or visual impairment, then on children with language disorders in the absence of hearing or visual loss.

1.2   DEVELOPMENT OF PERCEPTUAL SKILLS

To study developmental changes in perceptual skills, we designed standard tasks that varied in stimulus complexity, and could be presented under different sensory modality conditions in a uniform way across different age cross-sections.

   1. *Stimulus complexity:* The focus on stimulus complexity was inspired by Piaget's (1961/1969) discussion of perceptual mechanisms in which perceptual activity and its organization were differentiated. Piaget pointed out that the environment is structured, but that the structure of the environment is not perceived directly. To perceive it, Piaget (1947/1950, 1961/1969) insisted that the perceiver has to organize the input in an active way. Such organization is learned by the child and improves with age. Because such organization develops over time, the child will be able to deal adequately first with just simple structures, and later on with more complex ones. In general, Piaget's theory meant that children of increasing age can successfully deal with an increasing degree of complexity of stimuli. This assumption could be supported by showing that children at different ages give different responses to tasks of varying stimulus complexity.

   2. *Modality conditions:* We presented analogous tasks at similar complexity levels in the auditory, visual, and tactual modalities. Different sensory modalities were assumed to contribute to spoken language acquisition. It is known that children with profound hearing impairment fail to acquire oral language because they lack auditory input. Children with blindness are delayed in language acquisition (Fraiberg, 1977; Mills, 1993) because they cannot perceive the visual cues of speech signals. Children with language disorders without hearing or visual loss appear to have tactual or visual–tactual or sequential processing difficulties (Affolter, Brubaker, & Bischofberger, 1974).

1.2.1   Cross-Sectional Studies of Perceptual
Development in Normal Children

We designed Successive Pattern Recognition tasks and Form Recognition tasks to study perceptual development and the difficulties of children with language disorder in the first two cross-sectional studies.

Tasks were designed to meet several criteria, including the following:

- Refer to perceptual processing (i.e., be of a recognition kind with minimal demands on memory).
- Require a search for relevant information and provide feedback during the task instruction–learning process.
- Offer successive items or spatial features on different levels of complexity.
- Be testable in different modality conditions.

To study the difficulties of sequential processing of children with language disorders, we designed Successive Pattern Recognition tasks to meet the described criteria.

1.2.1.1 Successive Pattern Recognition in Normal Children

First we studied normal children to investigate the development of Successive Pattern Recognition.

1.2.1.1.1 Procedures.
Four series of patterns of increasing complexity were created and presented to 250 normal children in the age range of 4 to 14 years. Each child was tested individually and had to judge whether two consecutive patterns were the same or different. The number of elements in a pattern increased from one element per pattern (Series 1) to two, three, and four elements per pattern (Series 2, 3, and 4, respectively, as shown in Table 1.1).

Patterns were presented in the visual, auditory, and vibro-tactile[1] modalities. The stimulus features differed in two dimensions: two levels of intensity and frequency for the auditory patterns, two levels of brightness and color for the visual patterns, and two levels of intensity and two places of stimulation for the vibro-tactile patterns (see Table 1.2). All children included had been screened on perceiving the stimulus dimensions in the various modalities (i.e., intensities, colors, frequencies, and locations).

Instruction for Successive Pattern Recognition tasks consisted of five training items. Each item included two consecutive patterns, a standard pattern and a comparison pattern as shown in Table 1.1 for Series 1 to 4. After each item was presented, the children had to indicate (by speaking

---

[1]The term *tactile* refers to a kind of passive perception, as in Successive Pattern Recognition, where the child could feel the vibro-tactile stimuli without actively moving the fingers. The term *tactual* refers to a more active kind of perception, such as required in Form Recognition tasks, where the child has to actively explore the forms (see Section 1.2.1.2).

TABLE 1.1
Standard and comparison Patterns for the successive Pattern Recognition Tasks

| | *Series* | | | | | | |
| | 1 | | 2 | | 3 | | 4 | |
Item	SP	CP	SP	CP	SP	CP	SP	CP
1	R	R	gG	gG	gGG	gGg	RRrR	RRrR
2	R	G	RR	GG	Rrg[1]	Rrg	RRRR[1]	gggg
3	G	G	gr	Gr	Ggg	GGG	RGrR	RGrR
4	G	g	Gg	gG	grG	grG	GRGG[1]	RRGG
5	g	g	rr	rr	gGg[1]	rRr	RgRG	rgRG
6	G[1]	r	gg[1]	RR	RRR	RRR	ggGG	ggGG
7	g	r	GG	GG	Rgg[1]	Rgg	GrrG[1]	rGGr
8	R	r	Rg	Rg	gGG	GGG	grgg	grrg
9	r	r	GR	gr	Rrr	Rrr	RGRR[1]	RGRR
10	R	g	gr	GG	Rgg	ggR	rggr	grrg
11	R	R	gG	gG	gRg[1]	gRg	gGgG	gGgG
12	R	G	RR	GG	GgG	GgG	GGGG	gggg
13	G	G	gR	Gr	RGg	RgG	grGr	grGr
14	G	g	Gg	gG	gGr	rGr	gRgr	gRgr
15	g	g	rr	rr	rGr[1]	rGr	grRG	Grrg
16	G[1]	r	gg[1]	RR	rrg	grr	GgGG	ggGG
17	g	r	GG	GG	GgR	gGR	gGGg	GggG
18	R	r	Rg	Rg	rrr[1]	ggg	GgGg	RrrR
19	r	r	GR	gr	ggG	ggG	rGrG	rGrG
20	R	g	gr	GG	ggR	GrG	rRRR	RRRR
21					grr	rgr	RRRR	RRRR
22					rgg[1]	rgg	rggg	gggr
23					ggg	ggr	gGGG	gGGG
24					GRG	RGR	gGgg	gGGg

Note. From Affolter & Stricker, 1980, Table 30, pp. 142-143. Reprinted with permission of the publisher and the authors.
SP = Standard pattern; CP = Comparison pattern; R = bright red, or loud 500 Hz, or strong 125 Hz right thumb; r = dim red, or soft 500 Hz, or weak 125 Hz right thumb; G = bright green, or loud 1000 Hz, or strong 125 Hz right middle finger; g = dim green, or soft 1000 Hz, or weak 125 Hz right middle finger.
[1]Criterion items for continuation of testing. See text for discussion

or by gestures) if the patterns were the same or different. Critical dimensions were never pointed out to the children. Examiners acknowledged a correct response by saying "yes," or saying "no" for an incorrect one. This instructional approach allowed us to determine whether children could search for and select the relevant information on their own without being told what to look for. Such performance is typical of daily-life situations in which children have to evaluate stimuli and discriminate relevant from irrelevant ones in a spontaneous active way (see more details about the procedures in Affolter, 1970; Affolter, Brubaker, Stockman, Constam, & Bischofberger, 1974; Affolter & Stricker, 1980).

TABLE 1.2
Description of Stimuli for Successive Pattern Recognition Tasks

Modality Conditions	Dimensions			
	Intensity		Frequency/Location	
visual	dim	bright	red	green
auditory	soft (- 5dB)	loud (+ 5dB)	500 Hz	1000 Hz
Vibro-tactile	weak(- 3dB)	strong (+ 3dB)	thumb	middle finger

We expected the number of correct responses to decrease from Series 1 to 4 in all modalities (series effect), and to increase in all modalities as the children got older (age effect). We assumed that the pattern of the increase reflected development in the organization of perceptual activity as described next.

1.2.1.1.2 Results. The results revealed:

• Instruction: Children were able to learn the tasks with the instruction provided.

• A significant age main effect: The children showed a larger number of correct responses to all modality conditions as age increased. They were first successful in recognizing short successive patterns with one and two elements. Later on they were also successful in recognizing longer patterns with three and four elements.

• A significant series main effect: Correct responses decreased systematically as the complexity of the stimuli increased from Series 1 to Series 4.

• A significant modality main effect: Scores in the visual and auditory modality conditions were higher than those in the vibro-tactile condition. Likewise, ceiling scores were reached at an earlier age in the visual and auditory modalities than in the vibro-tactile modality condition.

• A significant triple age-by-series-by-modality interaction effect: This effect was due to the clustering of correct responses to Series 1 and 2 in all three modalities at about age 6, and the clustering of correct responses to Series 3 and 4 in the 12 to 14 age range. Ceiling scores were reached earliest at about 12 years for visual patterns followed in order by auditory and then vibro-tactile patterns at about 14 years.

• An item analysis: Patterns with maximum contrast (BB vs. rr) were recognized correctly before patterns with minimum contrast (bB vs. BB).

1.2.1.1.3 *Interpretations of Successive Pattern Recognition in Normal Children.* Instruction: The instructional approach showed that the children could select the relevant information without being told what to search for.

The *age effect* suggested a development in Successive Pattern Recognition. Because the stimuli remained the same for children at different ages, the score shifts across age implied changes in the children's ability to more adequately organize their search for relevant information in the stimulus patterns.

The *series effect* can be accounted for by the differences in complexity that corresponded to the number of elements included in the patterns for Series 1 to 4. The more elements there are to compare, the more complex the task.

The *modality effect* can be interpreted as an active search for information and an organization of perceptual activity: This effect seemed to be related to the amount of contrast between the two levels of a dimension, as measured by the amount of JNDs (Just Noticeable Differences) inherent in the dimensions (Affolter, Brubaker, Stockman et al., 1974). There were two levels of brightness and color in the visual patterns, two levels of frequency and intensity in the auditory patterns and two levels of intensity and places in the vibro-tactile patterns. The largest stimuli contrasts were between the visual stimuli followed by the auditory stimuli whereas stimuli contrasts were the smallest in the vibro-tactile stimuli. Such differences in the contrast of stimuli dimensions appeared to influence the recognition of patterns. Visual patterns, which had the largest contrasts, were recognized correctly from an early age; auditory patterns with smaller stimuli contrasts were recognized some time later, and vibro-tactile patterns with the smallest contrasting stimuli dimensions were recognized only by the oldest children.

Item analysis supported the interpretation that recognition success is related to amount of contrasts. Younger children recognized patterns with maximally contrasting features (e.g., rrr vs. BBB) before they recognized patterns with minimal contrasts (e.g., BBb vs. BBB). Such inherent contrasts in the stimulus arrangements appeared to influence the degree of task complexity, and thus success in all modality conditions in recognizing successive patterns. We infer: It is more difficult to extract adequate information when stimulus dimensions offer small contrasts. The smaller the contrast, the higher the demands on perceptual organization. Thus, children with a more elementary level of organization at the young ages recognize patterns with large contrasting dimensions before they recognize patterns with small contrasting dimensions.

The *triple interaction age-by-series-by-modality* can be accounted for by the pattern of increase of correct responses with age and the modality effect. The increase of correct responses with age showed two clusters. There were exposed gaps in the ages when children correctly responded to patterns with paired stimuli (patterns of one and two elements), but not to serial stimuli (patterns of three and four elements), and later when they correctly responded to both paired and serial stimuli. The marked gap suggests that grouping two elements in succession presents a different task than grouping three and four elements. In other words, a different kind of perceptual organization seems to underlie the recognition of paired and serial stimuli. There appear to be two levels of the organization of perceptual activity: A more elementary level that is sufficient for the recognition of paired stimuli, but not of serial stimuli, and a higher more complex level that is required for the recognition of serial stimuli. This interpretation relates to what Piaget (1947/1950, 1961/1969) described as a critical difference between pair and serial ordering. Pair ordering (e.g., putting A and B into a sequence AB), requires judging A as coming before B, and B as coming after A. In serial ordering (e.g., putting A and B and C into a series ABC), B takes the crucial place. It requires the judgment that B comes after A, and at the same time before C. Piaget and Inhelder (1956/1964) emphasized that such serial ordering requires consideration of multiple kinds of relationships indicated by the concept of "at the same time."

Piaget's (1961/1969) interpretation that search for information is of an active kind appeared to be supported by the modality effect and including the item analysis.

The interaction age-by-series-by modality refers to the observation that the increase of correct responses with age also depends on the modality. The gap in the increase of correct responses with age, we discussed, was observable earlier in the visual and auditory modality, and only later in the vibro-tactile. We infer that even when children are competent in organizing serial stimuli, the use of that competence is information dependent.

Behavioral observations: The children had to evaluate and select relevant dimensions for the comparison of patterns and to decide if two consecutive patterns were the same or different. To do this, children had to extract information inherent in the patterns. Small children often spoke aloud when solving the tasks. From their verbal remarks, we inferred that the children first considered the information in each of the elements within each of the two consecutive patterns. Then they ordered the elements in each pattern, and finally decided if the two consecutive patterns were the same or different. To illustrate, the stimulus elements in the visual patterns were differentiated by two colors in one dimension, and by two levels of brightness in the other dimension. When given a pattern such as rrr and BBB, children had to judge whether the two consecutive patterns were the same or different. In the pattern rrr, each of the three red elements could elicit the judgment that all elements were the same. In pattern BBB, the three blue elements could elicit the judgment that all the elements were the same. Besides color, all elements of pattern rrr were equally dim. Judgment: The three elements are the same. All elements of pattern BBB were equally bright. Judgment: The three elements are the same. Next, children had to compare the two successive patterns in order to arrive at a correct response. Because all the stimuli were the same within each pattern, order was not critical—the patterns were maximally contrasted. Still this was a difficult problem for younger children: Because the stimulus elements within the pattern rrr were the same, as were the elements of pattern BBB, the children had to change their judgment when considering two patterns instead of one at a time. They had to change the first judgment of "the same" to a judgment of "different." Young children were not able to make that change. They pointed out, "They are different—and they are the same" (see more examples in Affolter, 1970). At all ages, the children appeared to be perceptually active in responding to the patterns and their improved performance with age was interpreted as a development in the organization of perceptual activity.

It was interesting to note that correct responses to the Successive Pattern Recognition tasks increased up to the age of 14, covering the same 14-year span of language acquisition. We concluded, therefore, that there may be a relationship between recognition of complex successive patterns and language acquisition.

1.2.1.2 Form Recognition in Normal Children

Clinical observations of children with language disorders had revealed that besides the problems with sequential ordering, they also had difficulties with spatial relationships.

To study the spatial problems, we designed Form Recognition tasks. The forms not only had to be recognized visually, but they also had to be recognized tactually. The tactual condition allowed us to document the active search for information in a more direct way by observing the pattern of hand and finger movements. In addition to the modality-specific, visual and tactual conditions, a cross-modal, visual–tactual condition was included in which visually presented forms had to be matched with their tactually presented analogues. The cross-modal condition permitted study of intermodal connections (i.e., the transfer of information from one modality to another). Intermodal processes are very important in perception. Sherrington (1951) pointed out that humans are highest on the evolutionary scale because of the complexity of intermodal connections in the human brain.

1.2.1.2.1 Procedures. The choice of forms used in our study was based on Piaget and Inhelder's (1948/1956) design of stereognostic tasks.

Stimulus conditions: The first series included forms with topological features, such as, open versus closed, inside versus outside. A second series of simple Euclidean forms differed in roundness versus different angular shapes (triangle, rectangle, and so forth), and a third series included forms with complex Euclidean features like different crosses and a star (see Fig. 1.1).

Modality conditions: The three series of forms of different complexity were presented in the three different modality conditions (visual, visual–tactual, and tactual) to 140 normal children, 3 to 9 years (for more details, see Affolter & Stricker, 1980, pp. 148–152).

In the visual condition, children had to match two corresponding pictures of forms by looking at the pictures. In the visual–tactual condition, the picture of a form was presented visually and children had to search tactually for a corresponding wooden form among other forms, which were hidden from view within a cubicle. They could bring the selected form into their visual field and visually check its correctness. In the tactual condition, visual information was excluded throughout the task: The children had to tactually explore a template presented to them and search

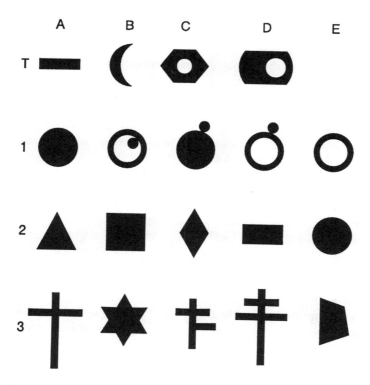

FIG. 1.1.   Description of Stimuli for the Form Recognition Tasks.

for the matching or corresponding wooden forms. Then the children had to insert the selected form into the template. A correctly chosen form would fit into the template, an incorrectly chosen form would not. Thus, the children received tactual feedback on the correctness or incorrectness of their selection.

Other observations: In addition to studying perceptual skills in the construction of spatial relationships of different complexity and in different modality conditions, the Form Recognition tasks allowed observations of the search for information as children manually handled the forms. Such handling can be registered and observed. We assumed that the handling of complex forms would require a more highly organized search for information than the handling of simple forms. The search for information was expected to be clearly observable on the tactual Form Recognition tasks. Normal children were expected to be very skilled in their finger movements during the search for tactual information and the patterns of finger movements would differ for exploring topological and Euclidean forms.

The tactual tasks could be solved by using either an exploratory or fitting strategy. Using the exploratory strategy, the child manually explores the different forms, selects, grasps, and inserts the selected one into the template; exploration and selection happen prior to insertion of the form. Using the fitting strategy, the exploratory part is left out; the child randomly grasps one of the forms and tries to insert it. If the form does not fit, the child puts that form aside, randomly grasps another one, and tries to insert it. It was expected that normal children would apply the exploratory and not the fitting strategy.

Instruction: Event knowledge is usually transmitted verbally by speaking, or visually by showing videos or films. Instead of providing verbal instructions for doing the tasks, we instructed the children by providing guided tactual information. Guided tactual information about events has rarely been used or studied. We assumed that tactual information can be used as an instruction means in all modality conditions of the Form Recognition tasks. To do this, the child's hands were guided to match four training forms presented in each modality condition. It was expected that normal children would be able to learn the tasks when provided with guided tactual information.

1.2.1.2.2 *Results.*

With regard to instruction, all children understood the nonverbal guided tactual instructions of the Form Recognition tasks in the different modality conditions, even when vision was excluded. Patterns of finger movements changed with age. Young children showed a simultaneously grasping pattern of finger movements when selecting topological forms of Series 1. This pattern was adequate for Series 1 but not for Euclidean forms of Series 2. Older children showed a different pattern. They explored contours and edges of the forms with their fingers in a successive kind of pattern. Finger movements were well coordinated and adjusted at all ages. Complex forms of Series 3 were explored for a longer time than forms of the other two series. All children used the exploratory strategy when selecting and inserting forms in the tactual condition (e.g., they grasped the forms and the fingers moved over and around the shape of the forms before they selected and inserted them). If successful, they had already selected the forms correctly before inserting them.

We observed the following:

- A significant age main effect was revealed in the increased number of correct responses with age in all task conditions.
- A significant series main effect was revealed in the decreased number of correct responses as stimulus complexity increased from Series 1 to Series 3; correct responses were observable first in the recognition of topological (Series 1) and simple Euclidean forms (Series 2), and later on in complex Euclidean forms (Series 3).
- A significant modality main effect was revealed in the high scores in the visual modality followed in order by scores in the visual–tactual and the tactual modalities.
- A significant age-by-series-by-modality interaction effect was revealed in the small visual score shifts with age and ceiling scores observed at 5 years of age. For other modality conditions, ceiling performances were reached at 9 years, but were observed earlier in the visual–tactual than in the tactual modality condition. The tactual modality condition also revealed a different age trend for Series 1 and 2 relative to the other modality conditions. Young children recognized topological forms in Series 1 more often than the simple Euclidean forms of Series 2. At about 6 years this performance pattern was reversed; children recognized simple Euclidean forms more often than topological ones. The complex Euclidean forms of Series 3 were the last to be recognized in every modality.

The item analysis revealed that in the topological series, young children differentiated only open versus closed features. In the simple Euclidean series, they differentiated only features of roundness versus angularity.

1.2.1.2.3 Interpretations of Form Recognition in Normal Children.
The understanding of the tactually provided instruction for Form Recognition tasks by all children suggests that being guided through a task provides enough *tactual information* to get to know about the respective *event*. A motor subsystem that enables self-initiated movement is not necessary for haptic (tactual) input to occur (Lederman & Klatzky, 1987). Normal children at all ages showed finger movements that were

skillful and adapted for inserting the forms. We infer that they were able to receive enough tactual information to evaluate and select relevant spatial relationships for comparison.

Age effect: The increase of correct responses to Form Recognition tasks in different modalities and stimulus complexity conditions across age can be interpreted as an increase in the *organization of perceptual activity.*

Results suggest that such an organization of perceptual activity is an *active* process. Children explored complex Euclidean forms for a longer period of time than simple forms. All children used an exploratory strategy in the recognition of tactually presented forms. This means that they correctly selected a form before inserting it based on active tactual exploration.

The organization of the search for information undergoes a development. This conclusion is supported by the series and modality effects, the item analysis, and the exploration patterns of finger movements.

Series effect: Younger children recognized the forms of Series 1 and 2, whereas the more complex forms of Series 3 were only recognized by older children (series effect). We can infer that the more complex forms of Series 3 require a higher level of perceptual organization than forms of Series 1 and 2.

Modality effect: Recognition of forms in the visual modality appeared to be easier than in the visual–tactual modality, and most difficult in the tactual modality (modality effect). It appears that children could combine visual and tactual information in the intermodal visual–tactual modality condition. This reminds us of the discussion of contrasts of the dimensions presented in the different modality conditions for Successive Pattern Recognition. It raises the question of whether forms presented in the tactual modality may present smaller contrasts than forms in the visual modality. This would allow the same interpretation as for Successive Pattern Recognition: Visual forms were recognized first because they presented larger contrasts and thus put less demands on the perceptual organization. The answer to that question for the stimuli of Form Recognition awaits further investigation.

Item analysis: The recognition of forms appeared to be related to the amount of contrast offered by the critical spatial relationship. The item analysis allowed us to reveal that topological relationships of open/closed and Euclidean relationships of round/angular are simpler, that is, offer larger contrast than topological relationships of inside/outside, or Euclidean relationship of triangular/rectangular (see Fig. 1.1). From the item analysis we can infer that recognition of forms with more complex spatial relationships within a series demands a higher level of perceptual organization.

Exploration patterns of finger movements: Organization of finger movements and their patterns when exploring forms appeared to change with age. This may also be an expression of a development of organization of search for information in levels. Young children showed a kind of simultaneously grasping pattern and more often recognized topological forms than simple Euclidean ones. In older children the grasping pattern typical of the younger children had disappeared. Instead, they began to explore more successively and systematically the angles and surfaces of the forms and they more often recognized simple Euclidean than topological forms. The implication is that these children might have reached another level of organizing their search for information.

1.2.1.3 Summary of Successive Pattern Recognition and Form Recognition in Normal Children

Instruction of the Form Recognition tasks revealed the possibility that event knowledge can be transmitted through guided tactual information.

Both recognition tasks required the children to search for information. Piaget (1961/1969) called it perceptual activity. For example, perceptual activity during Successive Pattern Recognition tasks consists of analyzing, evaluating, and selecting the information that is relevant to ordering and comparing the successive patterns. This activity was also expressed by the finger movements when exploring the forms in the tactual modality condition of the Form Recognition tasks. The interpretation of such a search requiring active processing was supported in both tasks by significant series and modality effects as well as item analyses and behavioral observations.

We conclude that both younger and older children analyze, evaluate, and try to select relevant information. They were all active in searching for information. Significant age effects in both tasks revealed that younger children were less successful than older ones. This outcome is interpreted as a difference in the organization of the search for information in children of different ages. Like Piaget (1961/1969), we conclude that the development of perceptual skills is due to a development in the organization of perceptual activity.

Such development of organization of perceptual activity appears to happen in levels. Evidence for levels is inferred from the age gap observed between recognition of successive patterns with stimulus pairs and recognition of patterns with three or more elements. In the Form Recognition tasks we observed changes in exploratory finger movement patterns with age. This change also suggests different levels of the organization of perceptual activity. Such an interpretation of data in terms of a distinction of levels of organization of perceptual activity is consistent with earlier research outcomes. Hirsh (1959) and Hirsh and Sherrick (1961), for example, supported Broadbent's (1958, 1971) classical distinction between a sensory simultaneously processing system within sensory modalities, and a perceptual successively processing system with supramodal features. Miller, Galanter, and Pribram (1960) described an elementary level of "re-sets" as being different from a more complex level of processing. Different authors have described in similar ways systems for modality-specific and for supramodal organization, although they utilized quite different terms (see Aaronson, 1967; Murdock, 1967; Wickelgren, 1967).

Thus, improvement of perceptual performances, as measured by the two recognition tasks, can be related to improvement of some kind of organization of perceptual activity, which is observable in different sensory modalities. The organization of perceptual activity develops in levels, reaching a ceiling at around 14 years for Successive Pattern Recognition, and 9 years for Form Recognition, and thus spanning the critical age range for language acquisition.

1.2.2 Cross-Sectional Studies of Perceptual Development in Children With Sensory Deprivation

The organization of perceptual activity continued to be an important aspect of our research focus. Piaget (1961/1969) suggested that some kind of experience underlies the development of perceptual organization. We were curious about what kind of information such experience might include. What role do sensory modalities play and how do they interact in the developing organization of perceptual activity? We expected to gain insight by studying children with profound hearing impairment who were deprived of auditory input, and children with profound visual impairment who were deprived of visual input. We predicted that children would get less experience in the deprived modality and low scores in that modality would reflect a deprivation effect. Conversely, we assumed that in the face of a deprivation effect, the same children would get even more experience in the nondeprived modalities, and therefore could score higher than normal in those modalities. This would reflect a compensation effect.

Literature had shown both deprivation and compensation effects (as well as similarities) in the development of children with sensory deprivation. Furth and Pufall (1966) found that 6- and 7-year-old deaf children were inferior to hearing children in the reception of successive visual and auditory stimuli. Withrow (1968) noted that deaf children, age 6 to 7 and 10 to 11 years performed poorer than hearing peers on immediate reproduction of successively presented visual stimuli. Kracke (1975) observed that deaf children, age 8;4 to 15;3 years, did not differ from hearing children in the recognition of vibratory patterns.

Form recognition did not differentiate deaf children from normal peers at ages 5 to 9 years (Affolter, 1954). Experimental data on pattern perception of children with blindness were scarce, especially for young children. Eaves and Klonoff (1970) observed no differences in tactile performances between blind and sighted children at ages 6;6 to 15;9. Davidson (1972) had shown both deprivation and compensatory effects in children with blindness, which were subsequently confirmed by Bischofberger (1989). In the few studies on the development of form discrimination, results have not been consistent. Hatwell (1966) observed that blind children, 8 to 16 years old, performed like normal peers on recognition of simple tactile forms. Hudelmayer (1970) reported that blind children, 9 to 15 years old, were inferior to sighted peers in learning strategies for tactile classifications. For a more detailed discussion of research findings available at the beginning of our research projects, see Affolter and Stricker (1980).

1.2.2.1   Successive Pattern Recognition
in Children With Sensory Deprivation

Several studies were done using the same Successive Pattern Recognition tasks that had been presented to normal children. The instructions used to orient the children to the task allowed them to evaluate and select relevant dimensions of the patterns, as already described.

Affolter (1970) compared 4- to 10-year-old children, 33 with normal hearing and 21 with a profound congenital hearing loss, on Successive Pattern Recognition tasks in visual and auditory modality conditions. All children were screened for the ability to discriminate the dimensions in each condition. Significant age main effects were observed in both the normal and hearing-impaired groups. They increased their number of correct responses as they got older. There was also a significant group main effect. As expected, children with hearing impairment made fewer correct responses to all series in their deprived auditory modality than did hearing children. They also made fewer correct responses in their nondeprived visual modality but just on the more complex patterns of Series 3 and 4. The differences between children with hearing impairment and those with normal hearing became greater as age increased.

The observation that children with hearing impairment performed more poorly than normal in a nondeprived modality on complex tasks was corroborated in a subsequent study of just the vibro-tactile modality (Affolter & Stricker, 1980). In this study, 16 children with profound congenital hearing loss were compared to 16 children with congenital blindness, and 20 children with normal hearing and sight on the vibro-tactile Successive Pattern Recognition tasks at two age levels, 7 and 11 years. Given that the vibro-tactile modality was not deprived for normal children or for hearing-impaired or blind children, deprivation effects were not expected in the children with sensory deprivation, rather compensatory effects were expected. At 7 years, there were no group differences on Series 1 and 2 (patterns with one and two elements) but there were differences on Series 3 due to lower scores for hearing-impaired and blind children than for normal children. None of the groups performed Series 4. At 11 years, a significant group main effect in all four series was due to lower scores for hearing-impaired and blind children than for normal children.

Bischofberger's (1989) study was designed to explore whether children with sensory deprivation simply needed more time to reach the ceiling performance levels, as had been observed in normal children. He compared 18 congenitally blind children, 10 to 16 years old, to 18 children with normal hearing and sight at comparable ages. No significant group differences were observed on either the vibro-tactile or the auditory Successive Pattern Recognition tasks in any series. Normal and blind children reached ceiling level (maximum performance) for Series 1 through 3 within the older age range observed.

All children were able to select relevant dimensions during instruction for the Successive Pattern Recognition tasks. Item analysis for both groups revealed that patterns with more contrasts were recognized before patterns with less contrasts.

1.2.2.2   Form Recognition in Children With Sensory Deprivation

Several studies were done (Affolter & Stricker, 1980; Bischofberger, 1989). All children with sensory deprivation understood the nonverbal tactual instructions provided for doing the Form Recognition tasks, as previously described. They all used the exploratory strategy in the tactual tasks by selecting and exploring forms before inserting them. Their finger movements, like those of the normal children, were well coordinated and skillful when handling the forms.

In one study (Affolter & Stricker, 1980), 14 children, ages 4 to 12 years, with profound hearing loss were tested with the Form Recognition tasks in all modality conditions. They were compared to the 140 normal hearing children from the original Form Recognition study as already described in Section 1.2.1.2. No significant differences between normal and hearing-impaired children were found. Correct responses regularly increased with age in hearing-impaired as in normal children. Visual tasks apparently were easier than visual–tactual and tactual tasks. Small score variations among series did not reveal a consistent effect. Thus neither compensatory nor deprivation effects were observable in children with hearing impairment.

In another study (Affolter & Stricker, 1980), 32 congenitally blind children, from ages 3;7 to 9;11 were age and gender matched to 32 sighted (normal) children and examined on Form Recognition in the tactual modality condition only, as this modality was not deprived for either group. Both groups increased their number of correct responses with age. However, there were group differences that varied with age and the complexity of the series. From 3;6 to 5;6 years of age, blind children had higher tactual scores than sighted children; they also recognized simple Euclidean forms more often than topological ones. In contrast, most sighted children at that young age recognized topological forms more often than simple Euclidean forms. From 6 to 8 years of age, there was no group difference. By 9 years, sighted children scored significantly higher than children with blindness on the most complex forms of Series 3, and maximum scores (ceiling effects) were more often observable in sighted than in blind children (Affolter & Stricker, 1980, pp. 34–35).

Again Bischofberger (1989) explored whether blind children simply needed more time to reach the ceiling level of performance that was observed in sighted children. He compared Form Recognition in 18 congenitally blind children, ages 10 to 15;11, with 18 sighted children of the same age range, as was done for the Successive Pattern Recognition tasks. There was no group difference at these older ages. This outcome indicated that blind children do reach ceiling performances but most of them with a time delay relative to normal children.

In all sensory deprivation studies, the item analysis for both groups showed that children differentiated topological relationships of opened versus closed before more complex relationships like inside versus outside, and Euclidean relationships of roundness versus angularity before Euclidean relationships of triangular versus rectangular.

1.2.2.3 Interpretations of Successive Pattern Recognition and Form Recognition in Children With Sensory Deprivation

Performances on both recognition tasks revealed similarities and differences between normal children and children with auditory or visual deprivation.

Instruction for Successive Pattern Recognition was understood and feedback (responses "yes" vs. "no") was usable for all children. For Form Recognition, children with sensory deprivation were like normal children in understanding guided tactual instruction, and they all used the exploratory strategy in the tactual condition. Fingers moved successively and showed skilled coordination and adjustment when exploring forms in the tactual condition. These observations and the findings of the item analyses suggest a similar kind of perceptual activity in sensory-deprived and in normal children. Age effects in all groups and both tasks allow the conclusion that such perceptual activity also develops regularly in children with sensory deprivation.

However, the results revealed important differences. *Deprivation* effects were observed in the *deprived* modality condition as expected. Hearing-impaired children scored lower on recognition of successive patterns in the auditory modality even when they were screened for perceiving the dimensions of these patterns. Blind children could not be tested on visual patterns.

There also were deprivation effects observable for hearing-impaired children in Successive Pattern Recognition, and for blind children on both tasks in their *nondeprived* sensory modality. For Successive Pattern Recognition, lower scores were found for vibro-tactile patterns of Series 3 at a younger age for children with sensory deprivation, but not for Series 1 and 2. At an older age, the deprivation effect was found in all series for both groups in the vibro-tactile modality. Deprivation effects were also found for Series 3 and 4 for the hearing-impaired in the visual modality. No deprivation was found on visually impaired for 10 to 16 year olds in the auditory modality. They scored like normal children.

Deprivation effects in a deprived sensory modality are understandable because one can expect reduced experience in that modality. But why are there deprivation effects in a nondeprived sensory modality? This deprivation effect was mainly expressed by low scores on recognition of complex patterns. Such findings raise the question of the kind of experience basic to the development of higher levels of perceptual organization.

The results also showed that in both groups with sensory deprivation a *compensatory* effect was missing in Successive Pattern Recognition. The only compensatory effect observed was for simple Form Recognition tasks in blind children at young ages. The absence of consistent compensatory effects implies that experience underlying the development of perceptual organization may not be related to an input from a specific sensory modality alone. If the development of organization of perceptual activity would depend entirely on modalities isolated from each other, we might expect children, who are deprived of experience in one modality, to have more freed capacity in their nondeprived modalities. As a result, a consistent compensatory effect due to added experience and therefore to improved organization of perceptual activity should result in higher than normal scores. But again, this was not the case.

We concluded that normal and sensory-deprived children showed similar performances in the recognition of simple successive patterns at young ages. Blind children reach ceiling levels in both Successive Pattern Recognition and Form Recognition. These findings suggest that basic experience underlying the development of perceptual organization is similar in all groups. Because the three groups share a nonimpaired tactual modality, it seems that tactual features may be an important aspect for such an experience. Because of the similarities of findings neither visual nor auditory input can be considered critical for such experience. But to explain the deprivation effect and the delay of ceiling effects one can argue that visual and auditory input may enhance experience. It seems then that the difference in experience between normal and sensory-deprived children is not of a qualitative (deviant) kind but of a quantitative (delay).

Deprivation effects were more obvious for the recognition of complex patterns and not elementary ones; compensatory effects were only found for elementary forms. These findings suggest a differentiation of a more elementary level of organization of perceptual activity as compared to a more complex level. Such an interpretation coincides with our findings regarding levels of development from our data on normal children.

1.2.2.4 Summary of Successive Pattern and Form Recognition in Children With Sensory Deprivation

Similarities of sensory-deprived and normal children in understanding instructions, in the outcome of item analyses of both tasks, in skilled patterns of finger movements, and in using the same exploratory strategy in Form Recognition tasks support the interpretation of a similar kind of perceptual activity in *all* groups. Significant age effects in all groups confirm our interpretation of a development of organization of perceptual activity. Deprivation and compensation effects support the interpretation that there are levels of organization of perceptual activity. The development of such organization of perceptual activity can be related to some kind of basic experience. Deprivation effects in nondeprived modalities in complex tasks, and missing compensatory effects suggest that such experience is not determined by visual or auditory modality specific activities. Children with sensory deprivation achieve ceiling levels. This suggests that their experience is qualitatively similar to the one of normal children. Tactual input present in all these children may be a critical feature of that experience. Normal children reach a ceiling level before sensory deprived children. This suggests that visual and auditory input may enhance the experience.

1.2.3 Cross-Sectional Studies of Perceptual Development in Children With Language Disorders

Two cross-sectional studies were done using the same procedures that had been used to study normal and sensory-deprived children. All children were screened for the ability to discriminate the dimensions in all three modality conditions in which the tasks were presented.

1.2.3.1   Successive Pattern Recognition
in Children With Language Disorders

One study (Affolter & Stricker, 1980) involved 44 children, 8 to 11 years, with reading and writing difficulties. They were matched to normal children at comparable ages. These dyslexic children attended a special program designed for them. They were presented the Successive Pattern Recognition tasks. They all could follow the instructions.

The number of correct responses increased with *age* in all modality conditions for Series 1, 2, and 3, but not for Series 4. Scores for Series 4 in the auditory and the vibro-tactile modalities at all ages showed 0% correct responses, and in the visual modality, correct responses never went above 50%. *Series* and *modality* effects were similar to the normal children. Responses to Series 1 in the visual and auditory modalities were similar in both groups; the number of correct responses in the vibro-tactile modality condition were lower for dyslexic children. Scores of correct responses in all modality conditions became lower for Series 2 and decreased even more as the series became more complex. No differences of groups were found in the item analysis.

In another study (Affolter & Stricker, 1980), 38 children with language disorders, at ages 5 to 15 years, were tested on Successive Pattern Recognition tasks in all modality conditions. They were compared with 13 children with hearing impairment, ages 4;9 to 9;11 years and 20 normal children in the same age range, who had been tested previously. Twenty-three children of mixed age failed to follow instructions and they were judged nontestable. Only 15 of the children with language disorders were testable. By contrast, all the normal and hearing-impaired children were testable.

The testable 15 language-disordered children exhibited *series* and *modality* effects on the Pattern Recognition tasks similar to the effects observed in the hearing-impaired and normal children. The number of correct responses decreased as the complexity of the patterns increased from Series 1 to Series 4; they were highest in the visual modality followed in order by the auditory and vibro-tactile modalities.

There was no significant *age* effect. The children with language disorders had low scores at all ages, especially for the recognition of complex patterns. The pattern of correct responses was not uniform either. Some children performed Series 1 and 2 in different modality conditions, but not the complex patterns of Series 3 and 4. Others failed in the recognition of both simple and complex patterns, especially in the vibro-tactile modality. Some performed all the series in just one condition, either visual or auditory, but failed to perform in other modality conditions (for details see Affolter & Stricker, 1980, pp. 37–82). Results of the item analysis did not differ in the three groups of normal, hearing-impaired, and language-disordered children.

1.2.3.2 Form Recognition in Children With Language Disorders

Of the 38 children with language disorders, who were initially screened for the Successive Pattern Recognition tasks in the study by Affolter and Stricker (1980), 29 were testable on the Form Recognition tasks. Nine children did not understand the guided tactual instructions. Some children did not use the exploratory strategy like the normal and the hearing-impaired children. They used the fitting strategy to solve the tactual tasks: They showed spatial disorientation. They grasped the forms without exploring them with their hands and fingers and thus without making a selection; they inserted them at random into the insert board. They would often say, "Does it fit or doesn't it?", suggesting they were able to abstract the rule corresponding to the fitting strategy, but could not organize the search for tactual features when holding a form in their hands as required by the exploratory strategy. All children with language disorders showed difficulties coordinating finger and hand movements in the tactual condition for inserting the forms. When a form did not fit, they released it and inserted another form selected at random.

The *modality* and *series* effects were similar to those previously described for the hearing-impaired and normal children on the Form Recognition tasks. But children with language disorders exhibited no significant *age* effect. Most of them recognized forms only in the visual modality at ages comparable to those of the normal children. However, the number of visual forms presented for comparisons had to be reduced to two at a time for some of the children. When children with language disorders were successful, they succeeded on simple Euclidean forms but not on topological ones.

For normal and hearing-impaired children the order of modalities was never critical. This was not the case for children with language disorders. For some of them performing the visual tasks before the tactual appeared to increase correct responses in the tactual modality.

Item analysis did not differentiate the groups. Like normal and sensory deprived children the language-disordered children differentiated topological elementary relationships before more complex relationships, and Euclidean elementary relationships before more complex ones.

1.2.3.3 Interpretations of Successive Pattern Recognition and Form Recognition in Children With Language Disorders

All children with language disorders showed difficulties *organizing their search for tactual information*. This was mainly expressed by spatial disorientation when searching and selecting forms inside the cubicle with

vision excluded, and failures in coordinating and adapting finger movements when grasping, holding, and inserting forms. Frequently they used
only one hand at a time, alternating the hands. This interpretation of difficulty in searching for information is further supported by the frequent
use of the fitting strategy instead of the exploratory one; it means that such
children left out the search for tactual information and relied exclusively
on the result of the fitting into the board. The frequent failure of following instructions in both tasks can also be related to poor organization of
perceptual input in children with language disorders.

But, there were similarities among groups of normal, sensory-deprived,
and language-disordered children as revealed by the item analysis, the
modality, and the series effect.

Item analysis: Language-disordered children, like normal and hearing-
impaired, recognized the patterns and forms with larger contrasts earlier
than those with smaller contrasts.

Modality effect: Language-disordered children reacted to modality conditions similar to the other children.

Series effect: When language-disordered children were successful in
both tasks, they were first successful on Series 1 and not on Series 2, 3,
and 4 of the Successive Pattern Recognition tasks, and on Series 1 or 2 but
not 3 of the Form Recognition tasks. When they were successful on Series
3 of both tasks they were also successful on the Series 1 and 2.

These findings are similar to those for other groups of children. They
support a differentiation of an elementary and a complex level of organization of perceptual activity in language-disordered children similar to the
other groups.

The missing age effect in both tasks underlies the interpretation of poor
organization of perceptual activity in language-disordered children of all
ages. We can hypothesize that poor organization in these children may be
due to a failure in critical aspects of basic *experience*. We discussed the
findings of normal and sensory-deprived children and argued that tactual
input may be a critical aspect in basic experience for the development of
organization of perceptual activity. Poor tactual exploration and performance in language-disordered children appear to support such arguments.
Failing the critical aspect of tactual input in the basic experience may
explain a qualitative failure in the development of organization of perceptual activity. Such a failure may create a deviancy, rather than a quantitative
delay. This interpretation appears to be supported by the missing ceiling
effects in children with language disorders.

The patterns of low performance of the children with language disorders on both the Successive Pattern and Form Recognition tasks did not

reflect a homogeneous pattern of failures, which suggests that children with language disorders are *not* a *homogeneous* group. Three subgroups emerged. These subgroups corresponded to the subgroups observed in the longitudinal studies described later in this chapter.

1. Subgroup 1 consisted of children with tactual problems who showed severe failures on vibro-tactile Successive Pattern Recognition and tactual Form Recognition tasks. They recognized simple Euclidean forms more often than topological ones. They often performed at age appropriate levels when matching visually presented forms (see Bischofberger & Sonderegger, 1974).

2. The children in Subgroup 2 exhibited intermodal perceptual problems (i.e. difficulties in relating tactual with visual and auditory information). For Successive Pattern Recognition they failed in grouping patterns presented successively in any one of the visual, auditory, and vibro-tactile modalities. This failure was often already observable for Series 1 when one-element patterns were presented and had to be judged consecutively. On the Form Recognition tasks, they recognized visual forms at about their age level. But they failed to recognize tactual forms when they were presented before the visual forms. They recognized tactual forms more often when the visual modality was tested first.

3. The children in Subgroup 3 exhibited serial perceptual problems. They failed to perform complex tasks requiring serial organization such as recognizing successive patterns of three and four elements in all modality conditions, and in recognizing complex Euclidean forms in all modality conditions (Bischofberger & Sonderegger, 1976). They matched visual forms when presented one at a time, but not when presented within a series. They usually abbreviated the Form Recognition tasks in the tactual condition by applying the fitting strategy: They left out the search for information through grasping and exploring the forms before inserting them, characteristic of the exploratory strategy (used by normal and sensory-deprived children). Instead they went directly to the inserting part trying to fit the form into the opening of the insert board. When they did start to succeed in the tactual condition, they were first successful in matching topological forms, later on Euclidean forms.

1.2.3.4 *Summary of Successive Pattern and Form Recognition in Children With Language Disorders*

Children with language disorders were active in both tasks. This interpretation was supported by the item analysis, modality, and series effects. Groups, however, differed in the organization of their perceptual activity.

They were active, but their activities appeared to be poorly organized. The failure of organization of perceptual activity in children with language disorders was reflected in their poor responses to learning task instructions, their frequent use of a fitting strategy instead of the exploratory, spatial disorientation, and difficulties with hand and finger coordination and adaptation. Pattern of failures revealed that children with language disorders failed more often tasks of complex series; it suggests that they fail more often in the organizational characteristic of a higher level than of a more elementary level.

A failure in development of the organization of perceptual activity may account for the low performance of children with language disorders on both tasks at all ages. When discussing normal and sensory-deprived children earlier in this chapter, we proposed that some kind of experience may underlie the development of perceptual organization. We considered that tactual input may be a critical aspect. Children with language disorders may fail in such tactual input. Thus, their experience becomes qualitatively different and deviant, and ceiling levels are not attained.

1.2.4   Conclusions About the Development of Perceptual Skills

The studies of perceptual skills in Successive Pattern Recognition and Form Recognition in different groups of children at different ages support several conclusions.

First, perceptual skills include perceptual activity as an *active search* for information. This conclusion is supported by item analysis, modality, and series effects.

Second, such a search of information has to be *organized*. Organization can be inferred by the responses of the children to task instructions. All normal and sensory-deprived children were able to evaluate and select relevant information during task instructions without being told what to search for. Many of the children with language-disorders failed to do so on the Successive Pattern Recognition tasks even though they met the screening criteria for perceiving the dimensions. Some also failed to understand the tactual instruction for the Form Recognition tasks. It was concluded that children with language disorders fail in organizing their perceptual activity in an adequate way. Patterns of finger movements and strategies used in Form Recognition tasks supported the interpretations of poor organization of perceptual activity.

Third, age-by-series-by-modality interaction effects in both tasks allowed for the distinction of *levels* of organization of perceptual activity. Such effects were observable in normal and sensory-deprived children. These children successfully performed Series 1 and 2 in both tasks before they performed Series 3 and 4. We inferred that patterns and forms of

Series 1 and 2 demand a more elementary level of organization in the search for information than do those of Series 3 and 4. Deprivation and compensation effects of sensory-deprived children as well as difficulties of language-disordered children supported such an interpretation of levels of organization of perceptual activity.

Fourth, age effects can be interpreted as a *development* of organization of perceptual activity. Correct responses increased in all Series and in every modality of both tasks in normal and in sensory-deprived children. The pattern of highly organized exploratory hand and finger movements in tactual Form Recognition of normal and sensory-deprived children also changes with age. Language-disordered children did not show an age effect, and difficulties coordinating and adapting their finger movements when exploring forms did not change with age.

Fifth, the development of perceptual organization may require some kind of *experience*. We observed deprivation effects in children with sensory deprivation. These effects were observable not just in the deprived modalities, but also in the nondeprived modalities especially for complex Successive Pattern and Form Recognition tasks. A compensatory effect was only observed for a short period in young blind children's tactual Form Recognition. Experience underlying the development of perceptual organization appears not to be directly related to a specific visual or auditory modality of input. Visual and auditory input appears not to be a critical aspect for basic experience because both groups with sensory deprivation reach ceiling scores. What may be needed is tactual input. Difficulties in tactual input may cause deviancies in such experience in children with language disorders. As a consequence they fail in development as supported by the missing age effect. Missing visual or auditory information can create a delay, but not a deviancy. Thus, visual and auditory input may have an enhancing function by stimulating basic experience.

1.3   THE LONGITUDINAL RESEARCH
ON CHILDREN WITH LANGUAGE DISORDERS

Before, during, and after the time we investigated perceptual performances in cross-sectional studies, we also made longitudinal observations of children with language disorders. Each disordered child was assessed annually for 8 to 10 years. A profile of different skill scores was established. Behavior in formal testing and in informal, naturalistic settings was videotaped.

We began with 57 language-disordered children, aged 2 to 10 years, who received therapy at our center. Twenty children with language disorders who were evaluated and received treatment elsewhere served as a control group (SNF projects 3.237.69; 3.448.70; 3.902.72; 3.2050.73;

3.504.75; 3.711.76; 3.929.078). Eight years later, the group receiving therapy at the center included 43 of the original 57 children (Affolter & Stricker, 1980, p. 84). The following discussion refers only to the treatment group at the center. For more findings, the interested reader is referred to other publications (e.g., Affolter, 1987/1991; Affolter & Stricker, 1980).

One goal was to follow the development of language-disordered children over several years and compare it to the development of normal and hearing-impaired children. The other goal of the longitudinal observations was to apply the research findings to intervention.

By doing so, we intended:

- To reveal that children with language disorders, even when changing over time, would continue to differ from normal children across the years of our observations;
- To gain knowledge about the verbal, and especially the nonverbal difficulties of children with language disorders over time; we expected to differentiate subgroups with specific performance profiles and to observe the stability of the characteristic patterns across time;
- To gain knowledge about the progress of children with language disorders over time; we expected to show that (a) progress occurs, (b) progress happens according to levels, and within a level, skills show some interrelationship, (c) progress follows the same sequence of levels, as observed in normal children.

Our expectancies were guided by Piaget's developmental model of hierarchical–consecutive levels of interrelated skills. Affolter, as Piaget's student at the University of Geneva, had compared deaf and normal children on the development of a variety of skills that included classifications; number concepts; form discriminations; conservation of liquids, of quantities, of volumes; spatial relationships, and so forth (Affolter, 1954; Piaget & Inhelder, 1948/1956; Piaget & Inhelder, 1956/1964). The data were convincing: Hearing-impaired and normal children showed analogous patterns of development for a variety of skills, and also showed the same sequence of levels. A higher level was reached at the same time in a variety of skills, confirming a strong interrelationship among those skills. For example, reversibility was observable at 6 to 7 years for different skills, such as classification and conservation. Children could now reverse an action in representation that they had previously done on a sensorimotor level (Piaget, 1947/1950). The ability to reverse was transferred to many concepts. This finding supported the notion that skills develop by hierarchical levels and skills of a given level are interrelated, as Piaget had described.

We turned to this developmental model of interrelated skills and hierarchically related levels in order to formulate a working hypothesis. We argued: Cross-sectional studies of Successive Pattern and Form Recognition revealed the development of perceptual skills throughout the period of language acquisition. To consider a relationship between perceptual processes and language acquisition for intervention became a logical consequence of such an argument.

The literature on normal babies and young children, and especially the work of Piaget, provided relevant leads for establishing hypotheses about perceptual processes that could guide our longitudinal research. Piaget (1936/1952) described specific visual, auditory, tactual, and intermodal performances in babies, which are observable before they sit, crawl, and babble. For instance, babies of a few weeks old are able to follow a moving object with their eyes (see also Aslin, 1981). From about 4 months babies begin to coordinate eyes and hand movements when they grasp. Around 6 months they look toward a sound source such as the mother when she calls. Such perceptual performances of a visual, auditory, and tactual kind are shown by the baby before motor performances like sitting, crawling, and babbling are observed. Thus, they seem to develop independently of those motor skills. If children have difficulties with such early perceptual performances, one can consider such difficulties as primary and intervention should focus on the perceptual problems. We hypothesized that as such children improve in perceptual performances, they also would improve in performances that appear later without direct treatment.

We hypothesized further that perceptual organization continues to develop after the sensorimotor stage, and that this continued development is important to the acquisition of nonverbal and verbal performances at higher levels of development (Affolter, 1981). For example, when a child of 6 or 7 years shows difficulties in reading and writing, and at the same time fails perceptual performances typical for that age, it may be that the perceptual problems are primary, and the reading and writing problems secondary. Based on such a hypothesis we collected and analyzed our longitudinal observations.

Following is a two-part discussion of the longitudinal findings. First, we describe the general behavioral characteristics of the children with language disorders, their performance profiles over the years, and some common characteristics that turned out to be significant for developing our theoretical perspective. Second, we describe how they progressed over the years.

1.3.1 General Behavioral Characteristics of Children With Language Disorders

Some of our test procedures included those that had been used to evaluate the nonverbal skills of normal and hearing-impaired children (Snijders, 1977). When children with language disorders were tested on those skills, their profiles were not linear as they were for normal and hearing-impaired children. There were gaps. For example, some skills on some children were above age level (e.g., motor skills such as climbing). Some were at age level (e.g., tasks requiring logical reasoning, such as classifying geometric forms when the forms were presented one by one, or tasks requiring the embedding of forms). There were skills that were significantly lower than age level (e.g., visual–motor skills and skills requiring spatial concepts, imitating, or arranging picture stories (Affolter, Brubaker, & Bischofberger, 1974).

Such discrepancies among above-age, at age, and below-age performances were typical of all children with language disorders throughout years of observation. Differences in skills showing discrepancies, however, suggested that children with language disorders were not a homogeneous group.

1.3.1.1 Performance Profiles of Children With Language Disorders

Within-group profile comparisons revealed that the children could be consistently divided into three subgroups. Each subgroup could be characterized by a different pattern of performance. When the patterns were analyzed for perceptual processes, children of the three subgroups seemed to present different perceptual problems: One subgroup had tactual perceptual problems (Bischofberger & Sonderegger, 1974), a second subgroup had intermodal perceptual problems (Affolter, 1975), and a third subgroup had serial perceptual problems. It is interesting to note that most of the children with intermodal problems were referred to our center with the diagnosis of autism (see Affolter, Brubaker, & Bischofberger, 1974).

A striking example of subgroup differences in perceptual deficits was the behavior of turning the head toward a sound source and looking at it. This localization behavior is observable in a normal baby at about 6 months of age. Children with tactual or serial problems did not appear to be delayed. Children with intermodal problems, however, were delayed in such a behavior for many years. As a consequence, these children were often diagnosed as deaf and fitted with hearing aids before their referral to us for treatment. When working with them, we noticed that their hearing was not the problem; their problem was an intermodal one (i.e., a deficit in connecting different sensory modalities). They could see and hear, but they could not integrate the two sensory modalities. Looking at a sound source requires auditory and visual input and a coordination of the two input modalities. These children seemed to fail in such supramodal or intermodal processing. Longitudinal clinical observations corroborated this initial interpretation. After several months or even years of intervention based on daily-life events without special training for sound localization, one could observe that children with intermodal problems started to turn their heads, and look behind themselves at a person entering the room.

Other critical performances were climbing versus going down a staircase. Children with intermodal problems appeared to be very skilled; some climbed like monkeys. Children with tactual problems failed in climbing. Going up or down unfamiliar stairs depends on visual and tactual information. It was observed that children with tactual problems and children with intermodal problems became very stiff and rigid, or even panic stricken in such a situation. We inferred that children with tactual problems panicked because they could not process adequate tactual information. Children with intermodal perceptual problems panicked because they failed to coordinate the tactual and the visual information.

Children with serial problems differed from the two other groups as they usually behaved quite normally in familiar situations. But their behavior became disordered whenever situations became more complex, as for example, in the presence of an unfamiliar person, or when performance required some speed. This dependency of performance on situation complexity was often overlooked by people around these children, and they were often considered to be unmotivated when they could not perform (Affolter, Brubaker & Bischofberger, 1974).

1.3.1.2 Discrepant Behavioral Difficulties as a Common Characteristic of Children With Language Disorders

One of the most interesting features of children with language disorders was their discrepant behavior. This feature was singled out earlier when we described how children with language disorders had difficulties walking up unfamiliar stairs in our center in contrast to their ease in walking up familiar stairs at home. Such discrepancies always impressed us. When these children failed to accomplish familiar tasks in unfamiliar territory they were called poorly motivated, causing problems at home or school.

Observations by family members and educators were quite consistent. For example, they reported that language-disordered children were able to discuss a problem or a task to be solved, but when asked to solve it, they refused. Some children were labeled hyperactive and were thought to have a short attention span or an attention deficit. Others had difficulties relating to people and were diagnosed as autistic. But the most difficult behavior to deal with even in an educational environment was the failure in interaction. Because of these difficulties the children were often called behaviorally disturbed, or even psychotic.

When such specific judgments were reported, we asked if this was always the case. Did these children always have a short attention span? Were they always hyperactive? To fully answer the question we made our own observations. Using examples from the data collected, we came to a surprising conclusion.

Among these examples we observed another feature. When language-disordered children had difficulty understanding commands, we took their hands and guided them until they continued alone. Some parents intuitively do the same thing. They take the hands of a child for guiding when the child has difficulty performing a certain task. We observed such situations: A family is playing hide-and-seek; the father takes his little boy by the hands and guides him to hide behind a tree (Affolter, 1987/1991). It is in this sense that some of the following examples refer to guided events.

Short attention span :

M., a 5-year-old boy, and language-disordered, is brought to our teaching program by a course participant. Reports of psychological diagnostic testing show an attention span of only a few seconds. We decide to use a real life activity: making chocolate pudding. The session is videotaped for further discussion with the course participants. The therapist guides M.'s hands through the event for about 20 minutes, thus providing him with tactual information about the event. Throughout this time the child's attention is fully focused on the event. When the therapist guides the child down from the chair to indicate the end of the event, M. gets back on the chair, obviously wanting to continue. The guided event is continued for another 20 minutes, again with M. fully attentive.

How can we explain this child's behavior which contrasts with the referring person's observations? Is it true that M. has a short attention span?

Hyperactivity:

R.,a 9-year-old boy, is in a normal children's classroom. He can hardly sit quietly on his chair, he twists his body wherever he is, has difficulty with concentrating; he speaks very rapidly. The psychologist describes him as hyperactive.

The teacher brings R. to see us. We advise the teacher to work with R. on the floor, sitting behind R. and guiding him whenever difficult actions come up. The teacher tries this out—R. becomes calm, working on his task. No hyperactive behavior is observed.

Poor motivation: First Example

B., a 12-year-old boy, and language-disordered, is often described as knowing what to do but poorly motivated. In a teaching situation, he is asked to
prepare a banana milkshake. Seated at a table he slices the banana and
opens the milk carton. Next he needs a bowl for mixing. The bowl is in a
cupboard across the room from the table where B. sits. B. looks at the
banana and the milk and says, "One needs a bowl," but he does not stand
up and walk across the room to the cupboard. The therapist approaches B.
to help him move the chair so he could stand up. But still B. does not move.
Is B. not motivated? He knows what problem needs to be solved. He himself has formulated the problem: he needs a bowl.

The therapist considers the situation. Then the therapist takes the milk
carton, puts it into B.'s hands so B. can feel it. He helps B. to stand up, ini-
tiating the action. B. continues the action, pushes the chair back, walks
across the room with the milk carton in his hand and gets the bowl.

Example Two:

D. is an 8-year-old girl, and language-disordered. She is in a special school
where educators have spent much time teaching her to sit quietly and work
at a table. She finally can do it. However, when her parents take her to a
restaurant she cannot sit still. She moves almost continually and they have
much difficulty making her sit down. Is this a lack of motivation?

Similar observations are frequently reported about our clinical population. Children with language disorders can talk about a problem, but they
seem unwilling to solve it. They show a specific kind of behavior in one
situation, but fail to show it in another one. This is interpreted as unwill-
ingness to act. So, psychologists, teachers, and therapists tend to judge
such behaviors as a sign of poor motivation. Is this interpretation correct?

Poor memory:

T., a 15-year-old boy, has severe language problems. His daily routine
includes occupational therapy followed by language therapy. He goes from
one place to the other through an extended hallway. When he arrives at the
clinician's room he is asked what he did in occupational therapy. Both therapists report that he never remembers. They say he has poor memory. Is this
interpretation correct?

In a teaching situation our course participants work with T. They ask him
to prepare a sandwich. One of them guides his body and hands to perform
the necessary actions. In this manner he receives tactual information about
the event.

Afterwards he returns to his school, has lunch, and then goes to his language therapy. When asked what he did with us in the morning, he could

tell the speech therapist what he had done. The speech therapist is amazed. Had she been wrong about T.'s poor memory?

Children with language disorders were referred to our center with different descriptive labels such as tactual–defensive, avoidance of contact, autistic behavior, emotionally disturbed, and personality problems.

Autistic-like behavior:

F. is a 14-year-old boy and language-disordered. The therapist reports that F. refuses to be touched for guiding. When, for example, the therapist takes F.'s hands to guide him to get a tomato to cut for salad, F. pushes away the therapist's hands. The therapist interprets this as tactual–defensive behavior.

We try to work with F. We put a bedspread into his hands, then start to guide him to put the fresh cover on his bed. We have his full attention on the task, not once does he push the guiding hands off.

Is this a child who refuses to be touched? How can we explain these examples of contrasting behaviors in the same child? In all these examples, the referral reports described the child as having a problem such as a short attention span, hyperactivity, poor motivation, poor memory, or autistic-like behavior. The descriptions were formulated in an absolute and general way: the child is hyperactive, is autistic, and so forth. No one reported attempts to change the testing situation and explore whether a short attention span was always observable, or to note if the child was always hyperactive, autistic, and so forth. Attention, motivation, and memory were considered to be primary skills, prerequisites for learning. Our clinical and teaching experiences suggested that what appeared to be a short attention span or hyperactivity was actually behavior dependent on the situation.

We argued that these contrasting observations of attention span, hyperactivity, motivation, memory, and tactual-defensiveness or autistic-like behavior, have a common cause. This cause is related to the available information in the situation in which a task has to be performed. We began to consider the availability of information as an important factor that influenced the performance in both test situations and in daily life.

We concluded that short attention span and hyperactivity were observable whenever a disordered child did not get enough information in daily-life situations. It was assumed that in guided events (e.g., making chocolate pudding), the child received adequate tactual information about the event. When tactual information was received, the child could focus his attention on the task. This meant that information is a prerequisite for sustained attention, as Broadbent's (1958) vigilance research suggested. He observed that whenever human subjects are in deprived situations in which they have to wait a long time for a relevant stimulus, they have difficulty sustaining their attention over time.

In our hyperactivity example, we referred to R., who had been called a hyperactive child. However, when he sat on the floor with the teacher behind him, he became quiet. In this position the environment provided more tactual information than when he was sitting on a chair. We inferred that hyperactivity was related to inadequate information. The lack of information appears to be the primary cause, hyperactive behavior a secondary effect.

In our poor motivation example, B. would not move from his chair to walk across the room to get the bowl. The therapist, watching and helping B., considered the kind of information B. had available to decide about the next action step. The bowl was in the cupboard at a distance from B. The sliced banana and the milk carton were on the table. B. had none of these objects in his hands. He did not touch them; he only saw them. But visual information was not sufficient to allow him to plan the next step of the event. When he articulated the problem of needing a bowl, he was functioning on a recognition level. Recognizing a problem does not mean that one can also solve it. Recognizing a problem and solving it are two different levels of behavior. The former is an elementary level and is made possible by visual and/or auditory information. The latter is more complex and requires previous tactual experience which is integrated, stored, and retrieved when the tactual information of the situation is perceived. Thus, when B. touched the milk carton, this seemed to help him retrieve corresponding tactual experiences and plan the actual steps to solve the problem of getting a bowl out of the cupboard across the room.

The second example was of D. sitting quietly in the therapy room, but moving around in the restaurant. With respect to information, the two situations differed greatly. Situations in the therapy room do not change much and changes that do occur are predictable. This is not the case in a restaurant where there are many unpredictable changes. There is also the matter of familiar versus unfamiliar situations. D. had difficulty differentiating relevant from irrelevant information and extracting adequate relevant information. The more complex the situation, the more pronounced this difficulty becomes. She was able to function in a familiar environment with few changes, but not in a complex and changing environment where she needed to extract the relevant information and delete the irrelevant. In this complex environment, we infer that she reached the limit of her capacity for processing information; she became tense and stressed, maybe near panic. Therefore, she moved around.

Thus, it appeared that the problem of these children was not a problem of motivation but a problem of information in a given task situation.

Reportedly, T. usually did not remember what he did only a few moments ago. Persons around him considered it to be a problem of short-term memory. However, when he was provided with more adequate tactual information by being guided through a sandwich-making event, he could remember afterwards, hours later, even when other intervening events had occurred. This observation suggested that T. remembers an event when he receives adequate input about that event by being guided. Conversely, whenever he does not remember an event, it is likely that he did not receive adequate information about the event and consequently could not store it. His problem appeared to be an input problem rather than a problem of subsequent processing. In other words, something that he does not perceive cannot be stored; something that he does not store cannot be retrieved. T. had, therefore, not a problem of memory but a problem of information input, of perception.

When F. was touched, he jerked. These movements were generally interpreted as signs of tactual defensiveness or avoidance. However, one can elicit similar reactions in normal people. Normal people also jerk when they are blindfolded, or put in a dark room, and are touched unexpectedly. When a baby is touched during the first weeks of life, the baby makes jerking movements too. We can conclude: Whenever one is touched by an unknown stimulus, one jerks. In an animal, jerking away from an unknown stimulus may mean saving its life. Jerking is, therefore, a normal reaction. What is not normal is the frequency with which jerking reactions were observed in children with language disorders (i.e., the frequency with which they judge a stimulus received tactually to be unknown or unfamiliar). A baby normally gets familiar with tactual stimuli by tactual experiences. Perhaps tactual stimuli are more often judged as unknown to the disordered child because of difficulty with adequate tactual information, which reduces tactual experience. However, when F. touched the object that he needed to solve a problem, as in the bedspread example, one could guide him. He seemed not even to notice that he was guided. It suggested that through tactual information he got to know about the goal and the event.

These examples emphasize the importance of (a) observing children's daily-life activities, (b) considering situation-dependent information, and (c) differentiating between competence and performance.

In summary, longitudinal observations of children with language disorders confirmed our predictions that the group is not a homogeneous one. Specific performance profiles emerged that reflected three subgroups. Such profiles characterized individual children consistently and could be observed throughout the years of observations. There also were behavioral features that characterized all children with language disorders. All of them exhibited discrepant performances. They were at age levels on some skills but not others. Their discrepant performances seemed to be related to the information in a situation.

1.3.1.3 Changes in Developmental Performance Over Time

All the children with language disorders had problems acquiring language. This was the reason they were referred to us. Longitudinal evaluations revealed that they also failed in symbolic play behavior such as pretending, recognition of events in graphic representations. Piaget (1945/1962) described these kinds of performances as expressions of a more general semiotic function.

1.3.1.3.1 From Sensorimotor to Semiotic Performances. Semiotic behavior is characteristic of the developmental level of intuitive intelligence, higher than the level of sensorimotor intelligence. Piaget described at length semiotic behavior as being different from sensorimotor behavior. He considered language as part of semiotic behavior, as opposed to the signal development that is observed at the sensorimotor stage. Semiotic behavior is shown when a form such as a sequence of speech sounds, or a gesture, or graphic forms can be used to represent a past or future event.

In contrast, signal behavior refers to actual events, and Piaget (1963) described such behavior as less complex than semiotic behavior. Understanding a verbal expression only in an actual situation can also be observed in nonhuman animals. Some children with language disorders in our research group did not perform on the semiotic level. They performed on a signal level. When one told them that they will go swimming tomorrow, they expected this event to happen right away. They went to get their swim suit and coat to go out. For them, "swimming tomorrow" meant "swimming now"; the event had to happen in the actual situation. This does not meet the criterion for semiotic performance. These children also recognized just pictures of objects. They did not recognize actions in pictures or understand fiction.

This important distinction of Piaget between semiotic behavior and signal behavior is seldom made in the literature about language acquisition. As a consequence, language acquisition is considered as something linear. Beginning around 9 months a child pronounces consonant–vowel sequences, continues with words for objects, and then acquires words for actions. Stockman discusses respective literature in the epilogue (see Section 4.2). She refers to competing interpretations of object-focused knowledge versus event knowledge as the basis of linguistic referential meaning. From the view of Piaget, such a competition may be due to a non-differentiation between levels. Object-focused meaning can be regarded as characteristic of a more elementary level of signal development. Performances of this level are already observable in the baby by 9 months. Event knowledge as event representation can be regarded as characteristic of a higher level. Performances of this level are observable from around 18 months on. It is a level of true language development as part of semiotic processes. According to Piaget (1945/1962), acquisition of signals is characteristic of sensorimotor performances, acquisition of semiotic performances characteristic of a higher level of intuitive intelligence. With this important differentiation between signal acquisition and semiotic performances in mind, we discuss respective findings of our longitudinal research.

Traditional language therapy does not distinguish semiotic and signal behavior. Therapists try to teach children language by teaching signal performance: For example, children have to match pictures to objects, spoken words to pictures, usually an exhausting and frustrating kind of work for both the teacher and the child. We soon stopped doing such exercises and went back to "sensorimotor activities" as we called them during the first few years. These were activities with real things. This stage of our thinking was followed by the intervention of guided event activities in daily life.

Thus, the longitudinal data revealed that children with language disorders had problems with perceptual processing, and also with semiotic behavior. We considered our hypothesis about the dependency of levels and argued: Perceptual processing, which belongs to the sensorimotor level, can be considered the primary deficit. So we worked with the children on sensorimotor performances of the previous stage (i.e., on real event activities). We observed progress on this level in daily-life behavior. Children began to show behavior that we called "doing with": When other children stood up, these children would now also stand up and go to eat, or go with the others to get their coats for going out. They showed increased understanding of spoken words in actual situations.

By continuing to work on improving these children's sensorimotor performances, the moment came when they almost suddenly showed understanding of past or future events referred to by spoken forms. Simultaneously these children began to speak and to understand actions in pictures. Vocabulary improved rapidly, which can also be observed in normal children when they discover semiotic performances around the second year of life. And all this happened without specific training of semiotic performances. Such longitudinal observations counter theories asserting that children will never learn language if they had not done so by age 6 (Lenneberg, 1967). In our longitudinal study, some children who were not on the semiotic level at the beginning of the research, discovered language as late as 12 and 14 years. (Affolter, 1987/1991).

Findings of the longitudinal studies confirmed the existence of levels and of some kind of interrelationship of skills. We could observe what Piaget (1936/1952, 1945/1962) called a transfer among skills. For the child who reached intuitive intelligence with the characteristics of semiotic function, different skills emerged at the same time. For example, they understood spoken language and graphically represented actions. Having obtained evidence for the concept of levels, we sought evidence for the sequence of developmental levels.

1.3.1.3.2 *The Sequence of Levels of Development in Children With Language Disorders.* We found a very regular sequence of developmental levels in normal and in hearing-impaired children, which corroborated Piaget's observations (1947/1950), and corresponded to developmental levels described elsewhere. However, we observed a different sequence of developmental levels for children with language disorders than is expected for normal children.

During the first year, babies normally engage in mouthing behavior. They put objects, which they have grasped, into the mouth. They also begin to babble during that time. Both kinds of behavior are present in the babies before they develop speech sounds and are often considered to be prerequisites to speech acquisition. But our children with language disorders did not babble like the normal children. They also failed to mouth objects, or they did so several years later than expected. Yet, in spite of missing the babbling stage, some children with language disorders developed speech (Affolter, Brubaker, & Franklin, 1978).

Piaget observed that normal children show direct imitation, before deferred imitation (Piaget, 1945/1962), and before they perform daily events such as getting some yogurt when they are hungry. Normal children also imitate movements, gestures, sounds, and behavior of others before true language appears. However, children with language disorders and intermodal perceptual problems were able to perform daily events before they manifested either direct or deferred imitation (Affolter, 1975). Children with language disorders and serial perceptual problems began with deferred imitation before they showed direct imitation.

Normal children begin symbolic play by using their own bodies (closing the eyes to pretend to be sleeping), and later on, they use objects (such as a doll) to represent scenes of daily life. Children with language disorders left out the first step—the use of their own bodies. Even when they used a doll to pretend, these children performed poorly.

Normal children will draw a human person on an elementary level at around 4 years. By contrast, language-disordered children were much older when they draw these pictures, and when they did, deviant drawings were often observable (Affolter, 1987/1991; Affolter & Stricker, 1980).

However, some children with perceptual intermodal problems began as early as 5 years to use perspective in their drawing. They drew three-dimensional houses. This use of perspective is not typically observed in normal children until much later, around 12 years, and is the most complex level of drawing.

In our ninth year of longitudinal observation, we were able to identify a consistent pattern of progress. Our children with language disorders at a given level performed skills that were also observable in normal and hearing-impaired children at that level. This supported our predictions that development can be characterized by levels, and that skills of a given level are somehow interrelated. However, at that time, we were not able to account for the irregularities in the sequence of levels of children with language disorders. These findings contradicted our expectation that language-disordered children will follow the same sequence of levels of development as normal children. We needed to reconsider existing theories of learning and models of development to account for our findings.

1.3.2   Implications of Longitudinal Research for Development and Learning

Our longitudinal findings showed that some progress or learning did occur among the disordered children who took part in our intervention programs. In the next sections we discuss the kind of progress we observed and the implications for describing relationships between and among skills and levels of development.

1.3.2.1   Interrelationships of Skills and of Levels

There were and still are two contrasting theoretical perspectives that underlie existing intervention and learning programs: those that assume the independence of skills, and those that assume an interrelationship between and among skills that develop in levels (Crain, 1980; Flammer, 1988; Kluwe & Spada, 1980).

Traditionally, intervention has meant skill learning. The most frequently used approaches continue to be oriented toward improving many different skills. They are guided by a model that views development as an accumulation of numerous independent skills. Given that there are a multitude of independent skills, a multitude of deficits are possible too. A deficit could affect any skill. A recently constructed model describes learning as module-specific (Fodor, 1983; Gardner, 1983). It suggests that each important set of skills has a corresponding module in the brain. There are specialized perceptual skills, specialized spatial skills, and so on. In this sense, skills, like attention, memory, and motivation, have been described as separate unique entities. They can be evaluated and impaired independently, and they can be learned separately in a cumulative manner.

A striking example is attention as a specific skill. Psychologists often report a short attention span in children with language disorders. They call it a sign of Attention Deficit Disorder. They also refer to the extensive literature on attention in general from a psychological, psychophysiological, and physiological point of view. In the field of learning, the discussion of attention is endless. There is discussion about selective attention, focal attention, directed attention, and so forth (Wingfield, 1979). Attention span is considered as something absolute. A child has an attention span of 2 minutes or for three digits, for example. Most learning theories assume that sustained attention is a prerequisite for receiving information and also for learning to occur. Attention span in a child also is expected to increase with age; it can be improved by training. There are specific remedial intervention programs with the purpose of improving the attention span.

Closely related to attention is the notion of motivation, which has also become an important concept when considering learning. In the field of education and learning, there is much discussion of motivation and how to improve it.

Such a theory of intervention and learning will also include different skills involved in memory. Memory has been studied in the context of many fields: physiology, neurology, and psychology. One can read about short-term memory, working memory, long-term memory, how to improve memory, and so forth.

Just as there are specific skills, there are specific disorders. For example, some children with language disorders are diagnosed as tactual–defensive, a disorder that is claimed to exist in addition and not related to their language problems. Psychologists and therapists describe this disorder as a kind of emotional disorder in which the child refuses to be touched, or refuses to enter into contact by being touched. Sometimes such behavior is interpreted as a sign of oversensitivity to tactual stimuli. There are special programs to help these children better accept tactual stimuli, or to reduce the assumed oversensitivity.

The concept of functional training belongs to this theory of skill learning (Arnadottir, 1990; Kratz, Tutt, & Black, 1987), and is frequently used in intervention. For example, perceptual learning means training discrimination skills; visual discrimination of color, size, shape, and surface texture; learning to distinguish cars, flowers, letters, and so forth; auditory discrimination of noises, sounds, and so forth. Motor learning means training specific movement skills. If a child has difficulty using a spoon, eating with a spoon has to be practiced. If a child cannot put on a coat, putting on a coat has to be practiced. For each child, a list is made of the different skills to practice. Such a list can grow long, and keep the teacher and the student very busy.

Our data contradicted the assumption that there are a multitude of independent skills and, therefore, a multitude of possible deficits. The data confirmed the existence of some kind of interrelationship among skills. However, the findings suggested that such an interrelationship could not be a direct one. We discussed the findings that children with language disorders presented patterns of deficient and nondeficient skills, that reflected certain performance profiles. These profiles were restricted in number and characterized three subgroups. These subgroups could be identified at different levels of development. These observations suggested that the relationship among skills of a specific level is not a direct one. Each pattern of profile appeared to be somehow related to a specific basic perceptual problem.

Related to the problem of interrelationship among skills was the problem of levels. Our longitudinal data gave evidence for the existence of levels in the development of skills. The view that development occurs in levels is supported by different researchers in the field of child development (Gesell & Thompson, 1934; Piaget, 1936/1952). Piaget insisted that such levels are hierarchically dependent. For intervention this meant that once a given level is reached by the child, different skills belonging to that level develop together without being trained for separately.

Our data confirmed the existence of levels in children with language disorders as well. However, the difference in the sequence of levels contradicted a hierarchical dependence of consecutive levels. This meant that our interpretation had to take into account such findings.

1.3.2.2   *The Need for a New Model of Development and Theory of Learning*

Having accepted the theory that skills are interrelated and their development is characterized by levels, we still questioned how development occurs. Development is related to progressing, and progressing expresses some kind of basic learning. Theories of such basic learning are strongly related to a specific model of development. For example, when one considers levels of development, the question arises as to how a child progresses from one level to the next. Or, more generally, how does a child functioning on a certain level learn the interrelated skills of the next level?

Learning is inferred from observing and interpreting specific changes in behavior as positive. Every approach to learning tries to elicit such changes and to make the changes permanent. But approaches toward eliciting such permanent changes differ.

An old but still in use theory, claims that changes can be elicited by trial and error (Thorndike, 1931). It is claimed that children learn by imitating parents, siblings, teachers, and members of a wider social group. Numerous independent skills are learned by imitating teachers, and following their verbal directives. It is generally accepted that imitation plays a critical role in learning and development. Thus, imitation is considered an important source of learning. Different means are used to enhance positive behavioral changes and to make them permanent, for example, classical conditioning (Watson, 1930), and frequent rewards or reinforcements (Mikulas, 1974; Skinner, 1957). Verbal praise and tangible tokens are popular procedures used to reinforce positive behavioral changes in special education programs.

Such theory assumes that knowledge can be handed over in a direct way like a gift to another person (Pfeiffer, Feinberg, & Gelber, 1987). This approach further assumes that children have direct access to the wisdom of life acquired by the social group, or that one is able to learn from history. In this view, the roles of parents, teachers, and social groups become well-defined and are considered to be of great importance.

However, because this kind of learning and development approach assumes that children learn because they can imitate, this theory does not account for our findings that children with language disorders who cannot imitate, nevertheless, did progress.

Piaget's model of development contrasts with the theory supporting an accumulative learning of many skills by imitation or verbal directives. Piaget (1936/1952) assumed that development happens by levels. Such levels are hierarchically dependent; what is acquired on one level has to be relearned on the next level; skills of an elementary level are prerequisites for skills of the next higher level. There are educators who try to apply Piaget's model of levels of development to teaching. They plan their teaching according to the level of development of a child; they try to enhance skills belonging to this level. This is done by creating respective situations so children can be active using their skills. It is expected that once skills of a given level are mastered the child will progress to the next level (Inhelder, Sinclair, & Bovet, 1974).

Our data, however, contradict a direct relationship between successive levels. The findings of an irregular sequence of levels in children with language disorders showed, for example, that some of these children did not exhibit imitation skills on a sensorimotor level as normal children do (see Section 1.3.1). This meant we were still faced with the problem of describing a source of learning and development. We could neither refer to imitation nor verbal advice nor consider skills of a given level as prerequisites for skills of the next level.

We were at the end of the longitudinal study when we had to face the problem of establishing a hypothesis about a new source of learning. This new source had to take into account the deviant sequence of levels and the absence of imitation skills (i.e., this source had to meet several criteria in order to account for our findings):

- It had to allow learning to occur without imitation.
- It had to present universal features; that is, the source had to be applicable to children all over the world in environments that are deprived, rural, or urban.
- It had to account for the regular sequence of development in normal, hearing-impaired, and blind children.
- It had to account for deprivation effects in children with sensory deprivation and for deviant performances in the children with language disorders.
- It had to include tactual information about events.

1.3.2.3 *Spontaneous Activities of Daily Life as a Source of Development and Learning*

To establish a new hypothesis of learning with the described criteria in mind, we reconsidered the available video recorded data, which had been collected across 10 years of longitudinal research. We concentrated on the spontaneous behavior that could be observed in natural settings for normal children, for children with hearing or visual deprivation, and for children with language disorders without hearing loss.

The amount of observable spontaneous activity in normal children and in hearing-impaired children was impressive. These children were not content to walk demurely down the street or on a sidewalk. As soon as they saw a wall along the street, they tried to climb the wall and walk it. Or they looked for something to jump over, a small crack or break in the sidewalk. If they saw a small opening in a fence, they tried to squeeze through. They were obviously delighted to throw stones into a creek or a pond. When adults tired of hiking and sat down to rest, these children usually maintained their level of activity.

Blind children engaged in activities that were similar to those of normal and hearing-impaired children, but they were less active. This was to be expected, because a lack of vision reduces the incentive to be active (Bischofberger, 1989; Fraiberg, 1977; Millar, 1994).

In contrast, language-disordered children showed different behavior in spontaneous activities. They would choose similar kinds of activities but the wall they would choose would be a low one. Or they would be still and watch other children perform. Their differences were supported by video recordings and reported observations by professionals and family members collected during the years of the longitudinal study.

Spontaneous activities observed in normal and hearing-impaired children seem to have universal character. When children anywhere in the world see a wall, a tree, or a rock to climb they will try to do it. They will throw stones and try to squeeze through small openings. In all these observed spontaneous activities, no exercise can be identified as the training for a specific perceptual skill.

Such spontaneous activities always involve some kind of search for information. Whenever children are involved with such a search, that search is oriented toward a goal that requires changes of topological relationships between body and environment, as in our examples of climbing and walking a wall. There appears to be a relationship between perceptual skills and everyday goal-oriented activities of children. Inasmuch as these activities always involve the two components, the body and the environment, it is appropriate to discuss interactions, activities that occur between (or inter-) child and environment. Daily activities of children can be termed interactive events.

We analyzed such everyday interactions and concluded:

- They do not require imitation skills.
- They are universal and observable in any social environment.
- They are applicable to all different groups of children and can account for the regularity of the sequence of levels of development in normal, hearing-impaired, and blind children.
- They can account for deprivation and missing compensation effects in children with blindness who grow up without the enhancing role of visual information.
- They require tactual information and consequently present specific difficulties to children with language disorders and thus could account for deviant aspects of their development.

These analyses, then, allowed for the hypothesis that daily-life interaction could function as a source of development and learning. It meets the criteria specified for such a source, which had emerged by the end of the longitudinal study.

1.3.2.4 Conclusions About Cross-Sectional and Longitudinal Studies

After a decade of research, we had collected data that contradicted some assumptions we made at the beginning of the research program. The findings put several constraints on a model of development and the respective theory of learning.

Cross-sectional developmental studies revealed a sensory deprivation effect on the most complex tasks for both hearing-impaired and blind children on Successive Pattern Recognition tasks and for just the blind children on Form Recognition tasks. Both deprived groups and normal children improved their performances with age. The age effect allowed the interpretation that the organization of perceptual activity becomes more adequate with increased experiences in normal and both sensory-deprived groups. In contrast, children with language disorders scored lower on all levels of complexity on the Successive Pattern and Form Recognition tasks. Their performances were patterned such that three subgroups with different perceptual problems were revealed. There was no significant age effect, which we interpreted as a sign of disturbances in the kind of experiences basic to developing organization of perceptual activity.

Longitudinal findings showed that children with language disorders were different from normal children in patterns of skills, and in sequences of developmental levels. These differences, again, did not appear to happen at random, but presented patterns typical of subgroups.

In summary, neither the theory of independent skills nor the theory of hierarchical–consecutive levels could account for these findings. The available theories of learning and their respective developmental models were not applicable as a basis for a theory of learning and a model of development, and thus not applicable for planning clinical intervention. To plan successful intervention we had to find a new source of learning and a model of development that fit our data. We hypothesized that experiences with daily interaction events meet the criteria for a source of learning, as inferred from our data. Therefore, daily interaction became and still remains a major focus of our research. What does interaction entail? This issue is taken up next.

1.4   DAILY-LIFE INTERACTION EVENTS
AS SOURCE OF DEVELOPMENT AND LEARNING

We are put into an environment; we move continually in a physical space. To behave adequately, we have to get to know our environment. Getting to know the environment means getting to interact by changing topological relationships between the body and the environment. A basic concept in the acquisition of such knowledge is the notion of support.

A support refers to the surface that carries the body (from the Latin *portare*=to carry), a surface that offers resistance to the effect of gravity on the body, on objects, and on other persons. Such surfaces can be the floor, a chair, a street, a hillside, and so forth. Support relates our own body to objects, to other persons and living organisms around us, and to the inert matter of the world. In other words, through this support, people and objects are topologically related. People interact to change such topological relationships. The notion of topology addresses spatial relationships that have to do with neighborhood in the sense of how things or persons are connected. The most elementary topological relations are being separate versus being together. To change from being separate to being together requires touching. For example, to sit down requires that I am together with the chair, so I have to touch the chair. To be together with another person requires that I touch that person. Touching provides tactual information. Tactual information is required to get to know about topological relationships and their changes. A more complex topological analysis is required when the relationship of being together includes situations like: inside versus outside, around something, at something, and through something (Piaget, 1970; Piaget & Inhelder, 1948/1956).

In considering topological relationships, the notion of the environment becomes important. The role of the environment in interaction has been discussed by several authors. Horowitz (1987) mentioned the long history of discussing the role of the environment in development. But he wrote that there is "no consensus on the questions of how critical, critical for what and when it is critical" (p.128). Often in psychological literature, environment is restricted to social environment. The physical environment is not considered at all or considered to be something very different. However, we agree with Ulvund (1989) who wrote:

It may be argued that from a developmental perspective a distinction between the physical and the social environment is a highly arbitrary distinction, which hardly has any counterpart in nature. One argument against such a distinction is that the responses the individual makes to the social environment are probably based on similar processes of attention, perception, and learning as the responses the individual makes to the physical environment. (p. 63)

Interaction is strongly related to cognitive behavior. Reed (1993) referred to cognitive behavior and perception which lead to knowledge about the environment. Taking Gibson's (1979) viewpoint, he wrote that, "Cognition is used to refer to any and all psychological processes that function to give an organism knowledge about its environments, and its situation within the environment . . . perception is cognitive because it yields knowledge" (p. 47).

Interaction, thus, includes perceptual and cognitive processes. Interaction between a person and its environment leads to knowledge, knowledge about ourselves as individuals, knowledge about the social part of the environment, and knowledge about the world around. Daily interaction thus becomes an important and complex kind of behavior. Piaget (1947/1950) considered interaction to be an active process and fundamental to development. Coming from the field of biology, Piaget described interaction by differentiating assimilation and accommodation.

1.4.1   Assimilation and Accommodation
as Parts of Interaction

There are two parts of interaction processes, an assimilation and an accommodation part. Both parts occur everywhere in the living world. The environment provides light. A plant, which needs light, will assimilate it. To do this, plants have to orient themselves toward the light source; they have to accommodate their position to the environment. Even a plant, which no longer has roots, can do so. Cut a sunflower, put it in a vase in the morning so that the head of the sunflower is turned towards the sun. When you return in the evening, the flower's head is turned towards the sunset. You can make inferences. The plant has interacted with the environment; it has assimilated something it needs from the environment, the light, and with the light, the warmth, and so forth. The plant has accommodated its position to the direction of the light source so that the most light can be assimilated by the plant's surface; the plant takes out of the environment what it needs, in this case, the light. In daily life we encounter similar phenomena:

> I peel an orange. At the beginning, the orange peel and flesh of the orange are together, the peel is outside, and the flesh of the orange inside. By peeling, I separate the peel from the orange. With this topological change, the orange changes. The peeled orange is not the same orange anymore; it has lost the peel. I assimilate that new kind of information; I can feel that what I hold in my hand is now juicy, soft, sticky. At the same time the orange changes, I have to change also; I have to accommodate my grip to the softness and stickiness of the object I am holding.

Learning requires both parts of interaction, assimilation and accommodation. In addition it requires a search for information that involves perceptual processes.

> K., an 11-month-old baby, is sitting for the first time in her life on a sandy riverbank. It is summertime and she is barefoot. Her feet and toes dig into the soft sand; the feet enter the sand and the toes move individually. She touches the sand with her fingers and attempts to grasp it. K. lifts her hands filled with sand and the sand flows away. She opens her fingers and looks at them. Her face shows surprise. Again she attempts to grasp the sand and her feet dig deeper into it. After a while she begins to pour sand over some nearby small rocks and watches the sand gliding down the rock. K. continues her exploration.

By observing K.'s behavior, one can analyze activities, some of which can be interpreted as assimilation and some as accommodation. She touches the sand and attempts to grasp it—the sand flows away. We can infer that K. assimilates the softness and the flowing of the sand through her fingers. She applies what she has learned about interaction; she touches, moves, grasps, tries to hold and to release by displacing. She does it with her feet and toes and fingers. She is continually involved in varying topological changes, and thus gets information about the sand. Searching for this information she continues to change topological relations within her environment: The sand flows away from the rocky support; it is not there anymore where it was a moment ago.

We can also observe activities that can be interpreted as accommodation: K. changes the movements of her toes, feet, fingers, and hands according to the touching of the environment in relation to the changes of topological relations. She accommodates her movements to the sand when grasping and holding it. She appears to continue such activities of assimilation and accommodation. She also increases the complexity of cause-and-effects: She explores first what happens between her body and that strange sandy support; later she includes parts of the environment such as the relationship between the sand and the rocks. She is changing her behavior, suggesting that she is learning by interacting.

Analyzing ongoing spontaneous activities of children in this way, we can view them as interacting with the environment. During these activities, children induce changes in their environment by changing topological relationships. As the environment changes, they have to accommodate their movements to the environment; they have to change too. Thus, learning is enhanced.

In summary, assimilating parts of the environment, such as light by the plant, food by us when eating, and so forth, can induce changes in the environment. On the other hand, the organism involved in assimilating always has to accommodate to certain conditions of the environment until equilibration (adaptation) is reached. This means, interaction activities involving changes of topological relationships between actor and environment create changes that affect the person interacting and the environment. In this sense, interaction can be described as a basis for evolution (Piaget, 1947/1950). Ongoing assimilation and accommodation activities also are involved in daily events as children continually interact with their physical environment: support, objects, persons. These everyday interaction events change something in the child as well as something in the environment. All these changes require the search for information. What this means for interaction is discussed in the next section.

1.4.2   Interaction and Information

In addition to assimilation and accommodation there is always some additional kind of information to gather in order to appreciate changes in the environment and in the person interacting. Piaget regarded the information available in the environment and utilized by the organism as essential for evolution. At an early age, Piaget (1911) became interested in interaction as basis for evolution: At age 14, he was spending the summer in the mountains. There he observed a kind of pond snail that he had also observed at Lake Neuchâtel. Comparing such snails from both locations more closely, he was surprised to notice specific differences and wrote his first paper describing them. To explain the differences he pointed to the differences in the environment. To assimilate what they needed, the snails had to adjust or accommodate to a somewhat different environment: the ones living at a high altitude had to accommodate to a mountain environment and those living below to a lowland and lake environment. From this time on interaction including assimilation, accommodation, and search for information as mechanisms for evolution remained a major concern for Piaget.

1.4.2.1 *The Necessity of Information When Interacting*

Each time a topological relation between the environment and the actor is changed during interaction, a search for information about that change is required. Piaget (1947/1950) pointed out that an organism takes that kind of information, which it can assimilate in a given interactive situation out of the structured environment. Piaget assumed that the kinds of information an environment may provide to a specific organism in an actual situation might well be specific to that organism. Thus, specific animals will take different kinds of information out of the environment. We refer the reader to descriptions of the concept of species specificity in Gibson's (1979), Kessen's (1993), and Lorenz' (1977) work. In Gibsonian terms information available in the environment and utilized by different species is called affordance.

Interacting in daily life is always connected with an actual situation. Situations in daily life change continually; situation A differs from situation B. Whenever something in the environment changes, we have to expect that the kind and amount of information available also change. This can cause success or failure in solving a problem. For example, I may be able to play a musical instrument. I may play certain compositions when I am at home and relaxed. I may not be able to play them in front of a large audience. The situation at home is different from that with a large audience. Being familiar with the situation at home, I can make all kinds of predictions. When there is a large audience, my predictions are poor. The difference of the two situations goes along with a difference in the need for information. In the second situation I need more information. The search for more information can cause a load on my processing capacity, and can lead to a breakdown of my performance. This interrelationship among situation, performance, and information is a very important one.

1.4.2.2 The Available Information When Interacting

Given that interaction between the child and environment is important and requires a certain amount and kind of information, the question arises: What information is critical for daily interaction to occur? Is it verbal or nonverbal? What is the relationship between language and interaction? What is the relationship between motor acts and perception? If perception is important, what are the necessary sensory modalities involved in interaction?

1.4.2.2.1 Nonverbal Daily-Life Interaction and Language. Probably the most widespread assumption about daily interaction is that it is verbally controlled, that language is required for adequate interaction with the environment (Piattelli-Palmarini, 1980; Vygotskii, 1962). Interaction also is usually studied from the viewpoint of social interaction in contrast to individuals in isolation (Granott, 1993), and therefore strongly related to verbal communication.

Piaget devoted considerable research to exploring the relationship between language and thought–cognition. That research included comparative observations of deaf and hearing children. Affolter (1954) and Furth (1966) found that profoundly deaf children with very little oral language not only performed at their age levels in cognitive skills such as problems of conservation, seriation, stereognostic tasks, and classification but also presented the same sequence of developmental steps as observed in normal hearing children. In 1963, Piaget published an important lecture about the connection between language and operations of intelligence. In this lecture he described his view that language cannot be the origin of intelligence. Rather, he emphasized, it is the other way around—intelligence, in the sense of adaptive behavior, is there first.

There is little reported research about the relationship between verbal language and interaction in daily-life events (Nelson, 1986). When observing children's daily activities, it appears that verbal language is not required for their spontaneous interaction in daily life (Affolter, 1968). Children can dress, eat, move from place to place, and find their own problems to solve without having oral forms for all these activities. Also, children with profound hearing impairment do not differ from hearing children in their performances of daily activities. This suggests that daily interactive events are independent of oral language, that daily interactive activities are basically of a nonverbal kind. Hence, throughout this book when we refer to daily interaction we refer to nonverbal interaction.

This leads us to the next question, "If daily interaction is not necessarily controlled verbally, then what kind of information is critical for adequate daily interactions?"

1.4.2.2.2 Nonverbal Daily-Life Interaction and Motor–Perceptual Aspects.
When normal children prefer to climb a wall and walk along it instead of walking nicely on the sidewalk, we assume that it is not the motor part but rather the perceptual novelty involved which makes the task interesting. Perceptual activity involved in daily activities can be more or less organized. One can expect that the more children interact, the more they learn to organize their perceptual activity, and thus they develop perceptual skills by interacting.

Although it is widely accepted that children learn by doing, it is the motor part of interaction that appears to be important to many educators and psychologists (see Anzai & Simon, 1979; Lawler, 1985). They assume that motor development is a requirement for cognitive development (Hong, Gabriel, & St John, 1996). So when children fail in motor production, they are also expected to be slower in development.

Psychologists were therefore puzzled when such expectancies were contradicted a few years ago. The onset of free walking in two groups of Hopi Indian children was studied. Children of a first group were raised traditionally: The babies were cradled most of the day, so they could not move, but were moved. Their mothers took them along on their everyday activities. Children of a second group were raised in a modern Western way: These babies could move freely all day long. At the age of 15 months, Dennis and Dennis (1940) compared the walking of the children in both groups. There was no difference; children of both groups could walk freely. The authors of that study could not explain the findings. They questioned whether walking is determined genetically. We present our interpretation in the next section when we discuss the tactual information in daily-life interaction.

Other observations also contradict the notion that the motor part plays an important role in interaction and in development: The development of children with cerebral palsy was studied. Because these children fail in adequate motor development, they could be expected to fail in interaction, and therefore in cognitive development. However, many of these children do develop age-appropriate cognitive skills. Some are able to have academic careers (E. Köng, personal communication, October 18, 1978; J. Oertel & V. Peschke, personal communication, November 16, 1997). Can we assume, then, that paralyzed persons cannot develop adequately because they have absent or severely impaired motor skills? We conclude that motor theories of learning by doing fail to account for such data, and it appears that one has to search for explanations other than a motor theory.

Some researchers consider the perceptual part of motor acts. Tolman (1949) raised the question about what is stored when one learns by moving. Is it a motor program or is it some kind of perceptual–cognitive information? In his first experiment, rats had to find their way by walking through a maze to find food without making errors. They all learned to do so. In a second experiment, he used a different maze with the same pathways but changed the situation: the pathways were filled with water so the rats had to swim. He hypothesized that if the rats had stored a motor program when learning by walking the first time, they would have to relearn to find their way when swimming was required, because swimming demands a different motor program than walking. If, however, they had stored perceptual–cognitive information, this information would still be available in the second experiment because the pathways with the different corners and dead ends were not changed. The results showed that the rats performed in the second experiment without errors, meaning they could directly apply what they had learned in the first condition. In conclusion, rats store and retrieve not a motor program, but perceptual–cognitive information. Tolman called it a cognitive map.

Many psychologists would agree that in order to perform daily activities, children need adequate perceptual information, and they need to combine that with action systems (Reed, 1982). Often they do not specify what they mean by perceptual information. They usually emphasize that, for daily-life behavior, the relationship between motor skills and visual information is important (Prinz & Bridgeman, 1996). They consider "visuo-motor" skills and "perceptual–motor" learning. E. Gibson (1967; 1988/1991) suggested, as an example, that the manipulatory skills of 6-month-old babies may be related to the possibility of their being in a sitting position, and thus getting a good view on the objects. Lawler (1985) referred to the theory of body-parts-mind and argued, "that some cognitive structures are descended from ancestors in the locomotive subsystems and others from ancestors in the visual subsystem" (p. 150).

If daily interaction can only occur when adequate vision and motor skills are present, one cannot account for the successful development of blind children (Fraiberg, 1977; Millar, 1994). Also, how does one account for adults with brain damage who retain good motor skills and have good sight but still present difficulties in nonverbal interaction (Affolter & Bischofberger, 1996; Affolter, Bischofberger, & Calabretti-Erni, 1996)? What explains the interactive difficulties of children with language disorders who can discriminate visual forms adequately? They also have the required motor skills, can recognize problems in daily nonverbal interaction, even talk about them, but when they should solve the problems, they do not move or move inadequately (Affolter & Bischofberger, 1993, 1996; Affolter & Stricker, 1980).

To find some answers to these questions, we continued to inquire about interaction and the kind of information involved in interactive events.

1.4.2.2.3 Nonverbal Daily-Life Interaction and Tactual Information.

We observed that in natural parent–child interaction, parents would often help children to learn a new task by taking their hands and guiding them through the task. Parents would not necessarily talk the children through the task, but literally guide their hands so the children could peel the orange or open the jar. We called this guiding a person through the interaction steps of a problem-solving event. We used this natural behavior as a clinical tool and applied such guiding to our children with language disorders (Affolter, 1987/1991). We also refer the reader to the previous discussion of cross-sectional research. The findings showed that one can recognize an event when perceiving guided tactual information. Tactual guiding developed into a successful clinical intervention method: Guiding patients to solve problems of daily life. We began to call this method Guided Interaction Therapy. Because this method worked so well with our patients we wanted to know more about how tactual guiding provided the necessary information to people for understanding daily events. What kind of information are people picking up in the guided activity? Is it the motor act or is it the input that is critical?

To answer that question, we first analyze input information when a change in topological relationship between leg and support occurs, a change that is frequently performed whenever we locomote in daily life. Consider the following two situations while keeping your eyes closed (because we intend to exclude visual information). Situation A: You lift your leg, then you put it down on the floor. Situation B: Someone else holds your leg, lifts it, then puts it down on the floor. Both situations have common features: The leg is lifted and one no longer feels the support with that leg. The leg is put down on the floor and the leg feels the resistance of the support. This resistance blocks the movement of the leg. We talk about a change in resistance: The leg is separate from the support—no resistance. The leg touches the support—total resistance. One experiences the same change of resistance in Situation A and in Situation B. This feeling of changing from no resistance to total resistance suggests that in both situations there is a common input phenomenon that seems important (see Day & Singer, 1964). The motor act is only needed to elicit the change of resistance felt between body and support. We conclude that people get the same kind of information whether they perform the motor act themselves, or they are guided in the act.

The second analysis of input information has to do with another daily event, taking off a wristwatch. This event requires a sequence of changes of topological relationships between arm and wristwatch. Each change in topological relationship elicits a change in resistance similar to the preceding example. A person is guiding another person to take off the wristwatch. The question arises: Is enough information transmitted through guiding so the person being guided recognizes the event?

> A person wearing a wristwatch is asked to close the eyes. You, the guider, want the person to take off the wristwatch, but you don't want to use verbal instructions. You guide the hands of that person and begin to take off the watch. The guided person perceives the different changes of resistance elicited by the changes of topological relationships between arm and wristwatch. The moment comes when the guided person takes over and continues the event correctly alone. We assume, that at this moment, the person has picked up enough information about the event to recognize it. The information available is tactual, and not visual or verbal.

These observations suggest that tactual information may be important when interacting. Our studies lead to the inference that neither vision nor hearing by itself is critical for daily nonverbal interaction to occur, but tactual information may be indispensable. Children with significant congenital hearing or visual impairment still develop adaptive nonverbal cognition and language despite their respective sensory deprivation. We concluded from clinical and research observations that visual–motor processes alone can not account for adequate nonverbal daily interaction. Guided intervention, where one provides tactual information about an event, appears to permit patients and children to perceive the event as if they acted alone. Tactual input, therefore, became an important concept in our work.

The importance of tactual information when interacting has been rarely mentioned. We searched scientific literature for some descriptions of tactual processing (Katz, 1989; Loomis & Lederman, 1986). But research about tactile or tactual input is very scarce. Most studies are done in physiology laboratories using artificial passive stimuli. For example, the perception of one versus two points on the skin is measured. Psychological investigations, if available, examine perception of texture (Goodwin & John, 1990) or vibro-tactile input (Blamey, 1990) or haptic manipulation of objects (Rolfe-Zikman, 1987; Schiff & Foulke, 1982). One of the best descriptions of the tactual sensory systems in daily-life use was done by Gibson (1962, 1966), who compared haptics with other sensory systems such as vision and hearing. He described that, in daily life, haptic perception, like visual and auditory perception, does not function randomly but is structured. In 1966 he referred to sensations coming from the joints and wrote:

> The human skeleton contains over 100 mobile joints, on the authority of medical encyclopedias. They are arranged in a hierarchy of the body, its members, and its extremities, as we noted in the last chapter. Their total

input is not a sum or a statistical collection. It follows geometrical laws, and the orchestration of this input to the central nervous system, simultaneous and successive, is not a collection of sensations but a structured perception. The angle of one joint is meaningless if it is not related to the angles of all the joints above it in the postural hierarchy. The branching vectors or directions of the bones constitute the "bone space" of the body and this is linked in turn with gravity and the ground. A certain pose of the body exists at any one moment, and the geometrical set of all body poses defines the set of all possible movements. Motor behavior consists of responses within this set. (p. 118)

But Gibson also stressed the uniqueness of the haptic system among the different sensory systems. In contrast to vision and audition, the haptic system is multimodal; several sensory modalities form the haptic system: temperature, pressure, and so forth; the whole body is involved in haptics. Taylor, Lederman, and Gibson (1973) argued that, "It is this multimodal nature of touching which gives touch the feeling of providing substance and reality to the perceived world" (p. 262). The haptic system is also unique in its functioning as a receiving and a performing system at the same time, according to Gibson. Another special feature of the haptic system is the stick phenomenon. Blind people apply the stick phenomenon when using the white cane—the important source of information switches from the hand to the point of the stick where the stick touches the environment. The stick phenomenon allows one to explore something behind, or something under something else. This is not possible to do by using vision. The stick phenomenon suggests also an explanation for the normality of Hopi babies and for children with cerebral palsy. These children are carried on the back, or on the mother's arms and by other persons who take care of the children. They are carried for daily-life activities. In these situations, the persons carrying the children function as a stick for the children. As a consequence, these children get tactual input about changes of topological relationships performed by the care givers in daily-life activities.

In general, studies of tactual processes refer to experiments removed from natural settings. Heller and Schiff (1991a) pointed to this fact and stressed the importance of studying naturalistic touch:

Aside from the early phenomenological descriptions from David Katz's classical observations . . . there has really been no serious attempt to develop a natural history approach to the study of touching behaviors. Perhaps it is time for such an approach to emerge. (p. 334)

Because we were concerned with daily-life interaction we began to explore the importance of tactual input in relation to daily events. First we had to define event. Our definition of events corresponds to the definition of Nelson (1986) who wrote:

> Events are sometimes defined as simply change, for example, the movement of a bouncing ball. The events we are concerned with here are of a more macro order; they involve people in purposeful activities, and acting on objects and interacting with each other to achieve some results. (p. 11)

Daily-life events involve interaction. Such interaction involves changes of topological relationships between a person and the environment, and within the environment. The sequences of changes of topological relationships are goal-oriented and have a beginning and an end. Daily-life events require continual input of information about the topological relationships between actor and environment and within the environment. This is necessary to judge the topological changes needed to accomplish the event, and to perform them until the goal is reached. The question arises: What kind of information is necessary? For example, I want to get the knife on the table to peel an orange. I move my hand toward that knife until I feel the resistance of the knife on the table. Now I grasp the knife. This suggests that changes in resistance are a basic source of information when touching the environment (Lorenz, 1977). It is this change from no resistance to resistance that allows me to judge that I am at the knife, or, more generally, that there is an object in the world around me and that my body touches that object. Touching goes along with a change in topological relationships: Before touching, my body is separate from the world/object around me, while touching, I am together with the world/object.

Piaget (1961/1969) referred to perceptual activity. Taking out of the environment that tactual information which is needed for interacting requires that the organism is actively perceiving. Furthermore, it requires that such active perception is organized. A very fundamental kind of organization has to do with the critical sources of tactual information.

1.4.2.2.4 The Need to Organize the Search for Tactual Information. We observed young babies' behavioral changes in interactive natural situations. We tried to determine if and how their movement patterns changed when they touched the environment. We assumed that such observations permit inferences about underlying perceptual processes. We claimed (Affolter, 1987/1991) that a baby's movements are goal-oriented from birth on. They are oriented towards a search for information about the interaction between the body and the environment. This point can be illustrated with two examples, a normal baby and a baby with brain damage. Because this search involves the whole body, we refer to leg and foot movements and not just to the hands in the examples.

Example 1: T. is a 2-month-old normal baby.

Situation 1: She is lying on her back on the floor. Her legs move in free space. Repeatedly, one foot touches the other one; the little toes of one foot move along the other foot.

Situation 2: Now her feet can touch a wall. After she has touched it once, she repeatedly stretches her legs and appears to search for that wall. Whenever she succeeds, she keeps in contact with the wall for a short moment. At each contact, her toes move individually on the wall's surface. This kind of movement pattern, that is, stretching her legs, staying in contact with the wall, and moving her toes along it, can be observed repeatedly, but now her feet are not touching each other.

Situation 3: Now the mother takes T. on her lap. First she lifts her and T. gets tense. Then she puts T. on her lap and T. snuggles her body along the body of her mother and becomes limp.

Example 2: S. is a 6-month-old baby with brain damage.

Situation 1: He is lying on his back on the floor. His body is rigid. His legs are stiff and move rigidly in the air. Not once do his feet touch each other.

Situation 2: His legs touch the wall once. His body becomes more rigid; he moves his legs faster and hits the wall once more but they do not stay in contact with it; his toes do not move separately.

Situation 3: The mother lifts S. and takes him on her arm. S.'s body becomes more rigid, and his legs hard like sticks. This condition does not change even when his mother takes him on her lap.

Let us first consider the three situations. They differed in the topological relations between environment and baby. In the first situation, the babies lay on their backs on the floor and did not touch the wall. In the second situation, the babies touched the wall. In the third situation, the babies were first in the air, then touched their mother's lap.

In the case of the normal baby, these changes of topological relations coincided with changes in movement patterns. We concluded that the changes of topological relationships were concurrent with the changes in movement patterns. We inferred that the normal baby, T., searched for information each time the topological relations changed, as when her separation from the wall was changed to being together with the wall. T.'s movement patterns changed. First one foot was together with the other one, the toes moving along the other foot. Then, when touching the wall, the legs stretched out towards that wall. When in contact with the wall, the toes stayed on the surface of the wall, suggesting that T. changed sources of information. When foot touched foot, the source of information was between the two feet. When foot and then toes touched the wall, the source now was between foot and wall, toes and wall. When lifted by the mother, the baby did not touch a stable environment, there was no stable tactual source, and as a consequence the baby became rigid. Sitting in the lap, the tactual sources now were between T.'s body and the mother's body. Also, through the lap of the mother the baby could feel the stability of the chair (see Gibson's stick phenomenon, Section 1.4.2) and got oriented toward a stable tactual source of information and her body relaxed. We concluded that T., a normal baby, appeared to turn her attention to those sources of tactual information, which corresponded to a specific change in topological relationships between the body and the environment.

We then observed S., the baby with brain damage. The observable change in movement patterns was a kind of hitting in the direction of the wall when the topological relationships changed from being separate to being together with the wall. The legs were stiff, and they were stiff before, during, and after the change of topological relation between the body and the wall. The observed increase in tension suggested that S. noticed that some topological relationships had changed. But the feet appeared unable to stay with the wall to explore that new source of tactual information. Similarly was the behavior when the mother lifted the baby and put him in her lap. The tension in the body of the baby observable when the topological relations changed did not disappear when sitting in the lap of the mother. It suggests that the baby could not explore that new source of tactual information created between the body of the baby and the lap of the mother, a stable source as the mother was sitting on a chair.

The ability to change and explore sources of tactual information, when changes of topological relations occur, may be an important basic organization in the search for information. T., at 2 months, already appeared to show changes of behavior that can be accounted for by changes in source of information. S., at 6 months, appeared to fail in such basic organization in the search for information.

1.4.3   Nonverbal Daily-Life Interaction as Problem-Solving Events

By observing and analyzing children's nonverbal interactive behavior, we began to differentiate activities that reflect processes entailed in searching for information from those that establish cause–effect relationships (Affolter, 1984; Affolter & Bischofberger, 1988). We assumed that both cognitive (cause–effect relationships) and information aspects were constrained by the task. Thus, interactive events appeared to have three main components: cognitive, information, and task.

The Cognitive Component: Reaching goals of daily life includes changes of topological relationships. This requires consideration of causes and effects, or cognitive processes. For example: I want to grasp an orange from a basket on a shelf. To do this I have to change the topological relationship between my body and its support in order to displace my body and approach the orange. Furthermore, I have to change the topological relationships between and among orange/basket/table/mutual support and my body.

To perform causes and effects in daily interaction requires hypotheses to be made. If children grasp the wall when climbing, then they can lift their bodies. To make such hypotheses, children apply rules that refer to previous experiences (Holland, Holyoak, Nisbett, & Thagard, 1987). Performing an activity according to the rules, children search for feedback to judge the adequacies of their activities. Assuming that solving problems requires a certain level of cognitive development, we agree with Holyoak (1990) who wrote:

> All normal people do acquire considerable competence in solving at least some of the particular types of problems they habitually encounter in everyday life. We might therefore suspect that problem solving depends on general cognitive abilities that can potentially be applied to an essentially unlimited range of domains. (p. 117)

The Information Component: Problems of daily interaction are always solved in an actual situation. This actual situation has to offer the possibility to gain a critical amount of information about the problem to be solved. When children are successful on a specific task in a certain situation, we can conclude that they have reached the cognitive level to deal with that task. However, they may fail to perform this task, if the situation changes. When this is the case, we may conclude that in the changed situation, the children still have the cognitive prerequisites for doing the task in their competence, but they fail to perform the task because they are unable to extract enough information in the given situation.

> K., a 6-year-old girl, likes to hike with us in the mountains. She can do it for several hours and is quite skilled at walking on stony, rough mountain trails. In this instance it is wintertime, but there is not much snow on the roads. So we decide to take the mountain bus up beyond the village. We get off the bus. There is a very strong wind. The wind has piled up the small amount of snow so the road is hardly visible, and the depth of snow can hardly be predicted. K. refuses to step into the snow and walk on that kind of road.

In conclusion, K.'s hiking skills are still in her competence, but K. fails in performance because she cannot extract enough information in the changed situation. To perform, one has to consider a strong interrelationship between cognitive skills and information available in an actual situation.

To make valid inferences about a child's cognitive level, we must differentiate between competence and performance. When children do a task successfully in a specific situation, they not only have the cognitive prerequisites in their competence, but they also have them in their performance. In that specific situation, they are able to extract enough information from the environment to use their competence to solve the problem and perform the task. Therefore, when children fail to perform a task, they may not have the required cognitive prerequisites; that is, they are not competent to solve the task. It can also be the case that they do have the competence but cannot perform, because the situation demands more information than they can search for (Affolter, 1987/1991).

The Task Component: The task provides the goal. To reach the goal, problems have to be solved. Kintsch (1977) wrote, "One talks about a problem whenever there is something that one wants to do or achieve, but it is not immediately clear how to go about doing it" (p. 426). For example, a child is going down the street and sees a wall. The child intends to climb on it and walk along the top. The task is walking along the top of the wall. To fulfill that task, the child has to solve several problems: How do I reach up? Where do I get a hold to lift my body, my hands, arms, feet? How do I balance my body once on top of the wall? In the solving of one problem, another problem appears.

Such observations suggest that children's spontaneous daily activities are oriented towards solving problems to reach a specific goal. Children are usually very skilled in predicting the extent of the problems. The wall they see has to offer some challenge; children will choose to climb a wall if that wall is difficult to climb. This choice is skillfully made according to their possibilities and the situation: the height of the wall, their body height, their climbing skills, presence of familiar persons to help, and so forth.

In summary, nonverbal interaction with the environment when solving problems of daily life includes causes and effects. The basic causes and effects in nonverbal interaction have to do with changes in topological relationships between body/support/objects/persons. Solving problems in daily life requires such changes. Children learn from the regularities of such causes and effects and establish certain rules.

1.4.4 Nonverbal Daily-Life Interaction as Rule-Regulated

Children and adults apply several rules in daily interaction. The notion of rule development has been applied to other domains, such as language acquisition. Chomsky (1957) described the creative aspects of grammar by referring to a finite set of rules that are used to create sentences appropriate to an unlimited number of situations. Analogously, children learn a finite set of rules that allow them to code, store, and retrieve an unlimited number of nonverbal interactive experiences.

Rules for interaction are derived from regularities in the changes of topological relationships. The most basic rules, the touching rules, appear to be the first ones the baby learns. They are basic, because changing topological relationships always requires touching the environment and the resulting changes of topological relationships between body and environment allow differentiation of support/side/object. The object is viewed broadly here to include anything that can be separated from the support, an inanimate object, a person, or any other living organism.

Touching rules are followed by handling rules. Elementary handling rules deal with sequences of changes in topological relationships between body/support/object/person. The more complex handling rules deal with multiple changes of topological relationships among body/support/objects/persons.

We assume that children acquire such basic rules for interaction during the sensorimotor level (i.e., during the first 18 months, and before they reach the representational stage of development). For example, babies locomote from about 7 months on. They try to reach objects by crawling along the support. They get to know that what is on the floor can be reached and touched by crawling along the floor. This becomes a rule that the child applies in actual situations.

Once children have reached the representational level, they have to relearn those rules on that higher level (see Section 2.4). Piaget has described such relearning on a higher level of what has been acquired on a lower level in many of his books. It means that basic rules for interaction are utilized also by adults on a representational level as described in the following example:

> You are on top of a mountain looking down to the valley. Across from that valley there is another mountain. You want to climb it. To do this you have to judge the distance. You imagine in your mind, that is, you "represent" that you walk along the support—down the mountain, across the valley and up the other mountain. You have to do this to judge if you have time enough for that hike.

Because children with language disorders move in the same physical world as normal children do, one can assume that they are involved with the same types of changes of topological relationships as normal children. They also experience similar kinds of causes and effects. Therefore, we can expect that they develop competence for a set of rules for nonverbal interaction which are similar to those for normal children.

We next consider the three most important touching rules. Their acquisition is followed by handling rules. These rules are acquired hierarchically such that the simple ones are embedded in the more complex ones. For example, touching rules are embedded in the handling rules.

1.4.4.1 *Touching Rules*

To interact one has to touch the physical environment. To keep nonverbal interaction going, one has to continue the touching process. Touching the environment leads to a sequence of touching rules: support rule, moving rule, and holding-lifting rule. These rules of touching are interrelated and interdependent. The support rule is acquired first. The moving rule includes the support rule, and the holding-lifting rule includes both the support and the moving rule.

As soon as a baby is born, the baby touches the environment. Touching the environment produces changes in the topological relationships between body and the environment. By following children through their sensorimotor experiences, we can describe touching rules by referring to increasingly more complex changes in topological relationships between body and environment.

1.4.4.1.1 *Support and Sides.* Because life in the physical world involves gravity, a baby's most elementary experience is oriented towards gravity and includes changes of relationships between body and support. We propose that the support rule is the first rule of nonverbal interaction that a child learns.

The relationship between body and support becomes a very important elementary relationship. Whenever there is a sudden change in that relationship, as in the case of an earthquake, even adults with normal perceptual experience fright and panic. To feel secure we need a stable support. Numerous observations of daily-life behavior confirm this assumption. Here are a few examples:

P. is a 12-year-old boy with problems picking up adequate tactual information. As soon as he is not actively involved in a task and has to wait, he rocks his body back and forth, lifting one foot and then the other. One day I observe him when he was going down an unfamiliar set of stairs. He slides one foot along the support step until he reaches the edge of the step. He follows the edge with the heel of his foot downward until he reaches the support of the next step. There he puts his foot down. Then the other foot performs an identical sequence of movements. At the same time, he is holding onto the railing of the stairs with one hand, and touching the wall at his side with the other one. This is how he walks down the stairs—in continual direct contact with the support, the steps, the wall, and the railing.

A few weeks later I observed M., an 18-month-old normal infant, who was also going down an unfamiliar set of stairs. At first she behaves like P., the 12-year-old boy described in the preceding example. She goes back to these stairs frequently during the next 3 days. Already by the second day she is able to behave differently. She can now step down by lifting her foot into free space and placing it on the next step.

One can make similar observations of normal adults under certain circumstances. How does one walk down stairs in the dark? And what about lecturers who are under stress in front of an audience? They begin to shift their body from the right leg to the left, from one side to the other.

The importance of a stable support in interacting activities is further emphasized by watching infants who are beginning to explore the environment:

N. is a 22-month-old girl, who likes to climb on chairs so she can reach things on the tables. For a few days she is in a room she does not know well. There are two chairs in the room that she could use for climbing—one is a wooden chair and very stable, the other one is covered with a cozy warm sheepskin and is rather unstable. After a few attempts at climbing on the less stable chair, she never chooses it again.

In addition to the importance of stable resistance offered by the support, one also has to consider the resistance from the sides. This helps us to realize that the world includes not only the support underneath but also what is next to us. See descriptions of observations of babies from this perspective in Affolter (1987/1991).

In conclusion, both kinds of experiences with the support and with stable sides can be considered basic for nonverbal daily interaction. I have to know where the world is around me and, at the same time, where my body is before I can act upon it.

1.4.4.1.2 Moving and Holding/Lifting.

After some experience with the changes between body and support, the child extracts regularities in changes of topological relationships between body–support, and objects or persons on that support. Children discover that they touch things that offer other kinds of changes of resistance. These things can be moved, embraced, held, and lifted. These experiences are basic to the notion of an object as something that can be separate from the support, and is different from it, and basic to the learning of more complex touching rules. They apply not only to inanimate objects but also to persons and other living organisms.

During the first few months, babies frequently produce a kind of scratching movement when touching a resistance (Piaget, 1936/1952), as for example when lying on their stomach, on the floor. For this kind of exploration they not only utilize their hands but may also use their feet or other parts of the body. We interpret such behavior as a search for a resistance, which differs from the resistance of the support or the sides. By such explorations, they often find something that resists the scratching movements: perhaps a fold in the blanket, or an object on the floor. They learn that there are different kinds of resistance: one kind, the support, does not move; another kind does move and appears to be different from the support. It can be held and lifted.

1.4.4.2 Handling Rules

There are other rules that include the touching rules, but go beyond them. They deal with topological relationships between and among body/support/objects/persons. Because they require manipulations, we call them handling rules. We differentiate elementary and complex handling rules. Elementary handling rules deal with sequences of changes of topological relationships between body and support and object. Complex handling rules deal with multiple changes of topological relationships between and among body and support and objects/persons; they deal with neighborhood or proximity relations among objects and support. We next discuss elementary and complex handling rules.

1.4.4.2.1 Elementary Handling Rules: Separating and Releasing-With-Displacing. When babies begin to explore releasing-with-displacing from 7 months of age, they already generalize the possibility of separation to any visually perceived spot on the support. Can one take off a spot which differs visually from the floor—separate it? They will explore such rules. When the spot turns out to be an object, they will grasp it, take it off, and release it at another location. That is, they displace the object. They are also interactive with people. They explore separating hair/head, glasses/nose/face of people around.

Daily activities almost continually require the application of such handling rules: I need an object, such as a knife, I grasp it at a specific location, such as the drawer, and displace it to another location, such as next to the orange on the table, and release it there. We talk about releasing with displacement. The discovery of such handling rules is related to the amount of previous grasping experiences the baby has acquired during the preceding 4 to 7 months. There is a time delay of several months between the appearance of moving and holding/lifting and the discovery of releasing with displacement.

Careful analyses of videotaped observations of 7-month-olds, who had discovered releasing, suggest that such rules of separating, releasing, and displacing are interrelated. They include sequences of changes of topological relationships with connected changes of sources of information. Explorations of such sequences allow the baby to discover releasing-with-displacing and to acquire extensive experience with the releasing rule: What I can take off at one location on the support, I can put back at another location on the support. The child grasps an object, lifts it, and then releases it at another place. Each of these steps elicits changes in resistance between object and support. Such changes in resistance still appear to be the basic tactual information for the child when applying elementary handling rules.

1.4.4.2.2 *Complex Handling Rules: Rules of Proximity.* These rules have to do with topological relationships and their changes between and among body/support/objects/persons. We talk about proximity. Our observations of babies reveal that they begin to consider multiple topological changes: They take something out of something else; put something into another thing; put a cover on a bottle, and take it off. Such exploration of changes in topological relationships becomes more and more complex, as, for example, when the child begins filling and emptying. Affolter (1987/1991) has described such a development at length.

Growing children, after 18 months of age, will continue to interact: They will continue to organize their experiences according to these rules. We assume, as did Piaget (1947/1950), that these rules become more and more internalized with age, and can be used when solving problems of daily life on higher levels of development.

1.5 SUMMARY OF THE PROBLEM

Our program of research was motivated by the broader question of how to account for the abnormal language development in children without hearing or visual impairment. We were initially guided by the hypothesis that their verbal deficits were causally related to their lack of adequate nonverbal perceptual skills, which typically emerge before language.

Research findings of *cross-sectional* studies of perceptual development on Successive Pattern and Form Recognition tasks revealed:

1. Increased successful performances with age in normal children and in children with deprivation of auditory or visual sensory input. The age effect was interpreted as a sign of increasing skill in the organization of perceptual activity.

2. Increased success in different modalities until a ceiling level was reached in normal and sensory-deprived children. These findings sug-

gested that a critical degree of experiences may be basic for improving the organization of perceptual activity.

3. A deprivation effect in the nondeprived modalities of children with hearing or visual impairment when responding to complex perceptual tasks. This finding suggests that the experience basic to the organization required for complex tasks requires something beyond visual or auditory modality specific input. Also, observations of ceiling performances of both groups of sensory-deprived children suggest that the absence of auditory or visual input appears to delay development but does not prevent it from occurring. However, tactual input, which was commonly experienced by the normal group and both groups with sensory deprivation, may be a critical source of input for achieving a normal organization of perceptual activity. We proposed that successful performance on complex perceptual tasks requires tactual experience enhanced by vision and audition.

4. Patterns of perceptual performances in children with language disorders that differed from normal and sensory-deprived groups. Their lack of systematic improvement with age suggested the lack of the type of experience that is critical to improving perceptual organization.

The *longitudinal* research revealed:

1. Performance profiles which consistently differentiated three subgroups over the years. This finding suggests that skills at different levels are related. Their relationship, however, appears not to be a direct one. They may be related to a more basic and common source of experience with different perceptual features.

2. A sequence of developmental levels in children with language disorders that differed from the sequence of levels in normal and sensory-deprived children. This outcome suggested that developmental levels are not directly dependent on one another.

Neither the model of independent skills nor the model of hierarchical dependent levels of development could account for all the findings from the cross-sectional and longitudinal studies of development. We hypothesized that a common source of experience with information of a tactual kind accounts for normal development, and, at the same time, for the deviations of language-disordered children. To explore this possibility, the videotaped samples of children's spontaneous activities in daily life in the longitudinal research database were analyzed. The spontaneous activities of normal and hearing-impaired children were compared to those of language-disordered children. The observations revealed that normal and hearing-impaired children were almost continually involved with problems of an interactive kind.

- Such interactive behavior has the characteristics of problem-solving behavior, is nonverbal, and appears to require basic tactual information processing.
- Such interactive behavior also can be described as rule regulated and those rules are similar in children who are normal, hearing-impaired, or language-disordered.
- Children with language disorders have difficulties with such interactive behavior and their difficulties appear to be related to a problem of information.

These conclusions from the first period of research led to the following related working hypotheses about the basis for language disorders in children:

- Children with language disorders fail in perceptual organization.
- Their inadequate perceptual organization prevents adequate nonverbal interaction with the environment.
- Deviant experiences of interaction can explain deviant development on the nonverbal and verbal levels.

The failure in nonverbal interaction suggests that children with language disorders have difficulty with solving problems in daily events. To confirm this assumption, it was necessary to ask another set of questions: What do we know about nonverbal problem solving in children? How can nonverbal problem-solving processes be described ? Do they differ for normal children and children with language disorders? Is there a development of nonverbal problem-solving activities in children with language disorders? If so, does it differ from normally developing children? Do observed differences reflect developmental delay or deviancy?

To address these questions, the cross-sectional Seriation study was planned. Several constraints were imposed on the design of the study:

1. The problem-solving task had to include a goal to attain and offer feedback information for helping the child to establish hypotheses, to reach conclusions, and to judge success or nonsuccess. Performance patterns had to allow for inferences about the use of interactive rules.

2. The instruction had to be nonverbal to control for language problems of the children with language disorders. Our earlier studies had shown that knowledge about an event (the task) could be transmitted through tactual information.

3. The task had to have the possibility of being presented in different complexity and modality conditions so that competence and performance

could be differentiated. Our earlier research had shown that performance varied with task complexity (cognitive competence) and with the modality of sensory information (perceptual activity). Competence could be judged as present when a child solved the task in at least one modality condition.

4. The findings had to be applicable to daily-life events, because clinical intervention was the ultimate reason to do the research. That is, the goal was to also relate the outcomes of the Seriation study to observations of daily-life behavior. Kessen (1993) pointed out the importance of "the shift from the classical experiment to the observational study of everyday behavior" (p. 276).

Hence, the Seriation tasks were selected because they met all the above task constraints. The Seriation tasks also combined serial and spatial perceptual properties, which had been focused on separately in earlier cross-sectional perceptual studies.

Problem Solving in Normal and Language-Disordered Children: The Seriation Study

Daily nonverbal interactions, as the proposed source of learning and developing, are goal-oriented. They are directed toward achieving a problem-solving goal. In this chapter, we reveal what was learned about nonverbal interactive problem solving in normal children and children with language disorders when observing their performance on Seriation tasks.

Problem-solving performance is usually described in quantitative terms, as expressed by success scores on one or more tasks. The Seriation study focused on more than task success. We also wanted to explore the problem-solving activities and processes that lead to success or the lack of it. We observed how children physically handled the stimuli (i.e., interacted with the physical environment) when trying to solve the seriation problem. This latter goal led us to explore whether Pitt and Brouwer-Janse's (1985) model of problem-solving activities, which had been derived from a verbal reasoning task with normal adults, could be adapted for coding children's manual activities during the Seriation tasks.

We focus on the problem-solving process to explore what is involved in learning. To demonstrate, we use Seriation tasks to differentiate between competence and situation-dependent performance. Thus, we revisit what had been learned from earlier studies about the differential influence of sensory modality, task complexity, age, and the nature of language disorders on nonverbal performances.

In general, we expected to show that the same problem-solving activities and processes characterize both normal and language-disordered children; but the expression of competence in problem solving within and across these two groups is influenced in different ways by age and the kind of information inherent in the Seriation tasks. Furthermore, we predicted that children with language disorders were not expected to be like younger normal children in the distribution of problem-solving activities. Given their presumed perceptual difficulties, children with language disorders were expected to be more depressed on those activities or components having to do with the search for information than with the logical–hypothetical aspects. Conversely, younger normal children were expected to be more depressed on problem-solving components having to do with the logical–hypothetical aspects than the search for information. The performances of both groups were expected to be differentially influenced by the sensory information inherent in the task.

2.1   GENERAL METHOD AND PROCEDURES

2.1.1   Description and Selection of Subjects

This study compared 240 normal children and 50 children with language disorders on nonverbal Seriation tasks (see Table 2.1).

The normal group, ages 3;0 to 14;11 years, was divided by age into 12 groups of 20 each. Equal numbers of boys and girls at each age were randomly chosen from day care centers, kindergartens, elementary, and high schools. The children had normal hearing, vision, and language. Those in school were considered at least average students, who followed the required curriculum without difficulties, as judged from the annual teachers' reports.

The language disorder group included 50 children, ages 4;3 to 19;6 years. They were selected from the longitudinal clinical research group described by Affolter and Stricker (1980, pp. 163–164 and 166–169). All children with language disorders were at least 2 years below age level in receptive and expressive language. All were enrolled in speech–language therapy and followed a special education program. Many of them could not respond to formal tests. Therefore clinical observations were used to describe their performance profiles. The status of the children on some linguistic measures is shown in Appendix A, Table A1.

On the basis of their profiles of nonverbal performances, the children with language disorders were divided into two subgroups (see Table 2.2). The profiles were established by test findings and clinical observations, as described by Affolter, Brubaker, and Bischofberger (1974). For the Seriation tasks the few children with serial perceptual problems reacted similarly to the TK children so they were grouped together.

TABLE 2.1
Number and Age of Subjects in the Normal and Language Disorder Groups

Normal Children (N = 240)	Age in Years	Mean[a]	SD	Children With Language Disorders (N = 50)	Age in Years	Mean (Months)	SD
Age group 1: n = 20	3;0 - 3;11	41.55	3.8				
Age group 2: n = 20	4;0 - 4;11	54.00	3.5				
Age group 3: n = 20	5;0 - 5;11	66.05	3.7	Age group 1: n = 21	4;3 - 8;0	76.00	13.2
Age group 4: n = 20	6;0 - 6;11	78.45	3.4				
Age group 5: n = 20	7;0 - 6;11	90.45	3.6				
Age group 6: n = 20	8;0 - 8;11	101.3	3.4				
Age group 7: n = 20	9;0 - 9;11	114.6	3.3	Age group 2: n = 17	8;1 - 11;0	114.1	10.5
Age group 8: n = 20	10;0 - 10;11	127.7	2.6				
Age group 9: n = 20	11;0 - 11;11	140.0	2.3				
Age group 10: n = 20	12;0 - 12;11	151.9	3.3	Age group 3: n = 12	11;1 - 19;6	160.5	31.2
Age group 11: n = 20	13;0 - 13;11	163.5	2.7				
Age group 12: n = 20	14;0 - 14;11	175.3	2.7				

Note.
[a]Mean age and SD in months.
3;11 represents 3 years and 11 months.

TABLE 2.2

Number and Age of Subjects in the Language Disorder Subgroups (N = 50)

Age in Years[b]	Tactual–Kinesthetic and Serial Perceptual Problems (TK/S: n = 27)[a]		Mean[c]	SD	Perceptual Problems in Intermodal Organization (IM: n = 23)		Mean	SD
Age group 1 4;3–8;0	n = 14		74.57	13.5	n = 7		78.86	13.3
Age group 2 8;1–11;0	n = 11		117.6	10.4	n = 6		107.8	8.0
Age group 3 11;1–19;6	n = 2		139.0	0.00	n = 10		164.8	32.7

[a]Including one child with serial perceptual problems in each age group (i.e., a total of three children).

[b]4;3 represents 4 years and 3 months.

[c]Mean age and SD in months.

76

The TK/S subgroup included 27 children, ages 4;3 to 15;7 years. They scored lower than their age level on tasks that rely critically on tactual information processing (e.g., tactual matching of identical forms). However, they scored at age level on tasks that critically require the processing of visual information (e.g., visual matching of identical forms; Affolter & Stricker, 1980, pp. 54–66).

The IM subgroup included 23 children, ages 5; 3 to 19; 6 years. They scored at age level or higher on tasks that require only visual (or auditory) information (e.g., visual matching of identical forms), but they scored below age level on tasks requiring intermodal information (e.g., tactual–visual matching of identical forms; Affolter & Stricker, 1980, pp. 54–66). For more behavioral description of these children, see Section 1.3.1.

2.1.2 Description of Tasks

The nonverbal seriation problem required replicating a version of a model: displacing bars of different lengths from one site to another and assembling them to construct a stair series with an even base line and a stair-like top line. The Seriation tasks, used by Piaget and Inhelder (1956/1964), were adapted to study problem-solving activities from different points of view in the same child. From a cognitive view, the seriation problem was presented under two different stimulus complexity conditions, the short stair series and the long stair series. From the view of problem-solving processes (Anzai, 1987) and from the view of information, the same seriation problem was presented in four different modality conditions: visual (v), visual–visual (vv), tactual (t), and tactual–visual (tv). Altogether six tasks were presented to each child.

For every task, there were stimulus forms (the bars) at a stimulus site. There was also a construction site. All the bars that the child had to choose from were present at the stimulus site. The child could touch and lift them in order to select one. This was considered picking up information about the initial state of the task. The selected bars had to be displaced and released at the construction site to be arranged there according to the requirements of the task: the goal state. It was expected that children would apply some criteria to judge the progression of the task. They would focus on subgoals. For example, the empty spaces at the top of the aligned bars became smaller and smaller, whereas the bottom line extended, so that the insert board appeared to be filling up.

2.1.2.1 Modality Conditions

To study how information affected performance, the Seriation tasks were presented in four modality conditions to each child. Two modality conditions offered only visual information; one only tactual information, and one both tactual and visual information combined.

2.1.2.1.1 Tactual–Visual Modality Condition.

In the tactual–visual (tv) modality condition, the children inserted the stimulus bars into the same insert board as in the tactual condition (see Fig. 2.1). They could see and feel the insert board (i.e., they could run hands and fingers over the insert board to feel the resistance and look at what the hands were doing at the same time). Therefore, they could control the insertion of the bars into the openings by both tactual and visual information.

2.1.2.1.2 Visual Modality Conditions.

In all the visual modality conditions, the child was shown a red drawing of a model or template of the stair-like ordered bars. This model and the respective individual bars were presented to the child (see Fig. 2.2). The model was the same size and shape as the short/long stair series that had to be constructed. The children were offered visual information for controlling their construction of the stair series. In one visual modality condition, the vv task, the children constructed the seriation or stair series by placing the bars directly on top of the stair-like model so that the bars covered the design. In the other visual conditions, the v and V tasks of the short and long stair series, respectively, the children had to construct the seriation or stair series by placing the bars next to the model (i.e., below the model on a white sheet of paper between the model and the child).

2.1.2.1.3 Tactual Modality Conditions.

The insert board and the respective bars were presented to the children from behind a screen (see Fig. 2.3) for both tactual tasks, t and T, which were respectively present-

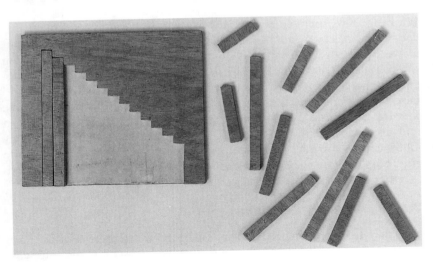

FIG. 2.1. Tactual–visual modality condition.

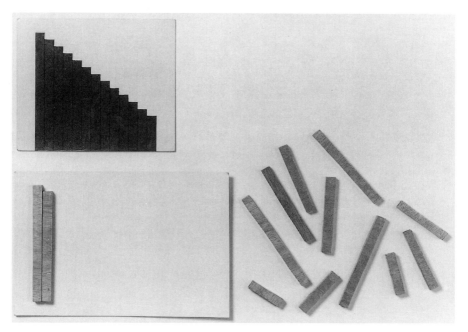

FIG. 2.2.   Visual modality conditions: Short stair series.

ed in the short and long stair series. The children had to reach through an opening covered by a curtain and to insert bars into the insert board. The children could touch the insert board; that is, they could run hands and fingers along the insert board and the bars to feel the resistances or effects of inserting the bars into the insert board. But, they could not look at what they were doing. Thus, only tactual information was available.

2.1.2.2 Task Complexity

The experiment included two complexity levels: the construction of a short and a long stair series. For the short stair series ABCDEF . . . , 13 bars ABC . . . had to be arranged so that their base line was straight and the top line was stair-like. The other series was called a long stair series because it consisted of 25 bars arranged in the series AaBbCcDdEeFf. . . . This long series, an insertion task, required that a new series, abcdef . . . (12 bars), be inserted into the first series ABCDEF . . . (13 bars). ABCDEF . . . was already constructed and presented to the children. See Figs. 2.4 & 2.5 for the long stair series.

In Piaget and Inhelder's study (1956/1964), children ages 4;0 to 6;0 years, arranged a series of bars ABCD . . . of increasing length by compar-

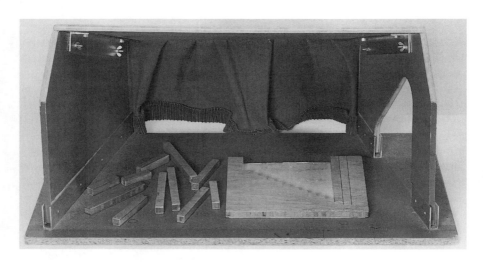

FIG. 2.3. Tactual modality condition: Short stair series.

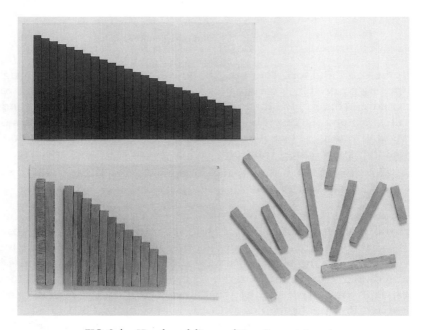

FIG. 2.4. Visual modality condition: Long stair series.

FIG. 2.5. Tactual modality condition: Long stair series.

ing pairs of bars. But they were unable to insert a second series of bars, abcd . . . between the bars of the first series so that the series became AaB-bCcDd. . . . To solve this insertion problem, the child needed to make multiple comparisons; B is at the same time shorter than a and longer than b—thus the sequence aBb. . . . Children older than 6 years were able to solve this insertion problem. Piaget and Inhelder inferred that these older children had reached a higher level of cognitive development.

2.1.3 Construction of Test Materials

The bars were made of plywood, 14×14 mm wide, varying in length from 50 to 170 mm. Length differences of 5 mm (for the long stair series) and 10 mm (for the short stair series) were easily discernible for both visual and tactual modality conditions, as observed in a pilot study.

For the tactual–visual and tactual modality conditions, a three-dimensional wooden board was used as a model form. The insert board offered tactual feedback to the children when inserting bars. The insert board for the short stair series (t and tv) was 87.5 mm wide, 178.5 mm long, and 14 mm thick. The insert board for the long stair series (T) was 101.5 mm wide, 318.5 mm long, and 14 mm thick. Stair series were cut out on each insert board so that the bars for both stair series would fit into the sawed out space. Cardboard backing was fixed to each insert board.

For the visual modality conditions (tasks v, vv, and V), a red drawing on cardboard corresponded to the exact size and arrangements of the bars as used in the tactual and tactual–visual modality conditions.

2.1.4   Test Situation

The examiner sat on the child's left side (on the side of the table at a 90°
angle). In this way he or she could easily guide the child's hands from that
side, and place the bars from the table into the child's right hand. In the tactual modality conditions, the material was hidden by a box-like screen to
prevent the child from getting any visual information. The box-like screen
opened away from the child's line of vision, so that a video camera could
record the hand activities and face, for example, eye gaze (see Fig. 2.6).

The models, representing the series of bars arranged as stairs, were presented to the children for replication. The stair series had an even base
line and a stair-like top line. The children were required to select one bar
at a time from randomly sorted bars and place it in the same order as was
represented on the model. In the visual modality conditions, the drawing
of a stair (visual model) was placed on the table before the children. They
had to place the bars in a stair-like order on (the vv task) or next to the
visual models (the v and V tasks). In the tactual modality condition, the
insert board was hidden within a cubicle with one opening covered by a
curtain but accessible to examiner observation from the other open side.
In the tactual–visual modality condition, the insert board was placed
before the child, so the child could watch as the bars were inserted.

FIG. 2.6.   Test situation.

2.1.5 Data Collection Procedures

Clinical experience had shown that some children with language disorders did not understand verbal instructions or could not initiate a required action. In these cases, it was desirable to take their hands and perform activities that other children can do spontaneously. We called this "guiding." This guiding method was explored in the study of Form Recognition tasks reported in chapter 1. Findings of that study supported the assumption that guided tactual information successfully transmits information about an event.

2.1.5.1 Instructions for Doing Task

The children were tested individually. No verbal instructions were given. The instruction was planned so that the child did not have to initiate any action. The examiner took a child's hands and guided them to interact with test material which provided "control-feedback information." In this manner, instructions were given by "doing with" the child, thereby providing tactual information about the problem to be solved.

The child received guided instructions for each modality condition (see Appendix A). When the child was judged "testable" (for criteria also see Appendix A) and started to solve a task but did not proceed correctly, the incorrectly placed bars were removed with the examiner's guidance, and the task was started again. If after the second attempt the child did not proceed correctly, then any performance was accepted. If the child did not proceed at all in a given task, the child was judged "instructable" but "nontestable" on that task and the next task in the sequence was started.

2.1.5.2 Task Sequence

Once the child was judged *testable*, the testing always began on two tasks of the short stair series (see Fig. 2.7). The sequence of the first two tasks was counterbalanced so that 50% of the children were tested first on task v (c) followed by t (d), and 50% were tested in the reverse order, task t (d) followed by task v (c). This procedure controlled for a potential modality effect. We were not sure whether prior visual information would influence later performance in the tactual modality condition.

The third and fourth tasks for all children were the tv (a) and vv (b) tasks. Children, who performed successfully on the short stair series of the v (c) and t (d) tasks, were tested further on the long stair series of the V (E) and T (F) tasks, respectively.

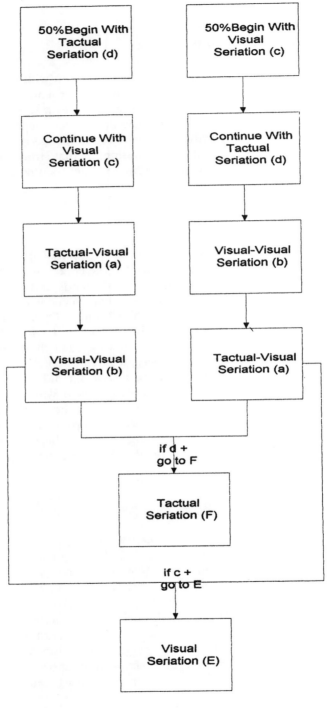

FIG. 2.7. Task sequence.

2.1.5.3   *Recording of Test Performances*

Each child was tested on each task by two examiners. One examiner interacted with the child; the other observed and recorded the behaviors. The examiners were the authors' clinical coworkers. They received two weeks of daily training sessions with normal children. The examiners had to learn how to guide a child through the nonverbal instructions, and judge and record the respective nonverbal behaviors in the test situation on the standard record form (see Appendix B, Table B1) for independent corroboration with the other examiner's observations.

Two normal children from the 20 in each age group were randomly chosen for filming. All 50 children with language disorders were filmed or videotaped during their problem-solving activities.

Record forms, films, and videotapes were analyzed by using criteria for judging the presence or absence of problem-solving activities relevant for solving the seriation problem (see Section 2.3.1, Table 2.7, Behavior Descriptions).

2.1.6   Data Analyses

This study analyzed nonverbal performances on the Seriation tasks in relation to four independent variables.

2.1.6.1   *Independent Variables*

One set of independent variables was guided by our basic goal of revealing if and how normally developing children differ from those with language disorders, and by the assumption that the clinical group is not homogeneous. Hence, one independent variable was defined by membership in a normal group, or in one of two language-disorder subgroups consisting of children with either tactual–kinesthetic/serial or intermodal perceptual deficits.

Another set of independent variables followed from a basic assumption derived from our earlier research: Cognitive competence should be differentiated from performance, as the expression of competence in an actual situation. Earlier studies had shown that performance could vary with age, an index of stored experiences and organization of perceptual activity. At a given age, performance can vary further with task conditions: the stimulus complexity, an index of cognitive demand; and the sensory modality of task presentation, an index of information demand. These three independent variables included age (3 to 6 levels), task complexity (2 levels), and sensory modality conditions (4 levels).

2.1.6.2   *General Structure of Data Analysis*

One or more of these independent variables were analyzed in relation to three types of dependent performance variables: success scores, problem-solving activities, and rule application. Thus, the first set of analyses focused on whether or not the children were successful on every task or some of the tasks in solving the seriation problem. The second set of analyses focused on their problem-solving activities and processes. The third and final analysis focused on the kind of solutions given to the seriation problem, as reflected in the configurations or products produced. From the configurations produced, we inferred the interaction rules that children used to reach the various solutions to the seriation problem. Statistical analyses of the data involved parametric multivariate procedures (analysis of variance; Wilkinson, 1990) and nonparametric procedures (Winer, 1971) where appropriate.

Analysis of each dependent variable was structured to reveal evidence for the competence–performance distinction. This was done for each of three levels of analysis (success scores, problem-solving activities, and rule application) by showing first how well children at different ages did on an overall measure of performance, which disregarded task complexity and modality of presentation. This general measure was interpreted as a broad index of competence. It was compared to task-specific measures of performance, which showed how well the children solved the seriation problem when the information and complexity conditions for doing the task were considered. Task-specific measures were viewed as evidence for the constraints on performance in an actual situation. We expected to show that a general index of competence does not accurately predict whether a child can solve the seriation problem. In the main, our larger goal was to show that children may have the competence to solve the seriation problem, but the expression of their competence as performance is dependent on the information in a particular situation. This is valid for normal children as well as language-disordered children.

2.2   SPECIFIC ANALYSES AND RESULTS: TASK SUCCESS

The goal of the Seriation tasks was the construction of a stair series. At the beginning of the task, all the bars were in one place, the stimulus site and the model in another place, at the construction site. One bar had to be chosen from all the others; the chosen bar had to be taken off the table (the support), displaced from the stimulus site to the construction site, and released there. The task was finished when all the bars were displaced from the stimulus site to the construction site.

2.2.1 Criteria for Task Success

A child was judged to be successful when the configuration created an exact replica of the seriation model. A score of 1 was given for success on a task, and 0 for any other configuration. No credit was given for a partial solution.

For each child, a cumulative success score was calculated. Because there were six tasks, the maximum possible success score was 6 (i.e., the child scored 1 on each of the six tasks: tv, vv, v, t, V, T). Success on just 3 of the 6 tasks (e.g., the tv, v, and vv modality conditions, yielded a score of 3). Success scores therefore could range from 0 (*no replication of the model in any of the six tasks*) to 6 (*replication of models in all six tasks*).

2.2.2 Data Analyses and Predictions for Task Success

The analysis of task success was guided by three main questions. The first question focused on how successful children at different ages were in solving the same seriation problem. The last two questions targeted specific task conditions that were expected to influence task success. We questioned whether success would vary with task complexity or with the kind of sensory modality in which the seriation problem had to be solved.

1. We examined for an *age* effect. Parents and professionals often do not consider a child competent to solve a problem until it can be done in all situations or tasks. Thus, we focused first on maximum success, which was attained when a child successfully solved the seriation problem in all six tasks (success score of 6).

If achieving task success were purely a cognitive problem, one could expect success regardless of task conditions. But if the conditions of performance are related to success, then success should vary with conditions. This outcome should result in both the number and types of tasks or situations in which the problem is solved. Hence, the second analysis made allowances for solving the problem in some conditions because we did not expect children to be successful on all six tasks at once. The analysis assumed that competence in solving the seriation problem is evident when a child succeeds even on one task. We asked if success scores shifted with age when success was not measured in an absolute or maximum way, and therefore included the full range of success scores of 1 to 6.

(a) For maximum success (success score of 6), it was expected that frequency does increase with age in the normal group (age effect), but not for children with language disorders (no age effect).

(b) For any success (success score range 1 to 6), it was expected that frequency does increase with age in both groups.

2.   To analyze the *complexity* effect, success on the short and long stair series was compared. The tasks yielding early versus later success were not expected to be random or unpredictable across children. We predicted that both normal and language-disordered children would become competent to do the short stair before the long stair series.

3.   To analyze the *modality* effect, success on tasks in the tactual–visual, visual, visual–visual, and tactual modality conditions was compared. Being competent to construct the short stair does not mean that children will solve the seriation problem all the time. Performing should still depend on the information inherent in the situation. We expected the normal children to be most successful in solving the short stair seriation problem when both tactual and visual information were available (tv task), and to be least successful when just tactual information was available (t task) while the results of the visual conditions (v and vv tasks) were expected to fall in between.

Children with language disorders were expected to differ from normal children and from each other. Those with tactual/serial deficits were expected to have the same sequence as normal children, but even lower scores on the tactual tasks than normal children and other language-disordered children with intermodal deficits. Those with intermodal deficits were expected to have a different developmental sequence than normal children and other language-disordered children with tactual/serial deficits. They would solve the seriation problem in a visual condition before doing so in the tactual–visual one, and their tactual–visual scores would be lower than those for other groups.

2.2.3   Results and Discussion of Success Scores

The score distributions are shown in relation to age for the normal children and for children with language disorders in Tables 2.3 and 2.4, respectively. Data for the normal children are shown only up to age 9, which includes just 120 of the 240 children studied between ages 3;0 and 15;0, because most normal children had reached maximum or ceiling scores by age 9.

2.2.3.1   *Maximum Success Scores in Relation to Age and Group Membership*

Table 2.3 shows that, for normal children, maximum success scores of 6 increased regularly with age. Below age 6, no child achieved maximum success scores. The percentages increased to 25% at 6;0 to 6;11 years (5 of 20 children) and 35% at 7;0 to 7;11 years (7 of 20 children), and at 8;0 to 8;11 years, 85% solved the seriation problem in all six conditions. Figure 2.8, which plots this age trend, shows that normal chil-

TABLE 2.3
Frequency Distribution of Success Scores 0 to 6 in Normal Children (n = 120)

Score (Age in Years)	3 to 4	4 to 5	5 to 6	6 to 7	7 to 8	8 to 9	Total
6	0	0	0	5	7	17	29
5	0	0	1	7	4	1	13
4	0	0	4	5	8	2	19
3	0	1	5	0	1	0	7
2	1	2	5	3	0	0	11
1	1	4	0	0	0	0	5
0	18	13	5	0	0	0	36
Total Number	20	20	20	20	20	20	120
% 6 Scores	—	—	—	20	20	20	29
% 1–5 Scores	10	35	75	25	35	85	55
% 0 Scores	90	65	25	75	65	15	36
% 1–6 Scores	10%	35%	75%	0	0	0	
				100%	100%	100%	

TABLE 2.4
Frequency Distribution of Success Scores 0 to 6 in Children With Language Disorders

Success/Age	4 to 8 Years	8 to 11 Years	11 to 19 Years	Total
6	0	4	5	9
5	0	0	1	1
4	1	4	2	7
3	0	1	0	1
2	5	0	1	6
1	2	2	2	6
0	13	6	1	20
Total number	21	17	12	50
% 6 Scores	--	23	42	9
% 1-5 Scores	38	42	50	21
% 0 Scores	62	35	8	20
% 1-6 Scores	38%	65%	92%	

dren obtained ceiling scores in the age range of 10 to 14 years. A statistically significant correlation was observed between age and maximum success scores ($r = .886 \; p < .001$). The high relationship leads us to conclude that age is a good predictor of how normal children will perform on Seriation tasks.

In contrast to normal children, Table 2.4 reveals that a lower percentage of the children with language disorders achieved maximum scores in all three age ranges, and score increments across age were small. This age trend is plotted in Fig. 2.9. No child below 8 years ($n = 21$) achieved maximum success scores. Between ages 8 to 11, 24% (4 of 17) of the children did so. At 11 years and older, 42% (5 of 12) had maximum success scores. Less than 50% of the children with language disorders obtained maximum scores in any age range.

The correlation between age and maximum success scores was positive, however it did not differ significantly from zero ($r = .23 \; p > .05$). We infer that age does not appear to be a good predictor of how children with language disorders will perform on Seriation tasks.

The regular increase of maximum success scores with age in normal children suggests that their success on the Seriation tasks was strongly influenced by their cognitive levels. Because all children were exposed to

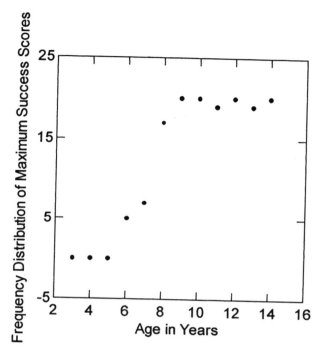

FIG. 2.8.   Frequency distribution of maximum success scores in normal children.

identical stimuli, we inferred that score shifts with age were also due to improvements in children's own ability to organize their search for relevant information needed to solve the problem.

Conversely, maximum success scores do not appear to be a good index of the cognitive competence in children with language disorders. In fact, given their low frequency of maximum success at every age relative to normal children, they could be viewed as generally cognitively incompetent to do the Seriation tasks, and as functioning at the level of younger normal children who also did not obtain maximum scores. If they were simply like younger normal children, there should have been regular maximum score gains as they got older, despite a time delay. But their depressed scores at every age and lack of regular shifts with age do not allow us to infer a simple delay in cognitive development. Other factors, besides cognitive level as indexed by age, appeared to influence the performance of language-disordered children. This interpretation was supported by data, which showed that they were competent to solve the seriation problem in some task conditions but not others, as revealed in the following analyses.

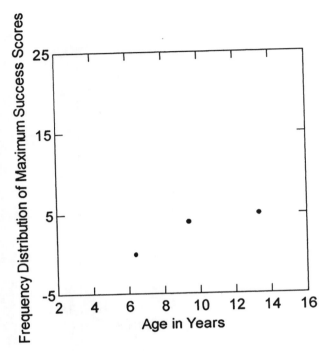

FIG. 2.9.   Frequency distribution of maximum success scores in children with language disorders.

2.2.3.2   Range of Success Scores as a Function of Age and Group Membership

In both the normal and language disorder groups, success scores ranged from 0 to 6 as shown, respectively, in Tables 2.3 and 2.4. A score of zero meant that a child did not solve the seriation problem in any condition, and it was interpreted as evidence for the lack of cognitive competence in solving the problem. Scores of 1 to 5 gave evidence that a child was cognitively competent to do the task, but that the expression of this competence was context-dependent.

Tables 2.3 and 2.4 show that in the normal and language disorder groups, the decreased frequency of zero scores across age corresponded with increased frequency of scores ranging from 1 to 6. In the normal group, no zero scores were observed at 6 years and older, and only 8% (1 of 12) of the oldest language-disordered children had zero scores at 11 years and older. The decreased frequency of zero scores means that the children in both groups became more cognitively competent with age, and this competence could be observed at earlier ages than maximum success scores predict.

At every age, the normal group included a few children who were cognitively competent on one or more tasks even though they did not achieve maximum success. As early as 3 years of age, 10% (2 of 20) of the children solved the Seriation tasks in at least one condition. That percentage increased to 35% at 4;0 to 4;11 years and 75% at 5;0 to 5;11 years. Given that there were no zero scores at 6 years and older, we can infer that all children by this age were competent to solve the problem in one or more conditions, although the majority did not achieve maximum success scores until 8 years or older.

The results for the children with language disorders were even more dramatic when competence was not based on maximum success scores. At the youngest ages observed (4 to 8 years), 38% or 8 of the 21 children were competent to solve the seriation problem in some conditions compared to 0%, using a maximum score criterion. The percentages of children with successful scores increased to 65% (11 of 17 children) at 8 to 11 years, and 92% (11 of 12 children) at 11 years and older.

It appears that maximum success scores underestimate the competence of both normal and language-disordered children. They do not take into account the differential influence of the performance conditions on expressions of competence. The following analyses identify which conditions of complexity and of modality favored successful performance and which ones did not in both groups, when children did not obtain maximum success scores.

2.2.3.3 Success Scores and Task Complexity

The Seriation tasks were presented at two levels of complexity: the short stair series with 13 bars and the long stair series with 25 bars. The results are presented in Tables 2.5 and 2.6 for normal and language-disordered children, respectively. In the tables, the tasks for the short stair series are represented as abcd (tactual–visual (tv); visual–visual (vv); visual (v); and tactual (t), respectively). The tasks for the long stair series are represented as E and F, visual (V) and tactual (T), respectively). By inspecting the lowest success scores of 1 to 3 we can infer which tasks for solving the seriation problem were easier and solved at younger ages. Lower success scores were generally associated with younger ages whereas higher scores were associated with older ages as shown.

Table 2.5 shows that all 23 of the normal children or 100% with scores of 1 to 3 were first successful in solving the seriation problem in one or

TABLE 2.5
Success Scores in Relation to Task Conditions (Complexity and Modality) in Normal Children ($n = 120$)

Tasks/ Success Scores	0	1	2	3	4	5	6	Age Range In Years
	3 to 4	3 to 4	3 to 6	4 to 7	5 to 8	5 to 8	6 to 8	
a[a]		5 (100%)						
ab			11(100%)					
abc				7 (100%)				
abcd					3 (16%)			
abcE					16 (84%)			
abcdF						1 (8%)		
abcdE						12 (92%)		
Total ($n = 120$)	36(100%)	a 5(100%)	ab 11(100%)	abc 7(100%)	abcd 3(16%) abcE 16(84%)	abcdF 1 (8%) abcdE 12 (92%)	29(100%)	

Note.
[a]Tasks:
a = tactual-visual modality condition (tv); short stair series.
b = visual-visual modality condition (vv); short stair series.
c = visual modality condition (v); short stair series.
d = tactual modality condition (t); short stair series.
E = visual modality condition (V); long stair series.
F = tactual modality condition (T); long stair series.

TABLE 2.6
Success Scores in Relation to Task Conditions (Complexity and Modality) in Children With Language Disorders (n = 50)

Tasks/ Success Scores	0 4 to 19	1 4 to 19	2 4 to 19	3 8 to 19	4 4 to 19	5 11 to 19	6 8 to 19	Age Range In Years
a[a]		1 (17%)						
b		4 (66%)						
c		1 (17%)						
ab			6 (100%)					
abc				1 (100%)				
abcd					1 (14%)			
abcE					6 (86%)			
abcdE						1 (100%)		
abcdF								
Total (n = 50)	20(100%)	a 1 (17%) b 4 (66%) c 1 (17%)	ab 6 (100%)	abc 1 (100%)	abcd 1 (14%) abcE 6 (86%)	abcdF 1 (8%) abcdE 1 (100%)	29(100%) 9 (100%)	

Note.
[a]Tasks:

a = tactual-visual modality condition (tv); short stair series.
b = visual-visual modality condition (vv); short stair series.
c = visual modality condition (v); short stair series.
d = tactual modality condition (t); short stair series.
E = visual modality condition (V); long stair series.
F = tactual modality condition (T); long stair series.

95

more of the short stair series. None was successful on either of the two long stair series. Therefore, the short stair series were overall less difficult than the long stair series at the youngest ages.

However, success as a function of task complexity was confounded by modality condition. The long visual stair series was easier for more children than the short tactual stair series. This confounding modality effect was found for the 19 normal children with a success score of 4. A significantly higher percentage of them (84%) solved the seriation problem in the visual long stair series (the abcE pattern) before the tactual short stair series was solved. A significantly lower percentage (16%) solved the seriation problem in all four short stair series, which included the tactual stair series for the abcd pattern, before any of the long stair series were solved.

The highest percentage of the 13 normal children (92%) with success scores of 5 had the abcdE pattern, which included the visual long stair series but excluded the tactual long stair series. This means that they solved the seriation problem in the short stair tactual task before they solved it in the long stair tactual series.

We infer a 5-step developmental sequence:

1. Failure to solve the problem in any complexity condition;
2. Solving the seriation problem in the tactual–visual and in both visual short stair series (abc);
3. Solving the seriation problem as in Step (2) and in addition in the visual long stair series (abcE);
4. Solving the seriation problem in all short stair series (including the short tactual stair series) and in the long visual stair series (abcdE);
5. Solving the seriation problem in all the short and the long stair series.

Table 2.6 shows that task complexity similarly affected the performance of children with language disorders and normal children. Low scores (1 to 3), observed between 4 and 11 years of age, corresponded with success on one or more of the short stair tasks. Success was never observed on either of the two long stair tasks. This observation suggests that the short stair series was easier than the long stair series. Again, complexity was confounded by modality of presentation. Early success on the short stair tasks was restricted to one or more of the tv, vv, or v conditions (i.e., a, b, and c). None was successful on the tactual short stair task (d). Of the seven children with score of 4, a higher percentage (86%) was successful on the short stair series (tv, vv, and v) and on the visual long stair series. Only a small percentage (14%) was successful on the four short stair series (including the tactual short stair series) but not on the long stair series. This observation, like that of normal children, shows that, in the visual modality, success occurred on the short before the long stair series.

In the tactual modality the evidence for a developmentally ordered complexity effect was similar. But it was less compelling than in the visual modality: Success on the tactual short stair series was barely represented in the data. When successful in the tactual modality, most language-disordered children were successful on both tactual modality conditions. Exceptions were the patterns, of one child with success score of 4 (abcd) and one child with success score of 5 (abcdE), which included only one tactual task (d). Both children showed success on the tactual short stair series (task d) and not on long stair series (task F). It is tempting to infer from the data that language-disordered children's failure to solve the tactual problem at either complexity level was followed by success at both levels of complexity, a different developmental pattern from normal children. A larger subject pool from different age cross-sections or longitudinal data would be needed to defend this interpretation.

In sum, the data supported the prediction that task complexity influences success on the Seriation tasks. In the normal groups, the short visual and the short tactual series were constructed before both long stair series in the respective modalities. In the group of children with language disorders the short visual series were constructed before both long stair series. This is not the case for the tactual series for most language-disordered children. If they constructed the tactual short stair series at all, they also constructed the tactual long stair series.

Normal children were older when they succeeded on the long stair series compared to the short stair series. This observation can be viewed as a cognitive gap, meaning that the construction of long stair series demands different cognitive skills than the construction of short stair series.

Since language-disordered children with success scores of 4 constructed the visual short *and* long stair series in the same testing session, we infer that cognitively they were able to perform a long stair series. But their failure to construct the tactual short stair series before the long one at younger ages suggests they could not utilize their cognitive competence because of difficulty with using tactual information.

2.2.3.4   *Success Scores and Modality Conditions*

The seriation problem was presented to the children under different modality conditions. They offered visual, or tactual, or combined tactual–visual information for replicating the model of the task. The outcomes can be derived from the data on normal and language-disordered children in Tables 2.5 and 2.6, respectively. Again, the ease or difficulty of the tasks can be inferred from the data shown in the tables for children with low success scores.

For normal children, Table 2.5 reveals that those who solved the seriation problem in just one modality condition did so only in the tactual–visual modality (a), which was presented in the short stair condition. In addition to the tv task, all the children or 100% with scores of 2 and 3 were successful on one or both visual tasks (a or b). As pointed out earlier, none of the low scores included success on a tactual task.

The ease of doing the visual task was reflected even among the normal children with higher success scores. Higher percentages (84% and 92% for scores 4 and 5, respectively) of them were more often successful on the visual task presented in the more complex long stair series than on the corresponding tactual task. Inspecting Table 2.5, once more, it can be seen that the majority of the normal children, 84% to 100%, were successful on task combinations that excluded one or both tactual tasks (cf. ab, abc, abcE, and abcdE).

Test results for language-disordered children are shown in Table 2.6. They were alike and different from normal children. They were similar in that they were less successful on tactual tasks than on tasks that included combined tactual–visual or just visual information. Note that just one child with a score of 4 did the tactual short stair task in an abcd task combination and one child with a score of 5 solved both the short and long stair tactual tasks in the abcdF combination. Otherwise success was demonstrated almost exclusively on task combinations that excluded tactual information.

The greatest difference between normal and language disorder groups was observed for children who were successful on just one task. Whereas all the normal children with the score of 1 were successful in only the tactual–visual condition, just one (16%) of the language-disordered children was successful on the tactual–visual condition. The highest percentage of language-disordered children (83% or 5 out of the 6) with a success score of 1 successful on a visual task. The vv task must have been easiest to do because it was solved by more children than was the v task. The vv task allowed the children to place the stimulus bars directly on the visual model of the serially arranged bars whereas the bars were placed beside the visual model in the v task.

Taken together, the results show that success on the Seriation tasks was dependent on the information inherent in the tasks for both normal and language-disordered children. We infer that both groups were able to pick up more information about solving the problem in the tactual–visual condition or visual conditions but not in the tactual condition. Although normal children seem to profit from combined tactual–visual information at an early age, language-disordered children may vary in the extent to which they can pick up intermodal information in the tactual–visual condition. Most often they solved the problem when just visual information was available.

The difficulty of the tactual tasks for all children suggests that less information was available in the tactual than the visual tasks (see discussions in Section 1.2.1). Even so, language-disordered children had more difficulty than did normal children in picking up the same amount of information in the tactual conditions.

These findings support our conclusion that the failure to perform a specific task in a given situation can be due to cognitive incompetence and/or to an information problem.

The modality effect indicates that performance as an expression of cognitive competence depends on "situational information" (Fischer & Bidell, 1991). Failures in performance are not necessarily failures in cognitive competence, although unsuccessful performances on psychological evaluations of children with language disorders are often interpreted as a delay in cognitive development. This is done without regard to the situational features or the context in which performance occurs.

2.3 PROBLEM-SOLVING ACTIVITIES AND PROCESSES

Task success is one way to look at problem-solving performances. Another way is to look at the activities entailed. By observing sequences of activities, we can make inferences about the underlying mental processes in problem-solving performances.

2.3.1 Analysis Procedures

The Seriation tasks were nonverbal tasks. The children had to solve the problems nonverbally by using manual activities.

To study how the children solved the seriation problems we had to observe and analyze their nonverbal manual activities. We had to judge which of these activities were relevant or irrelevant to the tasks. Such judgment of nonverbal problem–solving activities has rarely been made (Kluwe, 1987).

2.3.1.1 *Criteria for Judging Problem-Solving Activities*

Once we had decided about activities relevant to solving the seriation problems we had to code them. To find a coding system we turned to the problem-solving model of Pitt and Brouwer-Janse. Their model (see Pitt,

1977, 1983; Pitt & Brouwer-Janse, 1985; Brouwer-Janse, 1983; Brouwer-Janse & Pitt, 1986) was constructed from an assessment of the verbal problem-solving activities in high-school students, college students, and science professors. The model assumes that information processing and cognitive representation are complementary, as reflected in the Piagetian paradigm, and describes problem solving in "think-aloud verbal protocols" at two levels of analysis: an elementary level of individual component processes or subroutines (SR), and a level of grouped subroutines into eight problem-solving subprocesses (SP)—basics, evaluative, selective, hypothetic, feedback, patterning, action, and conclusion.

Because Pitt and Brouwer-Janse's model was designed to code "think-aloud verbal protocols" and not manual nonverbal activities, we had to alter the coding system to describe manual nonverbal activities as subroutines and subprocesses. This was a demanding and time consuming task. We had to decide which of the children's activities were relevant to solving the Seriation tasks and could be considered as subroutines, and which of the relevant activities were related to which problem-solving subprocesses, such as basics, evaluative, selective, and so forth. To do this, numerous observations, analyses, corrections, and controls were required.

2.3.1.2 Subroutines – a Primary Unit of Observation

In our study, the observable activities judged to be relevant to solving the seriation problem were coded as 25 subroutines (SR). A subroutine was defined as an action or a sequence of movements resulting in an observable change of topological relationships between the hands and an object/support, and also between and among objects and their support. For example, the hand reaching toward a stimulus bar and touching it changed the topological relationship between hand/body and object. First, the hand was separate from the object; after the action, hand and object were together. At the end of a subroutine one may observe a short pause or break in the movements.

The abovementioned example could continue; closing the fingers around the stimulus bar, lifting and displacing it, and finally releasing it on the support at the new site were also followed by a pause. Looking at an object often precedes the hand movements and can be considered part of that sequence. Thus, SR 1, touching an object, is an action involving a sequence of movements needed for the body (hands) to touch an object. SR 2, is an action involving touching and moving several objects on the support. SR 3 refers to sequences of touching the different items of the task: the model and/or bars at both sites, the stimulus and the construction site, respectively. SR 4 involves holding and lifting the object off the support (table). Each of these steps is a subroutine. These subroutines were viewed as elementary components of problem-solving processes. As shown in Table 2.7, our analysis included a total of 25 subroutines.

Two observers independently coded the data of each child for the analyses of the 25 subroutines, as shown in Table 2.7. Disagreements were discussed and resolved by consensus. A Pearson coefficient revealed a statistically significant correlation between the independent observers prior to discussion ($r = .85, p < .05$). This result was based on a randomly drawn sample of 25 of the youngest normal children (five from each of the five youngest age groups).

2.3.1.3 Subprocesses – a Grouping of Subroutines

Subroutines (SR) were grouped into the 8 subprocesses (SP) modeled by Pitt and Brouwer-Janse (1985): basics, evaluative, selective, feedback, hypothetic, patterning, action, and conclusion (see Table 2.7). A range of 1 to 6 subroutines defined each subprocess. For example, the cluster of six subroutines for the basics subprocess were SR 1, 2, 3, 4, 5, 6; the three subroutines for the evaluative subprocess were SR 7, 8, 9; and so on (see Table 2.7).

2.3.1.4 Task and Subject Selection Procedures

The analysis was based on a subset of the data. The data subset maximized the opportunity to observe remarkable differences within and across subject groups. Children selected from the normal and language disorder groups had the maximum frequency of 0 scores. These were the youngest children from both groups. For these age groups only children with success scores 0, 1, and 2 were included in the subset. This score criterion was chosen because children typically had demonstrated all of 25 subroutines by the time they reached success scores of 3 or higher. Only data from the short stair series were used. The long stair series were excluded because the children who successfully performed them were competent on all 25 subroutines and had reached ceiling performances on all tasks. Excluding the long stair series also meant that task complexity did not become a confounding variable in the analysis of the modality task conditions.

In the normal group, there were 39 children in age group 1 (3;0 to 3;11 years) and age group 2 (4;0 to 4;11years), who met the 0 to 2 score selection criterion (see Table 2.3). The language disorder group included 28 children, who met the 0 to 2 score selection criterion (see

TABLE 2.7
Description of Subroutines (SR) and Subprocesses (SP)

Subroutines SR#	Behavior Descriptions	Reference to Pitt's Model
SP BASICS		
SR 1	Looks at and/or touches display and several bars.	List given information
SR 2	Touches several bars and moves them on the support.	List assumptions
SR 3	Touches bars and model and grasps them spontaneously, or if that is not the case, can be guided to do so.	List questions
SR 4	Touches bar, holds it, and attempts to lift it (spontaneously or guided).	Define initial state
SR 5	Lifts the bar and releases it when touching the support. When guided, child continues the movements at every moment of the action.	Define subgoal
SR 6	Spontaneously displaces lifted bar from location 1 (stimulus site) to location 2 (construction site) and releases it there.	Define goal state
SP EVALUATIVE		
SR 7	Performs at least a global evaluation of length (short vs. long): that is, handles first a few short bars, or a few long ones.	Apply evaluative criteria
SR 8	Applies at least one of the proximity rules (displacing rules and side line rules).	Identify rules
SR 9	Works systematically: Each kind of behavior has to be applied to at least half of the bars.	Organize data
	Child takes several bars off of the stimulus location, chooses one bar, puts the others back, then places the chosen one on the construction site.	
	Child groups bars according to those she/he has already tried out and those not yet used.	
	Child keeps one hand on the bar placed last most of the time when searching with the other hand for the next bar.	
SP SELECTIVE		
SR 10	Takes placed bar off:	Select relevant and delete irrelevant information
	Right after having placed that bar, or after having placed one or two more bars.	
SR 11	Applies one set of rules to all bars.	Edit rules
SR 12	Applies one set of rules to at least half of the bars.	

Continued

TABLE 2.7
(Continued)

SP FEEDBACK		
SR 13	Applies displacing rule to all bars, bars touch each other.	Test reference
SR 14	Applies displacing rule and side line rule.	system
SR 15	Applies side line rule: Child refers to top line.	Identify feedback
SR 16	Applies side line rule: Child refers to base line.	Identify feedback
SR 17	Applies side line rule: Child refers to top line and at the same time to base line.	

SP HYPOTHETIC		
SR 18	Considers relationship between two bars.	Consider and establish relationships
SR 19	Considers relationships between a pair of bars in succession: Arranges bars in stair-like configurations.	
SR 20	Considers relationships among the sides of successively placed bars: Lines up bars.	
SR 21	Considers more than one relationship among bars at the same time.	

SP PATTERNING		
SR 22	Touches the base and/or top line of placed bars with some kind of adjustment several times.	Summarize relevant perceptual patterns
SR 23	Reverses any of the actions by taking off already placed bars or changing their location on the construction site. The effect has not to be a correct one.	Extract perceptual pattern from display

SP ACTION		
SR 24	Applies displacing rule to at least half of the bars.	Execute program

SP CONCLUSION		
SR 25	Stops when there are no bars at the stimulus site; all are now on the construction site.	Output Conclusions

Table 2.4), in the two youngest age ranges (4;3 to 8;0 years) and (8; 1 to 11; 0 years). Therefore, normal children included in the analysis were younger on the average than children with language disorders (cf. mean age = 41.49 months, SD = 7.0 and mean age = 87 months, SD = 24.5 for the normal and language disorder groups, respectively).

2.3.1.5 Structure of Data Analysis and Predictions

The coding system we developed by adapting Pitt and Brouwer-Janse's (1985) model of problem-solving processes was based on the assumption that development occurs in levels. What is learned on a lower level has to be relearned on a higher level (see Piaget, 1947/1950). What adults have available in problem-solving activities on a high verbal level was expected to be related to what children learn in problem-solving activities on a previous nonverbal level.

The first analysis focused on the "overall number of subroutines" used. A subroutine was counted just once regardless of how many times it was observed on the same task or different tasks. Each child's final score consisted of the proportion of 25 subroutines used overall in solving the seriation problem in some condition. This analysis was used to infer a general level of competence in solving the seriation problem without taking into account the effect of the sensory modality condition (or information) on performance in an actual situation. The overall number of subroutines was expected to increase with age in both age groups of normal but not language-disordered children.

The second analysis focused on whether children were overall more competent on some components or SP of problem solving than others, regardless of task. This analysis compared the children on 5 of the 8 subprocesses. Three subprocesses were excluded because they did not differentiate the children. The subroutines of the subprocesses basics, action, and conclusion had to be exhibited by all the children to be testable.

Proportions of the subroutines used in each of the five remaining subprocesses were compared: evaluative, selective, hypothetic, feedback, and patterning. We expected these proportions to increase regularly with age in normal children but not in language-disordered children.

We also expected uneven profiles due to the use of higher proportions of the SR for some problem-solving SP than for others. It was predicted that younger normal children with success scores of 0 to 2 would use higher proportions of SR involved with the search for information than for generating and testing hypotheses. The opposite trend was predicted for children with language disorders. We inferred from previous findings that processes associated with the search for information are related to perceptual processes, and children with language disorders appear to fail in perceptual processing (see chap.1). Therefore we expected lower proportions of SR use associated with the search for information than for generating and testing hypotheses.

A third analysis considered the proportion of SR use within each of five SP in relation to specific modality conditions. The proportion of SR used for the SP was computed separately for each of the short stair modality conditions: tv, vv, v, and t. Normal children were expected to show the highest proportions for all SP in the tv condition followed in order by the v, vv, and t conditions, respectively. Children with language disorders were expected to vary with the subgroups. It was predicted that the IM group would perform better in the vv and v than in the tv condition, which combined sensory input, although the least success of all was expected in the (t) tactual condition. Conversely, it was predicted that the TK/S group would perform best in the tv modality followed in order by the vv, v, and t conditions, but their (t) tactual performance would be even lower than that of children with IM perceptual deficits.

2.3.2   Results and Discussion of Problem-Solving Analyses

First, elementary problem-solving activities were analyzed as subroutines. Then, problem-solving activities were considered in each subprocess. Finally, problem-solving activities were related to task or modality condition.

2.3.2.1   Elementary Problem-Solving Activities or Subroutines

2.3.2.1.1   Within Groups.
The mean overall proportions of the 25 SR used by unsuccessful normal children and children with language disorders (also called clinical groups) as a function of age are presented in Table 2.8. For normal children, the average proportions of SR use increased from .81 for the youngest age group (3 ;0 to 3;11 years) to .91 for the older group (4;0 to 4;11 years). An ANOVA revealed that this age group difference was significant ($F_{1,38} = 9.44; p < .01$).

For the language disorder group the mean overall proportions of SR use by Age group 1 (4 to 8 years) $n = 18$; $\bar{x} = .86$ (SD $= .12$) and Age group 2 (8 to 11 years) $n = 10$; $\bar{x} = .89$ (SD $= .11$) did not differ significantly. Therefore both groups were pooled and then divided into clinical subgroups. The children with TK/S ($F_{1,18} = .283$) or IM perceptual deficits ($F_{1,8} = 3.231$) did not differ. The means were close to ceiling levels at .87 or higher in both groups. Therefore, the data for the subgroups of the clinical group were pooled to yield an average proportion of .87 for the whole group, as shown in Table 2.8.

2.3.2.1.2   Between Groups.
Significant group differences were observed when the overall mean proportion of SR use by the language disorder group (.87) was compared to the mean proportions at each of the two ages for normal children ($F_{2.75} = 6.04, p < .01$). Young normal children in Age group 1 (3;0 to 3;11 years) had significantly lower mean

TABLE 2.8

Overall Proportions of Subroutine Use by Normal and Clinical Groups

Group	Subgroup	Age Range	Mean (SD)
Normal children ($n = 39$)	Age group 1 ($n = 20$)	3;0–3;11	.814 (.101)
	Age group 2 ($n = 19$)	4;0–4;11	.906 (.090)
Children with language disorders ($n = 28$)		4;3–11;0	.874 (.119)
	Children with tactual–kinesthetic/serial perceptual problems ($n = 19$)	4;3–11;0	.869 (.131)
	Children with problems in perceptual intermodal organization ($n = 9$)	5;4–9;8	.880 (.090)

Note. 3;11 represents 3 years and 11 months.

proportions (.81) of SR use than did normal children in Age group 2 at 4; 0 to 4; 11 years (.91), and the pooled mean score of the language disorder group (.87). The language-disorder group spanned the ages of 4;3 to 11;0 years. Their scores were comparable to the older group of normal children.

Taking the overall number of SR as a sign of competence in solving problems, we concluded that normal children become more competent in problem solving as they get older such that by 5 years of age, they have all 25 problem-solving activities in their competence.

Children with language disorders also acquire competence in problem-solving activities because they scored at near ceiling levels, as did the normal ones at older ages. Therefore, their failure to systematically improve their seriation performances with age and achieve maximum success scores must be due to factors other than a general reduction of competence as measured by elementary problem-solving activities. Data interpretation was corroborated by an analysis of the overall problem-solving activities in each SP used, as described in the following section.

2.3.2.2 Problem-Solving Activities in Each Subprocess

In this analysis, SR were grouped according to five SP: evaluative, selective, hypothetic, feedback, and patterning. A SR was counted just once for each subprocess regardless of how many times it was observed on the same or different tasks. For each child the proportions of observable SR used were computed regardless of task, and averaged across children in the normal and language-disorder groups.

Table 2.9 shows the mean proportions of SR use for all five subprocesses for normal children in Age groups 1 and 2 ($n = 39$) and for children with language disorders ($n = 28$).

2.3.2.2.1 Within Groups. For normal children, a significant main age effect ($F_{11,38} = 7.85$; $p < .01$) was due to the increase in the proportions of activities used for each SP. Age group 1 achieved .62 for feedback, .725 for hypothetic and patterning, .797 for evaluative, and .828 for selective. Age group 2 achieved .768 for feedback, .803 for hypothetic, .868 for patterning, .928 for selective, and .982 for evaluative.

A significant main SP effect ($F_{4,160} = 15.488$; $p < .001$) indicated uneven profiles. Normal children had higher SR proportions for some SP than others. There was no age-by-subprocess interaction effect; the increase with age among SP was regular. For Age group 1 (3;0 to 3;11 years) the SP were ranked from high to low proportions in the order of the selective, evaluative, patterning, hypothetic, and feedback. For Age group 2 (4;0 to

TABLE 2.9

Mean Proportions of Subroutine Use for Each of Five Subprocesses in Normal and Clinical Groups and by Age Level in Normal Groups

Group	Subgroup	Age in Years	Subprocesses				
			Evaluative	Selective	Feedback	Hypothetic	Patterning
Normal children (n = 39)	Age group 1 (n = 20)	3;0–3;11	0.797	0.828	0.62	0.725	0.725
	Age group 2 (n = 19)	4;0–4;11	0.982	0.928	0.768	0.803	0.868
Children with language disorders (n = 28)		4;3–11;0	0.723	0.880	0.786	0.803	0.857
	Children with tactual–kinesthetic/serial perceptual problems (n = 19)	4;3–11;0	0.716	0.911	0.789	0.789	0.816
	Children with problems in perceptual intermodal organization (n = 9)	5;4–9;8	0.738	0.814	0.778	0.833	0.944

4;11 years) the SP were ranked from high to low proportions in the order of evaluative, selective, patterning, hypothetic, and feedback. We concluded that a normal unsuccessful child is competent earlier in information-seeking processes than in problem-solving processes of a more logical kind. This interpretation assumes that evaluative and selective processes reflect information-seeking activities and that hypothetic SP reflects logical cognition.

For the whole language disorder group, there was a significant overall SP effect ($F_{4,72}$ = 4.72, p < .01). Proportions were ranked from high to low in the order of selective, patterning, hypothetic, feedback, and evaluative subprocesses. Thus, the mean SR proportions, pooled across language disorder subgroups, were the lowest for the evaluative SP, suggesting difficulty with problem-solving components having to do with the search for information, as predicted.

The two subgroups, TK/S and IM, did not differ significantly ($F_{1,27}$ = 1.803). They both used all 5 subprocesses (see Table 2.9 for mean values).

2.3.2.2.2 Between Groups.

There was no significant difference in SR use between normal and language-disordered children ($F_{3,67}$ = 1.803, n.s.). However, a significant group-by-subprocess interaction effect ($F_{4,200}$ = 2.277, p < .05) indicated that the groups differed on different SP.

Neuman–Keuls comparison of means revealed that normal children, who were, on average, younger, had a significantly higher SR proportion in the evaluative SP than children with language disorders (cf. .887 and .723). Conversely, language-disordered children had a significantly higher SR proportion for the hypothetic SP than younger normal children (cf. .803 and .763). In addition, children with language disorders had a higher SR proportion for feedback and patterning SP than young normal children (cf. .789 and .857 vs. .692 and .795, respectively).

Thus, children with language disorders were not simply like young normal children. Disordered children were less adequate in the search for information, as was revealed especially by the evaluative SP. The subroutines for the evaluative subprocess (SR 7, 8, and 9 as shown in Table 2.7) involved arranging the bars, for example, handling a few short bars before handling a few long ones (SR 7) and then arranging them in a systematic way (SR 9). Both kinds of activities require a strong focus on information. We inferred that children with language disorders failed more often in these problem-solving activities because of perceptual problems.

The higher proportion of SP patterning in language-disordered children suggests they recognize errors more often than unsuccessful normal children do and try to correct them, but still fail. Clinical observations are consistent with this kind of behavior. For example, patterning included SR 22 (see Table 2.7). This subroutine was evident when the child positioned the bars to touch the base and/or top line of the construction, suggesting a search for tactual information; SR 23 coded any action that required some kind of correction.

2.3.3   Problem-Solving Processes in Relation to Task or Modality Condition

We assumed that the SR number applied to a given problem-solving task is related to the information inherent in the situation. When a task condition offers less contrasts in information, the search for relevant information was assumed to be more difficult (see Section 1.2). This reduces the child's capacity. In this case, the child is not able to use all the subroutines that may be available in competence. For this analysis, the problem-solving activities were examined in relation to four different modality conditions: tactual–visual, visual, visual–visual, and tactual in the short stair series.

Mean proportions of SR use for each of the five SP in each modality condition were computed separately for children in the normal group at two ages and in the language-disorder group for two subgroups. These results for the normal group at two ages and for the two language disorder subgroups are shown in Figs. 2.10–2.13 for the tv, vv, v, and t tasks, respectively.

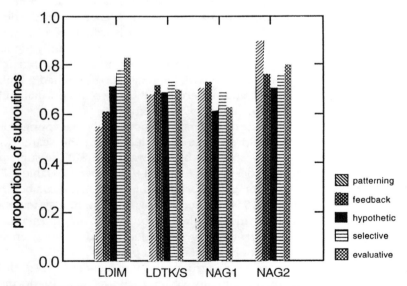

FIG. 2.10.   Proportions of subroutine use by normal and language disorder subgroups in the tactual–visual condition.

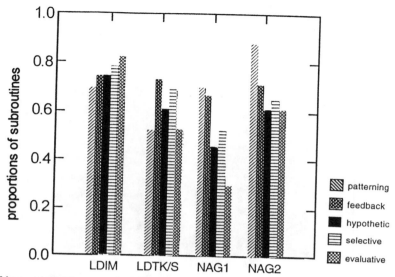

Normal children and children with language disorders

FIG. 2.11. Proportions of subroutine use by normal and language disorder subgroups in the visual–visual modality condition.

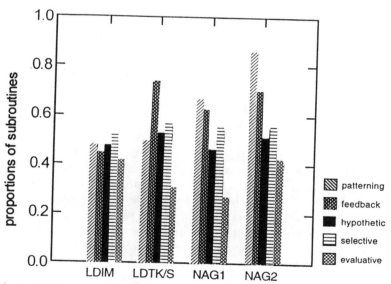

Normal children and children with language disorders

FIG. 2.12. Proportions of subroutine used by normal and language disorder subgroups in the visual modality condition.

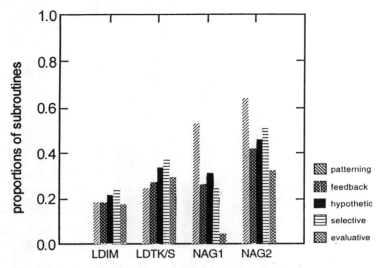

Normal children and children with language disorders

FIG. 2.13.   Proportions of subroutine use by normal and language disorder subgroups in the tactual modality condition.

2.3.3.1 *Within Groups*

For normal children, the proportion of problem-solving activities
increased with age for each problem-solving SP within each of the four
task conditions (age main effect; $F_{1,38} = 8.719, p < .01$).

The proportions were significantly higher for some problem-solving
subprocesses than others (SP main effect; $F_{4,148} = 36.1, p < .001$). The five
subprocesses were ranked in the order of the evaluative, selective, hypothetic, feedback, and patterning. However, the proportions of SR use for
each subprocess varied with modality or task conditions (modality main
effect; $F_{4,148} = 36.1, p < .001$). A significant subprocess-by-task interaction
($F_{12,444} = 6.4, p < .01$) indicated that rank order of the subprocesses in
mean proportions varied across modalities. The proportions of SR use for
the hypothetic, feedback, and patterning subprocesses were highest when
tactual–visual information was available and lowest when only tactual
information was available.

For children with language disorders, no significant overall age effect
($F_{1,27} = 0.008$) was observed when data were pooled across the two clinical subgroups with different perceptual deficits. There were significant
main effects for subprocess ($F_{19,513} = 18.576, p < .001$) and modality ($F_{3,27}
= 15.50, p < .01$). However, the significant subprocess-by-modality inter-
action ($F_{12,120} = 2.34, p < .01$) revealed that the rank order of the five sub-

processes in the proportion of SR use varied with the task or modality condition. Proportions of subroutines were highest in the visual–visual modality condition, followed by the tactual–visual, visual, and the tactual modality conditions in both the IM and TK/S subgroups.

This overall group trend, however, did not predict the rank order of the modality conditions for every subprocess in each disorder subgroup. Using the Neuman–Keuls procedure for the comparison of multiple means, a crossover effect was revealed for the evaluative subprocess. The TK/S group had a significantly higher SR proportion in the tv than in the vv task. The children in the IM group had the opposite effect. The proportion of SR use was higher in the vv condition than in the tv condition. For the selective subprocess, the difference was found in the v condition where the TK/S group had a higher SR proportion than the IM group. For the hypothetic subprocess, the two disorder subgroups did not differ significantly.

2.3.3.2 *Between Groups*

There was a significant main group effect ($F_{3,64} = 4.367, p < .01$) indicating that language-disordered children differed from younger normal children in the proportions of SR use for each subprocess within a modality. However, a significant interaction group-by-modality ($F_{12,200} = 4.176$, $p < .001$) revealed that clinical children in both subgroups did not exhibit lower scores than normal children in every modality. In some modalities they did exhibit higher scores (see Figs. 2.10 to 2.13).

Our data showed that modality conditions influenced the problem-solving activities of normal and language-disordered children. The search for information as expressed presumably by subprocess evaluative appeared to be most successful in the combined tactual–visual condition for normal and TK/S children. The search for information by SP evaluative was easier in a visual than a tactual–visual condition for IM language-disordered children. Information as expressed by SP evaluative in the tactual modality condition was the most difficult for all children, especially language-disordered children with tactual/serial problems.

2.4   SPECIFIC ANALYSES AND RESULTS:
RULE APPLICATION

This analysis focused on the actual products or outcomes of solving the Seriation tasks, not on scores but on patterns from which basic interaction rules could be inferred. In chapter 1, we argued that important rules for nonverbal daily interaction are derived from regularities in changes of topological relationships. Children learn these rules from interacting with the environment during the first years of life (Affolter & Bischofberger, 1988).

The Seriation tasks were created as tasks involving interaction (i.e., changes of topological relationships). This suggests that solving the seriation problems will also demand the application of rules of interaction; children have to represent such rules for solving the Seriation tasks. It was expected that the rules on a representational level can be related to the rules on a sensorimotor level. We further expected that the rules of interaction on a representational level be acquired in the same sequence as the ones on the preceding sensorimotor level.

In chapter 1, we discussed that babies are extremely active during the sensorimotor period. Continually, they change topological relationships between themselves and the environment. Thus, their activities fit the criterion for nonverbal tactual interaction. We assume that regularities in these interactive experiences allow the babies to acquire rules (Section 1.4.4). We described how babies start with the acquisition of touching rules. A very basic touching rule involves changes of topological relationships between body and support. Experiences with body/support/object follow; babies begin to move, embrace, and hold objects. They discover that objects differ from the support.

To be *instructable* on the Seriation tasks required that children present Subroutines 1, 2, and 3 of subprocess basics (see Appendix B). These requirements can be analyzed in terms of touching rules as they refer to touching, moving, and holding the bars. Representing these touching rules, therefore, was a prerequisite for being instructable. It meant, children had to know that bars are something different from the support, can be moved, embraced, and held.

As babies continue to interact on a sensorimotor level and acquire more experiences, a new set of rules begins to emerge. These new rules still require touching, but go beyond touching. With the object they are holding and lifting, babies now perform some actions called handling. An *elementary handling* rule refers to the topological change induced by separating an object from the support. But babies not only discover that objects can be separated from the support, they also discover that the object can be put back on the support, objects can be released. Releasing is first done quite accidentally. The baby grasps an object with one hand and focuses the attention on that interaction. Then the baby grasps another object with the other hand. The moment babies grasp the other object, their attention switches to that new interaction, and the first object is released. Thus, the first of the elementary handling rules is the *separation–releasing* rule acquired after the touching rules.

Accidental releasing is followed by a more complex kind of releasing. With increasing experiences of accidental releasing, babies discover the possibility of displacing. When they have grasped and released an object, the object is usually not where it had been before; the object has changed location on the support. This means, the environment has changed. Babies appear fascinated by that discovery. They begin consciously to produce and explore such changes. For people around those babies, a busy time begins. Babies will grasp whatever is within reach and release that grasped object by letting it fall on the floor. Such behavior is characteristic of a second elementary handling rule, the rule of *releasing-with-displacing*. This rule refers to the possibility that the location where the object is released is different from the location where the object has been grasped.

Once the children were judged to be instructable, guided tactual instruction on the Seriation tasks continued. To become *testable* the children had to perform more complex changes of topological relationships. Subroutine 6 of subprocess basics describes such topological changes and was considered one of the criteria to judge a child as testable (see Appendix B). The two elementary handling rules refer to similar topological changes: Children had to understand that bars had to be separated from the support at the stimulus site, displaced to the construction site, and released there. Children, therefore, had to apply not only the three touching rules, they had to be able to represent and apply the rules of separating–releasing and releasing-with-displacing. To be testable, then, children had to present five rules of interaction.

Being testable, however, did not mean that the children could construct a stair series. Displacing bars from the stimulus site and releasing them at the construction site was just the beginning of the construction of a stair series. For constructing a stair series children had to consider the models presented to them and try to replicate them. For solving the task some kind of product was required. To be successful, the configuration of that product had to present a short or a long stair series like the model.

Replicating a model is not a passive task, but an active and complex one. Children have to analyze the model presented to them. To realize the complexity of such an analysis, we turned to Piaget. Piaget and Inhelder (1948/1956) referred to the importance of assimilation processes in such analysis. We discussed assimilation in Section 1.4.1. Piaget and Inhelder investigated children's assimilation processes in numerous experiments. For example, they asked children to draw forms like the ones we used in the Form Recognition tasks (see Section 1.2.1). They observed that children draw forms according to the spatial features they had applied before when matching forms. Young children's drawings appeared to be primitive, incomplete, and not correspondent to the real forms—circles to represent topological features like closed versus open, inside versus outside. At some older age, they draw lines forming angles to represent a general angular feature of Euclidean forms such as rectangles, triangles, and so forth. When children were asked to compare their drawings with the real forms they insisted that their drawings were correct, even though they were primitive drawings.

Affolter (1954) confirmed such findings. She compared the development of spatial concepts in deaf and hearing children. Deaf children at different cognitive levels presented drawings of forms similar to the hearing children. Young children made primitive drawings, older children more complex ones. When asked, children at all levels would insist that their drawings corresponded to the real forms.

To investigate the problem of assimilation in the replication of the models of the stair series, we did a pilot study. Ten normal children, ages 4 to 9 years, were tested on the four short stair series of the Seriation tasks. Configurations of their 40 products were compared and seven different patterns of configurations could be distinguished (see Figs. 2.14–2.20). All configurations would fit 1 of these 7 patterns. The younger the child, the more elementary the configuration appeared to be. When children compared their products with the models, they insisted their product corresponded to the model. This was observed in all children, even when they were unsuccessful and their products did not show correct stair features.

To interpret the seven patterns of configuration, we applied Piaget's theory of assimilation. We assumed that children will assimilate the model according to interaction rules. Therefore, the configurations of the products should allow for making inferences about the interaction rules an individual child had available at the time of testing.

We analyzed the seven configurations according to rules derived from observing sensorimotor interactive behavior in children (see Section 1.4.4) as follows:

Configuration 7 was observed in the youngest unsuccessful children. We judged it to be the most elementary solution to the problem in the set. It shows a "piling up" of the bars, one on top of the other (see Fig. 2.14). This construction suggests that children applied the separation–releasing and the releasing-with-displacing rules. Each newly chosen bar was displaced and then released on the construction site. What is new for configuration 7 is the following: Children *generalized* these two rules to all the bars. We judged this behavior to be characteristic of a third elementary handling rule. Releasing the bars, children appeared to consider already displaced bars as being a "support" for the new bar. As a consequence, they constructed a product with the pile-up configuration. At this level, children consider changes of an elementary topological relationship between each bar and the support; they do not appear to consider more complex changes of topological relationships between and among bars.

A more complex set of rules was analyzed for configurations 6 and 5. To construct these configurations children had to consider changes of

FIG. 2.14.   The pile-up configuration.

topological relationships between and among objects/support. These children applied more *complex handling* rules. Rules still included the three
touching rules and the three elementary handling rules. But instead of
only considering topological relationships between bars and support,
children began considering topological relationships of neighborhood or
of proximity of objects. We call these complex handling rules proximity
rules. We differentiate four rules of increasing complexity. To gain some
knowledge about this new set of rules, we again observe children on a
sensorimotor level.

We discussed how children discover elementary handling rules. These
rules deal with just one object at a time. After a critical amount of experience with these rules, children learn that two objects can touch each
other. They begin to deal with neighborhood or proximity of objects. First,
they touch an object with another object without concern for where the
touching occurs. They use one object to pound on another without choosing a touching point. With increasing experience they begin to differentiate the place where the two objects touch each other. This place is the
source of the change of resistance they perceive when touching occurs
(see Section 1.4.2). They begin to explore the stick phenomenon
described by Gibson (1966) as unique to the haptic (tactual) system. By
taking a spoon or any longer object they use the tip to touch another
object and move it.

Increased experiences with changes of topological relationships between two objects enable children to discover that even more than two objects can touch each other; they begin to construct sequences (i.e., "strings of objects"), such as a train that moves. To construct a train requires that children differentiate places or sources where objects can touch each other. Finally, they are able to consider multiple topological relationships with multiple sources where objects can touch. Piaget (1936/1952) described how children first focus on just two touching objects. Later on, they consider relationships among objects. A famous example is Piaget's description of the a child finding a hidden object. Children find an object hidden under pillow A. But when the object is moved under pillow B they still look under pillow A before pillow B, even when they observed the change. At some older age they will look directly under pillow B, which suggests a growing consideration of multiple topological relationships among objects.

Analyses of configurations of the seriation products suggest a similar sequence of acquisition of proximity rules. Configurations 6 and 5 are called the "fill-in" and the "surface" configurations (see Figs. 2.15 and 2.16). Children arranged the bars to fill-in, or cover a surface. In addition to the three elementary handling rules of separation–releasing, releasing-with-displacing, and generalizing them, children now apply the first of the more complex handling or proximity rules. They consider that two objects, such as two bars, can touch each other. Such behavior requires changes of relationships

FIG. 2.15.   The fill-in configuration.

FIG. 2.16.   The surface configuration.

not only between object and support but between pairs of objects. Bars can *touch each other somewhere*, the particular touching place or source of information is not yet specified. When this new rule was generalized to all bars, the fill-in configuration 6 and the surface configuration 5 were created.

Configuration 4 is called the "lining-up" configuration. Children arranged the bars in parallel, so that they touched each other at their sides (see Fig. 2.17). Children did not take into account length, top line, or base line relationships. We infer that children apply a second kind of proximity rule. Bars touch each other at a *specified selected place* or source of information. For this configuration, the sides of the bars were chosen as source of information. This source was generalized to all the bars in a sequence; bars were lined up.

Configuration 3 is called the "stair-like" configuration, and configuration 2, the "base" configuration (see Figs. 2.18 and 2.19). The children arranged all the bars parallel to each other in such a manner that the top line of the bars was stair-like, but the base was not a straight line (configuration 3); or the base showed a straight line, but the top line was irregular (configuration 2). We believe that the children apply a third proximity rule. This new rule requires that two sources of topological changes are considered together, at the same time: Bars are lined up by touching each

FIG. 2.17.   The lining-up configuration.

FIG. 2.18.   The stair-like configuration.

FIG. 2.19.   The base configuration.

other at their sides, and in addition are grouped according to the top or the base line. These sources were generalized to all the bars.

Configuration 1 is called the "seriation" or correct configuration. The correct solution required the bars to be arranged in a series with a stair-like pattern on top and a straight line on the base (see Fig. 2.20). We infer that children applied the most complex of the proximity rules. This rule deals with multiple topological relationships among objects and support. The criteria for "multiple" comparisons in the Seriation tasks when arranging the bars are the consideration of three relationships at the same time: proximity specified for all the bars at their sides, on their tops, and at their bases.

2.4.1   Analysis Procedures

The application of rules was inferred from observed problem-solving activities and products or construction patterns of the stair series, called configurations.

2.4.1.1   *Criteria for Judging Rule Application*

When children pick up a bar from the stimulus site and put it down at the construction site, we presume they used some kind of interaction rule. Piaget and Inhelder (1956/1964) observed regular patterns in normal children's construction of series at different ages. Affolter (1954) described the same patterns in normal and hearing-impaired children.

122

CHAPTER 2

FIG. 2.20.   The seriation configuration.

2.4.1.2   Selection of Subjects and Tasks

Like our previous analyses of problem-solving activities, it was important to focus on children who varied in their performances on the Seriation
tasks. Unsuccessful children with success scores 0, 1, and 2 were selected
for this analysis because once a child was successful the child produced
configuration 1, and thus applied all the inferred rules of interaction.

For the normal children of Age group 1, 4 years of age, 20 children were
selected, and of Age group 2, 5 years of age, 19 children met the criteria.
Of the language-disorder group 28 children, age range 4;3 to 11 years, met
the criteria. Nineteen of these children presented tactual–kinesthetic/seri-
al problems, 9 children intermodal problems. Again, the task-specific
analysis of the modality or information variable was restricted to the four
modalities of short stair series where task complexity was held constant.

2.4.1.3   Types of Analyses and Predictions

There were three analyses performed. In the first analysis we looked at
the configurations of the children's products or solutions to the seriation
problem. In the second analysis, we looked at the overall proportions of
rule use in relation to age and subject groups, without considering modality conditions, and in the third analysis, we focused on the proportions of
rule use in the different groups in relation to task or modality.

The first analysis considered the *solutions*, such as the configurations
of the products, their patterns, and frequency of use. For each child four

solutions were evaluated, one for each of the four short stair series. When the solution for a specific task was not a product with a configuration pattern, the child was recorded as testable or instructable. In all, 156 solutions of the normal children and 112 of the language-disordered children were evaluated. Different predictions were made:

1. The configurations observed will be regular and restricted in number. Based on the findings of a pilot study, we expected seven different patterns of configurations. They would allow us to categorize the configurations and support the hypothesis that the reproduction of the model of the stair series is not done at random but express assimilation processes. This would permit an analysis of rules children may apply to solve the Seriation tasks. For more simple configurations we expected to detect more elementary rules, for more complex constructions more complex rules. Such rules would correspond to rules of a sensorimotor kind, already identified by observations of babies (see Section 1.4.4).

2. It was assumed that children in both the normal and clinical groups acquire sensorimotor interaction rules in a similar way, and that these rules are relearned on a representative level. We expected, therefore, that the configurations observed in normal children correspond to configurations observed in language-disordered children.

The second analysis focused on an *overall* estimate of potential *competence* in rule use as a function of age by disregarding the particular tasks or modality condition. Similar to the analysis of overall proportions of subroutines, the overall estimate was considered to provide a means to estimate the level of competence in rule application of the children.

It was assumed that the configurations produced when solving the Seriation tasks express assimilation processes; children have to assimilate the model of a stair series. Furthermore, such assimilation processes rely on interaction rules children have available in representation at the time of the testing. This means that the configurations can be analyzed according to interaction rules similar to those that babies learn during the sensorimotor level. Rule use, thus, was inferred by analyzing the different configurations. The seven configurations allowed us to infer rule use based on changes of topological relationships between support and object/bar, and between and among support and objects/bars. Table 2.10 shows that the seriation or correct solution was expressed by the product of the stair series presented as configuration 1. This configuration implies a maximum of 10 rules: Three touching rules, three elementary handling rules, and four proximity rules. Table 2.10 shows the different final solutions of the tasks and the respective inferred estimates of rule use.

We discussed that a child, who was instructable, presented three rules of touching. Table 2.10 indicates that such a child had a proportion of .3

TABLE 2.10
Descriptions of Solutions and Related Rule Application

Solutions	Touching Rules			Handling Rules Elementary - B1			Handling Rules Complex/Proximity - B2				# of Rules Cum	Overall Prop	Prop of Rules B2 per Task & Solution
	Sup	Mov	Hold	Sep/Rel	Rel/Disp	Gen	Any Place	Sides	Top or Base	Top and Base			
Instructable	X	X	X								3	.3	0
Testable	X	X	X	X	X						5	.5	0
Configuration 7 pile-up	X	X	X	X	X	X					6	.6	0
Configuration 6 fill-in	X	X	X	X	X	X	X				7	.7	.25
Configuration 5 surface	X	X	X	X	X	X	X				7	.7	.25
Configuration 4 lining-up	X	X	X	X	X	X	X	X			8	.8	.5
Configuration 3 top	X	X	X	X	X	X	X	X	X		9	.9	.75
Configuration 2 base	X	X	X	X	X	X	X	X	X		9	.9	.75
Configuration 1 stair-like	X	X	X	X	X	X	X	X	X	X	10	1	1

Note. Sup = Support; Mov = Moving; Hold = Holding; Sep/Rel = Separating/Releasing; Rel/Disp = Releasing/Displacing; Gen = Generalizing; Prop = Proportions.

of the 10 rules that could be applied. A child who was considered testable, presented the three touching rules and, in addition, two of the elementary handling rules, called B1 rules (i.e., the child had in all a proportion of .5 of 10 rules available). A child who produced the pile-up configuration 7 had all touching rules and the three B1 rules of elementary handling present (i.e., the child had a proportion of .6 of 10 rules available). A child who produced the fill-in configuration 6 or the surface configuration 5 had all touching and elementary handling B1 rules plus one of the proximity B2 rules available (i.e., altogether the child had a proportion of .7 rules available). A child who produced the lining up configuration 4 had all touching and elementary handling rules present in addition to two of the proximity B2 rules (i.e., altogether the child had a proportion of .8 rules available). A child who produced configurations 3 top line or 2 base had all the touching and elementary handling B1 rules present in addition to three of the proximity B2 rules (i.e., altogether the child had a proportion of .9 handling rules available). A child who produced configuration 1 stairlike, which was the correct solution, had all 10 rules available, the touching and the handling rules of an elementary and of a complex kind.

Because rules of a lower strategy were embedded in those of a higher strategy, we could estimate maximum competence or the highest proportion of rule use on the configuration that yielded the most sophisticated solution, regardless of task. Thus, to establish an overall estimate for each child, her or his most complex configuration was selected. In this way, each child received one score. The scores of the children were averaged, separate for each of the two age groups of normal children, for the language-disordered children as a group, and separately for the two subgroups.

We assumed that with increasing cognitive competence, a child would apply rules of interaction that reflect more complex changes in topological spatial relationships. The rules applied to the Seriation tasks presumably reflect interaction experiences on a sensorimotor level. These rules became internalized and can be used now by the normal and language-disordered children on a representative level to solve a problem like that offered by the Seriation task.

Because this measure of overall proportions of rule use is taken as a sign of competence in interaction rules it is expected that normal children at two age levels and children with language disorders do not differ.

The third analysis focused on the proportions of rule use in relation to the particular modality or *task condition*. For this analysis, we disregarded the touching rules and the elementary handling B1rules. These rules had to be present in a child to be considered testable, and to construct at least the pile-up configuration 7. Children who only had these rules present considered topological relationships between support and an object, but not between objects. To investigate the contribution of task condition or information on the assimilation processes when replicating a model we were interested in topological relationships between and among the bars (i.e., the relationships of proximity of bars). For this analysis, therefore, we scored and compared children on their use of just proximity rules. We discussed four proximity rules. Table 2.10 shows the proportions of proximity or B2 rules for each configuration. A child who was judged instructable, or testable, or constructed the pile-up configuration 7 for a specific task had none of the B2 rules available. A child who showed configuration 4 for a specific task had a proportion of .5 of B2 rules for that specific task. Each child received four different scores of proportions of B2 rules, one score for each task. For each task, and for each group, the proportions of rule use were averaged across children. This was done for the two age groups of normal children, for the language-disordered as a group, and for the two subgroups IM and TK/S separately.

It was expected that the use of B2 rules is information dependent. Both groups would be affected by modality condition. It was also expected that the modality effect would differentiate Age group 1 and Age group 2 of the normal children, and normal and language-disordered children.

2.4.2   Results and Discussion of Rule Application

We considered three analyses, the frequency of solutions observed, overall proportions of rule use, and proportions of rule use in relation to task or modality.

2.4.2.1   Frequency of Solutions Observed in Normal and Language-Disordered Children

Patterns of solutions observed and their frequencies are shown in Table 2.11. The table shows that:

1.   Seven different patterns of configurations were observed. They corresponded to the seven configurations found in the pilot study and described for the predictions. No other configurations were observed. Children who did not present a configuration were either judged to be testable or instructable.

These findings of regular patterns and a restricted number of configurations suggest, as predicted, that the reproduction of the models of stair series is not done at random but requires assimilation processes. As a consequence, interaction rules were inferred from the configurations as shown in Table 2.10. Table 2.10 indicates that for configurations 2 and 3, and 5

TABLE 2.11
Frequency Distribution of Final Solutions in Normal and Clinical Groups

Solutions / Age	Group: Normal Children (n = 39)	Subgroups: Age Group 1 (n = 20) 3;0–3;11 years	Age Group 2 (n = 19) 4;0–4;11 years	Group: Clinical (n = 28)	Subgroups: TK/S (n = 19) 4;3–11;0 years	IM (n = 9) 5;4–9;8 years	Total Solutions
Instructable	**0**	0	0	14 (13%)	8	6	14 (5%)
Testable	6 (4%)	5	1	1 (1%)	0	1	7 (3%)
Configuration 7 (pile-up)	3 (2%)	2	1	0	0	0	3 (1%)
Configuration 6 (fill-in) and Configuration 5 (surface)	9 (6%)	4	5	2 (2%)	0	2	11 (4%)
Configuration 4 (lining-up)	80 (51%)	47	33	45 (40%)	33	12	125 (47%)
Configuration 3 (top) and Configuration 2 (base)	48 (31%)	19	29	34 (30%)	24	10	82 (31%)
Configuration 1 (stair-like)	10 (6%)	3	7	16 (14%)	11	5	26 (9%)
Total solutions	**156 (100%)**	**80**	**76**	**112 (100%)**	**76**	**36**	**268 (100%)**

and 6, respectively, the same number of rules can be inferred. This suggests that they present comparable degrees of difficulty. As a consequence, they were pooled for further analysis of frequency and comparisons of groups.

2.   Normal and language-disordered children produced similar patterns of configurations with a similar distribution of frequency. The highest percentage of solutions involved configuration 4, the lining-up: 51% of normal children, and 40% of language-disordered children presented configuration 4. For both groups, the next highest percentage involved configuration 3 and 2: 31% of normal children, and 30% of language-disordered children. It appears, then, that the frequency distribution of configurations was quite similar in both groups.

Some exceptions were observed for more elementary solutions in only a few children of each group: The judgment of being instructable, but not testable was found in 13% of the language-disordered children, but not in normal children. Being testable was observed in 4% of the normal children, and 1% in language-disordered children. Configuration 7 was present in 2% of the normal children, and not observed in language-disordered children, These observations suggest a trend: When language-disordered children were considered testable they also performed a product and switched directly to the more complex configurations 6/5, leaving out configuration 7.

Our findings support the expectancies:

1.   Children with success scores 0 to 2 do not produce at random, but their constructions show a regularity. This regularity causes a restriction of possibilities, and allows for similarities of construction among children. The regularity and the similarity of the two groups in constructing seriation products underlie the similarity of the assimilation processes of both groups. We conclude that their basic interaction rule expressed by the configurations is in essence similar.

2.   Interaction rules inferred from the solutions can be related to sensorimotor rules (see Table 2.10) identified by observations of babies.

2.4.2.2   Overall Proportions of Rule Use

The overall proportions of rule use in two age groups of normal children present no significant differences with age ($F_{1,38} = 1.945$). At both age levels, mean overall proportions were .89 and .92, respectively. This means that normal children of Age group 1 and Age group 2 with success scores 0,1, and 2 do not differ, and are already high in competence of rule use. Being at success scores 0,1, and 2 appears to relate to factors other than competence in interaction rules.

There was no significant *difference* between normal (mean .91) and language-disordered children (mean .92) in the overall proportions of rule use ($F_{1,66} = 0.939$). This means that competence levels of rule use of unsuccessful language-disordered children are comparable to the levels of competence of unsuccessful younger normal children.

2.4.2.3 Proportions of Rule Use in Relation to Task or Modality

Results are presented in Fig. 2.21 for normal children, Age group 1 and Age group 2, and in Fig. 2.22 for language-disordered children in comparison to the normal children.

2.4.2.3.1 Within Groups.
ANOVA revealed for normal children a significant main age effect ($F_{1,37} = 4.801, p < .05$). Children of Age group 1 showed lower proportions of rule use (.325 in t, .538 in v, and .525 in vv) than children of Age group 2 (.526 in t, .605 in v, and .645 in vv), but they showed similar proportions of rule use in tv (.725 and .697, respectively).

A significant task effect was observed ($F_{3,111} = 22.843, p < .001$). The highest mean proportions of rule use were found in the tactual–visual (tv) condition (.712), followed by the two visual conditions (v and vv; .571 and

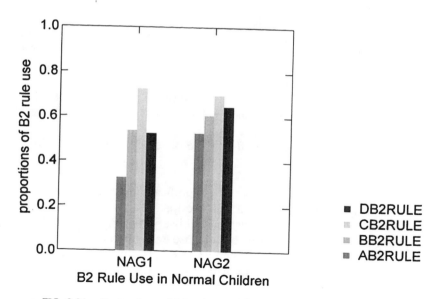

FIG. 2.21. Proportions of B2 rule use in relation to task or modality in Age group 1 and Age group 2 of normal children.

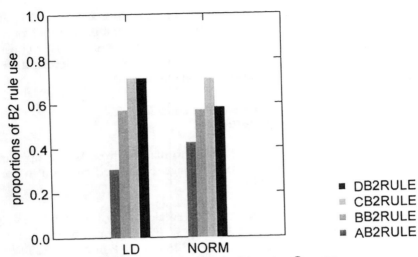

FIG. 2.22.   Proportions of B2 rule use in relation to task or modality in normal and language disorder groups.

.583, respectively). The lowest mean proportions of rule use were found in the tactual condition (.423).

A significant interaction task-by-age was observed ($F_{3,111}$ = 3.849, $p <$ .05). Lower proportions of rule use were observed in Age group 1 in the tactual condition (.325) and in both visual conditions (v and vv; .538 and .525, respectively), but not in the tv condition (.725).

Figure 2.22 reveals that in children with language disorders, a significant main task effect was found. The highest mean proportions of rule use were observed in the tv and vv tasks (.714 for both of them), followed by v task (.571), the smallest in the t task (.304).

No age effect and no group effect were observed in children with language disorders.

2.4.2.3.2   Between Groups.   No significant main group effect was observed between normal and clinical groups.

There was a significant main task effect observable ($F_{3,183}$ = 30.608, $p <$ .001). Highest mean proportion of rule use was observed in the tv task (.713), followed by vv task (.638), then v task (.571), smallest in t task (.373).

A significant interaction group-by-task was reflected by higher proportions of rule use in the t task in normal children (.423) than in language-disordered children (.304), and higher proportions of rule use in the vv task in language-disordered children (.714) than in normal children (.583).

Mean proportions of rule use were similar in the tv and v tasks in both normal children (.712 and .571, respectively) and language-disordered children (.714 and .571, respectively). As expected, rule use in both groups depends on information. For all children proportions were lowest in the tactual condition.

Looking at B2 rules and tasks we find an age effect in normal children in the visual and tactual conditions. Proportions of rule use in the tv condition were already close to maximum in Age group 1. This suggests that failure to succeed is not due to a competence problem in rule use but, rather, an information problem that interacts with the competence. This suggestion is supported by the interaction group-by-task when comparing normal and language-disordered children. For the tactual condition language-disordered children present significantly lower proportions of rule use than normal children. However, their proportions of rule use are higher than those for normal children in the vv task, suggesting that rule use in language-disordered children is differently affected by information than in normal children.

2.5 SUMMARY OF THE SERIATION STUDY

The Seriation study was a comparative study of nonverbal problem solving by normal and language-disordered children. Problem solving was considered an important aspect of the nonverbal interaction experience in daily-life events that was argued to be critical for development. The Seriation task was selected because it allowed us to observe the children's nonverbal physical behaviors online, as they manually interacted with stimuli under a variety of task conditions. This was important because not only did we aim to reveal the extent to which children were successful in solving the seriation problem, we also wanted to expose the factors that influenced success. In particular, it was important to show if low-task success by children with language disorders was related to cognitive competence in solving the problem as opposed to situational constraints on performance. Cognitive competence was not judged just by success in problem solving. We adapted Pitt and Brouwer-Janse's (1985) model of the problem-solving process to describe the kind of activities the children engaged in during the task, and we analyzed the sophistication of their solutions to the problems in terms of the type of interaction rules reflected. Given our hypothesis that children with language disorders have tactual/serial or intermodal perceptual problems, we were particularly interested in revealing the extent to which their problem-solving performance on the Seriation tasks was influenced by the type of sensory information available in the stimuli.

Therefore, normal and language-disordered children were compared on a variety of standard task conditions in which the complexity and the modality of presentation were varied. To separate out competence and performance issues, two types of data analyses were done. One analysis focused on overall activities without regard to task conditions as a general measure of competence; the other analysis focused on performance differences under different task conditions.

All the nonverbal problem-solving activities, subprocesses, and application of rules used in this study as global indices of competence were available in the repertoire of both normal and language-disordered children. Thus, language-disordered children with success scores 0 to 2 were similar to normal children with success scores 0 to 2 in overall problem-solving activities and overall rule use.

The influence of task complexity and modality of presentation on performance was clearly evident. In the Seriation study, both the normal and language-disordered children showed orderly development such that they became competent on one kind of task before another. They solved the seriation problem in the short stair before the long stair series, except for some language-disordered children who solved both stair series in the tactual modality at the same period. With respect to the problem-solving processes the language-disordered children had all the problem-solving components in their repertoire. Rule use of language-disordered children was similar to normal children. From the observed regularity and restriction of configurations of final solutions we inferred assimilation processes that were similar in both groups. Problem-solving activities of both groups were lower in the tactual modality than in a visual or combined tactual–visual modality condition. Also, both groups applied more rules in the visual conditions than in the tactual condition.

But language-disordered children were different from normal children in the lack of age effect. Also, effects of visual and tactual–visual conditions were different. Success was first observable in normal children in the tv task, for language-disordered in the vv task. Considering subprocesses, normal children with success scores 0 to 2 scored higher than language-disordered children with success scores 0 to 2 in evaluative subroutines, but lower in hypothetic, feedback, and patterning. For evaluative subprocess the two subgroups of language-disordered children were different. Children with intermodal problems did poorer on the tv task than the v task. Conversely, children with tactual–kinesthetic/serial problems did better on the tv task than the vv task. Rule use of language-disordered children with success scores 0 to 2 was lower in the t task than for normal children with success scores 0 to 2, but higher in the vv task.

The results were impressively consistent regardless of whether the analysis focused on task success, the problem-solving processes, or type of solutions or rules used to solve the problem. Results showed that even when a child is cognitively competent to deal with a short or a long series, cognitive competence still may not always show up in performance when there is a difference in information inherent in a task. In such cases, competence does not become performance.

Taken together, these outcomes strongly show the need to differentiate competence and performance. Children with language disorders did not demonstrate regularity in development over time or achieve maximum performance levels like normal children because their performance in an actual situation was depressed or held back by the difficulty of perceiving the adequate information for a particular task condition, because of their type of perceptual deficit.

The Seriation study is also significant in showing that a model of problem solving derived from verbal protocols could be adapted to study problem-solving activities on a nonverbal level. Data showed that the coding system worked. It served (a) to differentiate normal children at different age levels, (b) to describe a regular increase of activities of problem solving in normal children, (c) to show the deviancy of children with language disorders, (d) to differentiate two language disorder subgroups, and (e) to demonstrate that the structure of problem-solving processes observed in the children on a nonverbal level can be compared to the structure of problem-solving processes on a verbal level as observed by Pitt and Brouwer-Janse. We conclude that what children acquire for solving problems on a lower level is relearned by high-school students, college students, and professors on a higher level.

Clinical Implications

The ultimate goal of our many years of research was to improve clinical intervention for children with language disorders. To reach this goal, we not only studied language-disordered children but also those who were normal, congenitally deaf, or blind. We also studied adult patients with acquired brain damage. We claimed that developmental data collected on the different groups of children should fit a common model of development and also apply to the behavior of persons with acquired brain damage. This common model then should foster intervention programs for children with developmental language disorders and for adults with acquired or degenerative diseases of the nervous system.

In this chapter, we focus first on what our collective research outcomes mean toward meeting the criteria for a developmental model, as discussed earlier in Section 1.3.2. Second, we consider how existing models do not fit these criteria and a new model is introduced and described. Third, learning and intervention are approached with this new model in mind. Fourth, we describe ongoing and future research projects aimed at validating our model.

3.1 RESEARCH DATA AND CRITERIA FOR A MODEL OF DEVELOPMENT

We begin by acknowledging the consistency of findings across our multiple studies, which included Successive Pattern Recognition, Form Recognition, Seriation tasks, and the longitudinal studies. We discuss the relevancy of this consistency to existing models of development. Finally, we focus on outcomes of the Seriation study, which go beyond the findings of earlier studies.

3.1.1 The Interrelationship of Skills and Levels of Development

In chapter 1, two different models of development were identified. They differ in their assumptions about the relationship of developing skills and how skills are learned. According to the model of independence, skills are learned in isolation of one another in an accumulative way. One could argue that successful performance on the tasks used in all our studies required numerous and different kinds of skills. For success on the Seriation tasks one might consider, for example, classification skills, abstracting skills, and logical skills. The problem-solving activities could be divided into skills—those dealing with evaluating and selecting information when making visual and tactual discriminations, and those dealing with establishing hypotheses, using feedback, and patterning. The Seriation tasks also required spatial skills such as analyzing drawings, comparing lengths, and displacing bars. For rule construction, one can consider skills involved in establishing causes, judging effects, using memory, and so on. According to the model of independent skills, children would vary considerably in their scores on tasks that tap different skills. Some children would have high visual discrimination scores and others high tactual discrimination scores. Some would have high scores on certain spatial skills, but not others. Some children would score high on hypothetic skills and others high on comparing lengths. For children with language disorders, the model of independent skills would predict variable profiles of problem-solving skills without any recognizable patterns.

However, our data contradicted the model of accumulation of numerous independent skills. They supported some kind of *interrelationship among skills*. We observed regularity in the development of perceptual performance in normal, blind, and hearing-impaired children on the Successive Pattern and Form Recognition tasks. A similar regularity was found for normal children in their success scores, problem-solving activities, and rule use on the Seriation tasks across age.

Data for children with language disorders also contradicted the model of independent skills. When examining their profiles of problem-solving activities on the Seriation tasks, for example, language-disordered children showed similar characteristics which differentiated them from profiles observed in normal children. Normal children with success scores 0 to 2 had significantly higher proportions of subroutines (SR) for subprocess (SP) evaluative than did language-disordered children with comparable scores. In contrast, these language-disordered children showed higher SR proportions than did normal children for the hypothetic and patterning SP. So there appeared to be some common difficulty among children with language disorders that made them different from normal children. The model of independent skills does not account for such findings. Rather, findings support the notion of some kind of interrelationship among skills. Given that skills seem to develop in an interrelated manner, we asked if there are levels of development of such interrelated skills.

We have already discussed the research evidence for interpreting the pattern of increase of perceptual performances with age as an indication of levels (see Section 1.2). For example, the Successive Pattern Recognition study revealed an age gap between clusters of success in recognizing patterns with no more than two elements and patterns with three and four elements in normal children. We interpreted these findings as evidence for a development of perceptual organization by levels, an elementary level for paired patterns, which develops before a complex level for serial patterns with three or more elements. A similar interpretation was made for the Form Recognition task where children were first successful in recognizing topological and simple Euclidean forms before complex Euclidean ones, and where patterns of finger movements for exploring forms changed with age (see Section 1.2.1).

The findings from the Seriation study included features of relearning, another source of evidence for the existence of developmental levels. Piaget (1947/1950) referred to the process of relearning as characteristic of consecutive levels: What is acquired on a lower level has to be relearned on a higher level. There were two indexes of such relearning in the Seriation study. The first index was reflected in the coding of children's manual activities during the problem-solving task. Using Pitt and Brouwer-Janse's (1985) model, we showed that the same model used to account for verbal problem-solving processes in high-school students, college students, and university professors, could also account for the nonverbal problem-solving activities we observed in 3- to 14-year-old children. The implication is that there is similarity in the basic structure of problem-solving processes across the age span and for tasks in different performance domains. For the concept of developmental levels, this means that what children learn early on a nonverbal level is relearned on a verbal level later.

The second index of relearning was children's application of nonverbal interaction rules on a representational level, as could be inferred from their solutions to the seriation problem. Simple configurations can be related to touching rules, more complex configurations to elementary handling rules, and the most complex configurations to complex handling rules (see Section 2.4.2). These rules and their sequence of acquisition, expressed by the different configurations, were similar to the rules and the sequence of acquisition of younger children on a sensorimotor level. We infer that children acquire interaction rules first on a sensorimotor level in a regular sequence. This sequence first includes touching rules, then elementary handling rules, and afterwards, complex handling rules. After the sensorimotor level, children show similar interaction rules in a similar developmental sequence but on a mental representational level. The implication is that they relearn on a representational level what they had previously learned on a sensorimotor level, namely the rules for interaction. On the Seriation task, they used these rules to assimilate the models of the stair series and to perform their replication. Thus, our findings fit Piaget's description of relearning and his criterion for a sequence of levels. That is, they support the existence of developmental levels predicted by his model of interrelated skills and hierarchical levels of development.

However, our data on language-disordered children led us to question the claim that levels of development are hierarchically *dependent* on one another. The model of hierarchically dependent levels predicts that children with language disorders are merely delayed in development (i.e., they lack age-appropriate performances because of failure to perform at earlier prerequisite skill levels). If this is so, then their performance profiles should correspond to the profiles of younger normal children at earlier developmental levels. Consequently, an age effect ought to be observed. Children with language disorders should become increasingly more able to do the later learned skills as they get older and have more experience with prerequisite skills. But, this was not the case. All data from various cross-sectional studies were surprisingly consistent in showing the lack of a regular increase in performance with age in language-disordered children.

Furthermore, as discussed, the longitudinal study revealed deviant rather than delayed development (see Section 1.3). Some skills (e.g., perspective drawing), which are typically acquired late in normal children, were performed early by some language-disordered children. Conversely, some early acquired skills by normal children (e.g., direct speech imitation), were performed late by language-disordered children. This suggests that skills are not directly related, just as consecutive levels are not directly related.

In sum, our data indicate that skills are somehow interrelated and develop by levels, but the data do not support a dependent or direct relationship among skills and between levels. Therefore, the question can be raised about how to describe the relationship among skills and between developmental levels. To answer this question, we discuss the similarities and differences between normal and language-disordered children—their success, on problem-solving performances and rule use on the Seriation tasks. These data permit inferences that go beyond the earlier studies of Form and Successive Pattern Recognition Performances.

3.1.2 Similarities and Differences Between Normal Children and Children With Language Disorders on the Seriation Tasks

The seriation data revealed similarities and differences between normal and language-disordered children on all three types of analyses: success scores, problem-solving activities, and rule application in the problem solutions.

Success scores: Normal and language-disordered children were alike in that both groups were similarly affected by task complexity; namely, whether one had to solve the problem in the short or long stair series. Data supported the prediction that some children in both groups would perform successfully the short stair series, but not the long one. All children who successfully performed the long stair series also accomplished the short stair series. We interpreted these findings to mean that the short stair series put fewer cognitive demands on performance than did the long stair series for all children.

Differences were observable when success was evaluated in different modality conditions or tasks. Success for all children depended on the sensory modality condition or information. Normal and language-disordered children showed lower success scores in the tactual condition than in the visual conditions. But the groups reacted differently to the tactual–visual and visual conditions. Normal children were first successful on the tv task, language-disordered children on one of the visual tasks (more often the vv than the v task).

Group differences were also observed in the developmental features of success. The number of children who obtained maximum success scores in the normal group increased until an age at which all children were maximally successful. Children with language disorders did not show such a regular increase with age. Some children were unsuccessful on one or more tasks at every age level.

Problem-solving activities: When trying to solve the seriation problem, normal and language-disordered children engaged in similar activities as measured by the overall types of subroutines used. The activities of both groups reflected the three subprocesses (basics, action, and conclusion) that were required for being judged as testable. The problem-solving activities of both groups also included activities of evaluative, selective, hypothetic, feedback, and patterning subprocesses.

However, group differences were found when the development of problem-solving activities was considered. As already discussed, normal children with success scores 0 to 2 at different age levels presented higher SR proportions for the evaluative and selective subprocesses than for the hypothetic and feedback ones (see Section 3.1.1). This finding corresponds to observations of normal children dealing with problem solving in daily life. They show curiosity—they ask questions and investigate by searching for more information. Children with language disorders differed from normal children in SR proportions of subroutines for specific sub-processes; namely, the proportions of subroutines for the subprocess hypothetic and patterning were higher than in normal children as already pointed out. If such profiles like the language-disordered children were observed in younger unsuccessful normal children, one might infer that language-disordered children are simply immature or developmentally delayed. But because such profiles were never observed in unsuccessful normal children at any age, we infer that language-disordered children are deviant and not merely delayed in problem-solving activities.

Rule application: We observed similar patterns of configurations of the seriation products in normal and language-disordered children and inferred that they apply similar rules of interaction. The inferred sequence of rule application was similar as well. All children first applied touching rules to be considered instructable. In addition, two elementary handling rules were applied in consideration of testability. Patterns of configurations for both groups could be related to elementary handling rules only or, in addition, to complex handling rules. We inferred that one can relate the rules applied to the Seriation tasks to the rules that children had acquired on a sensorimotor level when interacting with the environment. This appeared to be valid for both groups.

Differences were found for rule use in children with success scores 0 to 2 in different modality conditions. For the tactual (t) task, language-disordered children used lower proportions of rules than normal children, but for the visual (vv) task they used higher proportions.

In sum, analyses of success, problem-solving activities, and rule use on the Seriation tasks revealed similarities and differences between normal and disordered children. They were alike when the analyses focused on overall processes that addressed competence. They were different on those analyses that focused either on different types of information or on development changes.

3.1.3   Interaction as Source of Development and Results of the Seriation Tasks

Basic experience and input features. When the Successive Pattern Recognition and Form Recognition studies were discussed in chapter 1, we considered the possibility that some kind of basic experience may underlie the development of perceptual organization. Such basic experience appears to have two characteristics, as revealed by our sensory-deprivation studies of congenitally blind and hearing-impaired children (Section 1.2.2). First, the quality of such basic experience appears unrelated to modality specific visual or auditory processes. Compensatory effects were not observed. Deprivation effects were observed not only in the respective deprived sensory modalities, as expected, but also on complex tasks in the nondeprived modalities, an unexpected result (see Section 1.2.2). But despite their severe hearing or visual deprivation, these children still increased their perceptual performance in a regular way such that they did eventually reach maximum or ceiling performances on the Successive Pattern Recognition and Form Recognition tasks, but with a time delay relative to normal children.

Second, similarities between normal and sensory-deprived children suggest that their basic experience has common input features that can be enhanced by visual and auditory information. But neither input source can be a critical feature of this basic experience because lack of such information did not prevent development from occurring in either sensory deprived group. Because these children commonly share adequate tactual input, it is considered that tactual input may be a critical source of basic experience. This hypothesis is strengthened when one considers that language-disordered children can see and hear, but still fail to show the same kind of regular developmental shifts as normal children and children with visual or auditory deprivation. Moreover, the difficulties of children with language disorders in tactual exploration and in understanding guided tactual instruction suggest difficulties in dealing with tactual features of basic experience.

Basic experience and interaction. Our observations, including the longitudinal findings, led to the hypothesis that spontaneous nonverbal interaction in daily life may be a source of development (see Section 1.4). The Seriation tasks were designed as interactive tasks to study aspects of nonverbal interaction. Thus, seriation data allow for the discussion and inferences about interaction as basic experience. Considering the similarities and differences described in the previous section, we can infer: Language-disordered children are similar to normal children in competence (cognitive processes expressed by complexity, problem-solving activities of different subprocesses, and the use of interaction rules). However, they are different whenever information and developmental changes are involved. We conclude that children with language disorders fail in task success and in adequate problem-solving activities because they fail in information-seeking processes. They fail to acquire adequate basic interaction experience because they fail in searching for information. Therefore, development becomes deviant.

With these conclusions in mind we searched for a model of development that would account for our data.

3.2   A NEW MODEL OF DEVELOPMENT

Neither a model of independent skill learning nor a model of hierarchical dependent levels could account for all our data. The independent skill model could not account for our observations of relationships among skills in development in normal, sensory-deprived, and language-disordered children. A developmental model of hierarchically dependent levels of skill could not account for the observations on children with language disorders whose levels of skills did not follow the expected sequence of normal children. Apparently, they can acquire skills of a certain level even though skills of the presumed prerequisite level are missing in the repertoire.

We searched for another model of development that would fit our data. In particular, the model had to show the lack of a hierarchical dependent relationship among developmental levels. The root of a growing tree offered a good figurative representation of our findings. The growth of the tree depends on the growth of its root. When the root is small as in a young tree, only a few branches are visible. The stronger the root gets, the stronger the trunk becomes, and the more branches that will grow. When the root gets sick, the branches get sick as a consequence. The branches are not related directly to each other; rather, they are related to the root. So their relationship to each other is an indirect one. Branches represent the levels of development. The growth of a branch represents the appearance of a given level with its respective skills (Affolter, 1987/1991). Just as the branches are indirectly related, so are the levels of development. They are indirectly related to each other through the root.

3.2.1   The Model of a Root of a Growing Tree

The root is the source of the tree's growth. The root stands for basic experience (i.e., for nonverbal interaction in daily life). We assume that nonverbal interaction in daily life fits the criteria of basic experience, as described at the end of chapter 1. Nonverbal interaction in daily life was defined as events with goal-oriented changes in topological relationships between a person who interacts and the environment. Interaction starts the moment an organism moves or is moved and touches the material world. Such interaction elicits changes of resistance, probably the most basic information of our existence (Lorenz, 1977). Such changes of resistance are elicited by changes of topological relationships. This means that perceiving such basic information involves causes and effects (i.e., cognitive processes). In this way information and cognitive processes are interrelated.

Our data suggest that children with language disorders fail in an adequate search for information while interacting. The model takes these findings into account. It assumes that children with language disorders fail in basic interaction experience. In our model, this means that their root is unhealthy or sick, and, as a consequence, the growth of the branches becomes deviant.

In this sense, a model of a root of a growing tree can represent development and its deviancies as well as the learning that occurs. In the next two sections we consider the model in relation to aspects of development and learning.

3.2.1.1   *The Model of a Root and Development*

As the child's nonverbal daily interaction experiences increase, the root grows and, with the root, the trunk and the branches grow too. As the size and strength of the root increase, both perceptual organization and cognitive processes are expected to improve. Knowledge about the world (cognitive and social) will expand.

Figure 3.1 represents this model of development. The circles refer to the size of the root, and the year rings of the trunk. Both are prerequisites for the appearance of specific branches. The dark arrows indicate the direction of growth in the root and the trunk. At each circle, arrows represent respective branches, which grow because of the size of the root. For example, when the child has experienced a critical number of nonverbal problem-solving events of daily life (see second circle at the center of Fig. 3.1), improvement of perceptual performances can be observed. Respective branches appear and will grow at least throughout childhood. As experiences in daily nonverbal interaction increase further, the trunk reaches another critical level of growth as represented by the third circle. Again new branches appear. These branches represent sensorimotor performances such as rolling over, sitting, standing, crawling, and so on. Again, further growth of these branches represents the growing of more complex sensorimotor performances such as signal acquisition and imitation. A further development involves the passage from the sensorimotor to the representation levels depicted by different branches. This means again, that branches, as developmental levels, are not directly related. For example, the passage from the sensorimotor level to the intuitive level does not happen in a "direct" way but results from the growth of the root or the growth in interactive experience. In this way development continues. Performances at higher levels will be observable as the tree grows and more and more branches appear.

One can also interpret the circles that represent the growth of the root and the trunk as signs of cybernetic processes in the form of dynamic equilibration systems. Brouwer-Janse (1983) described such equilibration systems of development. Thelen (1989) referred to a similar phenomenon in

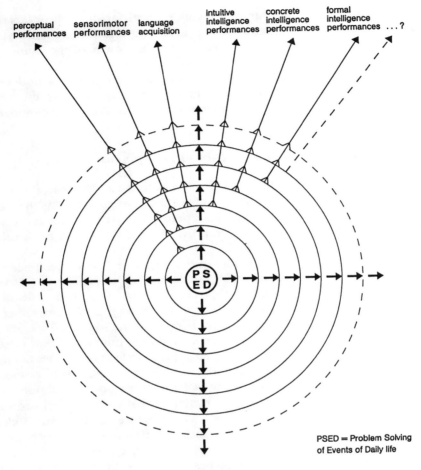

FIG. 3.1.   Model of development.

her theory of dynamic systems. Other authors pointed to self-regulatory processes (Edelman, 1987; Fentress, 1976). Piaget (1970) discussed self-regulatory processes involved in the equilibration systems. He wrote,

> The central problem of genetic epistemology concerns the mechanism of this construction of novelties, which creates the need for the explanatory factors, which we call reflexive abstraction and self-regulation. However, these factors have furnished only global explanations. A great deal of work remains to be done in order to clarify this fundamental process of intellectual creation, which is found at all the levels of cognition. (p. 78)

We argued earlier that the basic kind of nonverbal interaction experience, which is represented by the root, requires tactual information. Vision and hearing seems to enhance nonverbal interactive activity.

Such a model of a root can be considered to be valid for all people, irrespective of age or membership in a clinical group. As the tree depends on the root throughout its life, so adults still depend on a healthy strong root. In old age the root may start to get weaker, and soon, this weakness will be observable in the branches. But still, one can be aware of the root and try to keep it strong.

In summary, we can account for our data by comparing development to the growth of living plants such as trees. Tree branches are not directly related to each other. They are related to the root. In other words, skills characterizing different levels of development as noted in Piaget's work, for example, depend on a common source rather than a preceding skill or knowledge level (Affolter, 1987/1991). As the root grows, the trunk gets stronger and more and more branches appear. So different levels of development are related to the root (i.e., to the increase in daily nonverbal interaction experience, which is based on tactual information).

3.2.1.2 The Model of a Root and Learning

The model of the root of a growing tree can be applied to learning as well. Skills are like the branches of the tree. To make branches grow, the root must get stronger. This means that one cannot directly teach developmental skills. Teaching is done at the root.

The traditional approach requires educators, or therapists, or parents to hand over their experiences and their knowledge like a package to the child in a direct way. The Seriation study could be viewed from this approach. For each task, children were asked to look at the model of the to-be-constructed stair series. According to the traditional approach children should be able to use the visual information contained in those models in a direct way. They should try to replicate (i.e., to imitate the model when constructing the stair series by using visual feedback). In Section 2.4.2 we discussed our findings, which contradicted such assumptions. Instead of imitating the model step-by-step children assimilated the model according to their level of interaction rules. As a result, different configurations were produced as solutions to the problem.

The model of a root contradicts the traditional approach. Of course, the root needs soil just as children need parents, and teachers, and an environment. But the root assimilates; it takes out of the soil what it needs according to its actual level or state. For educators, this means, that all one can do is to offer children opportunities to interact (i.e., the respective environment). These opportunities should allow them to acquire basic knowledge about themselves and the environment.

To illustrate, take J., a 6-year-old, who is learning how to swim. Teaching swimming traditionally involves verbal instructions. The teachers demonstrate. The students look at them and try to imitate. Thus, the information provided is mostly auditory and visual, and imitation is the skill required. How could one change that approach?

There are two problems to solve when learning to swim, one is body position, the other is movement. Because many children with language disorders have difficulties in imitating movements but can swim, the aspect of imitation appears to be less important than body position (i.e., for swimming the body must learn to float in the water).

> I work on floating with J., giving her the opportunity to feel how her body floats. I help her feel how to inhale air into the lungs, and then put her body with the face down into the water—the body starts to float like a balloon. We do this for several days, a few minutes each time. J. starts to move her legs and her arms, trying to move her body forward, head once down, then another time up. She becomes more and more skilled. Then comes the day when she suddenly discovers swimming (i.e., inhaling air and moving forward like a duckling). "I did it all by myself," is her comment. Years later, she still tells about having discovered swimming all by herself.

This is a story about learning through interaction, getting tactual feedback directly connected to the task. In this way J. got the impression that she did it herself, that is, she discovered something new by feeling it (see Affolter, 1987/1991). When using this approach to learning, teachers often do not get credit from either the children or the public because the only thing teachers do when using this approach is to provide the child with situations for interacting, however difficult this is.

3.2.2   The Root and Nonverbal Daily-Life Interaction

The root in our model stands for the source of development and of learning. We mentioned that the root as a source of development and learning stands for nonverbal daily-life interaction. In Section 1.3.2, we discussed the criteria for such a source and that activities of daily life meet them. Now we focus on an additional criterion, which the Seriation study revealed. The description of nonverbal daily-life interaction as the source or root of development has to account for the similarities and differences between normal children and language-disordered children. They were similar in competence of cognitive processes, problem-solving activities, and rule application. They differed when they had to perform in actual situations and information became important. These demands on the root and thus on daily interaction are discussed in the next two sections under different aspects. We first focus on the notion of event, goal orientation, and hypothetical processes. The discussion of feedback information and rule application will follow.

3.2.2.1 The Model of the Root and Notions of Event, Goal Orientation and Hypothetical Processes in Daily-Life Interaction

In the Seriation tasks, activities were goal-oriented. To reach the goal, specific topological relationships had to be changed. Children had to make hypotheses about what changes were needed to construct the stair series, how to perform these changes, how to reach the goal. Once children reached success in the Seriation tasks, they had all the subroutines of hypothetic subprocess present; unsuccessful children had some of them, depending on their developmental level. The different subroutines of the hypothetic subprocess referred to hypotheses, which involved different degrees of complexity of topological relationships. We inferred their hypotheses based on the topological relationships between two bars, SR 18; between pairs of bars in succession, SR 19; among sides of bars for lining up, SR 20; and on more than one topological relationship at a time, SR 21 (see Table 2.7 in chap. 2).

Daily-life events also present goals. To reach these goals requires hypothetic processes. Almost continually, one has to consider demands including one's own needs, or the needs of the surrounding social group, the family, neighbors, coworkers, and so on. Making daily-life hypotheses requires collecting information about these demands. For a normal adult, such information involves all types of input, including visual, auditory, and tactual. The question arises about the basic, most-needed kind of information involved in establishing daily-life hypotheses. To suggest an answer, we turn to a few examples from our clinical populations.

Observations showed that children with language disorders, as do patients with acquired brain damage, often make incorrect hypotheses. Our interpretation is that such performances happen not because these persons are incompetent in establishing hypotheses, but because they may not receive adequate information in the situation. People around such patients usually talk to them and provide verbal–auditory stimulation, or they show them how to do a task and provide visual stimulation for them. Our findings (Affolter & Bischofberger, 1993, 1996) suggest that in these situations, patients are unable to make correct hypotheses because verbal–auditory and visual stimulation do not provide adequate information to them.

Mr. P. was in an accident and had suffered severe brain damage. In therapy
he is sitting on a chair. The therapist tries to make him change seats and sit
on a stool at a table. The stool and the table are close to the patient. The
therapist points with his hand to the stool and tells the patient to sit on it.
The patient does not move, even as he looks in the direction of the stool
and table. The therapist puts the stool closer to Mr. P. and guides the hands
of Mr. P. to touch the stool. Still the patient does not move. Now the therapist puts the stool so that it touches Mr. P.'s upper leg. After a short moment,
Mr. P. glides over to the stool and sits on it at the table.

What had happened? First, Mr. P. received visual and verbal–auditory
information from the therapist. He did not move; he was unable to make
the correct hypothesis. Then the therapist guided the hand of Mr. P. to
touch the stool. Mr. P. did not move; Mr. P. had still not reached a correct
hypothesis. He could feel the object, the stool, but this was not sufficient.
That feeling was not directly connected with the event. When the therapist pushed the stool so Mr. P. could feel it touching his upper legs/hips,
he moved over to sit on the stool.

The change of resistance Mr. P. felt the moment the stool touched his
upper leg/hips came from the same source that is critical when changing
from the chair to the stool. In other words, the change of resistance which
occurs at that source has to do with the first topological change required
for moving from a chair over to the stool: to separate legs/hips from the
chair and to connect legs/hips with the stool. Touching the stool with the
hands provides tactual information about the object but is not the source
of information about the event. To establish a correct hypothesis Mr. P.
needed tactual information about the beginning of the event (i.e., tactual
information coming from the source between stool and legs/hips).

A similar observation occurred with M., a 13-year-old with severe language disorders and diagnosed as autistic.

M. is stretched out on a long chair. The therapist tries to get him up and to
put him to work helping to prepare tomato salad. The therapist shows him
a tomato, and tells him to get up and cut the tomatoes—M. does not move.
Is he lazy? The therapist makes him touch a tomato. Still no reaction. Finally, the therapist brings a knife, puts the knife into M.'s hands and guides him
to cut the tomato. Immediately, M. stands up, goes into the kitchen and
works on preparing the tomato salad.

These examples explain why the children understood the instruction
for the Seriation tasks. The instruction did not simply consist of touching
the material. It consisted of starting the respective task by guiding the
child to perform the first changes of topological relationships. We expected that providing tactual information connected with the relevant sources

of information will enable the children to construct hypotheses about the task and the situation (see Appendix A). It turned out that this was possible for both normal and language-disordered children.

These observations suggest that, in order to establish highly probable hypotheses about an event, tactual information may be basic. But the tactual information has to be provided by the first changes of topological relationships of the event and its relevant sources of information. In other words, the basic tactual information has to do with the interaction part of the event, and not simply with touching an object.

There is another aspect to consider when establishing hypotheses, namely, the complexity or detour aspect. At the beginning of this chapter we discussed the complexity of relationships referred to by the subroutines of the hypothetic subprocess. Normal children and language-disordered children will first be competent to establish hypotheses for simple topological relationships between two bars, and only later for more complex, multiple topological relationships among the bars. Daily-life events often require hypotheses, which involve multiple topological relationships. Detours are such an example involved in daily life. How do I get an object from the top of a cupboard? I need to get a chair, to step on the chair, and then be able to reach out for the object. Getting a chair is a detour and is only indirectly related to the needed topological change, separating object from the cupboard. A striking example illustrates how a detour can increase the complexity of a daily-life event.

> Mr. S. is severely brain-damaged. He had a nap in his bed and now it is time for him to stand up for therapy. The therapist approaches the bed. He takes the patient's hand and begins to take off the blanket with him. The therapist expects that this provides enough information for the patient to make the hypothesis, "I have to get up." Mr. S. opens his eyes, takes the blanket and pulls it back over his body. The therapist tries again to guide Mr. S. to take the blanket off. Now Mr. S. starts to shout and hit. Does he not want to be disturbed, or is he just unmotivated to get out of bed?

After this had happened, we discussed the complexity of the topological changes, which were performed, their sources of information, and how they related to the real event. How does one get out of bed? By using the hands? No, this is a detour. If I take the blanket off as a first change of topological relationship, I do it because I know that afterwards I will move my legs out of the bed. That first change of topological relationship, separating blanket from body/bed, is not necessarily required for getting out of bed, that is, it is not directly related to the goal of getting out of bed. It is only indirectly related, and we call it a detour. That handling the blanket is a detour, not necessarily related to getting out of bed, becomes more understandable if I imagine myself being in bed, in the night, asleep. Unexpectedly somebody tries to pull my blanket off. My reaction will be, "Where is my blanket? It's gone and I am cold," and I will try to pull the blanket back over my body (just as the patient did). So we discussed the necessary topological change to get out of bed. To pull the blanket away from my body is not the necessary topological change. What is necessary is that I have to separate the body from the bed. This is critical to getting out of bed. It is done by using/moving the legs out of the bed. Thus, the therapist changed the approach.

> Instead of starting with the hands, this time he begins with the legs of the patient. Under the blanket he moves Mr.S.'s one leg close to the edge of the bed, and then the other one. The moment arises when the patient pushes the blanket aside by himself, sits up, reaches his hand out with a smile to greet the therapist, to get help sitting up and getting out of bed. The patient has established the correct hypothesis about the event.

This example corroborates the complexity aspect that is created when multiple changes of topological relationships, such as those required by detours, are involved. When working with patients, one may often need to reduce the number of changes of topological relationships by considering only the most important and necessary ones, and thus avoiding detours.

3.2.2.2 Changes in Resistance and Feedback Information in Daily-Life Interaction

Besides the hypothetical activities, the Seriation tasks were designed to observe feedback activities. Five different activities were coded as subroutines of subprocess feedback. To construct the stair series, children had to displace the bars. Displacing was described as moving the bars from the selection site to the construction site on the table, and releasing them so that in the case of already arranged bars, the displaced bars touch the others. Thus, three kinds of topological relations had to be changed: (a) between bars and support when taking off a bar for displacing it, (b) between this bar and the support when releasing the displaced bar, and (c) between that displaced bar and the arranged ones so that they are touching. Each change of such topological relationships elicited a change in resistance. Taking off a bar from the support changed the resistance between the bar and the support. Putting the displaced bar down on the support changed the resistance between bar and support. Arranging the bars so that they touch each other changed the resistance between bars. Each change of topological relationship happened at a specific place. This place became the relevant source for the change in resistance, which could be taken as feedback information.

Activities coded as feedback subroutines differed in regard to relevant sources of information. SR 13 was judged to be present when the children released the bars on the construction site so that the bars touched each other at any place; children did not have to identify a specific part of the bars as source. SR 14 being judged present required that the bars be arranged so that their sides touch each other; here the source of information was specified as at-the-sides. SR 15 and SR 16 referred to additional sources of information, such as the tops being stair-like (SR 15), or the baseline being straight (SR 16). SR 17 referred to the most complex displacing condition. To do this required a multiple of sources to be considered at the same time; tops of bars had to be arranged stair-like and at the same time the base line had to be straight. For the v and vv tasks, visual information could be utilized as feedback information; for the tv task, tactual and visual information could be used; for the t tasks only tactual information was available.

In daily life, the use of feedback information can be inferred in every event of daily interaction. I grasp the knife with my hand. The critical source, for knowing that I have the knife in my hand, is between my fingers and the knife. When I touch the apple with my knife I have to focus on the tactual sources between hand/knife/apple. When I cut through the apple on the cutting board with my knife, I have to focus on the tactual source between the apple and the cutting board. These changes of topological relationships involve changes in resistance and each time a respective source of information is created. In this way one can judge the effect of interactions (i.e., in our example the success of cutting/dividing the apple).

Judging changes of topological relationships among several objects in daily life can be quite difficult sometimes. Here are two examples:

> Imagine you are sitting in a train. The train stops in a station. There is another train on the next track. One of the trains starts to move. Since both trains are supposed to move, you are not able to decide which train is moving. However, if the position of your train allows you to face the building of the station, then you know immediately when your train moves. This is made possible because the station house offers the stable reference.

Piaget (1961/1969) described similar phenomena and referred to the relativity of perception. As another expression of such relativity, one can interpret the following example (Affolter & Bischofberger, 1993).

> R., a head-trauma patient, is sitting in his wheelchair. He has a pillow and a pillowcase on his knees. He tries to put the clean pillowcase on his pillow. The pillow, the pillowcase, and R.'s hands move. The knees also move. R.'s movements get faster and faster. His face and his whole body get tense. (p. 40)

Analysis: R. has the pillow on his knee. He handles the pillow and the pillowcase. Doing this, he has to move his body, his hands, and his knees. For all these actions, the moving knees are the reference, but they do not offer a stable reference. Because there is no stable reference, he can not detect relevant tactual sources of information needed to judge changes of topological relationships. Since he does not receive enough information, he searches for more, and his movements become rapid; the tension in his body increases. He appears close to panic.

> A therapist nearby notices R.'s difficulties and changes the environment. He gets a table for R.. Now, R. can put the pillow on the table. His movements become slower, and his face calmer. He continues his activities and reaches his goal successfully.

Analysis: The table provides a stable support as reference for the changes of topological relationships involved in the event. This is similar to the train station in our previous example. When R. feels something moving and at the same time he feels the stability of the table, he can take that stability as reference and decide that the moving thing is the pillow.

We conclude that adequate feedback information about relevant topological changes demands the reference to a stable source offered by the environment. The Seriation tasks allowed for such feedback information; the bars were moved and arranged always in relation to a stable support, the table. The insert board in the tv task offered an additional possibility of stable reference at the sides. It is suggested that this may have contributed to the success in the tv task as the first successful performance of young normal children. To get adequate feedback about topological changes, these changes must occur with reference to a stable environment.

3.2.2.3 Rules for Interaction in Daily-Life Events

We observed application of rules in the Seriation study and referred to interaction rules acquired by the children on a sensorimotor level. We expected that at the age children were tested with the Seriation tasks, they are acquiring rules similar to the sensorimotor rules, but belonging to a higher representational level. Solving the Seriation tasks required the application of touching and handling rules. We described such rules by analyzing the different configurations of the final solutions in the Seriation tasks (see Section 2.4). We differentiated rules by an increase in complexity of the topological relationships involved. These rules are acquired hierarchically (i.e., the simple ones are embedded in the more complex ones); for example, touching rules are embedded in the handling rules (see Section 1.4.4).

Subroutines of subprocess basics could also be related to rules. A testable child presented all the subroutines of subprocess basics. We inferred that they presented the touching rules and two of the elementary handling rules.

Children who were instructable were observed for presence or absence of touching and handling rules. The third elementary handling rule and proximity rules were not included in the subroutines of subprocess basics. We described and analyzed their use in the Seriation tasks by evaluating the configurations listed in chapter 2. The results of rule application were reported in Section 2.4.2.

The seriation data showed that the configurations of the seriation products of normal and language-disordered children were alike. One could identify all the described rules. We concluded that language-disordered children apply the same kind of rules in the Seriation tasks as normal children.

In daily-life events, we apply interaction rules all the time. Touching rules are important, for example, because the topological relationship between body and support is a critical elementary relationship. Whenever there is a sudden change in that relationship, as in the case of an earthquake, we experience fright and panic. To feel secure we need a stable support. In addition to the importance of stable resistance offered by the support, one also has to consider the resistance from the sides. It is helpful to hold on to a railing when going up a steep staircase. This helps us to realize that the world includes not only the stable base of the support but also what is next to us. We described our observations of babies from this perspective (Affolter, 1987/1991). Both kinds of experiences with the support and with stable sides can be considered basic for nonverbal daily interaction. One has to know where the world around us is and, at the same time, where one's body is before one can act upon it.

Even when children with language disorders are competent in the use of such interaction rules, they may fail to apply them adequately. We observed that rule use is information dependent in both normal and language-disordered children. Our findings revealed that language-disordered children reacted differently to information, as discussed.

Thus, in daily-life situations language-disordered children and other clinical people may fail to apply interaction rules adequately, not because they are incompetent, but because their search for information is not adequate. The problem often becomes apparent in releasing with displacing. We pointed out that babies from 4 months of age explore grasping and lifting objects for several months (see Section 1.4.4) before discovering voluntary releasing with displacing, usually around 7 to 8 months. Clinical experience supports such differentiation and time delay between holding/lifting and releasing. Some patients with severe brain damage will grasp objects within their reach but be unable to release them.

Patient X. had suffered a severe head trauma. He is being guided through the activities of squeezing an orange to make juice. He needs to hold a knife for cutting the orange in half. The grasping action requires separating the knife from the support and lifting it to cut. After the initial sequence of actions, the orange is cut in half and the knife is not needed anymore and should be released on the support. But patient X. keeps holding the knife in his hand—apparently not being able to release it.

The inability to release can occur in different situations. Affolter (1987/1991) has described more difficult events than the one just mentioned, as when, for example, children with language disorders want to make contact with another child by touching that child. When touching the hair, for example, they grasp some hair and are unable to release it. When this happens, they are often judged to be aggressive because the people around them do not have another interpretation. Our interpretation points to the difference in complexity between grasping and releasing. Releasing is more complex than grasping. This difference in complexity has been described by Affolter and Bischofberger (1993). They observed babies in the discovery stage of voluntary releasing around 7 months. A thorough analysis of these observations revealed that these babies performed sequences of changes of topological relationships between the object to release, the fingers holding the object, and the environment. Together with the described releasing goes the displacing rule. An object is grasped at a specific site on the support, then the object is brought to another site on the support and released there.

These sequences and the corresponding changes of resistance, which include changes of sources of information, underline the difference in complexity of information between grasping and releasing.

In summary, nonverbal daily-life interactive experiences, with changes of topological relationships and the corresponding changes in resistance, present certain regularities. On a sensorimotor level, the baby detects such regularities; they are fundamental to the baby's learning of interactive rules characteristic of the sensorimotor level of development. Babies first consider the touching of the environment with the touching rules: support rule, moving rule, and holding/lifting rule. All three rules of touching are interrelated and interdependent. The support rule is the most basic rule. The moving rule includes experience with the support rule, and the holding/lifting rule includes experience with the support and the moving rules. Once touching rules are discovered, the baby begins with the acquisition of handling rules. At a higher level of development, addressed in the Seriation tasks, these sensorimotor rules are relearned for representation. They are relearned in the same sequence as the sensorimotor rules. First the support rule is learned, then the moving and holding/lifting rules of the touching rules, followed by the handling rules.

The described rules that children in the Seriation tasks had to apply, also appear to be important in nonverbal daily-life interaction. They can be considered prerequisites for adequate nonverbal interactive behavior in daily-life events. To interact one has to touch the environment. To keep nonverbal interaction going, one has to continue the touching processes and apply handling rules. Daily events almost continually require that one takes an object, such as a knife, from a specific location such as the drawer, and displaces it to another location, such as putting the knife on the table. If a clinical person has difficulty applying these rules, that person has difficulty interacting and thus difficulty solving problems of daily events without special help.

3.2.3 The Root and the Dependency on Information in Daily-Interaction Events

We designed the Seriation tasks as interactive tasks requiring goal-oriented changes of topological relationships and expected that performing these changes depends on information as had been observed in the Pattern and Form Recognition studies.

Success and problem-solving activities were related to the modality conditions, which supported these expectations. Normal children were first successful on the tactual–visual (tv) task, and problem-solving activities were always highest in that modality condition as well. Findings suggest that normal children picked up more information about the Seriation tasks when both tactual and visual information were available than when just tactual or just visual information was available. For tasks in the tactual modality condition, problem-solving activities were low in young children, and success was only observable at older ages.

In language-disordered children with success scores 0 to 2, success and problem-solving activities were also related to information. They were first successful on the vv task. Like normal children with success scores 0 to 2, problem-solving activities were low in the tactual modality condition. For evaluative activities the two subgroups differed. Children with tactual/serial problems had higher proportions of evaluative subroutines in the tv task than children with intermodal problems. Children with intermodal problems had higher proportions of evaluative activities in the vv task than in the v task. These differences supported the existence of subgroups of language-disordered children with different perceptual problems.

Rule application was influenced by information for both groups with success scores 0 to 2, the normal and the language-disordered children. Proportions of rule use were lowest in the tactual modality condition for all children but lower in language-disordered than in normal children.

It appears that performance in daily-life events also depends on information. This dependency on information for success, problem-solving activities, and rule application observed in the different studies and in daily life became our focal interest. We began to differentiate between competence and performance. The importance of that distinction is the focus of the next section.

3.2.3.1 *Competence Versus Performance in Daily-Interaction Events*

Success or correct performance on the Seriation tasks did not solely depend on cognitive skills but also on situational conditions. Some children could perform a task in one situation (e.g., the tv modality), but not in another (e.g., the v modality). In these cases, failure and success were related to information inherent in the respective situations revealed by the modality effect. Such a modality effect was observable in both normal and language-disordered children. Thus, information was critical for both groups.

This means, then, that when dealing with performance, we must always consider both cognitive and informational aspects. The fact that a child was not performing the short stair series in the visual modality, for example, could mean the child was not able to construct a short series. This would have been a cognitive problem. But it could also mean the child was able to construct a short series in one situation but failed to perform it in another one. This would have been a problem of information. Our data showed both cases. There were children who did not construct the short series in any modality condition. We infer that these children fail in cognitive prerequisites. There were others who did not construct the short stair in the visual modality, but did it in the tactual–visual modality. We infer that they fail in picking up adequate information in that particular situation.

In these examples, one can apply the concept of competence in contrast to performance (Greeno, 1985; Greeno & Riley, 1987). Correct performances, as measured by the success scores, always imply competence and also the picking up of adequate information in the respective situations to do the task (i.e., children can utilize their competence successfully in an actual situation). Children who did not construct the short stair series in any modality can be described as incompetent in constructing the short stair series. Children, who failed the construction of the short stair series in the visual modality but did it in the tactual–visual modality, can be described as competent in constructing the short stair series. But their competence was manifested as performance only when tactual–visual information was available. Their competence did not become performance if only visual information was available.

The effect of modality on success, then, suggests that successful performances of children are dependent on cognitive skills, or competence, and on situational information. Competence becomes performance only when there is enough information picked up in the actual situation. These are situational features of task performance (see Fischer & Bidell, 1991). In other words, the regular increase in success scores of normal children in general (across modalities) can be interpreted as an increase in both cognitive and information-seeking processes.

Another analysis of problem-solving activities of the Seriation study showed that the overall SR proportions of language-disordered children with success scores 0 to 2 corresponded to older normal children with success scores 0 to 2. We submit that children with language disorders are not simply delayed in problem-solving activities and perform like younger normal children. Rather, their data suggest a wider gap between competence and performance than was observed in normal children with success scores 0 to 2.

In daily-life situations we encounter this relationship between cognitive and information aspects quite often, especially in situations where competence does not become performance.

> Riding on a city bus in my hometown may not require much information. But doing this in a foreign country may create problems for me. I apply rules acquired at home for riding the bus, but perhaps without success. If that is the case, I failed to make correct hypotheses. My competence has not become performance because of lack of information. To change rules and to establish new hypotheses I need more information.

In Section 1.3.1, we cited examples of children with language disorders and with difficulties in interaction who typically are diagnosed with short attention span, hyperactivity, poor motivation, poor memory, autistic-like behavior, and tactual defensiveness. We described two contrasting events for each child: A child reported to have a short attention span in one situation showed normal attention span in another. Likewise, a child reported as hyperactive in one situation behaved like a calm child in another. A child with poor motivation in one situation was motivated and performed a task in another. The common cause in all these examples appears to be the differences in information inherent in the respective situations. Disordered behavior occurs in the situation with inadequate information, and more normal behavior in the situation with more adequate information. By applying the concepts of competence and performance to these examples, one may report that such children have an adequate attention span, or calm behavior, or motivation in their competence. But their competence becomes performance only in situations which offer tactual information instead of auditory or visual.

3.2.3.2   Organizing the Search for Information in Daily-Life Interaction Events

Previous studies showed results, which we interpreted as an expression of an organization of perceptual activities. There were effects such as the series and modality effects, and effects of contrasts observed in our studies. An age effect was expressed by the increase of correct responses with age in both Successive Pattern Recognition and Form Recognition, with clusters of correct responses, and the change of patterns of exploratory finger movements. The difficulties of language-disordered children were interpreted as an expression of their difficulties in organizing perceptual activities.

This interpretation was also supported by the analyses of profiles of problem-solving activities in the Seriation tasks. As described earlier, profiles of the youngest normal children with success scores 0 to 2 always showed higher SR proportions in evaluative and selective SP than in the hypothetic subprocess. We discussed that the profiles of problem-solving activities of language-disordered children with success scores 0 to 2 did not correspond to profiles of normal children with success scores 0 to 2 at any age. They showed significantly lower proportions of SR of SP evaluative, and significantly higher proportions in SP feedback, hypothetic, and patterning. We concluded that language-disordered children were not delayed because they never performed like less mature normal children. We inferred that they were deviant in development of problem-solving activities. The deviancies were mainly due to their difficulties in evaluative activities, an important indication of a difficulty in organizing the search for information. We will shortly discuss such an inference by considering evaluative and selective activities addressed in the Seriation tasks.

The data showed increased SR proportions in both the evaluative and the selective SP with age in normal children with success scores 0 to 2. This regularity was observed in any task condition. It appears, then, that normal children master the organization of the search for information addressed by the two subprocesses equally well at any age and in any modality condition.

This was not so for language-disordered children with success scores 0 to 2. Their lowest SR proportions were observed in the evaluative subprocess, followed by higher SR proportions in feedback, in hypothetic, in patterning, and finally in selective. It appears that the two subprocesses of evaluative and selective address different aspects of the organization of search for information. These two aspects are handled differently in language-disordered and normal children.

For evaluative subprocess (see Appendix B for description of SR 7–9) the children had to choose a criterion for evaluating the arrangements of bars. One criterion was bar length. SR 7, for example, required that children perform at least a global evaluation of length—handling a few short bars before handling some long ones, or the reverse. Applying such a criterion requires a comparison between bars. There is a difference in grasping long or short bars. The source of information appears to be between the hand/fingers and the bar, which is grasped. For SR 8, children had to arrange bars so they touched each other along the side; the sides of the bars became the information sources for evaluation. Thus, evaluative activities required the choice of a criterion (i.e., a critical place where relevant information was picked up). We call this place the *source of information for evaluating the arrangements*. SR 9 required that children organize at least half of the bars according to a common source of information chosen as criterion in some systematic way. For example, comparing the length of several bars in order to choose one, and putting the others back on the selection site.

For selective subprocess (see Appendix A for description of SR 10–12) the children had to choose a criterion for *selecting bars according to a set of topological changes*. Taking off placed bars (SR 10) referred to the children's recognition that some bars were arranged according to some incorrect topological changes. SR 11 and SR 12 required children to select a common topological change and to apply that selected topological change as a rule to at least half of the bars (SR 12), or to all of the bars (SR 11). For example, children separated bars from the support at the selection site and put them together with the support at the construction site. The topological change, applied to the bars in this example, was separating bars from their support at the selection site and bringing them together with the support at the construction site (see pile-up configuration in Section 2.4.1).

There were similar effects of *task condition* for evaluative and selective subprocesses in both groups: SR proportions were lowest in the tactual modality condition.

In normal children with success scores 0 to 2 for both *evaluative and selective* subprocesses proportions of subroutines were highest in the tactual–visual modality condition. In this modality condition the visual information was combined with tactual information, when bars were inserted. When inserting, maximum changes of resistance could be elicited from *no resistance* to *total resistance*. When grasping the bar, the source of such maximum resistance was between fingers and bar; when lifting the bar, the source was between bar and support; when inserting, the source was between bars and support, bars and sides. Thus, such sources of maximum changes of resistance were between the bars and the support, between the sides of the bars and one side of the board, and between the tops of the bars and the board. In addition, children could see what they were doing. In this way, the tactual–visual modality offered maximum information of a tactual and visual kind for evaluating relevant sources of information and for select-ing task-relevant topological changes. It seems then, that for normal chil-dren, evaluative and selective activities depended on task condition in a sim-ilar way. They could evaluate relevant sources more adequately when tactual-visual information was combined with visual information.

The two subgroups of the language-disordered children with success scores 0 to 2 differed when they were compared on proportions of the two subprocesses and on changes in modality conditions.

For evaluative subprocess, children with tactual/serial problems showed higher SR proportions in the tv task than in the vv task. These chil-dren reacted to tv information in a similar way as the normal children. They could evaluate relevant sources more adequately when tactual–visu-al information was combined with visual information.

This was in contrast to children with intermodal problems. They had higher SR proportions of evaluative SP in the vv task than in the tv task. In the vv task the child puts the chosen bars directly on top of the bars of the stimulus stair. The child has to evaluate a relevant source of information by using this visual information. It appears that children with intermodal problems rely more on such visual information than on tactual–visual information provided in the tv task. This supports their difficulty in using intermodal tactual–visual information.

The subgroups also differed for *selective subprocess*: In the v task, chil-dren with tactual/serial problems showed higher SR proportions than chil-dren with intermodal problems. We remind the readers that in the v task the child looks at a drawing of a stair-like model and below it the con-structed stair. It can be argued that in this v condition the child gets a more general view of the two stair series than in the vv task. The higher scores of children with tactual problems suggest that they may have less difficul-ty to use such a general view when selecting relevant topological changes than children with intermodal problems.

We conclude that the difficulty of language-disordered children with success scores 0 to 2 can be related to the low SR proportions in the eval-uative SP. Evaluative activities but also selective activities separate the two subgroups; they appear to process a different kind of information when evaluating and selecting.

Daily-life nonverbal interaction also requires information, and an active organized search for it. In daily-life events, situations change con-tinually, and continually we have to search for information to deal with changing situations. In familiar surroundings we hardly realize the activi-ties we perform to search for information. We become conscious of these activities, however, whenever situations change. For example, I am staying overnight in an unfamiliar hotel: I have to find out where to park the car; if and where they serve breakfast; how the shower works. I buy a new computer or TV-set so I have to read the instructions that give me information about how to use it. Success in such situations requires adequate information. Such a search for information is connected to perception. We referred in chapter 1 to Piaget and Gibson who underlined the importance of perception being structured or organized. Furthermore, we described how nonverbal daily interaction requires changes of topological relationships between an actor and the environment and within the environment. Success in daily-life interaction depends also on information about such changes of topological relationships. Affolter (1987/1991) described numerous examples to illustrate the need for a search for information when topological relationships have to be changed, and the failure of adults with brain damage in that search. Here is one of these examples:

> Mrs. N. has acquired brain damage. For 6 weeks, the therapist has tried to teach her how to peel apples and how to spread butter on bread, all without success. The therapist tells me about Mrs. N.'s problems.

Consider the following: How long can one continue to peel an apple? The apple is round, and one can peel and peel until hardly anything is left in the hand. How long can one spread butter on bread? One can spread and spread for a long long time. How long can one go on drawing a circle? One can draw and draw. When peeling and spreading and writing, one elicits only minimum changes of resistance. This, in addition to some visual information, provides enough information for a normal person to decide when the apple is peeled or the butter is spread or a circle is drawn. However, the changes of resistance are too weak and do not give those who are perceptually disordered the information they need to reach such a decision. Perhaps this explains Mrs. N.'s difficulties and lack of learning. Could we change the situation? We tried.

> Instead of peeling the apple we begin by cutting it on a cutting board. We divide the apple in half; then we cut each half in two to get fourths. We continue dividing until there are many little pieces of apple on the table. Only now do we begin to take the skin off with a chop of the knife—one piece of apple after the other. With the first piece, we cut once and the skin is off. With the next piece, we cut once and the skin is off. Mrs. N. is beaming and exclaims, "I can do it." At the end, there are many pieces of apple, all peeled, on the table. (Affolter, 1987/1991, p. 142)

Performing successfully in daily life requires evaluative and selective activities, which are only adequate when there is enough information. The example has shown that, when an actor is provided with information, interaction can be successful. The need for helping disordered people in their search for information and how to do that is the focus of the next section.

3.3   THE WORK ON THE ROOT—
CLINICAL INTERVENTION ISSUES

The model of a root applies not only to normal children but also to persons with different types of disorders. If the branches of a tree get sick, it might be due to a sick root. The sickness of the root may be due to a disturbance of the soil, and the disturbance of the soil to disturbance of the air. The sick forests in mountain areas are a frightening example. The trees of those forests are sick because the air is polluted. The polluted air makes the soil sour, the root gets sick and, as a consequence, branches get sick. If the branches and the roots are sick, then in order to treat the sick branches, one has to treat first the roots and their surroundings, the soil and the air. It does not help to treat the sick branches. One has to focus the treatment on the primary problems, the sick root and the air. For us, the root represents experience in nonverbal interaction in daily life. The sick root represents disturbances of experience in nonverbal interaction in daily life. To help the root to get stronger and healthier, one has to work on the improvement of nonverbal daily-life interaction.

This principle of working on the root level so the branches will grow is valid for everybody: normal children, persons without difficulties, and those with difficulties, as in the case of children with language disorders and adults with acquired brain damage. The principle of working on the root is also valid for geriatric patients. The following discussion, therefore, includes at times examples of normal children and of clinical people other than language-disordered children. These examples are taken from research projects in progress (see Section 3.4) and should help to illustrate some important aspects of intervention, which are valid for all groups.

Intervention, which focuses on the model of a root, has been described previously in several publications (see Affolter, 1987/1991; Affolter & Bischofberger, 1993, 1996). The following sections summarize different aspects of such intervention by referring to discussions and examples presented in this book and elsewhere. We begin the discussion of intervention by focusing on some aspects of the evaluation, followed by aspects of interacting in daily life, and, finally, we discuss the expected outcome of this kind of intervention.

3.3.1   Aspects of Evaluation

The traditional approach: This approach to evaluating children with language disorders fits the described model of independent skills. As already discussed, this model assumes there are numerous skills, and numerous deficits or disorders (Hedge, 1995). The following example illustrates such an approach. It represents many similar ones:

From an early age, T. loved to meet other children. He would smile and run over to them, put his arms around their neck when greeting them, grasp their hair, pull it. Doing this, he would use too much force and the other children became scared of him. T. was always on the run, moving around. T.'s parents took him to see a psychologist when he was a 3-year-old. The psychologist diagnosed hyperactivity. T. was put into a special preschool program. When T. was 5, his speech was not at age level; he was diagnosed as having articulation problems and received speech therapy. After 2 years, his articulation had improved and he no longer received speech therapy. At 7 years he entered regular school. When he was 8, his parents were told he was dyslexic (i.e., he had difficulties in learning how to read and write). He received special help for his dyslexic problems. When he was a 10-year-old, his parents were told that T. had emotional problems because there were situations when T. showed high temper. He received special counseling for that problem. In the course of such a history of T., the parents became very depressed and frustrated. They had to face the problem of having a boy with a multitude of disorders and receiving a multitude of therapies.

Nobody involved in evaluating T. seemed to question the model of numerous independent skills and deficits, which they applied. No one considered the possibility that these different deficits might be secondary to a common primary and more basic problem.

We can argue that applying the model of a root of a growing tree changes the traditional approach to evaluation. Hyperactivity, articulation problems, and reading and writing problems can all be represented by different branches of the tree. These branches grow at different periods of life; hyperactive behavior is represented by a sick branch that often appears before the branch representing the growth of articulation skills is even observable. But both branches become sick because the root is sick; nonverbal daily interaction is disturbed because of failures in the search for information.

Evaluating the branches of a tree helps to identify a sick tree. The question is whether the branches indicate a normal, an immature, or a deviant tree. Similarly, one should ask if the development of a child is normal, immature, or deviant. We discussed several findings of children with language disorders in the Seriation study, which suggested deviant development: the lack of age effect and the deviant profiles relating to problem-solving activities.

The *time of evaluation*: Evaluation should be done at a young age and, if the child presents perceptual problems, intervention should begin early. This means that in the presence of deviancies, one cannot simply wait for intervention. Waiting, letting the years pass by, means that a child with language disorders will continue to present problems, as in T.'s case. This is similar to the tree with a sick root, which will continue to grow branches, but the branches will show deviancies as long as the root remains sick. Often, children with language disorders are seen at the age of 3 or 4 years when it has become obvious that their language acquisition is inadequate. Parents of such children often report that their children have had some difficulties since infancy; some parents illustrate their reports by bringing videotape-recordings they had made of their family at earlier times. They say they were told by pediatricians and nurses just to wait, that their baby was immature, or a slow learner, and would catch up in time. Such reports and documentation support our hypothesis that children with severe language disorders could be identified during the first two years of development. Research projects are in progress to study this hypothesis.

Delay versus deviancy: Traditionally, a disordered child or adult is evaluated by a clinician who applies a variety of testing procedures. The judgment is based on success scores of the child in different skills. Among the different skills tested are those that are assumed to reflect intelligence. This is done, for example, with IQ testing to determine if there is developmental delay (see Wingfield, 1979, p. 382). Such testing measures performance. Successful performance is interpreted as a sign of competence and serves to estimate a mental age.

Our Seriation study presented results of task success. We described the failures of the children with language disorders. They differed significantly in success from their peers. Psychologists also measure success in traditional evaluation and in the conclusion they draw: Children with language disorders are delayed. As a consequence, they are treated like children with a developmental delay.

Competence versus performance: We argue that the judgment of developmental delay in the case of the children with language disorder is a superficial interpretation and does not take into account the problem of information, and the need to differentiate between competence and performance. In traditional evaluation procedures, hardly any time or effort is spent analyzing the situational features of testing situations (Bischofberger & Sonderegger 1974, 1976), or on varying situational features to distinguish between competence and performance. Traditional evaluation procedures typically are based on the assumption that success versus nonsuccess can be measured in an absolute way without accounting for information in an actual situation that influences the performance (see Chandler, 1991).

We discussed in this chapter that both performance and competence include cognitive skills. But performance is more complex. In order for competence to become correct performance, relevant information, inherent in an actual situation, has to be available and picked up adequately. Successful performance requires both cognitive and information-seeking processes. In other words, failure in performance alone does not allow for differentiating between what is a failure in cognitive skills and what is a failure in information-seeking processes. In the present Seriation study, although all tasks were similar in that they entailed seriation problems, the situation differed discernibly in terms of the modalities in which information about the task was made available. Thus, for evaluation, situation variables must be weighed, in addition to task variables. This means that the variation and the analysis of information inherent in a task situation have to be an important aspect of evaluation.

Information: Information is critical not only in a task situation, but also in daily life. Performances in daily life are situational, and evaluation has to take this into account by investigating the degree to which information affects a child not only in a test situation but also in real-life interaction. We referred to examples of daily-life events where one could observe how a child's behavior changes with change in situational information (see Section 1.3.1).

Conclusion: The findings of the Seriation tasks confirm that success scores neither help us to identify children with language disorders, nor reveal their specific difficulties. We emphasized that children with language disorders are not delayed but deviant. Clinicians must take into account the differentiation between performance and competence for assessing children. When the children fail to succeed, their failure in performance does not necessarily equal failure in competence. Failure may be due to the situational information. In order to specify the kind of educational and/or therapeutic intervention required, it is not enough to know whether or not the children are successful. One has to be able to specify to what extent performances of individual children depend on information by varying situational features. Once information has been judged to be the critical factor in test situations and in daily-life interaction, one has to consider that the root of development is sick. We referred to the model of a sick root representing the basic problems of these children in nonverbal daily interaction. This suggests that one cannot simply wait but should initiate immediate help for these children in order to improve their interacting.

3.3.2 Interacting in Daily Life

The ideas of nonverbal interaction and daily life have appeared and reappeared in our discussion. These concepts even became the main focus of the last study, the Seriation tasks, and the findings of that study could be related to daily-life interaction. Several conclusions can be drawn. These conclusions are important for considering intervention and speak to the ultimate goal of doing our research, namely, the improvement of intervention.

If nonverbal interaction fails, as it happens when language-disordered children or persons with acquired brain damage interact with the environment, then we have to help those individuals to interact in a more adequate way. This is not easy to do, because interacting in daily life is so common to all of us that we hardly ever realize the complexity of the aspects involved. Therefore we have difficulties expressing them. This may also explain why there is so little research done on nonverbal daily-life interaction, and why its importance is almost totally neglected or overlooked by educators and therapists.

Interacting in daily life includes many aspects, such as cognitive and information features. We now describe the intervention part in daily-life interaction—creating the right environment, improving the search for information, and considering that interaction in intervention has to be event oriented.

3.3.2.1 Creating the Right Environment

With regard to creating the right kind of environment we discuss several aspects: the stimuli of the environment, touching the environment when interacting is occurring, the stability of the environment in order to allow for feedback processing, and gaining important knowledge.

3.3.2.1.1 The Stimuli of the Environment.   There is some discussion in the field of special education and rehabilitation about the relationship between environment and children. Quite often the question is raised if children with language disorders or other disabilities need more stimulation (i.e., an enriched environment). By enriching the environment, educators usually mean adding color, objects, sounds, and words. These educators do not differentiate between immature–delayed development and deviant development. They simply assume that by enriching the environment one can enhance progress in language-disordered children and in persons with brain damage.

Some educators refer to a perceptual overload in children with language disorders, emphasizing the importance of reducing stimuli, such as colors or sounds in the environment. Classrooms are sometimes painted gray; lights are dimmed. Some children are given ear protection to prevent distraction by acoustic stimuli; others are placed in acoustically treated rooms.

Such approaches either of enriching or of reducing stimulation in the environment consider that one perceives the environment in an absolute, direct, and passive way. Children perceive colors, light, and so forth, directly. If those stimuli are reduced, the child's perception will be reduced. If the child cannot concentrate, perhaps there are too many stimuli and the child may be able to pay attention when the stimuli are reduced. The child functions like a black box. Psychologists use this term to refer to the situation of taking photographic pictures with a camera, which looks like a black box. The corresponding theory claims that the mind of the child is like a camera. There is an opening through which the stimuli enter, and a film, which registers the stimuli entering through that opening.

Piaget and Inhelder (1948/1956) described numerous studies contradicting such a black-box theory. They demonstrated how children assimilate the world or space around them and absorb from the environment whatever corresponds to their developmental level. The findings of rule application in the Seriation study supported Piaget's and Inhelder's findings of assimilation processes (see Section 2.4). We cannot change children and adults, normal or disordered, directly. We can do that only indirectly by creating the right environment and giving them the opportunity to interact.

Language-disordered children fail in interaction not because they fail in competence, but because they fail in information-seeking processes (e.g., in evaluating stimuli present in an actual situation). Enriching or reducing visual or auditory stimuli does not improve the processes of picking up adequate information (i.e., the organization of input). Rather than enriching their environment or reducing the stimuli, these children need help in organizing their search for information in order to receive more adequate information when interacting.

We return to the aspect of the environment, introduced in chapter 1. When talking about the environment, many psychologists mean a social environment, where interaction is mostly verbal and happens between at least two persons (Lawler, 1985). Our notion of the environment and of interaction is different. When we discuss environment, we refer to the physical environment, an environment that one can touch. Such an environment includes objects, animals, plants, nature, and, of course, even something very special, the persons around us.

We defined interaction in the sense of changing topological relationships between an actor and the environment, such as changing from being separate to being together (see Section 1.4). This calls for an environment that is touchable (i.e., has a physical property). Our daily life continually demands this kind of interaction. One could not get out of bed in the morning without changes in topological relationships. So, touching is always included in daily-life nonverbal events.

This puts special requirements not only on the actor but also on the environment. Because the role of the environment in an interaction is easier to describe than the role of the actor, and, because the role of the environment is highly neglected, we begin by discussing the environment.

3.3.2.1.2 *Touching the Environment.*   In daily-life interaction the environment changes. Such changes have to be recognized. This requires information. When grasping the knife, I have to judge the grasping. In

order to do that, I need information. Information when interacting is the problem we have to tackle in intervention and not the problems of attention/distraction, motivation, or memory (see Section 1.3.1). Whenever children or adults fail in nonverbal interaction, we have to control the situation, and with the situation, the environment. The environment has to allow for a search for adequate information. This applies for working with the children or adults in a classroom, a therapy room, or in family surroundings. This means, that when a child or adult does not pay attention, we do not need to judge it as attention deficit or poor motivation. We have to consider whether the environment offers children or adults the opportunity to pick up relevant information about the event, so they can be attentive.

Once more we deal with the problem of information. Consider visual information. I am standing on the balcony looking down on a city street. I watch the many cars driving along, the people walking, the children playing. My eyes are busy getting all the visual information. My brain is active in considering what all these people are doing. I am active. But I can stand on my balcony for hours, and the world gets along if I look at it or not: I do not change anything in my environment. This is not the nonverbal interaction as we have defined it in this book: The person on the balcony is active, but not interactive. The analysis of auditory information is similar. I can listen to all the noises in the street, I do not change the environment. Again, I am active but not interactive. Neither visual nor auditory information is required for nonverbal interaction. Blind and hearing-impaired children, after a delay, reach the same level of perceptual skills of Successive Pattern and Form Recognition as normal children do (see Section 1.2.2).

We discussed that tactual information is absolutely necessary for nonverbal interaction to occur. Let us illustrate with a striking clinical example the importance of the environment in getting adequate tactual information when interacting.

We were teaching a course in a geriatric clinic and observed Mrs. R. She had suffered a severe head trauma some time ago. She was judged as not able to be rehabilitated and was admitted to this geriatric clinic.

When we met her, she was being pushed in her wheelchair down the hallway toward the elevator. She moved her body back and forth in the wheelchair, arms in the air, body tense. She talked and talked, sometimes comprehensibly, sometimes in incomprehensible jargon. What I could understand was that she was afraid that she would be put into prison, that somebody would come and kill her, or poison her. . . . She appeared to be in a panic. I was told that a few years ago she had come as a refugee from Eastern Europe and that she was severely disordered and agitated. Nurses and therapists were afraid to care for her as she panicked when touched or moved. In the bathroom she could not be alone even for a second because of her agitation.

Two of our student therapists were sent to observe Mrs. R.'s interactive behavior on the ward. They analyzed the situations when she was in the bathroom and in the dining room, when she was sleeping, when being dressed, and so forth.

Two hours later the students reported: The nurse put Mrs. R. on the toilet and said Mrs. R. could not be left alone for one second because of her agitation. The commode was placed in the middle of the bathroom. The students put Mrs. R. into a corner of the room, so she could touch the wall when moving her arms. As soon as she was in the corner and touched the wall, she became calm. The nurse, very surprised, asked the students if they had other magic tricks.

At lunch time Mrs. R. used to sit in her wheelchair at a table in the middle of the room, very agitated. First, the students pushed the table to a wall, so that Mrs. R. could sit in a corner. However, the armrests of the wheelchair were so high they did not fit under the table. This meant there was a gap between her body and the table, and she was not touching the table with her body. The students changed the wheelchair to one with lower armrests. Now Mrs. R. could touch the table with her body, touch one wall with her right arm, the other with her back. She became calm immediately, so calm that the students could guide her to drink. Then Mrs. R. looked around and said, "Today is a nice day."

Usually the nurse dressed Mrs. R. while she was on her bed. Only the head of the bed touched the wall while the sides of the bed were in free space. The students advised putting the bed into a corner, so the head of the bed as well as one side of the bed touched the wall and making sure that Mrs. R. was positioned in the corner touching both the head of the bed and the wall when being dressed. The next day the nurse told them that Mrs. R. got dressed in that changed environment—and she was calm.

What had happened? The changes in the environment allowed Mrs. R. to pick up tactual information, to feel the resistance offered by the environment while she was interacting. The students observed that when she was in the middle of the room, she was agitated. They inferred that in this position Mrs. R. received only visual information about the world around her. The resulting agitation was a sign of panic because the visual information did not allow her to perceive the environment as existing, and to know where she was (see also Affolter, 1987/1991). The changes the students created allowed Mrs. R. to touch the world around her, to elicit changes of resistance, thus providing her with tactual information. When Mrs. R. perceived the world around her and her body at the same time, she became calm.

These examples emphasize the importance of changing the environment so that the person interacting can touch the environment and, thus, extract important information from the touching.

3.3.2.1.3   The Stability of the Environment.   The Seriation study
revealed that children with language disorders apply the same kind of
touching rules as normal children. The most basic of these rules is the
support rule. Adequate touching requires the stability of the support. This
should be evident for everybody. Just imagine the extreme situation of an
earthquake, how frightening it is when the support begins to shake.

More complex touching rules were the moving and holding/lifting
rules, important for daily events. They are more complex because they
include additional sources of information at the side and more changes in
topological relationships. In order to apply these rules, one needs a stable
environment including support and sides. The stable environment also
serves as a reference for judging the moving and holding/lifting, the
changing of topological relationships between and among objects/persons
and support. We referred earlier to the relativity of perception. We discussed the example of two trains, each one supposed to move and myself
sitting in one of them. To judge which train moves one has to have a stable reference, such as the station house. We reported the example of R.,
who panicked when he attempted to put the pillowcase on the pillow and
everything was moving (see Section 3.2.2).

For purposes of intervention, this means when we change topological
relationships by interacting we have to find feedback information to judge
which parts of the environment are moving and which parts are stationary.
Thus, one has to make certain that children or adults are given the opportunity to perform interactive events within a stable environment. This
would include different kinds of supports, such as floor, table, chair, and,
if possible, even sides like a wall next to the actor.

We have already discussed constraints on the environment during interaction, and some ways to control the conditions of the environment. One
main condition is the opportunity of touching the world around when
interacting. A second main condition is the stability of the environment.
We provided an example of a geriatric patient. She became calm when she
touched the environment during her daily activities. Why?

3.3.2.1.4   The Knowledge About Where I Am and Where the Envi-
ronment Is.   We discussed that nonverbal daily-life interaction has not only
informational aspects but also cognitive ones. Mrs. R. became calm when she
touched the stable environment around her not just because she touched,
but because such touching allowed her to gain some important kind of
knowledge. This knowledge has to do with the "where" question. Where is
my body and where is the environment? Both questions are answered
together because the answer is a consequence of interaction when one is
touching the environment. I feel the wall, and at the same time I feel my
body. The source of information is there where I touch the wall, between the

wall and the part of my body involved with touching. This can be the hand, the back, the sides of the body, and so forth. The next example might help to describe the kind of knowledge to be gained:

> Luria (1987), a famous neurologist, described in his book an interesting case on the early stage of recovery of a lifelong acquaintance who had suffered brain damage after being shot in the head during World War II. Luria's patient was in the hospital, and Luria entered the patient's room. Later on the patient recalled that at that moment he did not know where he was. He heard voices and saw figures, but was unable to relate them to himself. Only at the moment when Luria touched him, did he become aware that it was the physician who was talking to him. The patient concluded that only when he was touched did he get to know where he was and where the world around him was. (pp. 8–10)

This example suggests that when somebody is in a stress situation, as this patient was, and cannot touch the environment, the person has difficulty organizing visual and auditory stimuli in that environment. The person does not know where the environment is and, at the same time, where his body is. It can be scary when this knowledge is missing. Such a cognitive aspect of touching a stable environment when interacting is very important and is often overlooked. Three more examples illustrate the panic or other difficulties that result when this knowledge is missing. Two of them show how behavior can change when touching the environment helps to provide that knowledge. Two examples are from classroom experiences, and one is from a family situation.

The first example is taken from a newspaper issue (Desegregation, 1996). The discussion focused on desegregation, the problem of schools in poverty areas, and how strenuous teaching can be in these areas.

Example 1:

> One afternoon, as J. (the teacher) led a grammar exercise, a girl turned her chair backward and rocked it back and forth. "LaQuita, please stop rocking and turn your chair around," he said.
>
> She looked at him, at the ceiling and continued rocking. J. continued the lesson, but eventually looked at her again. "LaQuita, please stop rocking and turn your chair around." She ignored him.
>
> "LaQuita, please stop rocking and turn your chair around." The fifth or sixth time, he said curtly, "Sit properly." She stopped long enough to shout, "I am. Damn!" and kept rocking. That was enough to earn her a trip to the principal's office. (pp. A10–A11)

What had happened? What is our interpretation of such an incident, and, based on that interpretation, what is its constraint on intervention?

To answer, let us analyze the rocking activity. We described P., a boy with tactual problems (see Section 1.4.4), who was rocking by lifting one leg, stamping it down, then lifting the other one. . . . Each time he was changing the topological relationship between body-support; off—together—off. . . . It was obvious to us that he was searching for information in order to know where his body was and where the support or the world was. We pointed out that a similar search for information is observable even in normal persons when they are under stress. We can also refer to rocking behavior in animals at the zoo. This behavior is often interpreted as a deprivation sign.

> Continuing our example of LaQuita, we noticed that in a picture taken of the classroom, the desks and tables where the students work are in the middle of the room. Earlier we cited the example of a patient in a geriatric clinic and described how therapists changed the environment to offer the patient the possibility of touching it when interacting. Now we apply this knowledge to LaQuita, and the conditions offered by that classroom. Where does she get tactual information when working in the classroom? We infer that she is receiving very little tactual information—and does not know where she is and where the environment is. As a consequence, visual and auditory information is not useful to LaQuita, as was the case for Luria's patient. So, she searches for tactual information—she rocks. In this way she changes resistance between her body and the floor, the chair being the stick which helps her to feel the resistance of the floor just like the blind person feels the resistance with her or his cane (see stick phenomenon, Section 1.4.2). And what kind of information does the teacher provide her? He talks to her, giving her verbal–auditory information. We have to consider that auditory information does not help LaQuita to know where she is and where the world around her is.

What could the teacher do differently? He could change the situation (i.e., the environment) so LaQuita can touch it. For example, instead of putting LaQuita in the middle of the room, he could put her at a table, or on the floor in a niche so she can touch the world around, just like the patient in the geriatric clinic we described.

Example 2:

A., a 7-year-old child with language disorders and hemiplegia (paralysis to one side of the body caused by brain damage). The teacher reported that A.'s hemiplegic arm tenses to such a degree that he lifts his arm, walks and moves around in this position, hardly ever lowering the arm. The doctors told the parents that they might have to consider surgery for A. to control the problem. We observe A. in the classroom. He arrives, takes off his jacket, and walks to his desk . . . his arm always raised.

We consider his environment. He performs his daily activities in the middle of the room. There he is unable to touch the world around. Consequently, he does not get tactual information to know where he is (where his arm is) and where the environment is. We change the situation.

Instead of putting children on chairs in a half circle around the teacher, in free space, we ask the teacher to line up the children, have them sit on the floor with their backs against the wall. In this position they are in direct contact with the support, the floor, and with the side, the wall. As soon as A. has changed his position, and is touching the environment, his arm comes down. Instead of removing or putting on his jacket standing in free space, we put a bench into a corner, and have A. sit down in that corner so he can touch a stable environment. As soon as he sits down on the stable bench, touches the wall behind and on the side, his arm comes down. He puts on the jacket without lifting his arm.

Touching his environment allows A. to turn toward relevant tactual sources of information. He changed the arm position. Turning toward sources of information created between his buttocks and the bench, between his back and the wall, he gets to know where his body is; he is sitting on a bench, and touching the wall. At the same time he becomes aware of his environment, the bench, and the wall. Then his body tone decreased and his arm went down.

Example 3 describes a family situation:

It is breakfast time. The two children N. and K. of family X. are both sitting at the table on a long bench along a wall. One end of the bench is in a corner, the other end is open. First all goes well. Then comes the moment when N. approaches and touches his sister K. Both are sitting in the middle of the bench. Father says, "N., move away from K". N. moves away for a few seconds. Then he touches his sister again. "N., I told you, let your sister go". Same reaction. This goes on for a few minutes.

I watch what happened. I conclude that N. is searching for information about where he is with his body and where the environment is. So I decide to change the situation. I get up, put a chair with a high back at the open end of the bench. That end is now like a corner. I make N. sit so that he can touch the back of the chair and sit in that new corner. I do the same with K.; I have her sit in the niche at the other end. All is quiet now and breakfast proceeds.

Focusing on the aspect of being in touch with a stable environment and getting to know where the environment is and where one is reminds us of the niche behavior we can observe in the children but also in the adult.

One feels secure in a niche. Children like to sit in a niche even when they have to crawl into it; adults going into a restaurant may prefer to sit in a booth like in a niche to eat (see also Affolter, 1987/1991).

3.3.2.2   Improving the Search for Information

We discussed, so far, the importance of the environment for touching when interacting. Often, however, this is not enough for adequate intervention. Touching the environment in an adequate way might be difficult for a disordered person. Simply putting disordered persons in an environment they can touch does not mean they will be able to change their sources of information according to respective topological changes. Thus, improving the search for information becomes an important goal of intervention. To be helpful we have to realize, for example, that we cannot teach the disordered persons to consider a tactual source in an absolute way without a goal. We insist on the importance of always changing sources in connection with an interactive event. This means, the changes have to be meaningful, to be related to the demands and the goal of an event and the respective situations. In the following sections we discuss how we can reach that goal. We discuss guiding as a tool for intervention. We describe what it means to work on a level of understanding and competence and not performance in intervention, and how to stimulate the changing of sources of information.

3.3.2.2.1   Guiding as a Tool for Intervention.   We often apply guiding as a tool in intervention with disordered persons. Guiding was used to instruct the children on the Form Recognition tasks (see Section 1.2.1) and the Seriation tasks (see Section 2.1.5 and Appendix A). We found that, through guiding, it is possible to transmit all the information needed to recognize an event. Guiding elicits the same kind of information one receives when performing the movements for interaction by oneself. With guiding we can intervene and enhance the selection of relevant sources of information and thus the picking up of adequate information while changing topological relationships. Guiding can be used with children at all levels of development and with adult patients at all stages of progress. Guiding somebody through an event means that we guide the body of that person and perform all the necessary actions of the event with that person.

How guiding is performed, from a technical point of view, is not the purpose of this book. Earlier literature (Affolter, 1987/1991; Affolter & Bischofberger, 1993, 1996) includes detailed descriptions of how to guide (i.e., providing information about Guided Interaction Therapy). This literature reviews the different kinds of guiding, for example, elementary guiding, intensive guiding, and guiding when nursing activities are performed.

We refer interested persons (e.g., family members, therapists, and teachers) to these books.

Guiding is possible whenever guided persons need information that they cannot pick up by themselves. Guiding can be used not only with disordered persons but also with normal children and adults whenever they do not know about an event, or they cannot perform daily activities. Guiding cannot be used when a person already knows about a task and can perform it (i.e., the task corresponds to the performance level of the person). If this is the case, the child or the adult will refuse to be guided. In intervention we do not plan performance situations because they are not learning situations. We have to focus on the understanding and competence level of the persons. In the next section we focus on the problem of competence as a contrast to performance, and how it applies to improving the search for information.

3.3.2.2.2 Expanding Competence. In regard to the search for information, the Seriation study has shown that language-disordered children are not comparable to younger normal children. Success scores of children with language disorders may be at a very low level. We discussed that success in the Seriation tasks revealed a performance level of the children. Such a performance level does not allow for inferences about their cognitive competence. These children may fail performing not because of a failure in competence but because they fail in the organization of the search for information. Some therapists do not realize that. They base intervention on children's performance levels and thus underestimate the cognitive level of these children; they may even use intervention techniques with older children, which are designed for babies or young children.

In order to plan intervention, we have to find the children's competence level as pointed out earlier in this chapter (see discussion of evaluation procedures). This is similar to teaching situations. Teaching should not be based on the child's levels of performance, but rather on the competence levels of the child. If the teaching approach is based on the student's performance level, the student will be bored because he or she can already do what is being taught. If the approach is based on expanding competence (i.e., the student's understanding of a problem that cannot yet be performed or produced), then the student can learn (Affolter, 1987/1991).

For intervention, therefore, we chose events that a child or adult has not yet in performance. In other words, they are not yet able to perform those events independently. We illustrate this by the following example:

> E. is a highly disturbed 5-year-old autistic girl with language disorder. Spontaneously she takes any paper she can find and tears it to pieces. The parents were advised to provide her with things she can take apart.

She is admitted to our school for perceptually disordered children where she receives Guided Interaction Therapy. She is guided in her daily activities: taking off her coat and shoes when arriving, opening her yogurt, cutting an apple to eat it, and so on. She can not perform any of these activities by herself, they are not within her level of performance. But she shows attention or understanding. We concluded that such guided events were building up her competence.

Thus, working on expanding understanding and competence in interaction events through guiding means working on the root. It includes cognitive and information aspects. As the root grows, branches grow, such as branches of perceptual skills. Search for information will improve and allow competence to become performance.

3.3.2.2.3 *Changing Sources of Information.* For intervention, it is important that we allow patients with disorders to feel the resistance of the environment when interacting. Feeling the resistance requires touching. Touching goes together with a change in source of information. The person guiding or intervening is responsible for helping patients improve their tactual input by changing sources of information. This has to be done while performing nonverbal daily events. To fulfill this requirement, the guider has to know about and control the kind of information inherent in the sequences of nonverbal interaction.

One kind of information has to do with the topological relationships between the body of the person who interacts and the environment. These topological relationships are essential to judge *body position.* Such topological relationships change each time an action is performed. These changes demand the search for information so the person who interacts can answer the question, "Where is my body now and where is the environment?"

I guide a patient to sit down on a chair. Once the patient sits on the chair I have to move the bottom of his body there where he touches the chair, so he can feel the source of information between the bottom of his body and the chair. In this way he gets the tactual information essential for knowing that he is sitting.

Thus, guiding considers not just the hands, but the whole body, when interacting. For instance, a needed object has fallen on the floor. To pick it up, one has to change the position of one's body. Or, somebody wants to clean the bottom shelf in a closet. To do this, one has to kneel on the floor. Or, an object has to be taken out of a closet from a high shelf. One may need to get a stool and climb on it to get the object. Each time one changes the body position, one has to change topological relationships between the body and the environment in a meaningful, goal-oriented way. And each time, one has to consider respective sources of information to answer the question "Where is my body now and where is the environment?"

The other kind of information is oriented toward the *event* and has to do with causes and effects. Each time the person who interacts has changed topological relationships between and among objects/persons/support, the person must be aware of whether the effects of those changes are achieved; for example, I want to write with a pen, the cap is on the pen. I take the cap off—is it separate from the pen? I have finished writing, I put the cap back on the pen. Is the cap together with the pen? In other words, the person who interacts has to change such topological relationships and search for tactual information respectively. He or she needs information to know what are the causes and what are the effects. It is important that I guide a person through events that require changes of topological relationships so they feel the changes of resistance. I will not guide a person performing actions, which do not require such changes in topological relationships (i.e., which are not considered to be interaction events as we have defined them). Thus, I will not guide a child for writing, or peeling, or spreading with the purpose of working on the root. I may help the child to write, but I am conscious that the child does not get the tactual information needed to change sources of information to improve experience in interaction.

These examples illustrate how I change sources of information in a goal-oriented way during a daily-life event. Disordered persons need help doing this. The purpose of my intervention is to provide such help. An example illustrates this approach to guiding as not just helping. The example describes, in a kind of slow motion, the event of picking up a knife from the support to cut an orange:

> Let the person feel the resistance of the knife, which moves in contrast to the stable resistance of the support (support and moving rules). Guide the hands of the person to press on the knife, then move the fingers of the person along the resistance of the knife until the fingers are closed around it (holding rule). Attempt to move the knife—to lift it (lifting rule). And by doing all these activities with the person, the person will feel the different changes of resistances included in the event. In this way the three rules of touching are applied for separating the object from the support.

Having cut the orange, the person has to release the knife. In order for the knife to be released, a similar sequence of interactive causes and effects has to occur. The earlier sequence is now reversed in the following manner:

> The knife is put back on the support (displacing rule); the stable resistance of the support is felt by the fingers of the child holding the knife. This information helps so that the fingers will loosen the grasp around the knife—and thus permit the release of the object on the support (releasing rule).

We have now discussed the two kinds of information one has to provide; one kind lets the patient know where he or she is and where the environment is; the second kind lets one know about the event and the topological changes involved.

These examples illustrate how we can initiate changes of sources of information when guiding a person to interact, to fulfill a primary goal of intervention: increase experiences in daily interaction by providing more adequate tactual information, and, thereby working on the root.

We considered the importance of touching the environment when interacting and how touching helps to change sources of information. We now consider that touching and changing sources of information have something to do with the event.

3.3.2.3 Daily-Life Events

Nonverbal interaction in daily life does not happen at random. It requires changes of topological relationships. These changes are oriented toward a goal of an event with a beginning and an end. This means we have to know about the structure of events. We discussed that daily life requires interactive events. For example, in order to get dressed, one has to change the environment and at the same time, change oneself. To get breakfast ready one has to change the environment again, and at the same time change oneself. Thus, it should be clear that visual and auditory information are not the primary kinds of information for nonverbal interaction. Visual and auditory information might be helpful in locating something or somebody, but the basic interactive information is of a tactual kind. When working on daily events we have to consider that we will do events not for but with the persons. Doing events with the persons means that we provide them with tactual information, and we stimulate problem-solving processes. These different aspects are discussed in the next sections.

3.3.2.3.1 The Structure of Daily-Life Events. To improve the growing of the root, we must examine experience in nonverbal interaction in daily life. Daily-life activities present the structure of events (Rock, 1986). Eleanor Gibson (1967) was conscious of the neglect of the notion of the event in the concept of direct perception. She pointed out that the perception of events, happenings over time, is a sadly neglected topic in perception. The importance of events of daily life for development in general cannot be underestimated (see also Aebli, 1987).

The structure of events is best described by comparison with a network. Events are always goal-directed. Such goals can be overall goals, subgoals, and sub-subgoals. In daily life one always deals with a hierarchy of goals: I want a drink of orange juice. The bottle of juice is right on the table, I open it and drink out of the bottle. But it can also be that the bottle is empty, and I have to go to the store to buy orange juice. The store is not within walking distance. The main goal is still the same, drinking. But now I have subgoals, which are hierarchically related. To go to the store means I first have to get the car out of the garage, or I may first have to get the key for the car. And again I have subgoals to consider. For intervention, this means I have to choose a goal to work on with a child or patient. I can choose just opening the bottle and drinking. Or, I can choose to go to the store and purchase a bottle.

3.3.2.3.2 Doing Daily-Life Events With but Not for the Person.

To involve disordered persons in daily events requires a change of attitude on the part of the people around them. We are all educated to help disabled persons, to be nice to them, to do things for them, such as opening a door when they have to pass through, bringing them objects they need, helping them to get dressed.

We argued that those persons can be helped in a more adequate way and it will not even take much more time to do so. Instead of opening the door for them, one does it with them. One takes their hands and guides them to open the door. In this way, they receive important tactual information about themselves and about the environment, about causes and effects involved in this event. An example illustrates the meaningfulness of such an approach:

> The lecture hall for our course was on the second floor. Three severely handicapped children with cerebral palsy were supposed to come to our room for practical work. There was no elevator in the building. The three children came in wheelchairs, unable to walk. How do we bring them up? Do we carry them? The oldest was already 17 and too heavy to be carried. In addition, we were teaching the participants that they should not do an event for the patients, but do the event with them. So we decided to guide these children to walk up the set of stairs. This we did, guiding them along the wall, step after step, higher and higher. I was standing at the top of the stairs on the second floor, when O., the first and oldest one arrived. The therapists were almost exhausted from the guiding. But O. looked at me and with a big smile, he pronounced with his gruff speaking voice, "That's the first time in my life I went up the stairs—I want to do it again."

I will never forget this statement. How can it be that in all his 17 years, no one ever realized that he was longing for this kind of interaction instead of being nursed?

> Later, I saw the three boys, on their way to lunch, having been guided to glide down the stairs and sit in their wheelchairs. This time I met the youngest, a 9-year-old. He looked at me with a big smile and said with his gruff speaking voice, "I am content."

3.3.2.3.3 *Stimulating the Processes of Nonverbal Problem Solving.*
Tasks of nonverbal daily life are problem-solving events. We have already discussed how information-seeking processes can be initiated by providing tactual information about nonverbal interaction events. We also mentioned that tactual information could transmit information about events. In this section we focus on how tactual information leads to establishing hypotheses. First, we present the example of guiding a normal child:

> M., a 2 1/2-year-old, wants to do everything by himself. He wants to butter his slice of bread himself, he wants to cut his own bread. When his siblings or parents want to help him, he refuses and says, "No, myself."
> I am in the kitchen preparing dinner. I need to pour some water into the grill pan in the oven. M. wants to do it. M. holds the pot to fill it with water. I stay behind M. I begin to guide his hands, which hold the pot. I guide him to fill the pot, to bring it to the oven, to pour the water into the grill pan. Then I let M.'s hands go. M. brings the pot to the sink. M.'s older sister enters the kitchen, sees M. and says, "Oh, did you help F.?" M. responds, "No, I myself."

The first requirement to stimulate hypothetic processes is that the information provided by guiding is event related. There has to be a goal that requires changes of topological relationships. Changing topological relationships requires touching. This is an example of the interrelationship between perceptual activity and cognition. Touching a person by guiding must be goal-oriented. This explains why M. refused to be guided by his parents or siblings. Their kind of guiding consisted of taking M.'s hands before the event had started, that is, before M. was touching the slice of bread to be buttered, or the knife for cutting. His refusal can be related to the hypotheses processes and to sources of information. The sources of tactual information were between the hands of the person who touched him and his hands, where he was touched. These sources of tactual information have nothing to do with the event. The sources were quite different when I started to guide M. to fill the pot with water. In this interaction, M.'s sources of tactual information were between the pot and his hands; they were sources providing tactual information needed for the event. In this situation I could start guiding M. to fill the pot with water. M.'s tactual sources were still between the pot and his hands when filling the pot with water. These were the most important tactual sources required for reaching the goal of filling that pot with water.

M.'s remark, "I myself," confirms our interpretation. Apparently, M. did not notice that I was guiding him. This can be observed again and again when one guides a child through an event the child cannot perform alone. Children with language disorders, who are guided, often respond similarly. It confirms what was pointed out already, that (a) being guided through an event and receiving tactual information about the topological changes included in the event allows one to perceive the same kind of information as when doing it oneself and (b) the important kind of information is not elicited by the motor act per se (Bischofberger, 1989; Day & Singer, 1964) but by the interaction. This means that touching causes changes in topological relationships and elicits changes of sources of information with changes of resistance. And this provides the information relevant for perceiving the event.

The next example supports the conclusion that guided tactual information stimulates hypothetical processes:

> B. is a 2-year-old normal child. She is being videotaped in a natural setting as part of a research project. She is putting on her slippers while sitting on the floor. One slipper is already on. The other foot is half in the other slipper; then difficulties begin. Her aunt D. is close by and sees the rising difficulties. She sits behind B., takes both of B.'s hands and finishes the event by guiding B. with no problem. B. stands up—her foot slips out of the slipper. B. sits on the floor between D.'s legs as she was before. D. takes B.'s hands and guides her to get the slipper, which is lying on the floor close by, in order to put it on again. The moment D. touches B.'s arms, B. shouts, wards off D.'s hands, and stands up, appearing to panic.

This kind of reaction when one intends to guide somebody is frequent. Usually when parents and therapists report this kind of behavior they say, "They refuse to be guided." Is this interpretation correct?

We analyzed the two videotaped situations carefully, the first one when D. could guide B., and the second one when D. could not guide B.. We detected an important difference between the two situations. The difference had to do with information, and consequently with establishing a hypothesis about the event.

In the first situation, B.'s foot was halfway in the slipper. The first important change of topological relationship of the event, putting on the slippers, was performed; the foot was together with the slipper. The source of information was between foot and slipper. It was not yet inside the slipper. This was the next change of topological relationship to occur, and this was done by guiding. When guiding, the tactual source of information was still between foot and slipper, thus connected with the event.

The second situation was different; topologically the foot was separate from the slipper. So the first change of topological relationship, foot separate—foot together with the slipper was missing. There was no source providing tactual information about the event, the foot did not touch the slipper. Aunt D. took B.'s hands. The source of information was now between the hands of the aunt and the hands of B.. There was tactual information, but not about the event. B. had no tactual information to establish a hypothesis about putting on the slipper. This topological relationship, hand of D. together with hand of B., had nothing to do with the event, putting the slipper together with the foot. This next step was apparent to D., but not apparent to B. So B. refused to be touched, to perform a topological relationship that was not required by the event.

The next example describes the strong relationship between information-seeking processes and establishing hypotheses. It illustrates processes we go through each time we start a daily event. In actual situations, there are many stimuli. Most of the stimuli are irrelevant to the event I have to perform. Only a few are relevant to the task. In daily life one has to order all the surrounding stimuli. We discussed assimilation and accommodation processes in chapter 1. It means that one has to actively structure the situation, evaluate all the stimuli, and discriminate the irrelevant from the relevant stimuli inherent in that situation. This is strongly related to establishing hypotheses. The following example illustrates how one can guide a patient to perform such structuring:

> J., a 14-year-old, has severe language disorders. She is guided to the refrigerator to take out cottage cheese to make sandwiches for a snack. The refrigerator is filled with many items. The therapist opens the door with J. They touch the milk, which is in front, and then they push the milk to the side. They touch a package of meat, push it aside. In this manner they touch several items, each time pushing them to the side, until finally, way in the back, they find the cottage cheese which they touch, grasp, and take out.

In this example, the therapist guided J. to find the cottage cheese among many other items in the refrigerator. The cottage cheese was the relevant thing, the other items were the irrelevant things. J. had to differentiate between the relevant information when touching the cottage cheese, and the irrelevant information when touching the other items. Evaluating and selecting relevant information was done together with evaluating, selecting, and deleting irrelevant information. And all this was connected with hypothetic and feedback processes. This kind of organization is more difficult than one usually admits. Often, especially when one performs events in a familiar setting such as taking a shower in one's own bathroom, one does not realize to what extent information is required. Only when staying overnight in an unfamiliar place does one realize what is entailed in learning how to manipulate an unfamiliar shower. For children with language disorders and adults with acquired brain damage, it is sometimes impossible to get information when they are on their own. And they may panic.

3.3.2.4 When Do I Talk?

Auditory information is needed to learn a conventional oral language system. This means that children have to get respective auditory input. But this is only part of language acquisition. Linguists differentiate between surface structure, conventional forms, and deep structure or the semantic part of language (see Chomsky, 1957; Fillmore, 1968). Experiences with tactual nonverbal events of daily life are considered to be the fundamental basis of deep structure or the semantic part of language (Affolter, 1968, 1987/1991), and the surface structure or conventional forms are the means to express internalized experiences of interaction. We refer the interested reader to this literature. For language acquisition we need to consider the semantic aspects represented in the deep structure, and the formal part of language. Research on the early acquisition of language by children shows that a normal child, at the early stages, does not talk while performing events, but speaks before or afterwards (Bloom, 1993). When adults talk to the children during their interactions, children will stop or reduce their activities. The same can be observed when talking to children at the same time that one guides them. They are unable to focus on the event; they are unable to pay attention to the tactual input. They are distracted. The same is true of the person guiding and talking. It is a capacity problem (see Affolter, 1987/1991). And because auditory–verbal information is not directly related to the respective topological changes, performance of the event may break down.

Spoken forms are used to refer to a semantic content. The semantic content is created by interaction events. These events are perceived basically through tactual information. That information is stored independently of the forms as part of deep structure (Affolter, 1968; Piaget, 1945/1962, 1963). This means that one should add linguistic conventional forms to tactual nonverbal events *after* the event has been performed. For intervention this means that whatever linguistic forms a speech therapist has to teach to language-disordered children (e.g., articulation skills, syntactic features, and so on), should be done after the child has experienced a guided tactual event. This should not be done before the event, or without connection to an event; otherwise the semantic part is missing. This same advice pertains for visual information when using graphic forms. Graphic forms are offered by drawings, pictures, and written forms of letters or numerals. These graphic forms can be compared to the conventional forms of oral language. Before using such graphic forms for teaching reading and writing, one has to make sure that the child has already experienced the respective tactual nonverbal events. This is not only valid for language but also for arithmetic. Forms used in arithmetic, such as numerals and signs to express addition, subtraction, multiplication, and division, always refer to stored tactual nonverbal events. Thus, arithmetic, as well as reading and writing, should be taught in relation to and after having experienced tactual events (see Affolter, 1987/1991).

3.3.3 Expectations When Working on the Root

So far we have discussed working at the root and have illustrated the work with examples of normal children, language-disordered children, and adult patients with acquired brain damage. We showed how their behavior depends on the interaction between actor and environment. We have discussed how to control the environment, how to help a person to improve the search for information, and how to change sources of information during interaction. We have discussed the importance of doing daily events with the person and thus stimulating problem-solving activities. Now the question arises: "What comes out of such experience of nonverbal interaction, of such work on the root?" In other words, "How do I recognize that the root is growing?" To answer that question, we refer to some effects of a short-term, which are observable during guided interaction events, and some long-term effects expressed by more permanent improvements in behavior suggesting the growth of the root and consequently the growth of branches.

3.3.3.1 Short-Term Effects of Intervention

Our goal of intervention is to provide the patients with more adequate interaction experience. This requires improvement of the organization of the search for information. Such improvement can not be observed directly. It has to do with input. The presence of input of information in another person can be observed only indirectly by observing certain changes in behavior. In this section we discuss some patterns of behavior we expect to change, and which we can interpret as a sign of more adequate input, in our words, as a sign that the work on the root is adequate.

A first and very important behavioral pattern deals with what we call *attention*. We all are more or less familiar with that behavioral pattern. For example, students are described as attentive when they show a certain degree of tenseness in their body position and their facial expression, when they sit without moving around much, when they stop irrelevant activities, and so on. The immediate improvement of attention is frequently astonishing in children with language disorders when one guides them through an event. This is so in the example of M., a 5-year-old making chocolate pudding. He focused for 40 minutes on the task, when in other situations, he could only focus for seconds (see Section 1.3.1). This example of M., with the reported extremely short attention span, shows that when we are able to give the child tactual information about an event, the child becomes able to focus his attention on the task. Thus, we agree with Broadbent (1958) and Posner (1986) that information is a prerequisite for attention. People who use Guided Interaction Therapy, therefore, are not concerned about reward. Reward usually is connected with the problem of motivation. In chapters 1 and 3, we described several examples of children and patients who refused to follow commands or refused to being guided. We raised the question about missing motivation (see Section 1.3.1). However, by analyzing the respective situations, we concluded each time that the problem was not one of motivation but one of information. This conclusion requires that one focus on the problem of changing the situation to improve the tactual information. This should allow child and adult patients to establish more adequate hypotheses and thus to pay attention.

Another behavior pattern concerns *body tone* and the change of sources of information. We reported some observations that children and adults get very tense when they appear to have difficulties in interaction (i.e., body tone increases). We discussed that the original tenseness or hyperactivity of a disordered person at the beginning of an event suggests that the person is searching for information but has difficulty in organizing sources of information and hyperactivity and/or tenseness are the effects. When, during the event, the person gets less tense (body tone decreases) and becomes more calm, one can infer that the person can now focus on sources relevant to the event. These are sources that provide tactual information according to the topological changes of the event.

We call the next behavior pattern *anticipation*. Anticipation is more than just input. Input is a prerequisite but anticipation demands an elaboration of the input, even some kind of memory. The following example illustrates this pattern.

A. is an 8-year-old girl with severe cerebral palsy. She spends much time every day attached to a device for standing. She can neither sit independently nor walk. She has never been guided for daily events. Everyday activities have been performed for her, not with her, except for attempts to walk with her.

We were asked to counsel therapists on how to work on the root in daily events. We guided A. to take an apple out of a drawer, to get a knife, to sit on a chair at the table; the therapist sitting behind her guides her to cut the apple. While doing this, I was told that A. does not eat apples. Daily-life events are social events directed toward not only one's personal needs but also the needs of people belonging to one's social group. So we decided that A. would give the piece of apple she had cut to the therapist sitting next to her. A. is guided to put the piece of apple into the therapist's mouth. This is done three times.

First time, A.'s eyes do not appear to follow the movement of her arms, even when she is guided to put the piece of apple into the mouth of the therapist.

Second time, A.'s eyes follow the movement of her arms. When she puts the apple into the therapist's mouth, her face shows intense attention—and then a smile appears on A.'s face as she watches the therapist chew the apple.

Third time, as soon as she raises her arm, A. looks at the therapist—and smiles. This smile happens before the apple reaches the mouth of the therapist.

On the third time A. anticipates that she will put the piece of apple into the therapist's mouth and the therapist will eat that piece of apple. We infer this by observing her smiling before the apple touches the mouth of the therapist. This means that A. has stored the first event tactually, the second event tactually and visually. Performing the third event, she retrieves what she has done before. She sees the therapist and feels her arm/hands touching the apple. Such tactual–visual information seems to help her to retrieve the event she has stored and anticipate the next similar event. A. seems to be able to learn; there is input, ability to store and also to retrieve. These observations suggest that with such guided events A.'s root will be expanding and growing.

Another immediately observable change has to do with *memory retrieval* (i.e., one takes out something from memory, or access to memory is working). We refer the reader to observations of retrieval in aphasics (Affolter, 1987/1991), such as improvement in speaking and writing when guiding them through daily events.

Usually, children with language disorders and patients with brain damage appear not to remember what has happened at home or in a previous therapy session. When their memory is evaluated with traditional testing procedures, they fail those tasks. Consequently, they are diagnosed as having poor memory (see example in Section 1.3.1). Thus, intervention programs for them include memory games, training for memory. Is it always true that their memory is poor?

Mrs. L. is brain damaged; she has severe aphasia. The language therapist tried very hard to get her to imitate lip movements as a prerequisite for training articulation skills, without success. Now, Mrs. L. is sitting at a table facing a mirror and a lipstick. The therapist guides her to open the lipstick and get it ready to apply it to her lips. Mrs. L. looks in the mirror while she handles the lipstick. Suddenly, her lips and her tongue start to move, to change position, to adjust and to get ready to apply the lipstick.

Watching these events, we concluded:

- When asked to imitate lip and tongue movements Mrs. L. looked at the mirror but failed to perform.

- When asked to perform lip and tongue movements within a daily-life event Mrs. L. could do it.

The difference between the two situations is the goal orientation. In the first situation, the lip movements had to be produced without a goal, without an event. Here the production failed. In the second situation, producing lip movements was embedded in an event. Here the lip movements were produced adequately.

Another example, described by Affolter (1987/1991) corroborates these observations:

> Mr. M., an adult with acquired brain damage, and severely restricted in motor performances, takes part in a course situation. The participants guide him to hang a bell over the entrance door so that one can ring the bell when a course session begins. First the hook has to be hammered into the wall. The patient's arm and hand, holding the hook, are guided up, farther up, until the right place is reached. The hook is drilled into the wall, still way up. Now, the patient's hands holding the bell are guided high up, higher, and higher until finally the hook is reached and the bell is fixed on the hook.
>
> That evening I gave a colloquium at the medical center. To illustrate course content, I showed some videos that included the video taken from the guided event with Mr. M. hanging the bell. It happened that Mr. M.'s physical therapist was in the audience. Watching how the patient's arm was guided higher and higher she shouted from the audience, "Hundreds of times I tried to get that patient to lift his arm—he couldn't do it, and here, look at that." (p. 172)

We concluded that when the patient is asked to imitate arm-lifting movements without an event, he reportedly fails. When arm lifting is embedded in a daily event, the patient is able to lift his arm. Such examples raise the question, "How do babies learn movement patterns?" Thelen (1995) studied movement patterns in young babies. She described how the patterns change according to tasks. In our own words, movement patterns of babies are embedded in daily-life events. So the next question arises, "How do young children retrieve movement patterns?"

> N., a 12-month-old, is videotaped as he is on top of a stair that leads down to a porch. There are several objects on the floor of the porch. A red bowl is close to the last step. N. looks at the bowl, then begins to climb down until he has reached the last step. Now he moves one leg toward the floor—and then that foot gets caught in the bowl. N. looks at what has happened, tries to lift his leg, but the bowl moves with his foot. Unsuccessful, N. sits down, his one foot still caught in the red bowl. He moves his hand to get the bowl off his foot, but still the bowl moves with his foot. N. makes several attempts; topological relationships between foot-bowl-body-support change and keep changing. Finally, N. is separate from the bowl; he crawls to other objects on the floor, interacting

with them for about 10 minutes. Then, he is again at the top of the stairs. He turns and gets a glimpse of the red bowl still on the floor. He climbs down to the red bowl, lifts his one leg and tries to put his foot into the bowl; it is obvious that he is trying to replicate the earlier event.

It appears that the resemblance of the actual situation to the previous one has helped the child to retrieve the stored interaction experience. Comparisons of the situations, in which the two patients and the normal child retrieved and applied what they have stored, suggest that retrieval is facilitated by similarities between stored interactive events and the actual respective event situations. Thus, important processes of memorizing (storing) and retrieving are stimulated, when people are provided with adequate tactual information in actual situations during daily-life nonverbal events (Fischer & Peschke, 1998). To enhance memory processes then, one has to go back to the root and then observe retrieval processes as short-term effects when experiencing tactual daily-life events.

We conclude that nonverbal interactive tactual experiences in daily life are important for disordered persons, not only for storing such experiences but also for helping them to retrieve previously stored similar interactive experiences. One can expect memory processes to improve.

Transfer is another phenomenon that can be observed. Transfer here means that an activity improves even if it had not been included in the actual guided interaction event. For example, guiding a patient through an event, even though the patient is sitting, can improve walking (Affolter & Bischofberger, 1993).

H., a patient with a head trauma, comes to therapy. Her physical therapist walks her through the room to a table and helps her sit down. The occupational therapist guides H. through the event to make an apple pie. Throughout the event, H. is in a sitting position. At the end of the event, the physical therapist comes to help H. to walk through the room again. He is astonished at the improvement in H.'s walking.

We infer that H. received tactual information when making an apple pie. H. had to change topological relationships, change sources of information and his body tone decreased. He also had to establish hypotheses. This is work on the root. Stimulating the growth of the root stimulates the growth of branches. Walking belongs to a branch, and walking improves as part of a branch. The phenomenon of transfer supports the model of a root. When one works on the root by experiencing nonverbal daily-life events, one can expect the root to improve. With the improvement of the root, branches grow even though they have not been directly involved in the actual event.

Thus, we observe short-term effects, like increase in attention span, decrease of hyperactivity and body tone, anticipation, access to memory, and transfer. They allow us to infer that our work on the root seems to be successful. In the beginning, these effects might not last long. They may just last during guiding. Then they will last for some minutes after guiding has been completed. Then they will last for hours. With time and growing experience in guided nonverbal daily-life events, these effects will last longer; they will continue beyond the guided sessions. They will be elicited more frequently and faster—signs that the root is growing. As the root gets stronger, more and more branches grow, and long-term effects are observable.

3.3.3.2 Long-Term Effects of Intervention

Just as immediate or short-term effects can be taken as signs that the root is growing, long-term effects can be taken as signs that branches are growing as a consequence of a stronger root. The same is true of real plants.

T., a 5-year-old child with language disorders and autistic behavior, did not speak. He never turned around to look at a sound source. He was diagnosed as having severe hearing problems in addition to other perceptual problems. He was fitted with two hearing aids when he was 3 years old. He did not imitate; he appeared not to be in social contact with other persons.

He was referred to the school for children with perceptual problems in our town. At school his perceptual problems were diagnosed as being of an intermodal kind (see descriptions of subgroups in Sections 1.3.1 and 3.2.3). The hypothesis was made that his localization failure could be explained by his intermodal problems. Localization performance requires an integration of two sensory modalities, the auditory modality for judging the direction of the sound source, and the integration of that auditory information with visual information for judging that what one hears is also something to look at. Perceptually, this placed T. below 6 months of age, since a normal baby is expected to look at a sound source by the age of about 6 months.

Work on the root was applied in the sense of Guided Tactual Interaction Therapy. It was expected that T.'s competence was far beyond that of a 6-month-old baby. T. was guided through daily events as they were relevant during the course of a day: getting undressed when arriving at school, emptying the school bag, preparing snacks, going to the store to purchase items, helping in the kitchen to get lunch ready, cleaning dishes, and so on. One could observe the short-term effects that we described in the previous section. But specific skills such as localizing a sound source were never practiced.

Six months later T. was making orange juice, working by himself at a table. It happens that he was videotaped for some staff discussions on that day. He is tending to his event when the door opens slowly with average loudness at his back and then somebody looks into the room. Very clearly, registered on the video, T. turns his head in the direction of the door and looks at the door. An amazing performance. T. localizes. He was not deaf. He had acquired perceptually the degree of intermodal integration necessary to turn his head in the direction of a sound source to look at it.

For us this was a sign that not only had the root grown, but new branches were appearing. Here, for instance, was a branch indicating perceptual development.

Another example illustrates long-term effects:

> B., diagnosed with severe language disorders and autistic behavior, was referred to the school for children with perceptual disorders when he was 6 years old. He did not relate to either adults or children. He did not speak or imitate. A normal baby begins to imitate movements and then sounds by the end of the first year. B.'s cognitive competence was judged to be well beyond the age of such babies. So he was guided through all kinds of daily events. This was work on the root. He was never trained to imitate nor to speak. However, all the described short-term effects, criteria for working on the root were observable.
>
> Time passed. When B. was 8, he began spontaneously to show the behavior of "doing with." For example, when other children stood up from their chairs to go to the other room to eat or to play, he would also stand now and do what they did. When other children put on their coats to leave for the bus, he would do the same thing. For people around B., this level or branch of social skills was very important. It allowed staff to integrate B. into a small group at school. At about the same time, B. began to understand verbal commands as signals in a respective situation (see Section 1.3.1); one could tell him to get his swimming suit when preparing for swimming, or put his shoes away, or go and play. When he was 10 he started to talk. He paid attention when one talked to him about a guided event of the past, or when one drew pictures about such an event. Language began to evolve.

These examples depict short-term effects, comparable to the growing of the root, and long-term effects, comparable to the growing of the root and the growing of the branches. These branches refer to developmental performances. First one can observe performances at more elementary levels of development. Localization was an example of branches of perceptual development. Then performances followed at more and more complex levels of development. An example is the behavior of "doing with." Lastly, language as the most complex performance began to appear.

For planning intervention, our model of a root with a growing tree seems meaningful. We have to help the patients to interact. We have to work on the root, not the branches. Our clinical experience and longitudinal findings strongly support the validity of this theoretical orientation and intervention (Affolter, 1987/1991; Affolter & Bischofberger, 1993).

3.4   RESEARCH IN PROGRESS

We expected the model of a root to be a valid account of normal development in young children, behavior and development of children with disabilities, and disturbances in behavior observed in adults with acquired brain
damage. Developmental data collected in normal children should therefore
help us to study persons with specific problems. Jackson (1884) described
the effect of acquired brain damage as a reversal of the sequence of levels
acquired in development. In Piaget's terms (1947/1950), this means that in
persons with acquired brain damage, functions are still present, but the
organization of the functions is disordered. This appears to correspond to
our observations that persons with brain damage do perceive, but they have
difficulties changing sources of information according to the topological
changes during interaction. They may get very rigid in such situations, and
often people in the environment do not realize the causes of the difficulty.
Such rigidity can lead to severe contractions (Lipp & Schlaegel, 1996). This
suggests that brain damage interrupts the primary organization of perceptual activity and, as a consequence, daily interaction is disturbed
(Bischofberger, Affolter, & Peschke, 1995). We assumed that the amount of
disturbance in perceptual organization is directly related to the severity of
brain damage (Affolter, Bischofberger, & Calabretti-Erni, 1996).

   In the following discussion we refer to projects investigating the validity of our model of a root. We present preliminary results. The projects can
be grouped into cross-sectional and longitudinal studies.

3.4.1   Cross-Sectional Studies

Cross-sectional studies in progress focus on nonverbal interaction activities of daily life in normal babies, the coding of such activities, developmental features, and the application to patients with brain damage. In
addition, the question about the validity of neuropsychological testing for
daily-life behavior and the evaluation of social interaction of adults with
acquired brain damage are addressed.

3.4.1.1   Development of Nonverbal Interaction
and Problem Solving in Normal Babies

   These studies were designed to focus on nonverbal activities of babies
in daily life. Within this framework attention is given to interaction features and to problem-solving activities. Normal, 0- to 18-month-old babies
were videotaped in daily-life activities such as diaper changing, eating and
spontaneous play behavior. It was assumed that movements of babies are
not produced at random but are goal-oriented.

In the first study we expected that (a) there are activities of the babies, which fit the criteria of interaction (i.e., the babies move for changing topological relationships between their bodies and the environment), (b) these activities can be grouped according to units of interaction in which elementary interactive activities are embedded in more complex ones, and (c) an increase in complexity of such units in a regular sequence in 0- to 18-month-old babies can be observed.

Video recordings of daily-life nonverbal activities of 54 normal 0- to 18-month-old babies were analyzed. The findings supported the expectancies. Interactive activities could be defined and grouped according to units, which increased regularly with age in complexity. Touching was first observable; then grasping/holding/lifting; then releasing with displacing; then sequences of topological relationships such as transporting, that is, lifting an object at a given location, locomoting with it for further interactions, as for example, pushing another object with that object and making it move or putting objects into one another (Affolter & Bischofberger, 1996).

A second study was based on the assumption that spontaneous nonverbal activities of daily life of 0- to 18-month-old babies, defined as interaction, are oriented toward solving problems. We expected that such nonverbal problem-solving activities increase in complexity with age.

The video recordings of 36 normal 0- to 18-month-old babies were analyzed and coded according to an adaptation of Pitt and Brouwer-Janse's (1985) model of problem solving and the coding system developed for the Seriation tasks. The findings supported the expectancies. The coding system allowed a description of regular increases with age in nonverbal problem-solving activities, grouped into 8 subprocesses in 0- to 18-month-old babies. By 18 months all the 25 coded activities were observable (Affolter & Bischofberger, 1988). This suggests that problem-solving activities can already be described in babies, that they increase in complexity, that the structure of problem solving on a sensorimotor level appears to be similar to the structure observable on both a nonverbal representative level (see seriation data), and on a verbal level as described for high-school students, college students and university professors (Pitt & Brouwer-Janse, 1985).

3.4.1.2 Developmental Data and Evaluation Procedures of Daily Activities of Adults With Acquired Brain Damage

We assumed that persons with acquired brain damage fail in daily-life interactions. We expected that the difficulties of brain-damaged patients in daily-life events could be evaluated by applying the coding system used for describing the increase of units of interaction in babies.

Videotaped spontaneous activities in daily life of 20 adults with different degrees of acquired brain damage were analyzed for presence of units of interaction. Findings support the possibility of differentiating brain-damaged adults on a wide range when evaluated on levels of units of interaction of daily activities. Individual patients consistently showed a specific level. Patients with only elementary units were more severely disturbed, whereas patients with more complex units presented less severe disturbances. Situational conditions of the interaction for some adult patients differed from babies: Adult patients started an event most often when only relevant stimuli were present in their field of action. Babies, however, began an event when both relevant and irrelevant stimuli were present in their field of action (Affolter, Bischofberger, & Calabretti-Erni, 1996). It appears, then, that the concept of units of interaction can be applied for evaluating adults with acquired brain damage.

3.4.1.3 Neuropsychological Testing Procedures and Interaction in Daily Life in Adults With Acquired Brain Damage

Neuropsychological test scores often do not predict how a patient functions in daily life. Also, patients are often judged to be nontestable and their performance is disregarded.

We decided to analyze the Form Recognition tasks in the tactual modality condition (see Section 1.2.1) for topological changes and length of the sequence of actions required. It was expected that (a) the coding system of units of interaction established for babies can be applied to evaluate performance on the Form Recognition tasks of testable and nontestable patients, and (b) both, the evaluation of interaction units and sequence of actions of the Form Recognition tasks of a patient, correspond to units of interaction and sequences of actions performed by that patient in daily-life events.

Video recordings of the performance of 10 patients with acquired brain damage tested in Form Recognition in a tactual modality condition and in daily-life activities were analyzed and findings supported the expectancies. The coding system used for babies was applicable to testable and nontestable patients and allowed differentiating them. The level of units of interaction and the length of sequences of action interpreted from test results corresponded to those in daily-life events (Bischofberger, Affolter, & Peschke, 1995).

3.4.1.4 Individual and Social Interaction in Daily Life in Adults With Acquired Brain Damage

It was assumed that social behavior involves interaction events, and thus requires goal-oriented changes of topological relationships. It was expected that when involved in reaching a common goal in a social group, patients with brain damage would vary in goal orientation and information needed for performing interaction events.

In a pilot study, four patients with acquired brain damage were videotaped. They were supposed to work toward a common goal in a group situation. It was observed that patient S. did not reach understanding of the main goal as the other three did. Patient H. showed spontaneous activities connected with the main goal and with other patient's needs (true social behavior). The activities of patients F. and J. were determined by individual goals, had to be initiated by guided tactual information, and objects needed had to be within the field of action. Patients F. and J. handed an object to another person in need of it (social behavior) only when asked. The findings suggest the possibility that such analyses allow for describing different levels of social functioning of brain-damaged patients in a group when they are expected to work on a common project (Hoffman & Söll, 1998).

3.4.2 Longitudinal Studies

There were two kinds of projects, one kind investigated changes over time in nonverbal interaction, memory, and other skills. The other kind of project focused on outcomes when patients received Guided Interaction Therapy and on comparisons of different intervention programs.

3.4.2.1 Improvement in Nonverbal Interaction, Memory, and Other Skills

Patients who receive Guided Interaction Therapy were expected to improve in understanding event goals, continue actions after having been guided, and perform events spontaneously. They were also expected to improve on other skills, such as memory and language performance.

In the first study, two patients, X. and Y. with acquired brain damage, received Guided Interaction Therapy for half a year, beginning 6 months after their brain injury. Four times during this period they were videotaped and evaluated on different aspects of daily-life interaction. They progressed from not understanding events in less familiar situations, to understanding such events when they received tactual information (by being guided), to understanding such events when visual or verbal information was provided. Spontaneous performance of events was not observed during this period. However, at the end of therapy they continued some actions when they had been guided through the beginning of the event (Trares & Stratthoff, 1998).

A second study focused on memory. Clinical observations support the assumption that memory retrieval is activated by Guided Interaction Therapy in daily-life events. For 6 months a patient with acquired brain damage received guided tactual interaction intervention. Neuropsychological tests at the beginning showed poor recall. Three times during the treatment period, the patient was evaluated on recall; he was videotaped when he performed events, matched on content, under two conditions: spontaneous performance and guided performance. The findings supported the expectancies. The patient did not recall any of the actions of the spontaneously performed events, but did recall the main steps of the guided event. Neuropsychological tests at the end of the period showed improved recall (Fischer & Peschke, 1998).

A third study focused on language and selected cognitive skills. It was assumed that Guided Tactual Interaction Therapy would improve not only interaction but also a variety of other skills. Children were expected to improve their scores on different nonverbal and verbal tasks.

Ten children at different age levels, with a motor–perceptual disorder, significant speech-language delay, and a variety of additional problems, received Guided Interaction Therapy three times per week for 8 months. The children were tested several times. As expected, focused attention and scores on cognitive and language tests improved, with gains ranging from 1 to 23 months. Gains were most notable for receptive language and basic concepts (Sweeney & Levine, 1998).

3.4.2.2   Comparisons of Intervention Programs

Observations of patients and children with language disorders receiving different intervention programs were collected over a period of time.

The first study included two patients with the same kind and degree of brain injury. Patient H. received only Guided Interaction Therapy; patient S. changed therapy programs. They were periodically videotaped and evaluated on interaction performances. Patient H. showed gradual improvement from understanding and continuing some actions of an event when tactual information was provided to understanding events when tactual *or* visual information was provided. After 10 months of treatment he was able to solve daily events successfully step-by-step.

Patient S. improved during a first period of Guided Interaction Therapy when tactual information was provided. He improved from understanding short daily habitual events to understanding daily events of a more complex kind, and continuing some actions on his own after guiding. He was dismissed at that time and received visual–auditory training for 41 months before he was referred back for Guided Interaction Therapy. He had regressed to his original level. After 6 months of Guided Interaction Therapy, he had recovered earlier gains. After 2 more months, he was functioning on a higher level. Daily activities in familiar situations were performed step-by-step when tactual or visual information was provided (Mohr & Nielsen, 1998).

In a second study two children with intermodal (autistic) perceptual problems were matched by diagnosis at age 5 years. Their performances reflected a similar low developmental level of interaction. Child A received Guided Interaction Therapy over 12 years, Child B, another kind of treatment. At age 17 both were reevaluated. Child A was integrated in a working group, had developed some language and was partially independent. Child B was found to function on the same low developmental level of interaction as at age 5, was totally dependent, and had no language (Bischofberger & Affolter, 1998).

A third study revealed the longitudinal outcome of two children with severe learning disorder. Each child went through periods of different intervention programs, both were followed over 15 years and periodically evaluated and videotaped. At age 5 both children were evaluated; they were inactive, visually oriented, touched objects but did not perform any goal-oriented sequence of topological changes as required in daily-life events.

A first period of 3 years of Guided Interaction Therapy followed. By the end of that period they understood and performed familiar events in familiar surroundings with tactual or visual information, step-by-step.

During a second period of about 6 years they received educational programs based on visual–auditory/verbal training procedures. By the end of that period both children showed severe behavioral disturbances and were dismissed from their programs because of psychiatric problems.

A third period of 3 years followed. They again received Guided Interaction Therapy. By the end of that period both were fully integrated in a group environment and showed adequate daily interaction (Affolter & Bischofberger, 1998).

We conclude from the research in progress that preliminary results appear to support the validity of the work on the root, that is, working with the disordered children and adults on nonverbal daily events by trying to improve their search for information. Guiding seems to be an important tool for intervention with both children and adults in the efforts to improve daily interaction. We recommend continued research within the described framework.

Epilogue: Language Learning and Nonverbal Interaction in Daily Events

Ida J. Stockman
Michigan State University

The overarching goal of this book is to present a theoretical framework of perception and cognition in which developmental language disorders can be explained and clinically remediated. This framework has evolved mainly from Affolter and Bischofberger's research and clinical observations of nonverbal performances in normal and clinical populations. It is based on four principal assumptions:

1. Nonverbal interaction with the physical environment in daily problem-solving events is the root of development;

2. Nonverbal interaction is critically dependent on perceiving information that is anchored by the tactual–kinesthetic input associated with elicited changes of topological relationships between the body and the environment;

3. Inadequate nonverbal interaction experiences hinder development of nonverbal and verbal skills when a central nervous system deficit prevents perceptual activity from being organized well enough to search for the relevant information;

4. Inadequate nonverbal interaction experiences can be impoverished by a variety of central perceptual deficits among children with language disorders, who are not a homogeneous clinical group.

These assumptions imply that language disorders are associated with perceptual difficulties that affect the central organization and processing

197

of information input. In this respect, Affolter and Bischofberger's thinking is attuned to the emerging emphasis on the information-processing demands on learning in language-disordered children. However, the primacy of "interaction" as a theoretical construct clearly sets their framework apart in two striking ways. First, the view that nonverbal interaction in daily events is the root or source of development means that a perceptual deficit can adversely affect nonverbal and verbal development only if it affects interaction experience. Thus, the causal relationship between perceptual deficits and aberrant development is indirect and not direct, as is usually assumed.

Second, physical interaction between the child and the environment sharply focuses the critical role of tactual input in the multisensory organization of perceptual activity. In contrast, visual and auditory input have been historically privileged in perceptual–cognitive theory. At the same time, a theoretical construct based on physical "interaction" does not confine perceptual processes to the sensory channel of experience. If interaction always includes the interrelationship between the person (actor) and also the environment, then what is perceived and learned must be necessarily influenced by the state of the perceiver (actor) and also the environment, inclusive of stimulus complexity in the actual situation. According to Affolter and Bischofberger, the perception of that complexity cannot be handed over to the perceiver in a passive, direct way. The perceiver must actively search for it and do so in an organized way.

Thus, what has emerged in this book is the sense that perception needs to be conceptualized more broadly than it is portrayed typically in the research literature on developmental language disorders. In Affolter and Bischofberger's view, perception is a multisensory process anchored by tactual information arising from learner–environment interaction, and mediated by cognitive and situational factors. It is relevant to ask whether this expanded view makes sense given the existing research on the nature of developmental language disorders, or whether it adds anything new to clinical intervention practices.

Such a critical discussion is needed from the vantage of language, and is the focus of this chapter. So far this book has had little to say about language per se because it has focused on the nonverbal performance of children with language disorders. Of course, its nonverbal focus is justified, as I pointed out in the introduction. Scholars are likely to agree that nonverbal perceptual–cognitive factors are relevant to fully understanding the language acquisition process, despite retreat from strong cognitive determinism in language acquisition theory (Bates, Benigni, Bretherton, Camaioni, & Volterra, 1979; Bowerman, 1989; Johnston, 1985; Rice & Kemper, 1984). Research on nonverbal skills and developmental language disorders has been pursued precisely because of what it might reveal about the nature of the language learning difficulty. Nonetheless, the search for nonverbal causative factors has been criticized for not yielding predictable linguistic outcomes (Johnston, 1991; Kamhi, 1993; Rice, 1991).

Skepticism about a causal relationship between language and nonverbal cognition has been fueled by a variety of observations. For one thing, the relationship between languages and the nonverbal experiences they code appears to be an arbitrary one, the notion of a universal grammar not withstanding. Languages are selective about which nonverbal experiences are coded and how they are coded. Some linguistic forms do not have obvious nonverbal cognitive correlates, but reflect instead conventional rules that may have evolved by historical accident.

Scholars also have been quick to point to the lack of congruity between verbal and nonverbal skills. For instance, it is commonly observed that children with language disorders can exhibit poorer verbal than nonverbal performances. More recently it has come to the fore that other children (e.g., those with Williams Syndrome) exhibit considerably better verbal than nonverbal performances. It is not surprising, therefore, that research has not shown a general dependency of linguistic knowledge on the prior emergence of nonverbal cognitive concepts (e.g., object permanence) that presumably were rooted in sensorimotor activity (Rice & Kemper, 1984), as Piaget's theory of cognitive development (Piaget, 1950, 1952, 1962) was thought to predict. Consequently, Piaget's waning influence on language acquisition theory has isolated the study of language from the kind of nonverbal physical interactive processes that Affolter and Bischofberger describe in this book.

Furthermore, severe motor and physical handicaps have always been the Achilles heel to a sensorimotor orientation to cognition (Segalowitz, 1980). Some children achieve a more mature stage of nonverbal cognition (Decarie, 1969) and language understanding (Bishop, 1993; Fourcin, 1975) than is predicted by their physical handicaps. Such outcomes suggest that development is not solely dependent on the usual amount of independent sensorimotor experience, which naïve interpretations of Piaget's cognitive development theory imply is necessary. According to Mogford and Bishop (1993), it is clear that:

> normal ability to perform actions on the world and note their sensory consequences is not necessary for linguistic development. (p. 249)

Not surprisingly then, clinical intervention practices for language-disordered children have stressed the necessity of working directly on language, and not on any nonverbal performances that are presumed to be prerequisites for its development. See Lahey (1988), for example. Movement-oriented treatment frameworks developed by occupational or physical therapists (cf. Ayres, 1972; Bobath, 1966; Delacato, 1963; Fisher, Murray, & Bundy, 1991) have not given a reason to alter this view. They have failed to yield consistently positive, or impressive treatment gains in linguistic or academic achievement (Daems, 1994; Hoehn & Baumeister, 1994; Roberton, 1981), despite their claims to do so. In some cases, the treatment frameworks have been discredited as theoretically misguided. See Cummins' (1988) critique of the Doman–Delacato methods.

In sum, contemporary views of language development and disorders do not encourage one to take seriously a theoretical framework that links language learning to nonverbal physical interaction processes, as put forth in this book. Although its usefulness for explaining and treating the disordered nonverbal behavior in language-disordered children may not be easily dismissed, the reason to view it as a serious explanation and alternative for treating abnormal language is less obvious.

In this chapter, therefore, it is important to speculate about what the linguistic consequences of Affolter and Bischofberger's conceptual framework might be for normal and abnormal language learners. I do so by first summarizing evidence for nonverbal deficits in language-disordered children that implicate the tactual–kinesthetic sensory system. This sensory system anchors information input in Affolter and Bischofberger's theory of nonverbal interaction. Then it is argued on intuitive and empirical grounds that nonverbal interaction in daily problem-solving events influences the perceptual processing demands for learning language in ways that may help to account for broad patterns of abnormal development. Finally, the implications of a nonverbal interaction framework for language intervention and further research are discussed.

4.1   PERCEPTUAL DEFICITS IN CHILDREN WITH LANGUAGE DISORDERS

If tactual input is important to the perceptual organization of language learning, then tactual–kinesthetic deficits ought to show up among the abnormal characteristics of children with language disorders. Fortunately there is corroborating evidence for Affolter and Bischofberger's claim that children with language disorders do exhibit deficits that implicate the tactual–kinesthetic sensory system. Such difficulties have been reported for children along the autistic spectrum (Leary & Hill, 1996; Sevin et al., 1995), and for children with less severe impairment—namely, those diagnosed with either specific language impairment (SLI; Bishop & Edmundson, 1987; Kamhi, 1981; Lahey & Edwards, 1996; Powell & Bishop, 1992; Stark & Tallal, 1981a, 1988), and those diagnosed with a learning disability (LD; Ayres, 1972; Chiarenza, 1990; Gillberg, 1989; Hadders-Algra &

Touwen, 1992; Henderson & Hall, 1982; Hoare & Larkin, 1991; Losse et al., 1991; Roberton, 1981; Rosner, 1981; Rourke, 1989; Rudel, 1985; Stone, May, Alvarez, & Ellman, 1989; Thompson, 1971; Wolff, Gunnoe, & Cohen, 1985; Wolff, Michel, Ovrut, & Drake, 1990).

A broad range of symptoms has been described on tasks requiring observations of (a) passive touch (e.g., two-point discrimination, dichhaptic stimulation, and so on); (b) rate and accuracy of executing fine and gross motor skills (e.g., balance, and hopping); (c) active touch in haptic tasks that combine tactual input with input from joint receptor stimulation during movement; and (d) clinical observations of goal oriented movement patterns in the routine daily-life activities of dressing, eating, and so on. Reduced sensitivity to tactual stimulation and slow, clumsy, and uncoordinated movement patterns have been reported. Poor haptic recognition has been observed, in addition to bizarre stereotypic motor patterns such as aimless flapping and rocking of the body and/or the lack of motor planning in daily living activities. Depressed motor performance amounts to more than a slow rate of executing rapid movements, as described by Stark and Tallal (1988). A motor skill such as static balance can be deficient as well (Powell & Bishop, 1992).

It is recognized that a causal interpretation is not justified by merely observing a correlation between disordered language and depressed tactual or sensorimotor performances. Depressed sensorimotor skills, in particular, are often simplistically viewed as just a motor problem—an additional deficit that is unrelated to a language disorder. Conceivably though, what are interpreted as motor deficits could be perceptual deficits that reflect the consequences of an inadequate search for information in nonverbal interaction events.

4.1.1 Movement as Perception

In the larger context of purposeful human action, motor acts are not isolated from perception, cognition, and knowledge acquisition. The view, that motor behavior is the product of context-dependent, physical and mental processes, is allied with dynamic systems theory, as applied to developmental cognition (Bushnell & Boudreau, 1993), neurobiology (Edelman, 1987), and motor skills (Thelen, 1995; Thelen & Smith, 1994). In a dynamic systems model of behavior, sensory and motor factors are among the fluid assembly of multiple factors that converge with prior knowledge and the information demands of a given situation to shape adaptive action and learning.

Dynamic systems theory provides a contemporary theoretical link to Affolter and Bischofberger's interaction framework. It is important to point out though that in their view, it is not movement per se, but rather the experience with goal-oriented nonverbal interaction events that is regarded as the root of development. Movement, whether independent or guided in interaction events, becomes important to learning about how the world works only insofar as it provides access to critical *perceptual* information that otherwise would not be available—namely, tactually anchored sensory input about changes of topological relationships between the body and the environment. In other words, movement is merely a means to an end.

Affolter and Bischofberger insist that motor acts leading to goal-directed touching of the environment mediate learning from real-world experience in a way that looking and listening cannot do. Neither looking nor listening can directly cause changes of state. Only by touching the environment does it become possible to change both the environment and the person doing the touching in a perceivable way. For example, to cut an apple, the change from an uncut to a cut state is an effect of interaction. Tactual information is experienced as a change of resistance that occurs with the separation of the apple into more than one piece. The change of resistance associated with the change of topological relations allows one to sense when the apple is cut and when the "cutting" act is completed.

There also are visual and/or auditory effects that normally co-occur with a change of state during an interaction event. For example, there are associated changes in the visual appearance of the cut apple as well as changes in how it smells, feels, and tastes. However, these changes are viewed as secondary effects of interaction. They cannot occur until the environment is first touched and a change of topological relationship is first achieved.

Still, learners must store the correlated secondary input of motor acts such as vision, audition, and so on in order to perceive the environment as familiar in the absence of the interaction event. This means that looking at a *cut* apple ought to yield more information about the object than what meets the eye as its color, shape, or size at a given moment. In an *intermodally* organized perceptual system, visual impressions, as effects of causative action, are connected to previously stored tactual information about the actions that created the state of a cut apple. There also is information about how cut apples smell, feel, or sound as effects of causative action. Such tactually anchored secondary input not only allows the perceiver to explain or predict how the effects came about, but it also allows one to do what is needed to recreate or prevent the same effects.

Understanding causes and effects also requires storage of information about the temporal order of causally related interaction events. Goal-oriented events, particularly the complex ones, involve more than a single change of topological relationship between the body and the environment. Typically there are multiple changes that are causally related to achieving a functional goal. For example, achieving the goal of cutting an apple may require the serial integration of many causally related interaction events, as when the same apple is cut into more than one piece and then eaten. A series of causally connected interaction events may precede or follow the cutting event. Before actually cutting an apple, a series of events may be required to get the knife and the apple. The events of cutting an apple will be followed by other causally related interaction events, if the larger goal is to bake an apple pie. The perception of serial information is necessary to fully understand the causal relationships among nonverbal interaction events.

Affolter and Bischofberger have argued in this book that perceptual deficits involving the *tactual* system or its *intermodal* or *serial* collaboration with other senses can adversely affect nonverbal daily interactions enough to alter the normal perceptual–cognitive organization of experience.

4.1.2 Types of Perceptual Deficits in Children With Language Disorders

Affolter and Bischofberger differentiate three types of language disordered subgroups based on the nature of the perceptual deficits. One subgroup includes children who primarily have a tactual–kinesthetic perceptual problem. Another subgroup consists of children with a primary intermodal perceptual difficulty (i.e., they have difficulty with integrating information from different sensory modalities). A third subgroup includes children with a serial perceptual problem (i.e., they have difficulty organizing sequences of sensory input). There are strong hints in the contemporary research literature that these three types of perceptual deficits may exist among children with developmental language disorders in the absence of impaired vision or audition.

4.1.2.1 *Tactual–Kinesthetic Perceptual Deficits*

In Affolter and Bischofberger's framework, some children with language disorders exhibit a primary perceptual deficit in processing tactual information. They require stronger than usual changes of resistance to detect such input. As a result, deviant movement patterns emerge as the compensatory search for more adequate tactual information when eliciting changes of topological relationship between the body and the environment. When interacting, for example, children may touch and release objects with too much force (Affolter, 1991); gait and posture may be unusual; knees may be bent toward the midline, or gravitational insecurity may become evident whenever the feet leave the support. Although children with normal and disordered language in the Seriation study had more difficulty solving the seriation problem in the tactual than in the visual or visual–tactual conditions, the language disorder subgroup with tactual deficits exhibited relatively more difficulty. At the school for children with perceptual deficits in St. Gallen, Switzerland, which Affolter and Bischofberger helped to establish in 1976, the tactual–kinesthetic subgroup typically comprises about 60% of the children according to its current principal, Herr Neuweiler (personal communication, September, 1997).

In the United States, professionals have struggled to find a suitable diagnostic label for such children. The terms, pervasive developmental delay (PDD) and more recently, multisystem developmental disorder (MDD), have emerged in response to this problem (Zero to Three/National Center for Clinical Infant Programs, 1994). The MDD diagnostic label was created in order to identify children who present serious nonverbal and verbal delays, but who unlike children with classic autistic characteristics, do develop affect and social skills. These children do not meet all the criteria for autism, and may have a better developmental prognosis than those who do. It is noteworthy that the criteria for the MDD diagnosis require significant dysfunction in the processing of visual–spatial, tactual, proprioceptive, and vestibular input. Children who fit the MDD diagnosis appear to be like those who have been described as having sensory-integration and tactual dysfunction (Ayres, 1972; Fisher et al., 1991). Still most children with a severe tactual–kinesthetic perceptual deficit are likely to get the diagnosis of atypical autism or autism not otherwise specified (NOS), using *DSM–IV* criteria (American Psychiatric Association, 1995). In other words, these children with tactual perceptual deficits in Affolter and Bischofberger's framework are judged as belonging to the spectrum of autistic disorders.

4.1.2.2 Intermodal Perceptual Deficit

Affolter and Bischofberger proposed that another subgroup has difficulty integrating input across different sensory modalities. These children presumably experience good tactual input, but it is isolated from what they see, hear, smell, and so on. An intermodal deficit can produce fearless climbers and movers who disregard visual information about potential hazards. Unusual stereotypic movement patterns are observed (e.g., rapid twirling and flapping of body limbs) that do not require coordinated visual control to be maintained. These children were less successful in solving the seriation problem in the cross-modal, visual–tactual condition than in either of the modality-specific, visual or visual–visual conditions.

The literature strongly hints that such behaviors are characteristic of children who present classic autistic symptoms (Rutter & Schopler, 1987). The overwhelming conclusion from more than two decades of research is that this group does not show difficulty with low level processing of sensory input in any modality, even in the face of mental retardation. See literature reviews of perception (Frith & Baron-Cohen, 1987) and cognition (Sigman et al., 1987). They show remarkable ability to process, store, and retrieve stimuli in near perfect raw form in each sensory field. Intact auditory perceptual skills are evident from the ability to reproduce or echo spoken sentences and musical patterns. Visual forms are faithfully reproduced in their drawings. On standard psychometric batteries, performance peaks on visual–motor subtests (e.g. block design, object assembly, and so on). Autistic children can fit puzzle pieces together quite well from feel alone when the edges of the puzzle pieces can be interlocked. So it seems that when the reproduction of stimuli in their original input form is sufficient to perform a task, children with autism may show intact or even superior skills in each sensory modality. The critical dysfunction is in deriving the necessary information to transform input into meaningful representation—a process that requires intermodal linkage of information from several sensory modalities. Frith and Baron-Cohen (1987) concluded that the autistic:

> use their intact lower level processing functions, which remain modality-specific, rather than higher level functions, which use abstract codes . . . (p. 93).

Recently Frith and Happe (1994) described the "central coherence theory" to explain the low level cognitive performances of persons with autism in the face of high level perceptual function in narrow sensory domains. This theory was based on earlier speculation by Frith (1989) that "autism is characterized by a specific imbalance in integration of information at different levels" (p. 121, cited in Frith & Happe, 1994). Normally, we draw together diverse information to construct higher level meaning in context (i.e., "*central coherence*"). It is necessary to get the gist of a verbal story or situation, because the actual surface forms are lost quickly and are more effortful to retain. This theory is compatible with the hypothesis that a canalized sensory system is a neurofunctional deficit in autism (Waterhouse, Fein, & Modahl, 1996).

There ought to be psychological evidence for a central coherence theory whenever autistic children have to perform intermodal tasks. Affolter and Bischofberger observed that children with language disorders and intermodal perceptual deficits performed more poorly when the Seriation task involved combined tactual–visual input than only visual. Similarly, Frith and Hermeline (1969) showed that autistic subjects performed as well as normals when just visually tracking a display and even better than normals when they tracked from just feel. Success decreased when they had to both look and feel. Smith and Bryson (1994) interpreted the autistic's inability to imitate other people's actions or movements as a cross-modal information-processing problem. An intermodal deficit has also shown up on tasks requiring the integration of just auditory and visual input (cf. Bryson, 1972; Casey, 1993), but this effect is not observed in every study (e.g., Walker-Andrews, Haviland, Huffman, & Toci, 1994). However, clinical observations often show that young autistic children are often diagnosed as deaf because they do not turn their heads in the direction of a sound source (i.e., localize sound), a skill that requires the integration of auditory and visual sensory input.

4.1.2.3 Serial Perceptual Deficits

Affolter and Bischofberger proposed that the primary perceptual problem of a third language disorder subgroup is exhibited whenever high temporal sequential processing demands are placed on performance. For example, when interacting with the environment, these children's movements can appear clumsy, if they are required to track and temporally sequence many movements, especially at a rapid rate. Yet, in familiar situations, movement patterns may appear normal. Consequently, these children typically appear less severely impaired than those with tactual–kinesthetic or intermodal deficits. Most are able to get by well enough to function in regular school settings, albeit with an LD or SLI diagnostic label that allows them to receive special help for language and other difficulties related to academic achievement.

A robust research literature now exists on the temporal processing difficulty of children with language disorders along the SLI–LD continuum. It has been hypothesized that they have difficulty processing rapidly changing temporal information (Merzenich et al., 1996; Stark & Tallal, 1988; Tallal, Stark, & Mellits, 1985; Tallal & Merzenich, 1996). Moreover, it is clear now that this is not simply an auditory processing problem, as was once thought. Visual and tactual sequential deficits also have been observed (Stark & Tallal, 1988; Tallal, Stark, Kallman, & Mellits, 1981). The latter observation has led to the conclusion that temporal processing is served by a supramodal mechanism that cuts across sensory modalities, as Affolter and Bischofberger have speculated in this book, and elsewhere (Affolter, 1991; Affolter & Stricker, 1980).

4.2   NORMAL LANGUAGE ACQUISITION AND NONVERBAL INTERACTIONS

In Affolter and Bischofberger's framework, the types of perceptual deficits described earlier are presumed to adversely affect language learning by impairing the organized search for information in nonverbal interaction events. Consequently, it is necessary to consider how nonverbal interaction experience, as the root of development, contributes to normal language learning. I propose that there are at least three ways, as considered next.

4.2.1 Nonverbal Interactions and the Context for Language Learning

First, nonverbal interaction events provide the natural contexts in which language typically is used, structured, and learned. People rarely experience words in isolation of the rest of what is going on in their daily life. People constantly elicit and respond to changes of topological relationships between themselves and the objects in the environment—both animate and inanimate. They do so all day long when they sit down, get up, move objects and physically touch others to achieve the functional goals of daily living—eating, dressing, going to the store, socializing, and so on. Such nonverbal events are not only contexts for language learning but they also complicate the process when their stimuli compete with linguistic input.

Children's socialization into a community requires them also to elicit changes in topological changes between their own bodies and the environment in order to achieve goals of daily living. The important point here is that nonverbal interaction events are the reason why people need and use words. They talk about what they have done, are doing, or are about to do. Normally developing children talk early and frequently about their own actions (Bloom, 1991), and they do so before they talk about the observed interactions of other people (Huttenlocher, Smiley, & Charney, 1983).

4.2.2 Nonverbal Interactions and the Conceptual Basis for Language Learning

There is a second way that nonverbal interaction experience may influence language learning. It should lead to conceptual knowledge about the world from which the semantic content of words and sentences is constructed. There is little doubt that learning the meaning of words draws on conceptual knowledge of the world (Jackendoff, 1996a, 1996b; Lakoff, 1987, 1994; Landau & Gleitman, 1985; Pinker, 1984, 1987). However, conceptual learning requires the baby to know not only about the environment outside of its body (the usual focus on knowledge acquisition in research), but also about its own body, and, in particular, how that body relates to other objects in the environment. This knowledge cannot be invested in a constant relationship between the body and the environment, if it is to represent reality. The reality of the natural world makes it necessary to ground such knowledge in the changing relationships between the body and the environment. One pushes on a door and there is an effect; the door opens. The "pushing" is the causative act; the change in the door is the effect on the environment. One touches another person and there is a different effect. The relationships between the body and even the same object can change continually: The child can put an object on a table, off, under, or near the same table, and so on. Such changes or transformations of reality result from nonverbal interaction events. They embed cause–effect relationships among objects and people as a central part. Tomasello (1995), drawing on the works of Piaget (1952), Mandler (1992), and Nelson (1986), stated:

> It is important to conceptualize the child's early cognition in terms of event structures with objects being no more prominent in the child's conception of the world than the activities and events in which they are embedded. (p. 137)

Languages have a sentence grammar because people talk about object relationships and not single objects. Cause–effect experiences, which arise from changes of topological relationships between body and environment, seem fundamental to understanding action relations expressed even in simple sentences (e.g., John cut the apple; John picks up the apple). They are equally relevant to the event relations expressed in complex sentences (e.g., John put the apple on the table so that he could *cut it*.); and in connected discourse, as rendered by the same speaker's narrative or across speaker turns in shared conversation (John washed and cut the apple. He ate the apple. Then he cut up more pieces to make the pie. He made the pie with—and, so on). Slobin (1985) proposed that the "manipulative activity scene" involving actor–action–affected object relationships in physical experience underlies the early use of transitive *(Subject (actor) plus verb (action) plus verb complement (affected object))* sentences in all languages. See also Hopper and Thompson (1980). Edwards (1974) even related the semantic relations (e.g., location, action, possession, and so on) expressed in early sentences to Piaget's stages of sensorimotor knowledge.

4.2.3 Nonverbal Interactions and Perceptual Organization in Language Learning

There is still a third way that nonverbal interaction experience may influence language learning, given that acquisition of any skill or behavior requires new information to be stored and retrieved. Beginning with the earliest development, nonverbal interaction events provide experiences with organizing perceptual input in ways that presumably lead to the adequate search for information in the input. For example, a nonverbal interaction event requires the organized search for tactual, intermodal, and serial information, which presumably underlies the learning of complex behavior including language. Organizing the search for information is important in Affolter and Bischofberger's view because they assume that information cannot be handed over from an outside source to the learner in a direct way. The learner must do some work by searching for it. The search for information (i.e., perceptual activity) must be organized.

If language learning is rooted in nonverbal interaction experiences as argued, then one can infer that it must depend on a perceptual organization that includes the same kind of features, that are required during nonverbal interaction events, namely, tactual, intermodal, and serial features. It is useful here to speculate about how the acquisition of linguistic meaning, form, and use may depend on the search for tactual, intermodal, and serial information.

4.2.3.1 Syntactic–Semantic Aspects of Language

Gaining access to the semantic–syntactic structure of a language requires children to figure out how words are matched to their stored experiences or world knowledge. Auditory input provides information about the sound patterns or phonological forms of spoken language, but carries little information about the content or meaning of words. In other words, merely hearing words will not clue children about their meaning, except for a few onomatopoetic instances, as Landau and Gleitman (1985, p. 14) pointed out. So obviously, learning a language requires the picking up of *intermodal* information about the relationship between the auditory forms of language, and the input from the other senses, which are the sources of input for linguistic meaning.

Tactual information becomes important when considering what these other input sources are for gaining access to linguistic meaning. Evidently, it has been assumed that children learn primarily by watching other people, because the visual sense has been emphasized in theories of conceptual and semantic development. Theories of semantic development have focused on lexical learning, and in particular, the words used for objects. The focus on objects, as the conceptual basis for linguistic meaning, has called attention to what can be visually observed about their static properties (i.e., shape, size, color, location, and so on). For example, see Clark's (1973) original perceptual feature theory.

This focus on objects could be justified by the observation that typical and atypical language learners seem to acquire noun words earlier and more easily than other types of words (e.g., action verbs; cf. Gentner, 1978; Kouri, 1994; Schwartz, Leonard, Messick, & Chapman, 1987; however, see a counter view in Bloom, Tinker, & Margulis, 1993). Although objects are naturally experienced as dynamic parts of events, they can be isolated from events and seen in the same place for an indefinite time after an event. In this durative, static state, nonanimate, concrete objects, in particular, are easy to single out and label with single words. Although in reality, this is an artificial state because most objects of daily life do move, and change their topological relations to people who move them. Consequently, it is questionable whether simple ostensive labeling of static objects leads to the depth of semantic representation reflected in a mature linguistic system.

Fortunately then, object-focused meaning now competes with growing consensus that linguistic referential meaning is grounded in event knowledge (Bloom, 1991; Nelson, 1986; Smiley & Huttenlocher, 1995; Tomasello, 1992; Tomasello & Merriman, 1995). Events incorporate more than objects; they include sequences of cause–effect action relations among objects and people as a central part. Therefore, events are invested in interaction relations, which are experienced with tactual input.

Interaction yields tactual–kinesthetic input, and associated input from other sensory systems (e.g., vision, audition, and so on) that feeds back perceptual information about the effects of causative action on the environment. Thus, tactually anchored visual input ought to be richer than is visual input experienced simply by looking at another person's action. To touch an object is to experience directly the force and change of resistance needed to cause it to change in some way (e.g., its location). On the other hand, visual observation of another person's action does not provide direct input about the intention to cause change even though the movements and the object can be seen. Direct bodily participation in events (self-action) makes causal relationships salient and enhances event recall (Slackman, 1985).

In a grammatical system, tactually anchored experiences show up in the conceptual content of actions, which typically is coded by verb forms. Bloom (1981) is among those who have argued that verbs are the centerpiece of a linguistic grammar because they condition the relational use of nouns and other grammatical markers in sentences.

Furthermore, there is support for Affolter and Bischofberger's argument that tactually anchored input is more critical than is vision for acquiring conceptual knowledge about causes and effects underlying a sentence grammar. Congenital blindness does not deny access to the development of spoken language. Landau and Gleitman (1985) reported that their blind subjects even encoded the same meaning as sighted children for color terms, whose acquisition ought to be especially dependent on visual input. Moreover, children with developmental language disorders can hear and see, but they still have difficulty acquiring a first language in any form. Visual perception is even a strength for some, as Affolter and Bischofberger observed in the Seriation study. It is their good visual perception that favors SLI children's successful performance on nonverbal intelligence tests, which can be disproportionately loaded with visual discrimination items (Johnston, 1982; Kamhi, Minor, & Mauer, 1990). It is reasonable, therefore, to ask why their good visual skills do not help them to be more successful at learning language.

The acquisition of syntactic/semantic features of language would have to rely on *serial* processes too. Linguistic forms consist of sequences or a series of sounds and words. These sequences map onto tactually anchored nonverbal interaction events, which also are serially organized. This is because most daily events involve multiple changes of topological relationships between the body and the environment that are causally connected to a goal, as pointed out earlier. Consider how many related causative acts are required to put on a shoe or cut an apple. And of course, discourse (multiply related sentences, as spoken by the same speaker in a story or narration, or by different speakers across conversational turns) comes to represent the sequential relationships of events. In sum, tactual, intermodal, and serial input are all relevant to acquiring the syntactic–semantic features of language.

4.2.3.2 Phonological Forms of Language

The complexity of spoken language task looms even larger, if the child also must search for tactual, intermodal, and serial information in order to acquire the phonological structure of words, grammatical meaning aside. *Serial* information is obviously important because children must process auditory input about the sequential properties of sounds to figure out where words begin and end.

However, the rate at which phonological forms are learned may well be enhanced by *intermodal* information. The blind child's delay in learning to speak suggests that the speed at which the sounds in the speech stream can be grouped into meaningful units is enhanced by the integration of auditory and visual input, although lack of vision does not prevent speech acquisition.

The rate of learning the phonological segments may be particularly enhanced by *tactually anchored* auditory input, as is possible only when a person can hear his or her own speech production. Babies who can hear, but who are unable to vocalize (Locke, 1993; Locke & Pearson, 1990) show at least temporarily depressed articulatory skills once they are no longer tracheostomized and can vocalize.

Furthermore, Bishop (1990) reported more global adverse effects on language acquisition among persons with a life-long, poor or absent ability to articulate speech sounds. Such persons with normal hearing are exclusively dependent on external auditory speech input which is not anchored by their own tactual experience; or at least the tactual input is poor for those persons with unintelligible articulation. Bishop's study included older hearing children with cerebral palsy and anarthria (lack of speech) and those with dysarthria (poor neuromotor control of speech). The lack of speech production experience did not prevent anarthric/

dysarthric subjects from performing like their normally speaking physical-ly handicapped controls on some tasks, namely, those requiring the audi-tory discrimination of real words or sentence understanding as measured by a forced choice picture recognition task. But the subjects with anarthria or no speech production experience were less successful in their audito-ry discrimination of nonsense words (the equivalent of unfamiliar word), and they had poorer receptive vocabularies (Bishop, 1990).

Knowledge of words requires an ability to segment the speech sound stream. Thus, the observations of poorer than normal performance among anarthric/dysarthric speakers were viewed as partial support for theoreti-cal models of working memory, which implicate "articulatory coding" in the short-term memory of new verbal material (Gathercole & Baddeley, 1990). Bishop (1990) stated that:

> We should not conclude that physical impairment of the speech apparatus has no impact on language acquisition process. Inability to repeat does not prevent vocabulary acquisition but may retard it. (p. 218)

Although the lack of normal speech in the deaf leaves no doubt that audi-tory input is critical for its development, tactual input may not play a trivial role in development. Self-produced speech could speed up the rate of learning speech if more precise sensory information about the individual segments is required to build an articulatory motor program for speech production than is required to recognize an auditory pattern produced by someone else. It is known that young children can have good auditory dis-crimination and recognition of other people's speech, but still make articu-lation errors (Bird & Bishop, 1992; Winitz, 1989). External auditory dis-crimination exercises do not necessarily improve impaired articulation in treatment either (Monnin, 1984). Some children have difficulty aurally dis-criminating just those sounds that they cannot produce (Aungst & Frick, 1964; Bird & Bishop, 1992; Locke, 1980). But poor discrimination of exter-nal auditory input is not expected in the face of excellent articulation.

It is understandable why just listening to speech (external auditory input) may not provide easy access to speech sound segments. The individual speech sounds (i.e., consonants and vowels) occur with such short duration that it is difficult to differentiate segments, unless they are deliberately pro-longed, as is characteristic of child-directed speech (i.e., motherese; Owens, 1996, p. 233). Even when children can comprehend other people's speech, it does not mean that they do so by precisely segmenting and recognizing all the words in the speech stream. They can rely on their world knowledge to figure out the meaning in context (Chapman, 1978; Paul, 1990).

When speech segmentation begins, typically developing children may perceive units that are larger than the phoneme or even the word. These early segments can reflect a gestalt representation of the slower temporal changes in the prosodic contour of speech (Waterson, 1971). This reasoning is consistent with the observation that at the outset, young normal children with immature speech can be successful at recognizing verbal routines—the kind that reoccur in near frozen auditory form across different speech events (e.g., "How are you?" "There you go." "Okay." "Bye bye"). Such verbal routines can be processed, stored, and retrieved as an auditory whole or gestalt, which need not require precise segmentation of individual speech sounds. One implication is that tactually anchored auditory input may provide the easiest access to individual speech sounds while observed or external auditory input may provide the easier access to the prosodic or more global sound patterns.

Given the previous discussion, gestalt processing ought to be most characteristic of auditory speech processing in children without self-produced speech or poorly articulated speech. This conclusion was reached concerning 5- to 6-year-old children with expressive phonological impairment (Bird & Bishop, 1992; Bird, Bishop, & Freeman, 1995). They showed depressed performances in phoneme categorization and rhyme generation for both real and nonsense words. The outcomes were not explained as a motor problem. Bird and Bishop (1992) reasoned that the children had difficulty doing a deep analysis of the phonological string or possibly a conceptual analysis that is independent of sensory or motor processes. It was concluded that "adequate auditory discrimination does not necessarily mean that the child's processing of phonological input is normal" (p. 309). Within Affolter and Bischofberger's framework, one could assume that a "deep analysis" or "conceptual analysis" of a phonological string, as referred to by Bird and Bishop (1992), requires tactually anchored auditory perception.

The possibility that the lack of speech production experience may slow the rate of language acquisition is not refuted by the fact that some persons with congenital anarthria can perform a variety of segmentation tasks in speech perception studies, as has been shown (Bishop, 1993; Bishop & Robson, 1989). The evidence for such successful performance has so far come from observations of older physically handicapped subjects with cerebral palsy. They ranged from ages 10 to 16 years in studies by Bishop and colleagues. In Fourcin's (1975) frequently cited case study, the 34-year-old anarthric subject with good speech comprehension and spelling ability was even older.

Although subjects may perform adequately at an older age, they may take longer than normal to reach that level. Performance at older ages reflects the cumulative effect of experience. As familiarity with words increases, so should use of this stored information to extract new segment patterns heard in the external auditory signal. However, in the absence of longitudinal observations beginning at a young age, it is not known if or how developmental rate may have been affected in these older subjects with physical–motor handicaps and good speech segmentation skills. Still, most of the anarthric and dysarthric subjects observed by Bishop and Robson (1989) performed more poorly than their physically handicapped normal speaking peers on some segmentation tasks, even at the older ages.

4.2.3.3 Language Use or Pragmatics

Language use or pragmatics may require the search for the most complex information of all. It incorporates and adapts form–meaning relations to different situations for talking. Intuitively, a high level of *intermodal* organization is required. All the tactual, intermodal, and serial input about the content and forms of language must be integrated with the multiple sources of information in the extralinguistic contexts for talking. These extralinguistic contexts, which include places, participants, times, activity sequences, and so on, require the search for additional tactual, intermodal, and serial information in order to perceive the event as one that requires the use of particular form–meaning relations.

We can infer that *tactual* experiences are also foundational for language pragmatics or use because understanding of causes and effects is required. A speech act is inherently a goal-directed causative act designed to have an effect on another person. The emergence of communicative intent (namely the discovery that one's own vocal actions can affect the actions of another person) is likely to be primed by cause–effect understanding (Harding & Golinkoff, 1979), which originates with the tactually anchored input from physical nonverbal interactions. The very nature of social communication involves contingent relationships between speech acts. A prior utterance or speech act causes the speaker to respond in a certain way (Prutting & Kirchner, 1983).

Besides communicative intent, pragmatics also requires one to know something about how to express communicative intent in different situations. Learning to use language appropriately or adaptively in different situations builds on knowledge of self and other people as causal agents in achieving nonverbal interaction goals in situations. The search for *tactual* information is essential because the contexts for talking are strongly identified by what people do when they come together. The *doing* context, whether cooking, eating, bowling, and so on, also inevitably involves *sequences* or *series* of changes in the topological relationship between the body and the environment. Active participation in a social context would require the child to elicit such changes, thereby picking up tactual information and the associated intermodal and serial relationships required to recognize events as familiar for using particular linguistic patterns.

4.3 ABNORMAL LANGUAGE
AND NONVERBAL INTERACTIONS

If normal language learning is rooted in the perceptual–cognitive consequences of nonverbal interaction experience as argued before, then it is reasonable to expect abnormal language learning to be similarly rooted. However, it is recognized at the outset that a broad perceptual processing framework, such as that proposed by Affolter and Bischofberger, is unlikely to predict knowledge and use of a single morphological inflection, word meaning, speech sound, or pragmatic device. There is just too much individual variability on this level even for grammatical morphemes, which are so commonly described as delayed in development (Lahey, Chesnick, Menyuk, & Adams, 1992). Nonetheless, a framework should account for why such individual variability exists and why language disorders are associated with broad recurring patterns of delay such as those described next.

First, children with developmental language disorders show a quantitative lag in the amount and complexity of language acquired. No matter what aspect of language is studied, the results so often show that they talk less than their age-matched peers (Johnston, 1988; Miller, 1991; Rice, 1991) and they make more errors when they do talk. Rarely do deficits show up at one level of language. Several skills typically are delayed at the same time. For example, phonological delay may co-occur with lexical and grammatical delays.

Second, asynchronous performance patterns within and across different domains of language performances have been observed (Aram & Nation, 1975; Conti-Ramsden, Crutchley, & Botting, 1997; Rapin & Allen, 1983; Tager-Flusberg, 1994; Wolfus, Moscovitch, & Kinsbourne, 1980) . They show up as remarkable gaps in performance that sometimes coincide with expected patterns of normal development and sometimes not. For example, children can show larger than expected differences between language comprehension and expression. Conversely, language comprehension can appear remarkably less well developed than the expressive use of linguistic forms (nonexpected direction). For example, the ability to echo well-formed sentences can exceed understanding of their conventional meaning. In addition, both language comprehension and expression can appear to be much better or worse than is nonverbal performance (cf. children with Williams Syndrome (Bellugi, Marks, Bihrle, & Sabo, 1994) and those with specific language impairment (Stark & Tallal, 1981b)). These variable patterns of delay imply that some abilities remain more intact than others.

In attempts to explain such widely ranging patterns of language disorders in terms of flawed information-processing mechanisms, little is known about how a broadened view of perception, such as that proposed by Affolter and Bischofberger, may fit into this picture. Information-processing accounts of disordered language are too simplistic when they imply that the source of the language learning problem is the overload of information. In stressing information overload, attention is focused on the inherent complexity of the stimuli that others select for the child to process in the environment outside of the child. The implication is that such linguistically complex stimuli can be handed over in a direct way to a perceptual processing system, which has a fixed or absolute capacity.

In contrast, Affolter and Bischofberger propose that one must also appeal to the child's own internally organized perceptual activity as the basis of poor information processing. Otherwise it is difficult to explain why in their studies, normal children's responses to the same stimuli varied as a function of age, and why children were able to process increasingly more complex stimulus events as age increased. Different responses to the same stimuli reflect the relative nature of the perceiver—not the external stimuli.

Consequently, Affolter and Bischofberger do not frame language disorders simply as a problem of information overload in external input. They frame the problem as the inability to pick up adequate information from the external input due to poorly organized perceptual activity. The emphasis is on the organization of the perceiver's search for information. Poor organization of perceptual activity is traced to inadequate experience with nonverbal problem-solving events of daily life. When the search for information from such events cannot be guided by adequate organization of tactual, intermodal, or serial input as a result of central nervous system pathology, then poor or deviant information is expected to result.

If Affolter and Bischofberger are right, then we can expect children with language disorders to approach the complex task of learning language without two benefits that should accrue from having adequately organized nonverbal interaction experience. First, they will approach the task with a perceptual system that is poorly organized to search for one or another type of linguistic information due to a tactual, intermodal, or serial deficit. Second, they will approach the task without age-appropriate knowledge of the world that can support the conceptual cognitive demands of language learning. As a result, children with language disorders should exhibit (a) a general language delay as a consequence of not picking up enough relevant information about what is to be learned by a given age, and (b) asynchronous patterns of language development as a consequence of picking up different types of inadequate information.

4.3.1 General Language Delay: A Consequence of Inadequate Information

General language delay is evident from the lack of age-appropriate linguistic skills due to late language onset and the use of a simpler grammar than peers at comparable ages.

4.3.1.1 Late Onset

Many children with language disorders say their first words later than normal. The most severe ones along the autism spectrum may not say words until 5 or 6 years of age or later, if at all. Some children say first words on time but fail to progress rapidly from single words to a multi-word grammar. The negative effects of late and slow development are cumulative, as less prior linguistic knowledge can be brought to bear on each new learning experience relative to normal learners. A general language delay ought to be a consequence of perceptual activity that is not organized well enough to pick up relevant information quickly. Whatever is meant by an adequately organized search for information, it is intuitively likely to include not only the ability to pick up critical types of information, but also the ability to pick up simultaneously multiple sources of critical information. The synchronization of multiple sources of sensory inputs, as does occur in nonverbal interaction events, should increase the *efficiency* of information processing. One effect of efficient processing ought to be an increased amount of input that can be processed at one time—an overall effect of a speeded rate of information processing.

There is evidence that children with language disorders are slower than their age-matched normal peers in the online processing of oral language (Lahey & Edwards, 1996; Montgomery, Scudder, & Moore, 1990; Weismer & Hesketh, 1996). Lahey and Edwards (1996) went so far as to propose that a neuromotor maturational lag explained why language-impaired children name pictures and execute nonverbal motor tasks more slowly than their age-matched normal peers. Language skills will not be at age-appropriate levels when the amount and type of information that can be processed at one time are less than what is typically done by certain ages.

4.3.1.2 Acquisition of a Simplified Grammar

The more complex the linguistic stimuli are, the more likely can relevant information be missed by inadequately organized perceptual activity to guide the search for information. It ought not be surprising then, that a simplified grammar is a common characteristic of all children with language disorders who get inadequate information of one kind or another. A simplified grammar means that complexity is missing. Typically, what is missing are the more advanced grammatical features, which also are the later appearing features in a typically developing child. In order to get all the critical features from complex input, the search for information must be more tightly organized than it is for simpler input. The need for a level of higher perceptual organization translates into later development because more experiences are needed over time in order to pick up all the relevant information.

If the demands for processing linguistic information are heavy relative to the perceiver's processing ability at the time, then linguistic input is simplified or sacrificed even for young language learners without perceptual problems. Bloom and Beckwith (1989) reported that normal children at the one-word stage did not talk and express affect at the same time. At a later age, when they did begin to do both things at one time, it was not without some linguistic cost. The children used only familiar, frequent, and well-practiced words while affect was expressed at low intensity and only with positive valence.

Similarly, children with language disorders may rely on simple verbal routines to express meaning. In the most severe cases, linguistic forms are used without conventional meaning. Articulation may break down as the length and grammatical complexity of utterances increase. It ought not be surprising that phonetically less salient features of the grammar in the ambient language like inflectional markers are often sacrificed, as has been observed across languages.

4.3.2   Asynchronous Patterns: A Consequence of Differential Access to Inadequate Information

Although simplification of grammatical patterns is generally characteristic of disordered language, children can differ in the kind of simplification patterns exhibited. Some variable patterns reflect individual differences because children bring varying experiences to bear on the learning of a particular linguistic feature or skill; for example, a grammatical rule or semantic category may be known at a certain age by one disordered child and not another one, because the feature happens to be more salient in a linguistic environment for some reason.

Other individual differences reflect systematic subgroup biases in performances (Aram & Nation, 1975; Wolfus et al., 1980), which may result from lack of access to one or another type of information. Despite differences among the many taxonomies that have been proposed for categorizing subgroups of language disorders, they all commonly reflect the unevenness in the performance profiles. That is, children in a given subgroup perform better in some areas than in others. These uneven profiles may reflect differential access to certain types of information.

Although the acquisition of linguistic meaning, use, and form was each argued to require the search for tactual, intermodal, and serial information, one aspect of language may be more heavily dependent than is another on a particular type of information. For example, I have proposed that pragmatics or language use may require the most complex level of intermodal integration. This claim predicts that children with intermodal perceptual difficulties would be particularly vulnerable to poor language performance in pragmatics, even though difficulties in all areas of language could occur. Hence, the performance patterns of language disorder subgroups could vary with whether a given performance domain requires the search for a greater or lesser degree of one or another type of information to which they are differentially vulnerable. This line of argument is pursued further in the discussion that follows. I speculate about what kind of language performance profile might be observed for children in each of the perceptual disorder subgroups that Affolter and Bischofberger described. In doing so, I present corroborating evidence for these performance profiles from the research literature on language disorder subgroups.

4.3.2.1 Tactual–Kinesthetic Perceptual Deficit

4.3.2.1.1 Semantic–Syntactic Disorders. As Affolter and Bischofberger have already described, children with a primary tactual–kinesthetic deficit require stronger than usual changes of resistance and associated changes of topological relationships in interaction events in order to get the essential information. Such children, therefore, should have difficulty judging when an object is touched or an action goal is reached. For this reason, fewer causative action relations may be successfully experienced or understood; and in turn, the acquisition of language content, form, and use is expected to be adversely affected.

The semantic–syntactic system ought to be particularly impoverished with pronounced gaps in the verb lexicon, given the assumed critical role of tactual input in gaining knowledge about causes and effects. Accordingly, language comprehension skills ought to be depressed even when the child is able to segment words in the sound stream or echo them with reasonable clarity.

In the research literature, a semantic–pragmatic subgroup with receptive language delay has been described for language-disordered children with autism (Rapin & Allen, 1983) and those without it (Conti-Ramsden et al., 1997). The difficulty that some language-disordered children have with learning action verbs, in particular, has recently come to the fore (Kelly & Rice, 1994; Rice & Bode, 1993; Watkins, Rice, & Moltz, 1993).

4.3.2.1.2 Phonological Disorders. In the most severe children with a tactual–kinesthetic deficit, deviant semantic–syntactic patterns are expected to coexist with phonological delay when disturbed nonverbal interactions affect oral body structures in addition to other body sites (e.g., limbs, torso, and fingers). These children may go through the stage of mouthing objects at older ages than expected. In addition, they may have difficulty making nonspeech movements of the oral structures on demand, or appear not to know where oral structures (e.g., the tongue), are in the mouth. Prelinguistic babbling may be absent or reduced too.

Once speech emerges, the pattern of phonological errors may reflect deviant rather than simple developmental delay. For example, vowels, which typically develop early in normal children, may be unintelligible, even when some consonants are accurately produced. Unusual phonological processes (e.g., spirantization, metathesis, epenthesis, and so on) may occur, along with abnormal prosodic patterns involving stress and rhythm. In other words, these are likely to be the kind of children with intractable speech articulation errors, which often are attributed to a developmental speech dysarthria or dyspraxia.

Developmental speech apraxia or dysarthria is still a controversial diagnosis (Shriberg, Aram, & Kwiatkowski, 1997b). It is often identified as a motor disorder in the absence of frank neurological insult. However, a tactual–perceptual rather than a motor basis for the difficulty also has been hypothesized (Shriberg, Aram, & Kwiatkowski, 1997a). Despite our inability to explain why they exist, phonological deficits have figured prominently in the efforts to identify language disorder subgroups. In some children, expressive language delay is restricted to the phonological domain (Aram & Nation, 1975). In other children, the phonological delay is part of a general expressive problem that also includes delays in formulation, repetition, and/or language comprehension (Aram & Nation, 1975; Conti-Ramsden et al., 1997; Rapin & Allen, 1983). The latter subgroup closely fits the language patterns predicted for the most severe children with tactual–kinesthetic deficits as described by Affolter & Bischofberger.

4.3.2.2 Intermodal Perceptual Deficit

Affolter and Bischofberger proposed that children with primary intermodal difficulties have difficulty integrating sensory input from different sensory modalities in nonverbal interaction events. As a result, their perceptual organization is predicted to be abnormally attuned to picking up information separately within each modality, whichever single input is most salient at the moment. Such an abnormal perceptual organization ought to adversely affect both the comprehension and expression of conventional linguistic meaning in a pervasive way.

Language, like all complex behavior, makes high demands on the search for intermodal information as argued earlier in this chapter. When learning language, intermodal or contingent relationships between different sensory inputs (tactual–kinesthetic and auditory) are required to access the spoken forms of language (i.e., solve the problem of segmenting the speech stream of sounds). A different set of intermodal relationships is required to make the form–content connections (i.e., solve the semantic mapping problem). Of the three language components, pragmatics or language use may place the most demand on the search for intermodal information. It incorporates meaning, form, and use relations in even the simplest speech act. The coordination of content, form, and use relationships then becomes very complex—requiring the coordination of multiple sensory sources.

A language problem could reflect a breakdown or reduction in the number and types of intermodal relations that are picked up within and across the different domains. In the most extreme case, the child may fail to acquire any aspect of language, given that even a single domain of language (e.g., speech sound articulation) requires search and storage of intermodal information. Children will appear less severe, if they can integrate information well enough within a single language domain, but cannot integrate multiple domains of input. In such cases, speech forms may be spoken or imitated in isolation of meaning or use, as Lahey (1988) described. Alternatively, children may reach a stage at which they can integrate information across two, but not three linguistic domains. For example, form–meaning relations may be comprehended and expressed, but inappropriately adapted to the context of use. For example, a child who announces in the classroom that he or she "*has to go pee*," conveys the proper form–content relations, but is not sensitive to the pragmatic context that requires different word choices and request manners.

Within a given language domain, dissociations may show up even when information is integrated well enough across domains to function at some level. With respect to language forms, children with intermodal perceptual deficits may be able to produce speech sounds with reasonable "clarity," but without the integration of additional input required for prosodic variation or affective expression. Speech may sound wooden and mechanical. With respect to linguistic meaning, the understanding of words may include the names of visible objects but not grammatical reference to cause–effect events, which requires the integration of visual and tactual–kinesthetic information. In language use or pragmatics, children may be able to generate appropriate content–form relations only in highly stereotypic or routine situations that are familiar, and especially if the familiarity can be cued by a single modality of input such as vision.

The children who fit these profiles are among those who present classic autistic symptoms and are described as having global impairment of receptive and expressive language (Aram & Nation, 1975; Wolfus et al., 1980) and semantic–pragmatic delays (Rapin & Allen, 1983). The pragmatic–affective delays in autism can be observed when other aspects of language seem relatively intact. Lahey (1988) described a language disorder subgroup in terms of the isolation of form, content, and use relations.

4.3.2.3 Serial Perceptual Deficit

Affolter and Bischofberger proposed that children with a serial integration deficit have primary difficulty tracking the sequential order of stimulus events. It is easy to see why children with serial problems could have some difficulty learning language, even when nonverbal performances seem intact. The combinatorial nature of spoken language forms makes very high demand on serial processing. Words are formed and recognized by the sequential order of speech sounds. For example, the words, *tip* and *pit*, include identical phonemes in converse sequential order to code their differences in meaning. To process a grammatical construction consisting of just two words with three sounds each (e.g., *come here /kam hir/*), at least six bits of information occurring in a particular order must be included in whatever input is registered by the nervous system. Perception of these forms is all the more difficult because each sound is so brief. If speech production requires more precise perceptual tracking of the individual speech sounds than does comprehension, then skills may be more depressed in the former than the latter for children with serial perceptual deficits. Thal et al.'s (1991) study of severe expressive language problems in young children is relevant here. The expressive language problems were more severe among 12- to 35-month-old children with focal injury to the left posterior than anterior rolandic area of the brain. The authors concluded that:

> During the period in which children are learning to produce speech, they have to analyze the speech stream in sufficient detail to permit the construction of a motor analogue. It is possible that the selectively greater problems in expressive language displayed by children with left posterior damage derive not from motor problems but from limitations on the kind of sensory analysis that is required for a precise sensory-to-motor mapping. (p. 525)

On the other hand, language comprehension ought to make less demand on the serial organization of perceptual activity than does expression. This is because children can use their nonverbal world knowledge to make sense of verbal events (Chapman, 1978; Paul, 1990), even if they are unable to differentiate all the segments that they hear.

Nonverbal performance may make even less demand on the serial organization of input than does language comprehension. In fact nonverbal performing and understanding of events can appear to be intact in the face of poor verbal understanding in many children diagnosed with language disorders along the SLI–LD spectrum. The temporal sequences of many nonverbal events change more slowly than verbal events, and fewer events may involve an obligatory order. When they do, the order makes sense in terms of cause–effect relationships understood from physical nonverbal interaction experiences, some of which are likely to be embedded in the familiar and routine daily-life events (Slackman, 1985). For example, all the nonverbal events involved in putting on shoes need not follow a strict order. One must put the sock on the foot before the shoe. However, it does not matter to the goal whether the sock and shoe are put first on the left or right foot; nor does it matter whether one foot is completely finished before the other one is begun. A child could choose to put the sock on each foot first and then the shoes—each time varying which foot is done first. One can observe or perform events related to each larger step in the event sequence before shifting to the next step. The sequences of such nonverbal events that frame the communicative contexts of daily life (eating, dressing, and so on) reoccur often enough to become familiar.

In contrast, the generative nature of spoken language leads often to novel word sequences rather than highly routinized or stereotypic ones. So the online serial processing demands ought to be higher for verbal than nonverbal events. Thus, it is understandable why some children can appear to have intact nonverbal performances but fail in language, as in the case of the so called specific language impairment syndrome or SLI. However, the same type of child could show depressed nonverbal performances if the task is serially taxing enough.

The research literature leaves little doubt that many children with language disorders exhibit serial processing difficulties, particularly those with SLI who score within the normal range on standard nonverbal intelligence tests (Stark & Tallal, 1981a, 1988; Tallal et al., 1981; Tallal et al., 1985; Tallal & Merzenich, 1996). Curtiss (1991) reported that SLI children performed more poorly than normal children on sequentially cued sentences than on the nonsequentially cued ones. Rapin and Allen (1983) described a clinical subgroup with a predominant expressive disorder and good comprehension that fits with the SLI-serial impaired child.

Thus, the appearance of intact nonverbal cognition and language comprehension skills may simply reflect less demanding processing of temporal sequences relative to language production, as discussed before. Nonverbal tests of cognition are loaded with visual discrimination items that do not challenge serial processing difficulties.

4.4 IMPLICATIONS FOR LANGUAGE INTERVENTION: GUIDED INTERACTION THERAPY

4.4.1 Principles of Language Therapy

Guided Interaction Therapy is anchored by the goal of improving the child's search for more adequate information in nonverbal, problem-solving interaction events, given that they are assumed to be the root for developing both verbal and nonverbal skills. Affolter and Bischofberger have already described what is entailed in working with patients at the root (i.e., facilitating nonverbal interaction experiences in daily problem-solving events). Here I focus broadly on how language intervention is integrated with such work. Although nonverbal interaction experiences are expected to build the perceptual–cognitive foundation for language learning, treatment at this level alone is not likely to be sufficient for disordered children to figure out how words map onto the content of these nonverbal experiences. The procedures for helping patients to pick up more adequate information from nonverbal interaction events (work at the root) do not require language; nor are they based on assumptions about how children come to match linguistic forms to nonverbal experience. At the same time, the relationship between the surface forms of a language and the content of nonverbal experiences is neither direct nor obvious. Therefore, it seems necessary to directly facilitate language learning. Affolter and Bischofberger agree, but the issue is how to do it.

Guided Interaction Therapy does not isolate the child's language learning from the natural interaction events of daily life. Therapists are expected (a) to help patients to pick up more adequate information from nonverbal interaction, and (b) to structure linguistic input and use of other symbols (e.g., pictures) around such events. In this way, words and other symbolic forms are always connected to the child's experience in a direct way. At the same time, therapists are expected to consider the situation-dependent nature of linguistic performance. The complexity of the linguistic task is controlled by choosing natural, functional event contexts for therapy, and simplifying the linguistic input, as discussed next.

4.4.1.1 Choosing Natural, Functional Event Contexts for Therapy

In established therapy approaches, a natural, functional context for intervention is one that allows spontaneous use of language in a socially interactive context, as opposed to drill work on isolated grammatical or phonological features. In Affolter and Bischofberger's interaction framework, a natural, functional intervention context is defined first in physical terms, although social interaction involving linguistic communication is typically a part of the range of rich experiences ordinarily associated with a natural physical interaction event in real world contexts. The therapeutic context must offer the possibility for a child to interact by eliciting changes of topological relationships between the body and the environment; and such changes must be elicited to achieve a functional problem-solving goal. The latter requirement is not met when, for example, a child opens and closes the same door, or even different doors all day long, as some severe children may do. In this case, the door opening and closing involve changes of topological relations between the body and the environment, but the change is not connected to a functional goal of daily life. Ordinarily, doors are opened or closed as part of a sequence of related events required to solve problems of daily life. For example, the room is hot; so the door is opened for ventilation. A sweater is needed for going outside, but it is located in a different room; so one opens the door to that room in order to get the sweater, and so on. More often than not, such natural contexts are connected to routine daily activities of dressing, washing up, watering a plant, and so on in which other people also participate. To get the functional part (the reason why one elicits a topological change) out of nonverbal interaction events, a higher level of perceptual–cognitive organization is obviously required than what is required to merely elicit a change of topological relationship.

There is value in structuring talk around a natural, functional context, as defined in Affolter and Bischofberger's terms. It should be possible to facilitate the acquisition of a linguistic repertoire that can serve the goals of daily living. Routine daily activities (e.g., eating, dressing, washing up, and so on), in particular, ought to be especially helpful for two reasons. First, they are culturally and socially meaningful. Consequently, the words connected to them are likely to be used by the child in functional situations and heard often in the ambient linguistic environment.

Second, routine daily activities are also likely to be familiar in the child's experiences. Structuring talk around familiar routines may also reduce the information load by allowing the child to set up expectancies about what will happen first, second, and so on in an event (Nelson, 1995). Therefore, processing capacity may be freed up enough to search for other information in the event, including the words that are spoken. In one experimental study, Farrar, Friend, and Forbes (1993) recorded the language spoken by young normal children in repeated episodes of the same event context over time. The significant increase in the amount and complexity of the children's talk was attributed to the increasing familiarity with the same event over time. So therapists are surprised, but should not be, when caregivers tell them that a child with language disorders talks a lot more at home than in the artificial contexts where most speech–language therapy is done.

Nelson (1986, 1995) proposed further that routine daily events provide the structure for conceptual categories that support nonverbal and verbal knowledge. Whereas the basic structure of a routine event may not change much from one time to another, changes within the event structure are inescapable, given the dynamic reality of daily living. For example, taking a bath has an action sequence for the young child that may include undressing, getting into the tub, splashing with the toy ducks, scrubbing the body, getting out of the tub, toweling down, and dressing (K. Nelson, 1995). But there can be changes in the bathing container, the person giving the bath, the bath objects (e.g., the type of toys, soap, towel used, and so on). Nelson (1986, 1995) described these changeable open-ended parts of the event as "slot fillers." They identify the roles that objects play in the event, and allow novel aspects of experiences to be conceptually integrated with what is already known and familiar. Objects and people that share the same role or slot in the event become conceptually linked. So that all the different types of soaps occupy the "thing used for washing the body" slot in the bath scene event, for example.

These are the same kind of elements in interaction events that language therapists could modify in the efforts to enrich a therapeutic context consisting of familiar daily routines. By introducing novelty into an event structure that also has familiar aspects, perceptual and cognitive processes are stimulated. At the same time, all these changes in the event are likely to require new vocabulary and sentence frames. After all, a word comes to represent a whole category of related experiences, which form a nonverbal conceptual category. For example, the English word, soap, symbolizes all the soap objects ever experienced. But it is their role in events that unifies and organizes the different experiences into conceptually and linguistically codable categories.

4.4.1.2   Simplifying the Linguistic Input

The complexity of the linguistic input is reduced in two ways within Guided Interaction Therapy. First, it is reduced by not talking to the child at the same time as the action is performed. Words and pictures are mapped onto events before, and especially right after one or more goal-directed changes of topological relations between body and environment are elicited. The reason is that a child's attention can be diverted from the information in nonverbal interaction events when the therapist talks at the same time. Talking also can divert a therapist's attention away from the guided interaction event that is being attempted at the same time. This is a processing capacity issue. At the same time, "true" symbolic representation is facilitated when words are experienced in the absence of the interaction events to which they refer.

The complexity of the language task is reduced further by putting comprehension instead of expression in the foreground. Language comprehension is less demanding for any learner because the responses do not have to be formulated at the level of complexity required for speech production. Therapists can rely on nonverbal means (e.g., pointing, eye gaze, affective expression, or performance of an action) to determine or observe whether the child recognizes and understands words. Thus, children are not required to imitate or say words as a measure of response change. Speech production is not discouraged, and it is even necessary when intervention aims to improve articulation clarity and other aspects of expression. However, the primary goal of the language intervention is the acquisition of unknown form/content/use relations. Achieving this goal requires comprehension to be in the foreground. Linguistic expression, on the other hand, reflects what a child has already learned.

Therapists make linguistic comprehension easier in a couple of ways. First, they can do all the things they usually do to simplify the linguistic input when teaching language. They can speak slowly, shorten and repeat sentences, and so on.

Second, therapists can choose words that map onto salient aspects of the felt cause–effect experience. Because events involve action relations between objects , words that refer to visual experience (e.g., color names), are not stressed in the input. Moreover, events are best represented by sentences and not single words. Sentences with action verbs code the object relations embedded in nonverbal interaction events. Verb-embedded simple word combinations may include the agent and/or object of the action referring to a single event frame of experience (e.g., *Mary cuts/ cuts bread/ Mary cuts bread*). Language can be elaborated by respecting the principles of teaching the rules of grammar and discourse, so long as talk is connected to real event experiences. For children on a production level, articulation therapy can be incorporated as well, but again in the context of meaningful representation of real events.

4.4.1.3 *Expected Outcomes of Guided Interaction Intervention*

When using Guided Interaction intervention, therapists are expected to periodically evaluate behavioral changes across time using tests or individually tailored protocols, as is typically done. Questions about progress are the same ones that are usually asked. For example, does a child now exhibit skills that were not in the repertoire before. Ideally, linguistic performance is assessed in several situations with different information processing demands. In this way, the competence and performance distinction is respected in making judgments about a child's level of performance.

Growth is expected on both nonverbal and verbal levels, given the holistic nature of the treatment. Multiple skills may emerge at the same time and may include some that have not been part of the therapy experience. This is because skills are assumed to be interrelated rather than independent—their relationships defined by the level of organized perceptual activity required to attain them as a result of nonverbal interaction experiences. Optimizing the development of multiple skill areas at the same time is desirable because children with language disorders often exhibit many aberrant verbal and nonverbal behaviors.

4.4.2   Comparison of Treatment Approaches

It is instructive to consider if and how the Guided Interaction treatment paradigm differs from existing approaches to developmental language disorders.

4.4.2.1   Overview of Established Treatment Approaches

At first glance, the Guided Interaction approach to language intervention does not appear to differ from the eclectic mix of existing strategies for teaching early language (Fey, 1986; Lahey, 1988; Nelson, 1993). The value of using tactual input, in addition to auditory and visual input for teaching language, is attested by several types of clinical intervention models. For example, co-active movement, used with the severely mentally retarded populations (Sternberg, McNerney, & Pegnatore, 1985), promotes a form of physical guiding, and Prompt Therapy (Chumpelik, 1984) emphasizes tactual cuing in treating severe articulation problems. Moreover, *focused stimulation* as an intervention procedure (Fey, 1986; Girolametto, Pearce, & Weitzman, 1996) emphasizes language comprehension instead of language production.

Natural contexts are regarded as a functional necessity for teaching language as a social communication skill. Although there is no uniform interpretation of what is meant by natural, there is the collective sense that a holistic, communicative context is needed in order to help children learn to use language in socially interactive ways. Such functional contexts for language treatment are embedded in concepts like *whole language* (for example, Norris & Damico, 1990), *classroom based assessment* and treatment (e.g., Nelson, 1993), and Milieu therapy (e.g., Kaiser & Hester, 1994). Constable (1986) went so far as to illustrate how language teaching could be structured around event scripts and slot-filler categories of functional everyday experiences, as conceptualized by Nelson (1986).

Furthermore, clinicians typically are taught that they can optimize linguistic input by altering its amount and salience. For example, they may simplify grammatical input and repeat the same words many times. Speech rate may be decreased and the targeted words may be stressed over others in sound stream. The acoustic spectrum of speech input may be altered to exaggerate or augment certain signal properties, as Paula Tallal and colleagues have recently shown could be done (Tallal et al., 1996; Tallal & Merzenich, 1996).

There is even growing sensitivity to the idea of orienting language therapy around action events. It is reflected in the emerging shift from noun to verb-focused therapy. The idea is not to replace nouns with verbs but to include verbs, which historically were less emphasized. Bloom (1970, 1981) was among the earliest scholars to argue that the verb is central to grammatical development. Recently, Rice (1991) and Watkins (1994) proposed that verbs should be the centerpiece of grammatical intervention. Many of the grammatical challenges for language-disordered children center on verbs and their arguments in sentences.

A verb-focused therapy ought to efficiently facilitate the learning of many linguistic features because the verb is central to a number of grammatical operations. For example, it conditions the agents and objects in sentences. Different sentences can be created around a single verb by changing its co-occurring noun arguments, for example, (Mary) (John) (she/he) stirs; (Mary and John) (they) stir; Mary stirs (it)(soup) (vegetables)(paint), and so on. In English, inflectional markers also pivot on the verb (e.g., stirs, stirring, stirred, has stirred, and so on). According to Watkins (1994), this type of verb-centered grammatical teaching will be most successful, if built around linguistic input that is tied to "real events," which inevitably will include nonverbal interaction events.

However, all of these different intervention procedures do not appear to be guided by a common theoretical framework that clarifies their rationale and unifies the relationships among them. Nor do they appear to be guided by common assumptions about the nature of language disorders or what is required to perceive and learn language. Established clinical intervention practices can be described as eclectic and fragmented. Clinical techniques may proliferate because each one is designed to focus on a different skill, which therapists assume can be adequately taught in isolation of other skills.

In contrast, Guided Interaction Therapy is a more holistic approach than are established approaches to language intervention. Skills or behaviors are assumed to be interrelated because of their dependency on a common root—namely, nonverbal interaction experience in daily events. The integration of the language input with input about nonverbal events in the same therapy session means that professional roles are redefined. Thus, more careful scrutiny leads to the conclusion that established clinical practices differ from Guided Interaction intervention on several fronts.

4.4.2.2   Comparison of Established Treatments
With Guided Interaction Treatment

Guided Interaction Therapy is guided by theoretical assumptions about the nature of development and language disorders that put constraints on language therapy—constraints on the timing, modality, context, and complexity of giving linguistic input in ways that differ from established practices. A few examples are singled out next.

4.4.2.2.1   When to Talk.   Therapists, who use conventional approaches, assume that for the child to learn language, one must talk all the time, and at the same time as the child is acting on the environment. It is not surprising, therefore, that the idea of talking after an event, as Guided Interaction Therapy requires, is not usually understood, or respected. This is the case, although studies show that in natural situations, children and their caretakers seem to instinctively reduce their talk, and even their affective expressions at the moment of the action (Bloom, 1996; Tomasello & Kruger, 1992).

4.4.2.2.2   Emphasis on Language Comprehension.   The emphasis of Guided Interaction treatment on language comprehension as opposed to production is not likely to be viewed as an adequate approach either. Many therapists (and parents too) are likely to conclude that a child is not progressing in language learning unless words are actually spoken. This is the case, although it is well known that language comprehension is very important to communication, and that all people have higher competency in language understanding than expression.

Of course, the emphasis on expressive language goals in established procedures extends beyond its obvious importance for participating in a social community. There is the issue of professional accountability, and how to measure it . Miller and Paul (1995) have pointed out that reliable ways to measure language comprehension, especially in natural spontaneous situations, are practically nonexistent or limited at best. They offer some ways to do better in this area.

4.4.2.2.3   Physical Interaction Events as a Central Focus.   More fundamental than the issues of when to talk in therapy or which language modality to emphasize is the structuring of the language therapy around nonverbal interactions in daily problem-solving events. Most professionals (and parents too) are likely to view such a treatment focus as not having anything to do with language. This is the case, despite the fact that language is rarely learned or used naturally in contexts that exclude nonverbal interaction events.

Physical guiding as a therapeutic procedure for facilitating the input of information from nonverbal interactions would be alien to most speech–language therapists. They are likely to erroneously view it as having a motor rather than a perceptual–cognitive goal, and therefore in the domain of occupational or physical therapy. Even were perceptual–cognitive development understood to be its goal, a child is still likely to be referred to other professionals (e.g., psychologists, special education teachers, and so on), given current definitions of professional roles.

The speech–language therapist's role seems to be dedicated just to putting words with what are assumed to be already stored experiences. Given this assumption, therapists do not make a point to work in the context of real events because they are not focally concerned with developing nonverbal cognition, or assume that they can do so in isolation of real events.

Instead of mapping words onto real events, as is done in Guided Interaction Therapy, therapists attempt to map words onto demonstrations of real experience. This often amounts to using pictures, toys, or games, which are themselves symbols of reality. Consider the recently developed Fast Forward intervention program. A child with language disorders is treated using computer video games in which the acoustic spectrum of speech signals is altered (Merzenich et al., 1996; Tallal & Merzenich, 1996; Tallal et al., 1996). Such a therapeutic context seems more artificial than real, given that children learn language in natural social–physical interactive contexts, and not at a computer desk. So Fey (1996) was right to question whether the dramatic gains in language comprehension, reportedly yielded by the Fast Forward auditory processing program, actually do generalize to natural situations.

The previous scenario suggests that what may seem similar about established practices and Guided Interaction Therapy—namely, the emphasis on functional, holistic contexts for therapy, is in fact very different. In established intervention approaches, physical interaction experiences are not in the foreground, if attended to at all. Functional contexts refer to the social interactive use of language. Strategies like recasts and expansions of a child's utterances are applied. To be successful then, a child must be already on a verbal level and even able to produce meaningful speech at some level.

Such approaches may work well enough for those children who have already reached a certain level of semiotic development so that nonverbal symbols (pictures, toys, computer games) are enough to retrieve their stored experiences for learning new words and grammatical rules. But what about children who do not recognize pictures, play with toys, or operate a computer appropriately, if at all?

4.4.2.2.4 *The Cognitive Referencing Issue.*

When there is evidence that the acquisition of linguistic skill is affected by conceptual deficiencies, Johnston (1988) proposed that clinicians "may need to wait for necessary cognitive growth or develop nonverbal t aining activities that would accelerate such growth." (pp. 707–708).

This proposal makes sense, except that established approaches to language therapy are not geared to promote such growth. If tactual input is essential to developing the perceptual–cognitive base of language, as Affolter and Bischofberger have argued, then looking at pictures or a therapist's demonstrations of action events are not sufficient forms of input for conceptual learning. Moreover, some children do not thrive when placed in therapeutic contexts that are not geared toward real events. When behavior is disruptive or inattentive, a therapist may conclude that a child is not cognitively ready to learn language, and therefore should not receive language intervention. Such a recommendation is reinforced when verbal performance is judged to be comparable to nonverbal cognitive performance.

The use of cognitive referencing for diagnosing a language disorder or denying access to services has been vigorously denounced by scholars and practitioners alike (Lahey, 1988, 1990; Nelson, 1993, p. 72). There is good reason to do so, not the least of which is the way cognitive competence is assessed. It is typically assessed in a static and absolute way, and the outcomes are interpreted as having a direct dependent relationship to the level of language skill attained. Furthermore, static measures do not assess a child's learning potential. They assess the competency that a child has already attained, and as can be demonstrated in a single context at that. Affolter and Bischofberger would argue that observing performance in a single situation may underestimate a child's real cognitive competence, not to mention the child's potential to solve problems were adequate tactually anchored information available while interacting. A single performance context does not take into account the differential effect of situation-dependent information on performance.

Furthermore, in Affolter and Bischofberger's nonverbal interaction framework, the nonverbal cognitive skills tested under any condition are not assumed to predict language learning in a direct way. Both verbal and nonverbal skills are assumed to emerge independently and as indirectly related outcomes of their common links to nonverbal interaction experience. Thus, in Guided Interaction intervention, language learning is not separated from efforts to improve nonverbal interaction.

Thus, cognitive referencing is not an inherently bad idea. After all, a therapist would not be expected to teach the formal rules of grammar to a typically developing 1-year-old child, partly because of cognitive limitations at this age. So why can't the same kind of reasoning also apply to a child with language disorders? The main reason is that cognitive referencing decisions about children with disorders may not be defensible, given existing views of nonverbal cognition and its assumed dependent relationship to language, measurement issues aside. Affolter and Bischofberger's interaction framework offers an alternative view of these relationships that could turn out to be clinically useful in dealing with this issue.

4.5   THE EMPIRICAL CHALLENGE

In this book, it has been argued that the acquisition of nonverbal and verbal behavior in normal and clinical groups can be interpreted within the nonverbal interaction framework proposed by Affolter and Bischofberger. The relevance of their framework to learning language has been emphasized in this chapter, in particular. Much of the argument rested on speculation and indirect empirical evidence from existing research. Such evidence is probably most useful for raising new research questions. Demonstrating that nonverbal interactions in daily problem-solving events impact on language learning, as argued in this chapter, presents an empirical challenge. Meeting this empirical challenge is not without difficulty.

It has been difficult to design studies that unequivocally separate an hypothesized cause of language disorders from the hypothesized effect. That is, investigators have not known for sure whether an observed effect was the cause or consequence of the language disorder. Besides that, perception is inherently difficult to study as a causal factor because it cannot be observed directly. It must be inferred from behavioral observations. It is especially difficult to identify a cause–effect relationship between language and a multifactor model of perception such as that proposed by Affolter and Bischofberger. They view nonverbal interaction experience as the primary source or root of development, and perception as one of the factors that contributes to successful interactions. In fact, a perceptual deficit is assumed to be related to language learning only indirectly and by virtue of its effect on interaction. This point of view has far reaching research implications for (a) the types of questions and hypotheses that could be posed about language-learning principles and their clinical application to children with language disorders, and (b) the types of methods used to investigate them, as considered next.

4.5.1   Questions and Hypotheses

Issues of normal and abnormal language learning are considered first, followed by issues dealing with clinical application.

4.5.1.1   *Learning and Development Issues*

Obviously, there are still many questions that should be asked and answered about the contribution of nonverbal interaction experience to nonverbal perceptual–conceptual development in normal children. The contemporary literature continues to reflect the debate on whether conceptual development is favored by visual perceptual categories or by functional categories, which are rooted in interaction events. This debate was recently reviewed by Booth (1998). It is worth noting that her study showed that young infants were more likely to learn, and learn faster, the visual distinctions between categories when they had produced the motions themselves than when they had merely seen either static or moving visual images.

The larger issue here is to what extent language learning for any child, normal or not, is driven by physical nonverbal interaction experiences in daily events. A suitable test of any theory hinges on the validity of its principal construct. In this case, that construct is nonverbal interaction experience in daily events. Fortunately, the questions do not have to be pitched at so basic a level as whether interaction exists in the sense that Affolter and Bischofberger have defined it. Although we may not know now how to quantify nonverbal interaction events well enough, it is not so abstract a notion as the Language Acquisition Device in Chomsky's earlier theory of generative syntax. A nonverbal interaction event is easily observed in ordinary situations. In the simplest form, it is apparent whenever a child or an adult deliberately touches the environment in ways that create a perceivable change of topological relationship between the body and the thing touched. The more difficult challenge is determining whether a causal relationship exists between such nonverbal physical experiences and the acquisition of language, as claimed.

Establishing a causal link between nonverbal interaction experiences and linguistic knowledge is not expected to be as simple a task as sampling behavior during nonverbal interactions and determining if and how language is related. As I understand it, nonverbal interaction experiences benefit language learning *indirectly* by organizing perceptual–cognitive experiences in ways that can effectively guide the search for information in the linguistic input. But how is such organization observed or measured?

It is harder to answer this question directly than it is to inquire about the validity of the assumptions on which perceptual organization is based. Here I call attention to two related basic assumptions of the theoretical paradigm described in this book. One assumption is that the normal organization of perceptual–cognitive experiences requires bodily participation in solving problems of daily interaction events. Mere visual observation of other people's interactions is not enough. A related second assumption is that a child, who is unable to interact alone to solve problems of daily living, can be physically guided by someone else to experience the same kind of input that is received when interacting alone. At the core of these assumptions is the importance of self-action and the tactually anchored, integrated sensory input it provides for learning. The following discussion addresses the empirical challenge of revealing the relationship between language learning and goal-directed interaction experiences.

4.5.1.1.1 *Nonverbal Interaction and Language Development.*
Research aimed at documenting the role of interaction in language learning could focus on whether unguided participation in interaction events facilitates language acquisition. One issue is whether this kind of experience actually facilitates acquisition of grammatical meaning, as reflected, for example, in the understanding of action verbs. There seems to be limited evidence that it might. For example, Mitchell-Futrell (1992) studied children with normal language. In one condition, they heard a novel action verb used to refer to guided interactions with objects in a blindfolded condition. In the other condition, they heard a novel action verb used to refer to a seen action that was done by another person. The children were better able to visually recognize the action for the new word when they had experienced the action in the blindfold condition than when they had just watched the action being performed.

However, other research outcomes suggest that language-disordered children do not respond the same way to different types of input. Olswang, Bain, Dunn, and Cooper (1983) reported that 2 of their 4 subjects with language disorders learned nouns and verbs better in an "object manipulation" than in a picture identification condition. One child learned best with picture identification whereas another one learned as well under either condition. Clearly the role of self-action in the learning process deserves further study.

Similarly, the question arises as to what effect self-production of speech might have on learning the forms of spoken language. One issue is whether self-production of speech facilitates the segmentation and retention of novel words, as has been suggested. It has been shown that a lack of speech production experience does not prevent speech perception and comprehension at some levels, but it may affect the rate at which children acquire such skills (Bishop, 1990). Earlier in this chapter, I proposed that internal and external auditory input may provide the easiest access to different aspects of the sound stream—the individual sound segments in self-produced input and the slower changing prosodic features in external input. These are hypotheses that could be tested experimentally by exposing different subject populations to foreign linguistic forms under conditions in which external and internal (self-produced) auditory inputs are manipulated.

In another vein, research on babies' mouthing exploration of the environment should be done. According to Affolter and Bischofberger, "mouthing" experiences represent interaction events that provide important input about objects and the spatial differentiation and organization of oral structures. If so, then research can address whether the timing or quality of mouthing exploratory interactions can be described well enough to predict who may end up babbling late or producing unclear speech later on.

4.5.1.1.2 Unguided and Guided Self-Action.

The validity of manual "guiding" as an instructional procedure would be supported by evidence that the patterns of brain activity, which correlate with such learning attributes as attention and memory, are generated in both guided and unguided conditions. Using EEG and other measures of neural activity, it should be possible to compare brain activity under guided and unguided conditions in the same child under different problem-solving conditions.

When patients fail to produce speech sounds because of a suspected tactual perceptual problem, therapists cannot manually guide the oral body structures, as it is possible to do for the rest of the body. To get at the potential effect of tactual input on speech performance, research studies can focus on whether articulatory patterns are improved by applying tactual cues to the face and neck, as is done in Deborah Hayden's Prompt therapy (Chumpelik, 1984), as opposed to just listening or looking at place cues provided by someone else. Cinematographic measurements of articulatory patterns following tactual, auditory, and visual cues could be compared. The goal would be to determine whether the different forms of input yield measurable differences in articulatory patterns.

4.5.1.2 Clinical Efficacy of Guided Interaction Intervention

It is worth considering whether Affolter and Bischofberger's three broad categories of tactual, intermodal, and serial perceptual deficits can help to make sense of differences within and across language disorder subgroups. These diagnostic categories may be particularly useful because subgroup differences are based on proposed areas of underlying perceptual deficits. In contrast, most taxonomies for classifying language disorder subgroups are geared toward describing the particular type of language performance affected and not the reason for the performance deficits, at least as specified in perceptual terms. Affolter and Bischofberger's taxonomy is useful too because it offers a perceptual explanation of the difficulties presented by children along the autism–PDD spectrum and those along the SLI–SD spectrum. Unfortunately, the autistic, SLI, and LD clinical subgroups continue to be studied in isolation of each other. To study clinical subgroups with tactual–kinesthetic, intermodal, and serial perceptual deficits as Affolter and Bischofberger have described, their research protocols must be first translated into behavioral measures that many professionals can use reliably. Once it is possible to do so, questions could be asked about if and how subgroups might differ in their respective linguistic profiles and responses to language intervention modeled around nonverbal interaction events.

There is another researchable issue. Ample evidence supports the coexistence of developmental language impairment with the kind of nonverbal deficits that implicate the tactual system. But the boundaries of this relationship are not known. Not all children with language difficulty exhibit obvious tactual deficits. The question is whether particular subgroups of language-disordered children are prone to do so, and if so, how stable or transient the relationship is across age and task complexity. Would the linguistic profiles of such children differ from those of other language-disordered children who do not display obvious tactual deficits in the manner argued earlier in this chapter? More generally, there is the question of whether any abnormal language group can be distinguished from normal learners in the number and complexity of topological changes that they elicit during nonverbal daily interaction events.

4.5.1.3 *Therapeutic Efficacy of Guided Interaction*

The speech–language pathology profession has been long concerned about clinical efficacy and the lack of clinical trial data to document how well a clinical intervention procedure works. It is fair to say that many established intervention practices have not been subjected to a broad or rigorous test of efficacy in the actual delivery of services. Guided Interaction Therapy seems to be no different. The most systematic data are available at the School for Perceptual Disorders in St. Gallen, Switzerland. There is documented evidence from school and clinical records, including an extensive video archive, that children with language disorders do progress, using the Guided Interaction approach. They develop a range of semiotic performances that include not only language but also drawing, picture recognition, symbolic play, and other forms of nonverbal symbolic representation. Sweeney (1996) reported significant language gains for children with language disorders, who were given Guided Interaction treatment in a pre–posttest study design. Clearly more efficacy studies are needed.

However, it is recognized that measuring long-term effects of any language intervention has always been difficult to do in a rigorous way because uncontrollable and unknown extraneous factors could influence the outcomes of the study. This challenge may be even more difficult to meet for Guided Interaction Therapy than for other treatments, and it is not obvious that the problem can be fixed by resorting to single-subject designs. This is because Guided Interaction Therapy is event-centered and

not specific skill-centered. Work on language (e.g., grammatical morphemes) occurs within the context of mapping language onto real events
in which children participate. Although one may have the goal or hope
that some aspect of grammatical morpheme knowledge will develop, the
therapy does not set out to teach just this specific grammatical feature in
isolation of everything else that goes on in a natural event. Therapists may
give linguistic input that includes morphological markers, as appropriate
to the interaction event, and after a period of therapy, assess whether the
grammatical markers in question appear in the repertoire. Even if they do
appear in the repertoire, it may be difficult to attribute their use just to the
therapy, when specific skills are not stressed as learning goals, and are not
deliberately worked on in a focused way.

The expected effects of the therapy are further complicated by the
expectation that multiple skills will emerge at the same time, even when
therapists do not work on them directly. But it is not yet predictable which
ones might be observed in a given child at a given time. If not, then it is
impossible to get baseline or pretherapy data on all the skills that could
turn up as therapeutic effects, but which cannot be detected in the
absence of knowing whether they were there all along in some performance context.

On the other hand, immediate therapeutic effects, which can be
observed within a single session, may be more easily documented and
attributed directly to the treatment. These include changes in verbal comprehension and expression before and after the guided event, in addition
to changes in attention, body tonus, event recognition, and planning.

In sum, controlled clinical efficacy studies are needed. We need to document (a) the rate and type of linguistic changes that result from Guided
Interaction Therapy; and whether it (b) yields different language outcomes than other established therapies, or (c) is equally effective in facilitating all aspects of language learning. The latter issue is particularly relevant, given Affolter and Bischofberger's claim that Guided Interaction
Therapy specifically aims to facilitate acquisition of the deep structure or
semantic base of language. But what about the formal grammatical properties that do not appear to be conceptually motivated? Some morphological markers are simply not semantically motivated. For example, the
difference between the phrase, "he goes" and "he go" and between "two
shoes" and "two shoe" is not a conceptual one. Both the standard and
nonstandard forms mean the same thing. Their differences reflect the formal properties of different English dialects, which may have evolved by
historical accident. There now are theoretical models that claim to predict
the type of features, which children are likely to honor when learning language, and why they do so (e.g., MacWhinney, 1989a, 1989b). It would be
instructive to know if such predictions apply to the types of grammars that

emerge in children who receive Guided Interaction Therapy as opposed to other types of interventions.

4.5.2   Investigative Approaches

Three types of methodological issues are relevant to further research on language disorders as conceptualized in the Affolter and Bischofberger framework. They concern the way behaviors are measured, the type of contexts for studying populations, and the type of subject populations observed. Taken together, they encourage the use of more complex methodologies in research designs than have been used typically to study children with language disorders. They also encourage the development of creative ways to measure and document behavioral changes.

4.5.2.1   *Measuring Behavior*

Meeting the measurement challenge will require more adequate measures of nonverbal perceptual–cognitive performance, and semantic–pragmatic knowledge of language.

4.5.2.1.1   *Measuring Nonverbal Interaction Performances.*   The relevancy of a nonverbal interaction framework for understanding development will hinge on how well we come to understand the tactual system. Tactual input not only is likely to add to the amount and complexity of information to be processed in the service of language learning; but it also appears to add information that may be difficult to process relative to the focal sensory inputs of audition and vision. The tactual system, which functions to detect the changing topological relations between the body and environment, is extremely complex. It is far more complex than is the passive tactual experience that is measured by the skin's sensitivity to touch (e.g., two-point discrimination). It includes force perception and the intermodal integration of multiple sources of information arising from skin, joints, and muscles, as Affolter and Bischofberger have pointed out. The input from the skin, which covers the entire body as the largest receptive field of all, is made even more complex because the JND (just noticeable difference) thresholds are higher at some body sites than others (Stuart, 1996). Because one or more body parts are always in contact with at least one support surface in the environment, the brain must continually register and integrate input from multiple body sites, and it must do so across different thresholds of sensitivity. It ought not be surprising that tactual input reportedly is processed more slowly (Heller & Schiff, 1991b; Streri & Pecheux, 1996) than are inputs from other modalities.

Such complexity no doubt contributes to why even normal children's performance is the lowest in the tactual modality, as described in this book, and elsewhere (Montgomery, 1993). Unfortunately, such lower performances also lead to the impression that a tactual system is inherently inferior to the better studied visual and auditory systems for processing information about the world. Thus, the tactual system, as a critical source of input for acquiring cognitive–linguistic function, is likely to remain one of the most controversial aspects of Affolter and Bischofberger's framework. Still, children cannot escape the consequences of processing this difficult input in nonverbal interaction events, if the development of complex skills including language depends on it, as has been argued to be the case in this book. To demonstrate the relevancy of a nonverbal interaction for understanding language pathology, we need better ways to measure tactual function for research and clinical purposes.

Studies are needed that focus on the dynamic interface between sensory and motor processes in purposeful problem-solving activity. This focus means that the measures used must go beyond sensitivity to static sources of tactual function (e.g., two-point and dichhaptic discrimination). They also must go beyond the focus on discrete motor skills such as balancing, hopping, and skipping. Although studies of haptic performances, which do involve dynamic sensorimotor interactions, have been done, they have not stressed the nature of the exploratory activity itself as a performance factor. For example, in a study by Kamhi (1981), poor haptic performance among children with SLI was attributed to the inability to mentally represent a visual image. Later on, Montgomery (1993) proposed that poor haptics in SLI children was caused by inability to scan and maintain a mental image rather than generate one. Although the latter study interpreted haptic performance in terms of information processes, no consideration was given to the possibility that memory stability and scanning are linked to the exploratory activity required to extract tactual input. Locher (1985) has gone so far as to claim that haptic input alters attentional demands enough to modify impulsive behavior and attention in learning-disabled children.

Affolter and Bischofberger described a novel way to code and quantify haptic exploratory activity. In their more recent work on the nonverbal interactions of babies, they have further elaborated the notion of an "interaction unit" as a metric of observation. If an interaction unit can be equated with a single goal-directed change of topological relationship between the body and the environment, then it may be possible to quantify task complexity in terms of the number, type, and ordering of interaction units involved in daily problem-solving events. Consider how many changes of simple topological relationships involving touching, grasping, displacing, and releasing are involved in the nonverbal interaction event of washing the hands as opposed to a dish or a window. Moreover, Affolter and Bischofberger's adaptation of the Pitt and Brouwer's model offers an alternative way to analyze problem-solving activities online (i.e., while interacting to solve a problem). This approach to nonverbal problem-solving performance may be a more sensitive and sensible index of problem solving in real life events than is the visual discrimination experimental paradigm used in a number of problem-solving studies (see Kamhi et al., 1985; Kamhi et al., 1990). However, replication of Affolter and Bischofberger's methodology in other studies is needed.

At the same time, seeking ways to dynamically measure neural and kinematic properties of sensorimotor activity during various types of nonverbal problem-solving interaction events is likely to be helpful. It can lead to better diagnostic accuracy in identifying language-disordered children with different types of tactually anchored perceptual deficits.

4.5.2.2 *Measuring Linguistic Performances*

Demonstrating the relevancy of a nonverbal interaction framework to language learning will depend on how well certain aspects of linguistic knowledge can be measured. Although there are prolific ways to assess knowledge of grammatical forms, there is less success in penetrating the depth of semantic and pragmatic knowledge, using standardized measures. This is partly due to the difficulty of measuring these areas of knowledge. Yet, intuitively, these two aspects of language, semantics in particular, seem more closely linked to nonverbal interaction experiences than are the syntactic and phonological forms of a grammar.

Most standardized measures of semantic knowledge have taken the form of vocabulary tests in which children point to pictured objects or actions. Only one of several possible meanings of a word is probed in frequently used tests such as the Peabody Picture Vocabulary Test (Dunn & Dunn, 1981). A more serious limitation of such single word vocabulary tests is that understanding word meaning in the context of sentences is missing from the usual measurement criteria. In fact semantic–syntactic relational meaning is treated and studied separately from word meaning or vocabulary development. This is the case even though words are less often experienced in isolation than in combination with one another. Research suggests that the normal acquisition of word use is influenced by the sentence context . For example, two longitudinal studies (Stockman, 1992; Stockman & Vaughn-Cooke, 1992) focused on the emerging use of locative words such as *off* and *on* in sentences that refer to changes of object location (e.g., "take that bug off me" or "put food on my plate"). Their findings suggested that the pattern of emergent word use was influenced by their semantic relation to the verbs in the rest of the sentence for both normal children and children with impaired language. Stockman (1991) revealed further, that the same word (e.g., off) emerged earlier in sentences that referred to movement or change of location than in those that did not.

Taken together, these studies suggest that the verb-conditioned meaning of words in sentences is likely to reflect the underlying semantic organization of the lexicon. It is possible that the depth of semantic knowledge could be more readily revealed by integrating observations of word and sentence meaning in further research. This kind of depth in describing semantic knowledge may be needed to capture the effect of Guided Interaction Therapy on the acquisition of linguistic knowledge.

4.5.2.3   Contexts of Observation

The methodological issue of how to measure tactually anchored perceptual performance extends beyond the parameters of measuring the sensorimotor activity itself. The context mediates performance outcomes in Affolter and Bischofberger's framework. Many contemporary voices (e.g., Fischer, Bullock, Rotenberg, & Raya, 1992; Thelen & Smith, 1994) point out that theories of competence have been fundamentally flawed by their failure to recognize the contribution of context demands on performance. Throughout this book, Affolter and Bischofberger have pointed out the need to distinguish competence from performance in evaluating children with language disorders. Discrepant performances can be accounted for by the lack of adequate information, given the context demands of a given situation and the maturity of the perceptual organization used to search for information in that situation. Consequently, it is possible that language-disordered children may not show deficits when they are observed on isolated sensory or motor tasks. But the same child may show pronounced difficulty when trying to organize movement to solve problems in a real-life situation. In this respect, Mulder and Geurts (1991) expressed concern about the simplicity of the laboratory contexts for studying human movement. Such contexts severely limit the "degrees of freedom with which one is allowed to operate" (p. 565).

Although basic mechanisms of motor control might be demonstrated in a tightly controlled laboratory context, the same results are not necessarily obtained in more complex, real-life conditions. In real life, movements are connected to events in which people participate. How one walks, runs, or hops can vary with whether an object is in the hand, or one is talking at the same time, and of course why one is doing the event.

Future research should expand the contexts of observation to include behaviors that occur in natural problem-solving situations. We do not know how children with language disorders approach the problem of trying to put on a shoe, open a door, and retrieve a distant and hidden toy.

Under what conditions are they likely to pay attention to words when they also are involved in a physical action? In the typical research study, a clinical group is compared to one of more nonclinical or normal groups. For example, children with specific language impairment or SLI are compared to normal language peers at the same chronological age and to younger normal peers at comparable language levels. In such quasi-experimental studies, procedures must be standardized in order for the comparative analysis to yield valid outcomes. Therefore, observations of behaviors in spontaneous situations are discouraged.

Yet observations of natural, spontaneous behavior may provide relevant leads about how children manage or fail to manage all the information that arises in natural situations in which input is available from language and nonverbal interaction events. Useful methodologies have been developed for studying spontaneous behavior in terms of the distribution of attentional resources in typically developing children. Bloom and Beckwith (1989) described a sequential lag time method for analyzing the temporal relations among children's actions on objects, spoken words, and affective expression. Other research has exposed the nature of children's verbal scripts for daily events (Nelson, 1986, 1995), or shown how spontaneous manipulative actions are deployed to solve logical problems like classification for both human and nonhuman primates (Langer, 1994, 1996). Although these methods have been used so far to study typically developing children, they have not been applied to atypical clinical groups with language disorders, but could be.

Paying attention to the performance context in multiple ways is important to designing research studies and interpreting their outcomes. This is especially needed when the research requires different subject groups or performances to be equated. The context variability of behavior creates the need to distinguish between competence and performance in a given situation, as Affolter and Bischofberger have demonstrated in this book. Their research suggests that researchers must not only take stock of processing demand in terms of stimulus and task complexity, as is typically done, but they also must consider the sensory modality of stimulus presentation, which is less often considered. Failure to regard multiple aspects of the performance context means that context equivalencies may not always be achieved for comparing different performance domains. Consequently, observed outcomes may be confounded by differences in task demand. For example, the observation that nonverbal cognition is lower or higher than verbal cognition could result from context differences. Discussion of the relationship between verbal and nonverbal cognition has been recently refueled by the observation that children with Williams Syndrome have much better verbal skills than expected, given their nonverbal cognition (Bellugi et al., 1993; Bellugi, Wang, & Jernigan, 1994).

Yet I am struck by the relative simplicity of most tasks used to test language in a standardized way relative to those used to test cognitive skills. In the former, children were required to select pictures that corresponded to a closed forced choice linguistic response on the Peabody Picture Vocabulary Test (Dunn & Dunn, 1981). Such standardized tasks require visual discrimination and recognition of pictures. In contrast, the standardized tests for cognitive performance seemed intuitively more complex and abstract. Here subjects had to generate patterns from stored mental representation (e.g., seriation and conservation tasks involving number, quantity, and weight). Although natural spontaneous samples of spoken language were described for subjects, spontaneous samples of nonverbal interactions in daily problem-solving events were not.

Thus, one is left wondering whether the gap between verbal and nonverbal performances is more a reflection of task demands than "true" competence in the respective areas. This is an important issue because big gaps between verbal and nonverbal performances are often interpreted as evidence for a modular view of behavior. In the extreme, language can be viewed as an encapsulated domain having little or nothing to do with nonverbal cognition. Such a view, however, seems counterintuitive if linguistic forms map onto conceptual knowledge acquired from nonverbal experiences. It also runs counter to Affolter and Bischofberger's contention that behaviors in different domains are related, albeit indirectly. Analogously, Kamhi (1993) pointed out that young normal children are capable of expressing quite sophisticated spontaneous language before they are able to do the nonverbal serial processing tasks used in research laboratories. Such an outcome should not lead to the conclusion that serial processing is unimportant to language learning. There is reason, then, to be mindful of the criteria used to achieve task equivalence when measuring performances in different domains.

4.5.2.4   Subject Populations

The study of language disorder groups should be expanded to include different age levels and clinical subgroups. The age factor is expected to explain some of the confusion in the literature about what is or is not characteristic of a particular clinical population. But developmental studies of language disorders seldom are done in either cross-sectional or longitudinal form. Typically, children with language disorders are compared with normal children at a single age point. Affolter and Bischofberger reported that the perceptual performances of their subjects with language disorders did not improve significantly with age. This outcome is surprising. Age, as a global index of prior experience, has been used to explain why older language-disordered children have been able to meet information processing demands on some tasks but not others and why, as a group, they may out-perform their younger language matched peers on some tasks. Clearly the role of age in performance needs further investigation.

One area worth exploring is the relationship of age to clinical categories of language impairment. Different clinical diagnoses may reflect different behavioral manifestations of the same underlying difficulties in changing performance contexts across age (Maxwell & Wallach, 1984). For example, once children turn 5 years or so in cultures with compulsory schooling, language must be used in an academic context. Literacy is a principal goal of schooling. Therefore, children learn written language, a modality of expression with different context demands than those required for oral language use at home. The distinction between children with specific language impairment (SLI) and learning disability (LD) appears to reflect such a distinction. SLI denotes a problem with oral language and is often diagnosed before school age. LD denotes a problem with school language, and it can include oral language as well. The same child, who is diagnosed with SLI as a preschooler, can later be diagnosed with LD. At even earlier ages (e.g., before 3 years), the same child may be diagnosed as PDD, if nonverbal performance also is poor. Scholars do view SLI and LD as a continuum of language difficulty. Yet the research on developmental language disorders has evolved along separate lines for children with SLI, LD, and PDD. Approaches to treatment are likely to be affected by whether the clinical categories are viewed as separate difficulties as opposed to different contextual faces of the same underlying difficulty.

Much may be learned about what the underlying differences are by comparing different language disorder populations with each other, as Affolter and Bischofberger have done. Comparative observations of different clinical subgroups will be important to determining whether the three categories of perceptual impairment they identified are differential diagnostic markers, as I have argued in this chapter. One rare comparative study of auditory serial processing in children with SLI and autism (Lincoln et al., 1992) already has revealed the possibility that these two groups have different perceptual deficits.

More research on the language and perceptual–cognitive performances of physically handicapped children is needed. They have proven to be a critical test of the relevance of perceptual–motor processes to language and cognitive development. Studies of these populations have not been designed to rigorously assess the functional effects of the physical handicap on nonverbal interaction experience in daily events. The opportunity to interact in daily events may be the important determinant of development and not the severity of the physical handicap.

Studies of children in the cerebral palsy population at different ages also would be helpful in trying to figure out whether a physical–motor handicap slows the rate of speech–language development, as I have argued. Most studies showing exceptional performances have been done with older children, possibly because it is easier for them to respond to standardized tasks than younger children. Although these studies can answer the question of whether a certain developmental level is reached in the face of a physical–motor handicap, they do not answer the question of how long it takes to get there. Studies at younger and older ages are needed to answer the latter question, and preferably longitudinal ones on the same child. Conceivably, physical handicaps do not prevent normal development but they may slow its pace or rate.

CHAPTER FIVE

Concluding Remarks

Ida J. Stockman
Michigan State University

In this chapter, I have tried to show how Affolter and Bischofberger's non-verbal interaction framework may be related to language learning. To do so, it has been necessary to argue that language learning depends critically on a perceptual/cognitive organization of experiences that includes tactual, intermodal, and serial features, which also are characteristic of non-verbal interaction experiences. Much research needs to be done. However, it is instructive to comment on how Affolter and Bischofberger's framework fares so far in rebutting the reasons for not taking seriously the notion that language learning is connected to tactually anchored nonverbal interaction experience.

One argument pivots on the incongruity between nonverbal and verbal performances in development. Normal language acquisition has not been shown to be dependent in a general way on the prior emergence of sensorimotor skills that were viewed as prerequisites, given interpretations of Piaget's theory of hierarchically dependent levels in developing cognition. The second argument follows from the first—namely, that some children with severe physical and motor handicaps still develop normal nonverbal cognition and language despite their physical limitations. The third argument calls attention to movement-oriented interventions developed by occupational and physical therapists. They have not proven effective in remediating language and academically related skills. The framework described in this book, however, accounts for these negative outcomes without abandoning the claim that physical nonverbal interaction experiences are critical to development.

5.1   INCONGRUITY OF VERBAL AND NONVERBAL SKILLS

In Affolter and Bischofberger's nonverbal interaction framework, congruity between verbal and nonverbal skills is *not* expected. As reported in this book, the authors also were misguided initially by a developmental model, which predicted a hierarchically dependent relationship among levels that emerge at different times. Although their research did support the assumption of interrelated levels, it did not support the assumption of a hierarchical dependent relationship among skills. In their longitudinal research on children with language disorders, some nonverbal skills (e.g., direct imitation of body gestures), which emerge before language in typically developing children, did not do so until after language onset in some children with language disorders. Some nonverbal skills (e.g., perspective drawing), which emerge late in typically developing children, were observed earlier than nonperspective drawing in some language-disordered children. Affolter and Bischofberger reasoned that nonverbal and verbal levels are not directly related to each other. They are indirectly related. This indirect relationship stems from the relationship of verbal and nonverbal skills to a third more basic source of development, namely, the nonverbal interactions of daily problem-solving events. Therefore, nonverbal skills are not expected to include prerequisite skills for verbal development or language acquisition. The emergence of some nonverbal skills before verbal ones or verbal before nonverbal ones has to do with the kind of perceptual organization that is required to pick up the information about one set of skills as opposed to another.

Bates et al. (1979) also hypothesized that nonverbal and verbal skills have a common or homologous origin. They concluded from their research findings that a homologous model must be viewed in local and not global terms. A local homologous model leads to narrowly rather than broadly correlated verbal and nonverbal skills. This explanation can account for the observation that some verbal skills seem to have a contingent relationship to the prior emergence of a nonverbal concept whereas others do not. For example, children's conceptual knowledge of object permanence precedes the use of "disappearance" words such as *all gone* in young normal children, but it does not precede the emergence of first words.

5.2   SEVERE PHYSICAL–MOTOR HANDICAPS

The fact that some physically handicapped children develop normally is not incompatible with Affolter and Bischofberger's framework either. The focus on interactive problem-solving activity as the root of development simply leads to different questions about why physically handicapped children may or may not develop. The question is whether these children have the means to experience changes of topological relations between their body and the environment in solving daily problems. This experience is not assumed to be dependent on the ability to move the body independently or in conventional ways. Thus, these children could still develop normal cognition and language understanding if an intact sensorium registers tactually correlated visual and auditory input when children are moved by caregivers or the children move themselves spontaneously in unconventional ways.

Nonetheless, Lewis (1987) pointed out that it is rarely the case that physically handicapped children have absolutely no means to interact with the environment or even to do so on their own at some level. However, the manner of interaction may be unconventional. For example, the mouth or feet may substitute for hands. In Decarie's (1969) study, 27 of the 30 subjects exhibited normal cognition as measured by object permanence and social understanding, despite congenital limb malformations due to thalidomide exposure in utero. But they were not deprived of independent means to physically interact with the environment. Most could even bring their limb stumps to the midline and one or more digits were attached to the stumps.

Among children with cerebral palsy, the opportunities for independent spontaneous interaction naturally vary with the severity of the physical challenge. Spastic cerebral palsy (lack of movement) is associated with greater risk for normal development than is athetosis (too much uncontrollable movement; Cruickshank et al., 1965; Lewis, 1987; Marks, 1974). Quadriplegia (four affected limbs) is associated with more risk than when fewer limbs (i.e., paraplegia, hemiplegia, or monoplegia) are affected. Even when four limbs are impaired, the head can be used as an instrument of causative action, and enough movement control is sometimes available in one limb or eye to operate a switch as an instrument of causative action in order to reach a goal requiring changes of topological relations between the body and the environment.

Many children with congenital quadriplegia, however, do not develop normally. Sensorimotor cognitive milestones, although achievable, may be reached at later ages than normal (Eagle, 1985). The physical disability need not be the sole risk culprit though. Lewis (1987) pointed out that the quality of interaction experience is likely to be a better predictor of development than is the severity of the physical handicap.

5.3 EFFICACY OF MOVEMENT-BASED THERAPIES

The third concern pertains to the efficacy of movement-oriented interventions for children with developmental learning disabilities. It should be pointed out that Guided Interaction intervention is not a movement-based therapy. Skilled movement is not its goal. The acquisition of knowledge is the goal. Guided Interaction is best described as a perceptual–cognitive approach to therapy. Movement enters into the picture because we must move to touch the environment in ways that elicit perceivable information about goal-directed changes of topological relations between the body and the environment when solving problems of daily life. Thus, movement is a means to an end and not an end of itself.

Perhaps the therapies developed by occupational and physical therapists would also claim that movement skill is not their end goal either. But they do not seem to be conceptually framed to deal with issues of mental development—neither nonverbal nor verbal cognition. Some therapies have been conceptually framed in ways that isolate motor patterns from perception and cognition (Delacato, 1963). Other therapies have framed motor patterns in sensory–perceptual terms but they are either isolated from cognition (Ayres, 1972; Bobath, 1966), or from the natural problem-solving contexts of daily life (Ayres, 1972). None is based on specific assumptions about language. Sensory integration therapy by occupational therapists is probably the best known approach in the United States. In their book on sensory integration, which was written to honor Jean Ayres, Fisher, Murry, and Bundy (1991) had this to say about cognition:

> It is surprising that no formal conceptualization of how mental and neurobehavioral phenomena are related has been developed and applied to the theory of sensory integration. Ayres' original work in developing the theory of sensory integration was based on a literature that did not grapple significantly with the problem of mind-body relationships, or, worse, considered it to be an insignificant problem. (p.30)

The authors go on to say that the complexity of the mind–body relationship must be understood in practicing occupational therapy based on sensory integration. As a perceptual–cognitive approach to rehabilitation, the Guided Interaction Therapy developed by Affolter and her colleagues ought to fare better than these earlier established approaches.

5.4   CODA

Affolter and Bischofberger have conceptualized information processes within a framework that casts a broad explanatory net. The challenge is to determine whether its theoretical specification is tight enough to yield new predictions about developmental language disorders—predictions that can avoid the pitfalls encouraged by a broad explanatory framework and stand up to rigorous empirical tests. This is the empirical challenge. It may be met if the notion of tactually anchored, nonverbal interaction experience is taken seriously enough to study its links to all forms of intelligent behavior with a fresh eye.

Appendix A—
Experimental Design

SUBJECT INFORMATION

The linguistic status of language-disordered children who were selected for the present study is represented in Table A1.

Previous research findings corroborated clinical observations that children with language disorders do not function as a homogeneous group. There are two main subgroups, which differ in perceptual processing (see Table 2.2 chap. 2).

THE TASKS, DETAILED INSTRUCTIONS
FOR EACH OF SIX TASKS

There were six tasks in all, four tasks of the short stair series, one in the tactual–visual, two in visual modality conditions, and the fourth one in the tactual modality condition. There were two long stair series, one in the visual modality and the other in the tactual modality condition. In the following section, instructions are described for each task separately. For each task the material is represented on respective Figs. 2.1 to 2.5 in chapter 2. The examiner provided the child with guided tactual information. If the examiner could not guide a child in any sensory condition, this child was judged as noninstructable for the given sensory condition.

TABLE A1
Subject Description—Children With Language Disorders

	General Descriptors			Language performances							
Subject Nr	Age at First Evaluation	Gender	Year of Selection	Actively Vocalizes Pleasure With Crowing or Cooing	Adjusts to Commands	Follows a Short Sequence of Similar Commands	Asks With Words (Intonation Patterns)	Names One or More Objects	Speaks in Short Sentences	Calls Himself With First and Family Names	Articulates Correctly all Vowels and Consonant Blends
1	2;0	M	1972[1]	p	p	—	nj	—	—	nj	nj
2	2;0	M	1976	p	—	—	—	—	—	nj	nj
3	2;0	F	1972	p	p	—	—	—	—	nj	nj
5	2;3	F	1972	p	—	—	—	—	—	nj	nj
6	2;10	M	1975	p	p	—	nj	p	—	nj	nj
7	2;10	M	1972[1]	p	—	—	nj	—	—	—	nj
9	3;1	M	1972[1]	p	p	—	nj	—	—	—	nj
10	3;2	M	1972[1]	p	p	p	—	p	—	—	nj
11	3;3	M	1975	p	p	—	—	—	—	—	nj
12	3;4	M	1972	p	p	—	—	—	—	—	nj
13	3;6	M	1976	p	p	p	—	p	—	—	nj
14	3;8	M	1974	p	p	—	p	p	p	—	nj
15	3;9	M	1972	p	—	—	nj	—	—	—	nj
17	3;11	M	1972[1]	p	p	—	nj	p	—	—	nj
18	3;11	M	1972[1]	p	—	—	—	—	—	—	nj
19	3;11	M	1976	p	p	—	—	—	—	—	nj
20	4;1	M	1975	p	p	—	—	p	—	—	nj
21	4;2	F	1975	p	p	—	—	—	—	—	nj
22	4;3	M	1975	p	—	p	—	—	—	—	nj
23	4;4	M	1975	p	p	—	p	—	—	—	nj
24	4;5	M	1972	p	p	—	—	—	—	—	nj
25	4;5	M	1975	p	—	—	—	—	—	—	nj

Continued

TABLE A1
(Continued)

26	4;5	M	1975	p	p	p	p	p	ⁿʲ
27	4;7	M	1975	p	p	–	–	–	ⁿʲ
28	4;8	M	1972	p	p	–	p	p	ⁿʲ
29	4;9	F	1972	p	p	p	p	p	ⁿʲ
30	4;11	M	1974	p	p	p	p	p	ⁿʲ
31	4;11	M	1972	p	p	p	p	p	–
32	5;0	M	1972	p	p	p	p	p	–
33	5;0	M	1972	p	p	p	p	–	ⁿʲ
34	6;0	F	1972	p	p	p	p	–	–
35	6;1	M	1972	p	p	p	p	–	–
36	6;2	F	1972¹	p	p	p	p	ⁿʲ	–
37	6;3	F	1972	p	p	p	p	p	–
38	6;6	M	1974	p	p	p	p	p	–
39	6;6	F	1972	p	p	p	p	p	–
40	6;6	M	1975	p	p	p	p	p	–
41	6;8	M	1976	p	p	p	p	p	–
42	6;11	F	1972¹	p	p	–	–	–	–
43	6;11	M	1972	p	p	p	p	ⁿʲ	–
44	7;0	F	1972¹	p	p	p	p	ⁿʲ	–
45	7;1	M	1974	p	–	–	p	ⁿʲ	–
46	7;4	M	1972¹	p	p	–	–	ⁿʲ	–
47	7;8	M	1972	p	p	p	p	p	–
48	11;3	M	1972¹	p	p	–	p	–	–
62	11;4	M	1972	p	–	p	p	p	–
86	11;6	M	1972	p	p	–	–	–	–
88	11;8	M	1972	p	p	–	–	–	–
89	11;10	M	1972	p	–	–	–	–	–
90	11;1	M	1972	p	–	–	–	–	–

Note. Adapted from Affolter and Stricker (1980, pp. 165–167). Reproduced with permission of the authors and the publisher.
1 = subjects also had hearing loss; see text for discussion.
p = performance present.
– = performance absent.
ⁿʲ = performance not judgeable; see text for discussion.

253

Tactual–Visual Modality Condition—
Short Stair Series (tv Task)

All material was touchable and visible to the subject. The insert board composed of 13 bars for the short stair series was used. The examiner put the insert board and the 13 cut-out bars in front of the child on the table (see chap. 2, Fig. 2.1).

1. The examiner guided the left hand of the child to touch the model form. The hand stayed there throughout the task. The examiner guided the right hand of the child with the palm side to feel the surface of the model form filled with the bars.

- The examiner guided one fingertip of the right hand of the child to feel the linear base of the inserted bars.
- The examiner slightly lifted some bars with the right hand of the child to create small gaps between their tops and the model form. The left hand stayed on those moving bars. The examiner guided the fingertips of the child's right hand to make the child feel these gaps and the corresponding step-like pattern of the model form.
- With the child's right hand, the examiner pushed the bars back into their correct position. Guiding the right fingertips of the child, the examiner made him or her feel the even baseline again.
- Guiding the right hand of the child, the examiner emptied all the bars out of the model form and piled them up at random at the right side of the model form; the left hand was still touching the model form.
- Guiding the right hand of the child, the examiner explored the inside of the now empty model form; with the fingertips he made the child feel its step-like pattern.

2. The examiner guided the child's left hand to touch and hold the model form. The examiner grasped the longest bar A with the right hand of the child and released it in the correct position in the model form. Now, the left hand touched the inserted bar A in addition to touching the model form. The examiner did the same with the second longest bar.

- Each time the examiner made the child feel with one hand that the bar did fit at the top and was lined up with the bottom of the insert board, while the other hand held the bars down.
- After having inserted two bars, the examiner guided the child's hands so that the left hand held the model form and the already placed bars and the right hand rested on the bars to choose from on the stimulus site. Then, the examiner took his or her hands off of the hands of the child expecting the child to take over and to continue.

If the child did not continue the task, the child was judged nontestable on the tv task. If the child did continue, the child was judged testable and the examiner removed his or her left hand.

If the child continued, but placed the bar incorrectly, the examiner started to guide again: The left hand stayed with the placed bars AB on the model form. With the right hand of the child the examiner removed the incorrectly placed bar. Then the cycle (take the next longest bar and put it next to the already chosen bars) was started again. If after the second attempt the child continued but did not proceed correctly, any solution was accepted. If the examiner could not guide a child in any sensory condition, this child was judged as noninstructable for the given sensory condition.

Visual–Visual Modality Condition—Short Stair Series Constructed on the Picture Model (vv Task)

All the material was visible to the subject. The cardboard with a line drawing of the 13-bar stair series called the picture model was on the table in front of the child, the bars on the stimulus site to the right. The picture model was also the construction site for the stair in this task (see chap. 2, Fig. 2.2). The examiner guided both hands of the child at the beginning of the task using his or her left hand on the child's left hand and his or her right hand on the child's right.

The examiner guided the left hand of the child to touch the picture model where the longest bars have to be placed. With the right hand of the child the examiner grasped the longest bar A and put it on the corresponding site on the picture model so bar A completely covered the longest drawn bar on the model. Then the examiner guided the child's right hand to pick up the next longest bar B and placed it next to A on the picture model so that it completely covered the second longest bar drawn. The baseline for bars A and B had to be at the same level and the top line of A and B had to show a stair-like step. The right hand of the child was guided to feel this pattern. Then the examiner guided the child's right hand to the bars and removed his or her guiding right hand. With the left hand he or she still guided the child to touch A and B on the picture model expecting the child to continue the task.

If the child did not continue, the child was judged to be nontestable for the vv task. If the child did continue, the examiner also removed his or her left hand. If the child continued, but placed the bar incorrectly, the examiner started to guide again: the left hand stayed with the placed bars A and B on the picture model. With the right hand of the child the examiner removed the incorrectly placed bar. Then the cycle (take the next longest bar and put it next to the already chosen bars) was repeated. If after the second attempt the child continued but did not proceed correctly, any solution was accepted.

Visual Modality Condition—Short Stair Series
Constructed Next to the Picture Model (v Task)

All the material was visible to the child. The same picture model of a short stair series made of 13 bars was used as in visual condition 1, in addition to a blank piece of cardboard of the same length as the cardboard with the picture model. The examiner put the picture model and the blank piece of cardboard next to each other in front of the child on the table (see chap. 2, Fig. 2.2). The examiner guided both hands of the child as in visual modality condition 1, but instead of putting the chosen bars on the picture model, the bars were placed on the blank cardboard below the picture model.

The left hand of the child was guided to touch the blank cardboard, the right hand to take the longest bar to place it on that cardboard, and the left to push it down. The left hand still held the longest bar A in place on the cardboard, when the right hand already grasped the next longest bar B and placed it next to bar A on the cardboard. The two longest bars were now placed on the cardboard and held down with the left hand. The right hand was guided to feel that the baseline for A and B was at the same level and the top line of A and B showed a stair-like pattern. With the left hand still on the bars on the cardboard, the examiner again guided the child's right hand to the location of the bars at the stimulus site and removed his guiding right hand expecting the child to continue.

The instruction period continues as described in vv task (see Section 2.2).

Tactual Modality Conditions—
Short Stair Series (t Task)

The children became familiarized with the cubicle, which later served to hide the test material before the testing instruction began; they could touch the cubicle—from the outside, from the inside, and peek through the openings.

When testing began, the material was not visible. It was hidden within the cubicle. It included an insert board for the short stair series and 13 bars (see chap. 2, Fig. 2.3).

The examiner seated the child on the chair with the cubicle in front of the child. Then the examiner guided the hands of the child through the opening into the cubicle where the material was placed according to the conditions depicted in Fig. 2.6.

1. The examiner guided the left hand of the child to touch the insert board. It stayed there throughout the task. The examiner guided the right

hand of the child with the palm side to feel the surface of the model form filled with the bars.

- The examiner guided one fingertip of the right hand of the child to feel the linear base of the inserted bars.
- With the right hand of the child the examiner slightly lifted some bars to create small gaps between their tops and the insert board. The left hand stayed on those moving bars. The examiner guided the fingertips of the child's right hand to make the child feel these gaps and the corresponding stair-like pattern of the model form.
- With the child's right hand, the examiner pushed the bars back into their correct position. Guiding the right fingertips of the child, the examiner made the child feel the even baseline again.
- Guiding the right hand of the child, the examiner emptied all the bars out of the model form and piled them up at random on the right of the cubicle; the left hand was still touching the model form.
- Guiding the right hand of the child, the examiner explored the inside of the now empty model form; with the fingertips he made the child feel its stair-like pattern.

2. The examiner guided the left hand of the child to touch and hold the model form. The examiner grasped the longest bar A with the right hand of the child and released it in the correct position in the model form. Next, the left hand touched the inserted bar A in addition to touching the model form. The examiner did the same with the second longest bar.

- Each time the examiner made the child feel with one hand that the bar did fit at the top and was lined up with the bottom of the model form, while the other hand held the bars down.
- After having inserted two bars, the examiner guided the child's hands so that the left hand held the model form and the already placed bars and the right hand rested on the bars to be chosen from the stimulus site. Then, the examiner took his or her hands off of the hands of the child expecting the child to take over and to continue.

If the child did not continue the task, the child was judged nontestable on the t task. If the child continued, the procedure was the same as described for the previous tasks.

Visual Modality Conditions—Long Stair Series
Constructed Next to the Picture Model (V Task)

The picture model of the long stair was on the table; the 13 bars of the short stair were already placed on blank cardboard (construction site) in order ABC . . . next to the picture model (see chap. 2, Fig. 2.4). The other

12 bars abc . . . were placed randomly on the stimulus site to the right of the construction site.

The examiner guided the child's right hand to take the longest of the bars abc . . . (i.e., bar a). With the guided left hand of the child he pushed bar A on the construction site to the left, thus creating a gap between A–BCD. . . . The examiner inserted bar a with the guided right hand into this space. Then the examiner moved both bars A and a with the guided left hand until they touched bar B. In this way the sequence AaBCD . . . was constructed, with the base presenting a straight line and the tops looking like steps. Then the examiner guided the right hand of the child to grasp the next longest bar b, guided the left hand of the child to push bars AaB to the left and inserted bar b in the gap with the right hand of the child, thus constructing the series AaBbCD. . . . Then the child was expected to continue. If this was not the case, the child was judged non-testable on the V task.

If the child continued, but placed the bars incorrectly, the procedure was as described for the previous tasks.

Tactual Modality Conditions—
Long Stair Series (T Task)

The material in the cubicle was similar to the tactual modality conditions—short stair series, except that the model form was twice as long to fit the bars of the long stair. The model form for the long stair series already contained the series of the short stair series ABC, its bars inserted in their respective places. In this manner, there were gaps between the bars A-B-C . . . , so that bars of the series abc . . . could be inserted (see Fig. 2.5). The bars of series abc . . . were placed to the right side of the cubicle on the stimulus site.

The following series of activities were conducted:

1. The examiner guided the child's hands. With the left hand of the child the examiner held the inserted bars down on the support so they would not move. With the fingertips of the right hand the examiner made the child feel the gap between bars A and B, its beginning and its end, and the corresponding step of the model form.

2. With the right hand of the child the examiner grasped bar a, the longest bar. The examiner helped the child to put bar a into the gap between the already placed bars A and B. While the right hand was still in touch with bar a, the examiner guided the child's left hand, which was on the model form, to push bars AaB tightly into the model form. Then, with the child's right hand the examiner grasped bar b and placed it between B and C. With the child's left hand the examiner pushed bars AaBb tight-

ly into the board. The right hand went back to the bars in order to make the next selection while the left hand rested on the inserted bars. Next, the examiner freed the hands of the child and expected that the child would take over the activity and continue the task.

If the child did not continue, the child was considered nontestable on the T task. Otherwise, procedures were followed as described for the previous tasks.

Appendix B—
Measurements

DESCRIPTION OF SUBROUTINES AND THEIR GROUPING
ACCORDING TO SUBPROCESSES

Problem-solving activities that children performed in order to elicit changes in topological relationships were inferred from the observed manipulations of the bars. For example, subroutine 5 (SR 5) can be described in the following way: A child moves the hand, holding a bar downwards until the hand with the bar touches the support. Before that action, the bar was separate from the support, after the action the bar is together with the support. This means the child changed the topological relationship between bar and support from being separate to being together (see Piaget, 1970, for more discussion on the topic of topological relationships and their importance in early development).

For developing a coding system for problem-solving activities, we applied Pitt and Brouwer-Janse (1985) model of problem solving. The coding system they used served to code verbal think-aloud protocols. We had to change that system to adapt it for coding nonverbal activities of our children. We recorded children's activities on a standard record form (see Table B1).

The following section describes 25 elementary components or subroutines grouped according to eight subprocesses or strategies. There were six task conditions. For each task condition there was an instruction period (see chap. 2 and appendix A) and during that period activities were observed which allowed us to infer for the child the presence or absence

TABLE B1
Record Form

Records and Descriptions of Activities

Name and social security number
Testing sequence
Manner in which test was administered
Success
Procedure chosen—followed throughout task
Procedure chosen—followed and nearly completed
                          —changed beyond midway
Sequences of procedures applied
Both relationships: stairs and base
One relationship: stairs
One relationship: base line
Works systematically
Starts at one end or the other
Differentiates between short and long
Compares two bars
Measures, using three or more bars simultaneously
Reverses any actions
Corrects any poor choice
Corrects a poor choice immediately
Begins a given task anew

---

of the subroutines of subprocess basics, subprocesses action and conclusion. The outcomes allowed us to judge if the child was testable or not for
that specific task condition. When a child showed the presence of all subroutines of subprocess basics, action, and conclusion for the tv task, the
child was tested on that task. If not, that child was not tested on the tv task,
and was judged to be nontestable on that task.

In other words, all children who were testable had all six subroutines
of subprocess basics, one of subprocess action, and one of subprocess
conclusion present.

Basics (Subroutines 1–6)

Clinical experience has shown that there are children with language disorders who cannot understand verbal instructions or cannot initiate a required
action. In these cases it is still possible to take the body of the child and perform activities that another child would do spontaneously. We call this "guiding" (Affolter, 1987/1991). Being guided means that somebody takes, for
example, the hands of another person, in our study, the child, and guides
them to touch the display. Perceptually, in both conditions one perceives the
same kind of tactual and visual information whether guided or performing
the activity alone. The criterion for "successful guiding" is fulfilled when the
child does not "refuse" being guided.

Activities required for subroutines 1 to 5 of subprocess basics are judged to be present regardless of being performed spontaneously or by guiding. Only the last of the subroutines of subprocess basics, subroutine 6 (SR 6) requires that the activities had to be performed spontaneously.

Subroutines 1 to 3 serve as criteria for judging instructability, meaning that one can continue to instruct a child. Presence of SR 6 is used as one of the criteria to judge a child as being testable on the respective Seriation task. Testability meant that the child presented the prerequisites for solving the respective Seriation task. It did not mean that the child would have success. Since subroutines 1 to 5 are embedded in SR 6, the activities coded by these subroutines can be considered "basic" for attempting to solve the respective Seriation task. Basics refer to activities that are observable before and during the instructions of each of the six tasks.

SR 1 refers to looking at and touching any part of the display. For starting any action with an object one has to touch it. The child does this spontaneously or is being guided.

SR 2 requires that the child touches several bars at the construction site and moves them on the support (see chap. 2).

SR 3 demands a beginning of differentiation of the stimulus display by requiring touching model and/or bars at both sites, the stimulus and the construction site, by performing a sequence of touching–moving. The activity includes, first, touching–moving one or more bars at the stimulus site, second, touching–moving bars at the construction site, and then returning to the bars at the stimulus site. This sequence is repeated. The child is guided to perform these activities.

If Subroutines 1 to 3 are judged to be present, it means that one can guide the child, and the child is considered instructable. If not, guiding is discontinued and the child is dismissed as a subject. If judged to be present, instruction by guiding is continued.

SR 4 includes holding a bar and attempting to lift it. Lifting an object requires, topologically, that one knows the object is something separate from the support. Observations of head-injured patients and of normal babies indicate the importance of this knowledge expressed by the sequence: touching, holding, and lifting (Affolter & Bischofberger, 1993).

SR 5: The hand now holds a bar, lifts it (see SR 4), and moves it away from the first location, the stimulus site—through free space and downward—until the hand with the bar touches the support. The bar is then released on the support. SR 5 also includes an additional requirement to be judged present, the switch from guided activity to what we call "continuing" an activity. This is a precursor of beginning an action step spontaneously (coded by SR 6). After guiding the child through the activities of SR 5 several times, the child is expected to take over the movements. For example, when the examiner guided the child to touch, to hold, and to lift the bar, we expected the child to continue moving the arm through free space and approach the support to release the bar. When guiding somebody, one can feel distinctively when this moment arrives. The child's tonus increases in his or her arms and hands. He or she takes over moving the hand. If this is the case, one releases the guided hand to give the child a chance to continue the movements of the action. If the child continues the sequence of movements as described, SR 5 is judged to be present.

SR 6 marks the end of the instruction period. After guiding the child several times through the sequence of grasping a bar at the stimulus site, moving through the air and releasing it at the site, we talk about displacing (see chap. 2). It is expected that the child performs now that sequence of displacing spontaneously.

Pitt and Brouwer-Janse (1985) coded in their think-aloud protocols some verbal statements as "list given information," "list assumptions," "list possible questions," "define initial state," "define goal state," being part of a basic strategy or subprocess.

Considering nonverbal activities as expressions of the problem-solving process we may identify the code according to Pitt and Brouwer-Janse:

SR 1 looking and touching any part of the display can be described as "list given information."

SR 2 touching and moving bars as "list assumptions."

SR 3 touching model and moving bars at both sites as "list possible questions."

SR 4 touching bars and lifting one can be interpreted as "defining an initial state." Initial state here refers to the knowledge that at the stimulus site there are bars, which one can hold and attempt to lift (topologically "separating").

SR 5 continuing guided action such as releasing the bar can be interpreted as "define subgoal" (i.e., understanding that one does something with the bar and then releases it on the support).

SR 6 present means that the child spontaneously performs the actions of grasping, lifting, displacing and releasing, and that stimulus and construction sites are differentiated. We can infer that the child has by this point "defined the goal state."

Evaluative (Subroutines 7–9)

Pitt and Brouwer-Janse (1985) described evaluative processes as "applying evaluative criteria," "identifying rules," and "organizing data." We chose three activities to judge the presence of evaluative processes in our study. They were coded by subroutines 7 to 9.

SR 7 codes "applying evaluative criteria." It refers to the consideration of the length of the bars as an evaluative criterion. The criterion is met when the child handles a few short bars before he or she handles a few long ones, or the reverse.

SR 8 codes "identifying rules" such as the identification of proximity rules (see Section 2.4). Relevant activities consist of arranging bars according to any proximity rule. For example, the child lines up several bars so they touch each other at their sides.

SR 9 refers to "organizing data" (i.e., evaluating information in a systematic way). For example, a child takes several bars off at one time, then chooses one of these bars, puts the other bars back, and places the chosen one on the construction site. Or, the child arranges bars on the stimulus site by separating those he or she has already handled from those not handled. Or, while the child keeps one hand on the last placed bar, he or she searches for the next bar with the other hand. Any of these or other "organizing" activities must be observed several times and be applied to at least half of the set of bars to be called "systematic" and to judge SR 9 as being present.

Selective (Subroutines 10–12)

Pitt and Brouwer-Janse (1985) described selective processes as selecting relevant and deleting irrelevant information. We chose three kinds of activities to support the inference that a child used selective processes.

SR 10 refers to a selection based on a set of topological changes (i.e., "select relevant and delete irrelevant information"). For example, the child places one or two bars, and immediately after that he or she takes these bars off. We infer that the child has recognized that some bars were arranged according to some incorrect or irrelevant topological changes. This may be a correct or an incorrect action. If this can be observed, SR 10 is judged to be present.

SR 11 refers to any rule that is applied by the child to all bars. The child "edits rules." It is inferred that the child identifies a set of available procedures.

SR 12 requires the application of that rule to at least half of the bars (SR 12 is less complex than SR 11).

Feedback (Subroutines 13–17)

We are asking what kind of information a child uses to judge what he or she has produced. We consider three levels of reference systems. They are coded by the five subroutines of this feedback subprocess.

SR 13 refers to elementary kinds of feedback. The child "tests a reference system." One kind refers to changes of resistance between the support and the bar. This information is assumed to allow children to judge lifting the bars from the support, and then releasing them again on the support. On the construction site bars have to touch each other, place of touching is not specified.

In SR 14 we code a more complex feedback reference system. The child "identifies feedback." The children have to consider changes of resistances along the sides of pairs of bars when they are placed on the support of the construction site (side line rule). Bars are "lined-up."

Subroutines 15 and 16 require differentiation and comparison of parts of bars generalized to all bars. SR 15 includes comparisons of the vertical lines of the bars lined up so that the top line is stair-like. SR 16 includes comparisons of bars by their vertical lines and codes the placing of the bars so that their bases form a straight line.

In SR 17 we code the most complex feedback information that the children will use. The child combines feedback of SR 15 and 16 by specifying the configuration of the bottom and the top line at the same time. The child places the bars so that their bases form a straight line and at the same time their tops form a regular stair-like configuration.

Hypothetic (Subroutines 18–21)

Making hypotheses involves predictions about causes and effects. In the present study these predictions are oriented toward changing topological relationships by arranging series of bars so they present stair-like patterns. Predictions may involve elementary topological relationships or more complex ones, being conceived one by one or in multiple ways. The coding of activities to make hypotheses has to take that into account. Activities were chosen that allow for inferences involving different levels of complexity for each relationship.

In SR 18 we code activities dealing with at least one relationship between two bars, such as, between the sides/lengths or between the tops of two bars. The child "considers and establishes relationships." For example, the child puts one bar next to another one, already placed, so that they touch each other. Touching can occur at different parts such as at the sides or at the tops (side to side, top to top). While watching the child placing the bar, we can infer his or her hypothesis, "I can push that bar on the support until it meets resistance on its top or at its side/length." The solution of "piling-up" is not considered for judging SR 18 present; it is inferred that this solution does not allow for the interpretation of considering topological relationships between pairs of bars, but rather, between support and a bar.

The relationships referred to by Subroutines 19 and 20 are more complex. They consist of considering relationships between pairs of bars in *suc-*

cession. SR 19 specifies that the child arranges the bars so that the top configuration has some resemblance to a stair and SR 20 so that the bars touch each other at the sides, and the bases of the bars are on one line.

SR 19 considers relationships between pairs of bars in succession. In SR 19 we coded activities which deal with a product or configuration that has some resemblance to a stair series. For SR 20, the child pushes each individual bar so that its side touches the side of other bars until all the bars are lined up.

In SR 21 we code activities, suggesting that a hypothesis the child is now applying reflects multiple kinds of relationships. The child places bars next to each other so that they touch each other, that their tops look like a stair and, at the same time, so that their baseline is straight. The criterion "at the same time" indicates the multiple kinds of topological relationships the child has to consider. In this sequence of a series, the bars have to be arranged according to their length AaBbCc . . . , so that bar a is at the same time shorter than A and longer than B. This kind of hypothesis is required for the child to be able to construct a series AaBbCc . . . , where a is shorter than A and at the same time longer than B (see Piaget & Inhelder, 1956/1964).

Patterning (Subroutines 22–23)

Patterning refers to the reactions observed when children consider their products. Such reactions appear to allow for inferences about relevant perceptual patterns analyzed and summarized by the children. Pitt and Brouwer-Janse (1985) described patterning processes as "matching data to prediction, and extracting patterns from data."

SR 22 refers to the touching of the base and/or top line of the construction and doing some kind of adjustment of the bars several times.

In SR 23 we code any action of removing bars, which involves some kind of correction (e.g., removing bars and starting all over again). The effect has not to be a correct one.

Action (Subroutine 24)

If the child displaced at least half of the bars from Location 1, the stimulus site, to Location 2, the construction site, this was interpreted as "execution of the program," and SR 24 was judged to be present. If the child displaces the bars to locations other than the construction site, SR 24 is judged to be absent. SR 24 had to be present as another criterion, besides presence of the six subroutines of subprocess basics, for judging the child to be testable.

Conclusion (Subroutine 25)

A task was ended when all the bars were displaced to the construction site and none was left on the stimulus site. We inferred: The child made "output conclusions." Whenever a child reached that conclusion and stopped his or her activity, SR 25 was coded as present. The presence of SR 25 in a child was another criterion, besides subroutines of basics and action, for judging the child to be testable.

RECORDING

For each child there was a standard record form, which was used and discussed in Section 2.1.5.3 (see also Appendix B, Table B1). The standard record form was utilized for judging and recording subroutines according to the previous description.

References

Aaronson, D. (1967). Temporal factors in perception and short-term memory. *Psychological Bulletin, 67*(2), 130–144.

Aebli, H. (1987). Development as construction: Nature and psychological and social context of genetic constructions. In B. Inhelder, D. de Caprona, & A. Cornu-Wells (Eds.), *Piaget today* (pp. 217–233). Hillsdale, NJ: Lawrence Erlbaum Associates.

Affolter, F. (1954). *Opérations infralogiques: Comparaisons entre les enfants normaux et sourds* [Infralogical operations: Comparisons between normal and deaf children]. Unpublished master's thesis, University of Geneva.

Affolter, F. (1968). Thinking and language. In G. Lloyd (Ed.), *International research seminar on vocational rehabilitation of deaf persons* (pp. 116–123). Department of Health, Education and Welfare, Washington. DC.

Affolter, F. (1970). *Developmental aspects of auditory and visual perception: An experimental investigation of central mechanisms of auditory and visual processing.* Unpublished doctoral dissertation, Pennsylvania State University.

Affolter, F. (1975). *Autistische und intermodal geschädigte Kinder. Longitudinale Beobachtungen bei einer Gruppe intermodal geschädigter Kinder*, S. 108 [Autistic children—children with perceptual intermodal problems. Longitudinal observations in a group of children with perceptual intermodal problems]. Ordo Humanus, Separatdruck.

Affolter, F. (1981). Perceptual processes as prerequisites for complex human behavior. *International Rehabilitation Med, 3*, 3–10.

Affolter, F. (1984). Development of perceptual processes and problem-solving activities in normal, hearing-impaired, and language-disturbed children: A comparison study based on Piaget's conceptual framework. In D. S. Martin (Ed.), *Cognition, education, and deafness* (pp. 44–46). International Symposium on Cognition, Education, and Deafness, Washington, DC.

Affolter, F. (1991). *Perception, interaction and language.* New York: Springer. (Original work published in 1987)

269

Affolter, F., & Bischofberger, W. (1988). Perception and problem solving activities. In M. Kalmar, S. Jackson, K. Donga, & J. Nagy (Eds.), *Abstracts of the Third European Conference on Developmental Psychology* (p. 298). Budapest: Hungarian Psychological Association.

Affolter, F., & Bischofberger, W. (1993). Die Organisation der Wahrnehmung, Aspekte der Entwicklung und des Abbaus [Organization of perception, aspects of development and regression]. In F. Affolter & W. Bischofberger (Eds.), *Wenn die Organisation des ZNS zerfällt—und es an gespürter Information mangelt* (pp. 24–55). Villingen/Schwenningen: Neckar-Verlag.

Affolter, F., & Bischofberger, W. (1996). Gespürte Interaktion im Alltag [Tactual interaction in daily life]. In B. Lipp & W. Schlaegel (Eds.), *Wege von Anfang an* (pp. 77–99). Villingen/Schwenningen: Neckar-Verlag.

Affolter, F., & Bischofberger, W. (1998, July). *Outcome of daily life nonverbal interaction in two severely learning impaired children with different intervention programs: A longitudinal study.* Poster session presented at the 15th Biennial meetings of the International Society for the Study of Behavioural Development (ISSBD), Berne, Switzerland.

Affolter, F., Bischofberger, W., & Calabretti-Erni, V. (1996, September). *Nonverbal interaction in babies and brain-damaged patients.* Poster presented at the symposium: The growing mind—La pensée en évolution, Geneva, Switzerland.

Affolter, F., Brubaker, R., & Bischofberger, W. (1974). Comparative studies between normal and language-disturbed children. *Acta Oto-laryngologica* (Suppl. 323).

Affolter, F., Brubaker, R., & Franklin, W. (1978). Developmental features of speech sound production in language impaired children. *Journal of Psycholinguistic Research, 7,* 213–241.

Affolter, F., Brubaker, R., Stockman, I., Constam, A., & Bischofberger, W. (1974). Prerequisites for speech development: Visual, auditory and tactile pattern discrimination. *Medical Progress in Technology, 2,* 93–102.

Affolter, F., & Stricker, E. (Eds.). (1980). *Perceptual processes as prerequisites for complex human behavior.* Bern: Huber.

American Psychiatric Association (1995). *Diagnostic and statistical manual of mental disorders* (4th ed.). Washington, DC.

Anzai, Y. (1987). Doing, understanding, and learning in problem solving. In D. Klahr, P. Langley, & R. Neches (Eds.), *Production system models of learning and development* (pp. 55–99). Cambridge, MA: The MIT Press.

Anzai, Y., & Simon, H. A. (1979). The theory of learning by doing. *Psychological Review, 86,* 124–140.

Aram, D., & Nation, J. (1975). Patterns of language behavior in children with developmental language disorders. *Journal of Speech and Hearing Research, 18,* 229–241.

Arnadottir, G. (1990). *The brain and behavior: Assessing cortical dysfunction through activities of daily living (ADL).* St. Louis: Mosby.

Aslin, R. N. (1981). Development of smooth pursuit in human infants. In D. F. Fisher, R. A. Monty, & J. W. Senders (Eds.), *Eye movements: Cognition and visual perception* (pp. 31–51). Hillsdale, NJ: Lawrence Erlbaum Associates.

Aungst, L., & Frick, J. (1964). Auditory discrimination ability and consistency of articulation of /r/. *Journal of Speech and Hearing Disorders, 29,* 76–85.

Ayres, J. (1972). Types of sensory integrative dysfunction among disabled learners. *The American Journal of Occupational Therapy, 26,* 13–18.

Bailey, A., Phillips, W., & Rutter, M. (1996). Autism: Towards an integration of clinical, genetic, neuropsychological, and neurobiological perspectives. *Journal of Child Psychology, Psychiatry and Allied Disciplines, 37,* 89–126.

Bates, E., Benigni, L., Bretherton, I., Camaioni, L., & Volterra, V. (1979). *The emergence of symbols: Cognition and communication in infancy.* New York: Academic Press.

Bellugi, U., Marks, S., Bihrle, A., & Sabo, H. (1993). Dissociation between language and cognitive functions in Williams syndrome. In D. Bishop & K. Mogford (Eds.), *Language development in exceptional circumstances* (pp. 177–189). Hillsdale, NJ: Lawrence Erlbaum Associates.

Bellugi, U., Wang, P., & Jernigan, T. (1994). Williams syndrome: An unusual neuropsychological profile. In S. Broman & J. Grafman (Eds.), *Atypical cognitive deficits in developmental disorders: Implications for brain function* (pp. 23–56). Hillsdale, NJ: Lawrence Erlbaum Associates.

Bird, J., & Bishop, D. (1992). Perception and awareness of phonemes in phonologically impaired children. *European Journal of Disorders of Communication, 27*, 289–311.

Bird, J., Bishop, J. V. M., & Freeman, N. H. (1995). Phonological awareness and literacy development in children with expressive phonological impairments. *Journal of Speech and Hearing Research, 38*, 446–462.

Bischofberger, W. (1989). *Aspekte der Entwicklung taktil-kinaesthetischer Wahrnehmung* [Aspects of development of tactual-kinesthetic perception]. Villingen/Schwenningen: Neckar-Verlag.

Bischofberger, W., & Affolter, F. (1998, July). *Outcome of two different intervention programs, nonverbal tactual interaction in daily activities and visual-auditory training procedures in two autistic children: A longitudinal study.* Poster session presented at the 15th Biennial meetings of the International Society for the Study of Behavioural Development (ISSBD), Berne, Switzerland.

Bischofberger, W., Affolter, F., & Peschke, V. (1995, October). *Neuropsychologische Testleistungen und alltägliches Interaktionsgeschehen—eine Leitstudie* [Neuropsychological test performances and interaction in daily-life events—a pilot study]. Individual poster presented at the Schweizerischer Kongress der Sozialwissenschaften in Bern, Switzerland.

Bischofberger, W., & Sonderegger, H. U. (1974). *Ausfälle taktil-kinaesthetischer Leistungen* [Failure in tactual-kinesthetic performances]. In Schweizerischer Verband für Taubstummen- und Gehörlosenhilfe (Hrsg.). Wahrnehmungsstörungen - Elektroencephalographische und Elektrocochleographische Audiometrie. St. Gallen: Tschudy. 19–29.

Bischofberger, W., & Sonderegger, H. U. (1976). *Seriale Leistung—ein auditives Problem?* [Serial performances—an auditory problem?] In Bommer AG-Rexton (Hrsg.). Vorträge gehalten am III. Audio-Symposium, Zürich.

Bishop, D. (1993). Language development in children with abnormal structure or function of the speech apparatus. In D. Bishop & K. Mogford (Eds.), *Language development in exceptional circumstances* (pp. 220–238). Hillsdale, NJ: Lawrence Erlbaum Associates.

Bishop, D. V. M. (1990). The relationship between phoneme discrimination, speech production and language comprehension in cerebral-palsied individuals. *Journal of Speech and Hearing Research, 33*, 210–219.

Bishop, D. V. M. (1992). The underlying nature of specific language impairment. *Journal of Child Psychology, Psychiatry and Allied Disciplines, 33*, 3–65.

Bishop, D. V. M., & Edmundson, A. (1987). Specific language impairment as a maturational lag: Evidence from longitudinal data on language and motor development. *Developmental Medicine and Child Neurology, 29*, 442–459.

Bishop, D. V. M., & Robson, J. (1989). Unimpaired short-term memory and rhyme judgement in congenitally speechless individuals: Implications for the notion of "articulatory coding." *The Quarterly Journal of Experimental Psychology, 41A*(1), 123–140.

Blamey, P. J. (1990). Multimodal stimulation for speech perception. In M. Rowe & L. Aitkin (Eds.), *Information processing in mammalian auditory and tactile systems* (pp. 267–281). New York: Wiley-Liss.

Bloom, L. (1970). *Form and function in emerging grammars.* Cambridge, MA: MIT Press.

Bloom, L. (1981). The importance of language for language development: Linguistic determinism in the 1980's. In H. Winitz (Ed.), *Native language and foreign language acquisition* (pp. 160–171). New York: New York Academy of Sciences.

Bloom, L. (1991). *Language development from two to three.* New York: Cambridge University Press.

Bloom, L. (1993). *The transition from infancy to language: Acquiring the power of expression.* Cambridge, MA: Cambridge University Press.

Bloom, L. (1996, March). *The integration of expression into the stream of everyday activity.* Lecture presented at Michigan State University's Symposium: Movement and Action:
Links to Intelligent Behavior, E. Lansing, MI.

Bloom, L., & Beckwith, R. (1989). Talking with feeling: Integrating affective and linguistic
expression in early language development. *Cognition and Emotion, 3,* 313–342.

Bloom, L., Tinker, E., & Margulis, C. (1993). The words children learn: Evidence against a
noun bias in children's vocabularies. *Cognitive Development, 8,* 431–450.

Bobath, K. (1966). *The motor deficit in patients with cerebral palsy.* London: Heinemann.

Booth, A. E. (1998). *The role of functional information in the development of concepts of
objects in infancy.* Unpublished doctoral dissertation, Pittsburgh: University of Pittsburgh.

Bowerman, M. (1989). Learning a semantic system: What role do cognitive predispositions
play? In M. L. Rice & R. L. Schiefelbusch (Eds.), *The teachability of language* (pp. 133–
169). Baltimore, MD: Brookes.

Broadbent, D. E. (1958). *Perception and communication.* London: Pergamon.

Broadbent, D. E. (1971). *Decision and stress.* London: Academic Press.

Brouwer-Janse, M. D. (1983). *The concept of equilibrium in cognitive development.* Unpublished doctoral dissertation, University of Minnesota.

Brouwer-Janse, M. D., & Pitt, R. B. (1986). *Knowledge acquisition: Methodological issues
and problem-solving profiles.* Paper presented at the 7th European Conference on Artificial Intelligence, Brighton Centre, England.

Bryson, C. (1972). Short-term memory and cross-modal information processing in autistic
children. *Journal of Learning Disabilities, 5,* 25–35.

Bushnell, E. W., & Boudreau, J. P. (1993). Motor development and the mind: The potential
role of motor abilities as a determinant of aspects of perceptual development. *Child
Development, 64,* 1005–1021.

Casey, B. J. (1993). Dysfunctional attention in autistic savants. *Journal of Clinical & Experimental Neuropsychology, 15,* 933–946.

Chandler, M. (1991). Alternative readings of the competence-performance relation. In M.
Chandler & M. Chapman (Eds.), *Criteria for competence: Controversies in the concep-
tualization and assessment of children's abilities* (pp. 5–18). Hillsdale, NJ: Lawrence
Erlbaum Associates.

Chapman, R. (1978). Comprehension strategies in children. In J. Kavanaugh & W. Strange
(Eds.), *Language in the laboratory, school and clinic* (pp. 309–327). Cambridge, MA:
MIT Press.

Chiarenza, G. A. (1990). Motor-perceptual function in children with developmental reading
disorders: Neuropsychological analysis. *Journal of Learning Disabilities, 23,* 375–385.

Chomsky, N. (1957). *Syntactic structures.* The Hague: Mouton.

Chumpelik, D. (1984). The prompt system of therapy: Theoretical framework and applications
for developmental apraxia of speech. *Seminars in Speech and Language, 5,* 139–156.

Constable, C. M. (1986). The application of scripts in the organization of language intervention contexts. In K. Nelson (Ed.), *Event knowledge: Structure and function in development* (pp. 205–231). Hillsdale, NJ: Lawrence Erlbaum Associates.

Conti-Ramsden, G., Crutchley, A., & Botting, N. (1997). The extent to which psychometric
tests differentiate subgroups of children with SLI. *Journal of Speech and Hearing
Research, 40,* 765–777.

Crago, M. B., & Gopnik, M. (1994). From families to phenotypes: Theoretical and clinical implications of research into the genetic basis of specific language impairment. In R. Watkins & M. Rice (Eds.), *Specific language impairments in children* (pp. 35–52). Baltimore: Paul Brookes.

Crain, W. (1980). *Theories of development.* Englewood Cliffs, NJ: Prentice-Hall.

Cruickshank, W., Bice, H., Wallen, N., Lynch, K., Podosek, E., & Thomas, E. (1965). *Perception and cerebral palsy.* Syracuse, NY: Syracuse University Press.

Cummins, R. A. (1988). *The neurologically impaired child: Doman–Delacato techniques reappraised.* London: Groom-Helm.

Curtiss, S. (1991). On the nature of the impairment in language impaired children. In J. Miller (Ed.), *Research on child language disorders: A decade of progress* (pp.189–210). Austin, TX: Pro-Ed.

Daems, J. (1994). *Reviews of research in sensory integration.* Torrence, CA: Sensory Integration International.

Davidson, P. H. (1972). Haptic judgments of curvature by blind and sighted humans. *Journal of Experimental Psychology, 93,* 43–55.

Day, R. H., & Singer, G. (1964). The relationship between the kinesthetic spatial aftereffect and variations in muscular involvement during stimulation. *Australian Journal of Psychology, 16,* 200–208.

Decarie, T. G. (1969). A study of the mental and emotional development of the Thalidomide child. In B. M. Foss (Ed.), *Determinants of infant behavior* (Vol. IV, pp. 167–187). London: Methuen.

Delacato, C. H. (1963). *The diagnosis and treatment of speech and reading problems.* Springfield, IL: Charles C. Thomas.

Dennis, W., & Dennis, G. M. (1940). The effect of cradling predicates upon the onset of walking in Hopi children. *Journal of Genetic Psychology, 56,* 77–86.

Desegregation. Teacher tries to balance compassion, accountability. (1996, March 17). *The Minneapolis Star Tribune,* pp. A1, A10–A11.

Dunn, L. M., & Dunn, L. M. (1981). *Peabody Picture Vocabulary Test–Revised.* Circle Pines, MN: American Guidance Service.

Eagle, R. S. (1985). Deprivation of early sensorimotor experience and cognition in the severely involved cerebral-palsied child. *Journal of Autism and Developmental Disorders, 15,* 269–283.

Eaves, L., & Klonoff, H. A. (1970). Comparison of blind and sighted children on a tactual performance test. *Exceptional Children, 37,* 269–273.

Edelman, G. M. (1987). Action and perception. In G. M. Edelman (Ed.), *Neural Darwinism: The theory of neuronal group selection* (pp. 209–239). New York: Basic Books.

Edwards, D. (1974). Sensory-motor intelligence and semantic relations in early child grammar. *Cognition, 12,* 395–434.

Farrar, M. J., Friend, M. J., & Forbes, J. (1993). Event knowledge and early language acquisition. *Journal of Child Language, 20,* 591–606.

Fentress, J. C. (1976). Dynamic boundaries of patterned behavior: Interaction and self-organization. In P. P. B. Bateson & R. A. Hinde (Eds.), *Growing points in ethology* (pp. 135–169). Cambridge, MA: Cambridge University Press.

Fey, M. (1986). *Language intervention with young children.* Austin, TX: ProEd.

Fey, M. (1996, November). *A critical evaluation of fast forward research: A response to Merzenich and colleagues.* American Speech-Language Association Convention, Seattle, WA.

Fillmore, C. J. (1968). The case for case. In E. Bach & R. T. Harms (Eds.), *Universals in linguistic theory* (pp. 1–88). New York: Holt, Rinehart & Winston.

Fischer, K., Bullock, D., Rotenberg, E., & Raya, P. (1992). The dynamics of competence: How context contributes directly to skill. In R. Wozniak & K. W. Fischer (Eds.), *Development in context: Acting, thinking in specific environments* (pp. 93–117). Hillsdale, NJ: Lawrence Erlbaum Associates.

Fischer, K. W., & Bidell, T. (1991). Constraining nativist: Inferences about cognitive capacities. In S. Carey & R. Gelman (Eds.), *The epigenesis of mind: Essays on biology and mind* (pp. 199–237). Hillsdale, NJ: Lawrence Erlbaum Associates.

Fischer, L., & Peschke, V. (1998, July). *Recall in a brain-damaged adult: (a) of spontaneously performed events, (b) of "guided" events providing tactual input: a longitudinal study.* Poster session presented at the 15th Biennial Meetings of the International Society for the Study of Behavioural Development (ISSBD), Berne, Switzerland.

Fisher, A., Murray, E., & Bundy, A. (1991). *Sensory integration: Theory and practice.* Philadelphia: F. A. Davis.

Flammer, A. (1988). *Entwicklungstheorien: Psychologische Theorien* der menschlichen Entwicklung [Developmental theories: Psychological theories of human development]. Bern: Huber.

Fodor, J. A. (1983). *The modularity of mind.* Cambridge, MA: MIT Press.

Fourcin, A. J. (1975). Language development in the absence of expressive speech. In E. Lenneberg & E. Lenneberg (Eds.), *Foundations of language development* (Vol. 2, pp. 263–268). New York: Academic Press.

Fraiberg, S. (1977). *Insights from blind: Comparative studies of blind and sighted infants.* New York: Basic Books.

Frith, U. (1989). *Autism: Explaining the enigma.* Oxford: Basil Blackwell.

Frith, U., & Baron-Cohen, S. (1987). Perception in autistic children. In D. J. Cohen & A. M. Donnellan (Eds.), *Handbook of autism and pervasive developmental disorders* (pp. 85–102). Silver Spring, MD: V. H. Winston.

Frith, U., & Happe, F. (1994). Autism: Beyond "theory of mind." *Cognition, 50,* 115–132.

Frith, U., & Hermeline, B. (1969). The role of visual and motor cues for normal, subnormal and autistic children. *Journal of Child Psychology and Psychiatry, 10,* 153–163.

Furth, H. G. (1966). *Thinking without language. Psychological implications of deafness.* New York: The Free Press.

Furth, H. G., & Pufall, P. (1966). Visual and auditory sequence learning in hearing-impaired children. *Journal of Speech and Hearing Research, 9,* 441–449.

Gardner, H. (1983). *Frames of mind: The theory of multiple intelligences.* New York: Basic Books.

Gathercole, S. E., & Baddeley, A. (1990). Phonological memory deficits in language-disordered children: Is there a causal connection? *Journal of Memory and Language, 29,* 336–360.

Gentner, D. (1978). On relational meaning: The acquisition of verb meaning. *Child Development, 49,* 988–998.

Gesell, A., & Thompson, H. (1934). *Infant behavior: Its genesis and growth.* New York: McGraw-Hill.

Gibson, E. J. (1967). *Principles of perceptual learning and development.* New York: Appleton-Century-Crofts.

Gibson, E. J. (1988). Exploratory behavior in the development of perceiving, acting, and the acquiring of knowledge. In E. J. Gibson (1991), *An odyssey in learning and perception* (pp. 599–607). Cambridge, MA: MIT Press.

Gibson, J. J. (1962). Observations on active touch. *Psychological Review, 69,* 477–491.

Gibson, J. J. (1966). *The senses considered as perceptual systems.* Boston: Houghton Mifflin.

Gibson, J. J. (1979). *The ecological approach to visual perception.* Boston: Houghton Mifflin.

Gillberg, I. C. (1989). Children with preschool minor neurodevelopmental disorders V: Neurodevelopmental profiles at age 13. *Developmental Medicine and Child Neurology, 31,* 14–24.

Girolametto, L., Pearce, P., & Weitzman, E. (1996). Interactive focused stimulation for toddlers with expressive vocabulary delays. *Journal of Speech and Hearing Research, 39*, 1274–1283.

Goodman, R. (1989). Infantile autism: A syndrome of multiple primary deficits. *Journal of Autism and Developmental Disorders, 19*, 409–424.

Goodwin, A. W., & John, K. T. (1990). Tactile perception of texture: Peripheral neural correlates. In M. Rowe & L. Aitkin (Eds.), *Information processing in mammalian auditory and tactile systems* (pp. 7–19). New York: Wiley-Liss.

Granott, N. (1993). Patterns of interaction in the co-construction of knowledge: Separate minds, joint effort, and weird creatures. In R. H. Wozniak & K. W. Fischer (Eds.), *Development in context: Acting and thinking in specific environments* (pp. 183–211). Hillsdale, NJ: Lawrence Erlbaum Associates.

Greeno, J. G. (1985). *Competence for solving and understanding problems.* Pittsburgh, PA: Learning Research and Development Center, University of Pittsburgh.

Greeno, J. G., & Riley, M. S. (Eds.). (1987). Processes and development of understanding. In F. E. Weinert & R. H. Kluwe (Eds.), *Metacognition, motivation and understanding* (pp. 289–317). Hillsdale, NJ: Lawrence Erlbaum Associates.

Hadders-Algra, M., & Touwen, B. C. L. (1992). Minor neurological dysfunction is more closely related to learning difficulties than to behavioral problems. *Journal of Learning Disabilities, 25*, 649–657.

Harding, C. G., & Golinkoff, R. M. (1979). The origins of intentional vocalization in prelinguistic infants. *Child Development, 50*, 33–40.

Hatwell, Y. (1966). *Privation sensorielle et intelligence* [Sensory deprivation and intelligence]. Paris: PUF.

Hedge, M. N. (1995). *Pocket guide to assessment procedures in speech-language pathology.* San Diego, CA: Singular Publisher Group.

Heller, M. A., & Schiff, W. (1991a). Conclusions: The future of touch. In M. A. Heller & W. Schiff (Eds.), *The psychology of touch* (pp. 327–339). Hillsdale, NJ: Lawrence Erlbaum Associates.

Heller, M. A., & Schiff, W. (1991b). *Psychology of touch.* Hillsdale, NJ: Lawrence Erlbaum Associates.

Henderson, S. E., & Hall, D. (1982). Concomitants of clumsiness in young school children. *Developmental Medicine and Child Neurology, 24*, 448–460.

Hirsh, I. (1959). Auditory perception of temporal orders. *Journal of the Acoustic Society of America, 31*, 759–767.

Hirsh, I., & Sherrick, C. (1961). Perceived order in different sense modalities. *Journal of Experimental Psychology, 62*, 423–432.

Hoare, D., & Larkin, D. (1991). Kinesthetic abilities of clumsy children. *Developmental Medicine and Child Neurology, 33*, 671–678.

Hoehn, T. P., & Baumeister, A. A. (1994). A critique of the application of sensory integration therapy to children with learning disabilities. *Journal of Learning Disabilities, 27*, 338–350.

Hoffman, W., & Söll, J. (1998, July). *Social behavior of 4 brain-damaged adults when solving problems of daily event as a group.* Poster session presented at the 15th annual meeting of the International Society for the Study of Behavioural Development (ISSBD), Berne, Switzerland.

Holland, J. H., Holyoak, K. J., Nisbett, R. E., & Thagard, P. R. (1987). *Induction: Processes of inference, learning, and discovery* (2nd ed.). Cambridge, MA: The MIT Press.

Holyoak, K. J. (1990). Problem solving. In D N. Osherson & E. E. Smith (Eds.), *Thinking. An invitation to cognitive science* (pp. 117–147). Cambridge, MA: MIT Press.

Hong, C. S., Gabriel, H., & St John, C. (1996). *Sensory motor skills for early development.* Oxon, England: Winslow Press.

Hopper, P. J., & Thompson, S. A. (1980). Transivity in grammar and discourse. *Language, 56,* 251–299.

Horowitz, F. D. (1987). *Exploring developmental theories: Toward a structural/behavioral model of development.* Hillsdale, NJ: Lawrence Erlbaum Associates.

Hudelmayer, D. (1970). *Nichtsprachliches Lernen von Begriffen* [Nonverbal learning of concepts]. Stuttgart: Klett.

Huttenlocher, J., Smiley, P., & Charney, R. (1983). Emergence of action categories in the child: Evidence from verb meanings. *Psychological Review, 90,* 72–93.

Inhelder, B., Sinclair, H., & Bovet, M. (1974). *Learning and the development of cognition.* Cambridge, MA: Harvard University Press.

Jackendoff, R. (1996a). *Languages of the mind: Essays on mental representation.* Cambridge, MA: MIT Press.

Jackendoff, R. (1996b), Word meanings and what it takes to learn them: Reflections on the Piaget-Chomsky Debate. In R. Jackendoff (Ed.), *Languages of the mind: Essays on mental representation* (pp. 53–67). Cambridge, MA: MIT Press.

Jackson, H. J. (1884). Croonian lectures on evolution and dissolution of the nervous system. In *Selected papers* (Vol. 2). New York: Basic Books.

Johnston, J. (1982). Interpreting the Leiter IQ: Performance profiles of young normal and language-disordered children. *Journal of Speech and Hearing Research, 25,* 291–296.

Johnston, J. (1985). Cognitive prerequisites: The evidence from children learning English. In D. Slobin (Ed.), *The cross-linguistic study of language acquisition* (pp. 961–1004). Hillsdale, NJ: Lawrence Erlbaum Associates.

Johnston, J. (1988). Specific language disorders in the child. In N. Lass, L. McReynolds, J. Northern, & D. Yoder (Eds.), *Handbook of speech-language pathology & audiology (pp. 685–715). Philadelphia: B. C. Decker.*

Johnston, J. (1991). Continuing relevance of cause: A reply to Leonard's specific language impairment as a clinical category. *Language, Speech and Hearing Services in Schools, 22,* 75–80.

Johnston, J. (1994). Cognitive abilities of children with language impairment. In R. Watkins & M. Rice (Eds.), *Specific language impairments in children* (pp. 107–122). Baltimore: Paul Brookes.

Johnston, J., & Smith, L. (1989). Dimensional thinking in language impaired children. *Journal of Speech and Hearing Research, 32,* 33–38.

Kahneman, D. (1973). *Attention and effort.* Englewood Cliffs, NJ: Prentice-Hall.

Kaiser, A., & Hester, P. (1994). Generalized effects of enhanced milieu teaching. *Journal of Speech and Hearing Research, 37,* 1320–1340.

Kamhi, A. (1981). Nonlinguistic symbolic and conceptual abilities of language-impaired and normally developing children. *Journal of Speech and Hearing Research, 24,* 446–453.

Kamhi, A. (1993). Children with specific language impairment (developmental dysphasia): Perceptual and cognitive aspects. In G. Blanken, J. Dittmann, H. Grimm, J. Marshall, & C.-W. Wallesch (Eds.), *Linguistic disorders and pathologies* (pp. 625–640). New York: Walter de Gruyter.

Kamhi, A., Catts, H., Koening, L., & Lewis B. (1984). Hypothesis testing and nonlinguistic symbolic abilities in language-impaired children. *Journal of Speech and Hearing Disorders, 49,* 169–176.

Kamhi, A., Gentry, B., Mauer, D., & Gholson , B. (1990). Analogical learning and transfer in language impaired children. *Journal of Speech and Hearing Research, 55,* 140–148.

Kamhi, A., Minor, J., & Mauer, D. (1990). Content analysis and intratest performance profiles on the Columbia and the TONI. *Journal of Speech and Hearing Research, 33,* 375–379.

Kamhi, A., Nelson, L. K., Lee, R. F., & Gholson, B. (1985). The ability of language disordered children to use and modify hypotheses in discrimination learning. *Applied Psycholinguistics, 6,* 435–452.

Kamhi, A., Ward, M. F., & Mills, E. A. (1995). Hierarchical planning abilities in children with specific language impairments. *Journal of Speech and Hearing Research, 38*, 1108–1116.

Katz, D. (1989). *The world of touch.* Hillsdale, NJ: Lawrence Erlbaum Associates.

Kelly, D. J., & Rice, M. L. (1994). Preferences for verb interpretation in children with specific language impairment. *Journal of Speech and Hearing Research, 37*, 182–192.

Kessen, W. (1993). Rumble or revolution: A commentary. In R. H. Wozniak & K. W. Fischer (Eds.), *Development in context: Acting and thinking in specific environments* (pp. 269–281). Hillsdale, NJ: Lawrence Erlbaum Associates.

Kiernan, B., Snow, D., Swisher, L., & Vance, R. (1997). Another look at nonverbal rule induction in children with SLI: Testing a flexible reconceptualization hypothesis. *Journal of Speech and Hearing Research, 40*, 75–82.

Kintsch, W. (1977). *Memory and cognition.* New York: Wiley.

Kirchner, D., & Klatzky, R. (1985). Verbal rehearsal and memory in language disordered children. *Speech and Hearing Research, 28*, 556–564.

Kluwe, R. H. (1987). Executive decisions and regulation of problem solving behavior. In F. E. Weinert & R. H. Kluwe (Eds.), *Metacognition, motivation and understanding* (pp. 31–64). Hillsdale, NJ: Lawrence Erlbaum Associates.

Kluwe, R. H., & Spada H. (Eds.). (1980). *Developmental models of thinking.* New York: Academic Press.

Kouri, T. A. (1994). Lexical comprehension in young children with developmental delays. *American Journal of Speech-Language Pathology, 3*, 79–88.

Kracke, I. (1975). Perception of rhythmic sequences by receptive aphasia and deaf children. *British Journal of Disorders in Communication, 10*, 43–51.

Kratz, L. E., Tutt, L. M., & Black, D. A. (1987). *Movement and fundamental motor skills for sensory deprived children.* Springfield, IL: Charles C. Thomas.

Krueger, L. E. (1982). Tactual perception in historical perspective: David Katz's world of touch. In W. Schiff & E. Foulke (Eds.), *Tactual perception: A source book* (pp. 1–54). New York: Cambridge University Press.

Lahey, M. (1988). *Language disorders and language development.* Philadelphia: MacMillan.

Lahey, M. (1990). Who shall be called language disordered? *Journal of Speech and Hearing Disorders, 55*(4), 612–620.

Lahey, M., Chesnick, M., Menyuk, P., & Adams, J. (1992). Variability in children's use of grammatical morphemes. *Applied Psycholinguistics, 13*, 373–398.

Lahey, M., & Edwards, J. (1996). Why do children with specific language impairment name pictures more slowly than their peers? *Journal of Speech and Hearing Research, 39*, 1081–1098.

Lakoff, G. (1987). *Women, fire and dangerous things: What categories reveal about the mind.* Chicago: University of Chicago Press.

Lakoff, G. (1994). What is a conceptual system? In W. F. Overton & D. S. Palermo (Eds.), *The ontogenesis of meaning* (pp. 41–90). Hillsdale, NJ: Lawrence Erlbaum Associates.

Landau, B., & Gleitman, L. (1985). *Language and experience: Evidence from the blind child.* London, England: Harvard University Press.

Langer, J. (1980). *The origins of logic: Six to twelve months.* New York: Academic Press.

Langer, J. (1994). From acting to understanding: The comparative development of meaning. In W. F. Overton & D. S. Palermo (Eds.), *The ontogenesis of meaning* (pp. 191–213). Hillsdale, NJ: Lawrence Erlbaum Associates.

Langer, J. (1996, February), *Manipulative action and the origin of logic.* Symposium on Movement and Action: Links to Intelligent Behavior, Michigan State University, E. Lansing.

Lawler, R. W. (1985). Computer experience and cognitive development: A child's learning in a computer culture. Chichester, England: Halsted/Wiley.

Leary, M. R., & Hill, D. A. (1996). Moving on: Autism and movement disturbance. *Mental Retardation*, February, 39–53.

Lederman, S., & Klatzky, R. L. (1987). Hand movements: A window into haptic object recognition. *Cognitive Psychology, 19*, 342–368.

Lenneberg, E. H. (1967). *Biological foundations of language.* New York: Wiley.

Leonard, L. (1987). Is specific language impairment a useful construct? In S. Rosenberg (Ed.), *Advances in applied psycholinguistics* (pp. 1–39). New York: Cambridge University Press.

Leonard, L. (1994). Some problems facing accounts of morphological deficits in children with specific language impairment. In R. Watkins & M. Rice (Eds.), *Specific language impairments in children* (pp. 91–106). Baltimore: Paul Brookes.

Lewis, V. (1987). How do children with motor handicaps develop? In V. Lewis (Ed.), *Development and handicap* (pp. 82–103). Cambridge, England: Blackwell.

Lincoln, A. J., Dickstein, P., Courchesne, E., Elmasian, R., & Tallal, P. (1992). Auditory processions abilities in non-retarded adolescents and young adults with developmental receptive language disorder and autism. *Brain and Language, 43*, 613–622.

Lipp B., & Schlaegel, W. (Eds.). (1996). *Wege von Anfang an* [Paths to follow: 5 years of clinical experience]. Villingen/ Schwenningen: Neckar-Verlag.

Locher, P. (1985). Use of haptic training to modify impulse and attention control deficits of learning disabled children. *Journal of Learning Disabilities, 18*, 89–93.

Locke, J. (1980). The inference of speech perception in the phonologically disordered child: Part I. A rationale, some criteria, the conventional tests. *Journal of Speech and Hearing Disorders, 45*, 431–444.

Locke, J. (1993). *The child's path to spoken language.* Cambridge, MA: Harvard University Press.

Locke, J., & Pearson, D. (1990). Linguistic significance of babbling: evidence from a tracheostomized infant. *Journal of Child Language, 17*, 1–16.

Loomis, J. M., & Lederman, S. J., (1986). Tactual perception. In K. R. Boff, L. Kaufman, & J. P. Thomas (Eds.), *Handbook of perception and human performance.* Vol. II: Cognitive processes and performance. Section VI: Perceptual Organization and Cognition (pp. 31–41). New York: Wiley.

Lorenz, K. (1977). *Behind the mirror: A search for a natural history of human knowledge.* London: Methuen.

Losse, A., Henderson, S., Elliman, D., Hall, D., Knight, E., & Jongmans, M. (1991). Clumsiness in children—Do they grow out of it? A 10 year follow-up study. *Developmental Medicine and Child Neurology, 33*, 55–68.

Ludlow, C., Cudahy, E., Bassick, C., & Brown, G. (1983). The auditory processing skills of hyperactive, language impaired and reading disabled boys. In J. Katz & E. Lasky (Eds.), *Central auditory processing disorders: Problems of speech, language and learning* (pp. 163–184). Baltimore, MD: University Park Press.

Luria, A. R. (1987). *The man with a shattered world: The history of a brain wound.* Cambridge, MA: Harvard University Press.

MacWhinney, B. (1989a). Competition and teachability. In M. Rice & R. Schiefelbusch (Eds.), *The teachability of language* (pp. 63–104). Baltimore, MD: Brookes.

MacWhinney, B. (1989b). The competition model. In B. MacWhinney (Ed.), *Mechanisms of language acquisition* (pp. 245–308). Hillsdale, NJ: Lawrence Erlbaum Associates.

Mandler, J. (1992). How to build a baby: II. Conceptual primitives. *Psychological Review, 99*, 587–604.

Marks, N. C. (1974). *Cerebral palsied and learning disabled children.* Springfield, IL: Charles C. Thomas.

Maxwell, S. E., & Wallach, G. P. (1984). The language-learning disabilities connection. Symptoms of early language disability change over time. In G. P. Wallach & K. G. Butler (Eds.), *Language learning disabilities in school-age children* (pp. 15–34). Baltimore, MD: Williams & Wilkins.

Menyuk, P. (1971). *The acquisition and development of language.* Englewood Cliffs, NJ: Prentice-Hall.

Merzenich, M. M., Jenkins, W. M., Johnston, P., Schreiner, C., Miller, S. L., & Tallal, P. (1996). Temporal processing deficits of language learning impaired children ameliorated by training. *Science, 271,* 77–81.

Mikulas, W. L. (1974). *Concepts in learning.* Philadelphia: W. B. Saunders.

Millar, S. (1994). *Understanding and representing space: Theory and evidence from studies with blind and sighted children.* Oxford, England: Clarendon Press.

Miller, G. A., Galanter, E., & Pribram, K. (1960). *Plans and structure of behavior.* London: Holt, Rinehart & Winston.

Miller, J. (1991). Research on language disorders in children: A progress report. In J. Miller (Ed.), *Research on child language disorders: A decade of progress* (pp. 3–22). Austin, TX: Pro-Ed.

Miller, J., & Paul, R. (1995). *The clinical assessment of language comprehension.* Baltimore, MD: Brookes.

Miller, L. (1984). Problem solving and language disorders. In G. P. Wallach & K. G. Butler (Eds.), *Language learning disabilities in school-age children* (pp. 199–229). Baltimore, MD: Williams & Wilkins.

Mills, A. (1993). Visual handicap. In D. Bishop & K. Mogford (Eds.), *Language development in exceptional circumstances* (pp. 150–164). Hillsdale, NJ: Lawrence Erlbaum Associates.

Mitchell-Futrell, K. (1992). *Action verb learning in observational and manipulation contexts.* Unpublished master's thesis, Michigan State University.

Mogford, K., & Bishop, D. (1993). Five questions about language acquisition considered in the light of exceptional circumstances. In K. Mogford & D. Bishop (Eds.), *Language development in exceptional circumstances* (pp. 239–260). Hillsdale, NJ: Lawrence Erlbaum Associates.

Mohr, S., & Nielsen, K. (1998, July). *Outcome of two kinds of therapeutic intervention in two brain-damaged adults: (a) nonverbal guided tactual interaction in daily activities, (b) visual-auditory training procedures: a longitudinal study.* Poster session presented at the 15th Biennial meetings of the International Society for the Study of Behavioural Development (ISSBD), Berne, Switzerland.

Monnin, L. (1984). Speech sound discrimination testing and training: Why? Why Not? In H. Winitz (Ed.), *Treating articulation disorders: For clinicians by clinicians* (pp. 1–20). Baltimore, MD: University Park Press.

Montgomery, J. (1993). Haptic recognition of children with specific language impairment: Effects of response modality. *Journal of Speech and Hearing Research, 36,* 98–104.

Montgomery, J., Scudder, R., & Moore, C. (1990). Language-impaired children's real-time comprehension of spoken language. *Applied Psycholinguistics, 11,* 273–290.

Mulder, T., & Geurts, S. (1991). The assessment of motor dysfunctions: Preliminaries to a disability-oriented approach. *Human Movement Science, 10,* 565–574.

Murdock, G. A. (1967). *Recent development in short-term memory.* Unpublished paper, Toronto University.

Nelson, K. (1986). *Event knowledge: Structure and function in development.* Hillsdale, NJ: Lawrence Erlbaum Associates.

Nelson, K. (1995, November). *Events as basic building blocks for concept development.* A lecture presented at the Symposium on Movement and Action: Links to Intelligent Behavior, Michigan State University, E. Lansing, MI.

Nelson, N. (1993). *Childhood language disorders in context: Infancy through adolescence.* New York: Macmillan.

Neville, H., Coffey, S., Holcomb, P., & Tallal, P. (1993). The neurobiology of sensory and language processing in language-impaired children. *Journal of Cognitive Neuroscience, 52,* 235–253.

Norris, J. A., & Damico, J. S. (1990). Whole language in theory and practice: Implications for language intervention. *Language, Speech, and Hearing Services in Schools, 21*, 212–220.

Olswang, L., Bain, B., Dunn, C., & Cooper, J. (1983). The effects of stimulus variation on lexical learning. *Journal of Speech and Hearing Disorders, 48*, 192–201.

Owens, R. (1996). *Language development: An introduction.* New York: Macmillan.

Paul, R. (1990). Comprehension strategies: Interactions between world knowledge and the development of sentence comprehension. *Topics in language disorders, 10*, 63–75.

Pfeiffer, K., Feinberg, G., & Gelber, S. (1987). Teaching productive problem-solving attitudes. In D. E. Berger, K. Pezdek, & W. P. Banks (Eds.), *Applications of cognitive psychology: Problem solving, education, and computing circumstances* (pp. 99–109). Hillsdale, NJ: Lawrence Erlbaum Associates.

Piaget, J. (1911). Les Limnées des lacs de Neuchâtel, Bienne, Morat et des environs [Limneae (snails) in the lakes of Neuchâtel, Bienne, and Morat and their environments]. *Journal de cinchyliologie, 59*, 4e série, t. 13, 311–332.

Piaget, J. (1950). *The psychology of intelligence.* London: Routledge & Kegan Paul. (Original work published in 1947)

Piaget, J. (1952). *The origins of intelligence in children.* New York: International Universities Press. (Original work published in 1936)

Piaget, J. (1962). *Play, dreams and imitation in childhood.* New York: Norton Library. (Original work published in 1945)

Piaget, J. (1963). Le language et les opérations intellectuelles [Language and intellectual operations]. In *Problèmes de psycholinguistique.* Neuchâtel: Symposium de l'association de psychologie scientifique de langue française, 1962. Paris: PUF. 51–61.

Piaget, J. (1969). *Perceptual mechanisms.* London: Routledge & Kegan Paul. (Original work published in 1961)

Piaget, J. (1970). *Genetic epistemology.* New York: Norton Library.

Piaget, J., & Inhelder, B. (1956). The child's conception of space. London: Routledge & Kegan Paul. (Original work published in 1948)

Piaget, J., & Inhelder, B. (1964). *The early growth of logic in the child: Classification and seriation.* New York: Harper & Row. (Original work published in 1956)

Piattelli-Palmarini, M. (Ed.). (1980). *Language and learning.* Cambridge, MA: Harvard University Press.

Pinker, S. (1984). *Language learnability and language development.* Cambridge, MA: Harvard University Press.

Pinker, S. (1987). *Learnability and cognition: The acquisition of argument structure.* Cambridge, MA: MIT Press.

Pitt, R. B. (1977). Toward a comprehensive model of problem solving: Application to solutions of chemistry problems by high school and college students (Doctoral dissertation. University of California at San Diego, 1976). *Dissertation Abstracts International, 37-09*, 4730-B (University Microfilms no 77-4218, 145)

Pitt, R. B. (1983). Development of a general problem-solving schema in adolescence and early adulthood. *Journal of Experimental Psychology: General,* Vol. 112, No. 4, 547–584.

Pitt, R. B., & Brouwer-Janse, M. D. (1985, April). *Problem-solving heuristics in adolescence and early adulthood.* Poster presented at the Society for Research in Child Development, Toronto.

Posner, M. I. (1986). Information processing: Overview. In K. R. Boff, L. Kaufman, & J. P. Thomas (Eds.), *Handbook of perception and human performance.* Vol. II Cognitive processes and performance. Section V: Information Processing (pp. V-1–V-10). New York: Wiley.

Powell, R. P., & Bishop, D. V. M. (1992). Clumsiness and perceptual problems in children with specific language impairment. *Developmental Medicine and Child Neurology, 34*, 755–765.

Prinz, W., & Bridgeman, B. (Eds.). (1996). *Handbook of perception and action. Vol. I: Perception*. San Diego, CA: Academic Press.

Prutting, C., & Kirchner, D. (1983). Applied Pragmatics. In T. Gallagher & C. Prutting (Eds.), *Pragmatic assessment and intervention issues in language* (pp. 29–64). San Diego, CA: College-Hill Press.

Rapin, I., & Allen, D. (1983). Developmental language disorders: Nosology consideration. In U. Kirk (Ed.), *Neuropsychology of language, reading, and spelling* (pp. 155–184). Orlando, FL: Academic Press.

Reed, E. S. (1982). An outline of a theory of actions systems. *Journal of motor behavior 14*, 98–134.

Reed, E. S. (1993). The intention to use a specific affordance: A conceptual framework for psychology. In R. H. Wozniak & K. W. Fischer (Eds.), *Development in context: Acting and thinking in specific environments* (pp. 45–77). Hillsdale, NJ: Lawrence Erlbaum Associates.

Reed, T. (1994). Performance of autistic and control subjects on three cognitive perspective-taking tasks. *Journal of Autism and Developmental Disorders, 24*, 53–66.

Rice, M. (1991). Children with specific language impairment: Toward a model of teachability. In N. Krasnegor, D. Rumbaugh, R. Schiefelbusch, & M. Studdert-Kennedy (Eds.), *Biological and behavioral determinants of language development* (pp. 447–480). Hillsdale, NJ: Lawrence Erlbaum Associates.

Rice, M. (1994). Grammatical categories of children with specific language impairments. In R. Watkins & M. Rice (Eds.), *Specific language impairments in children* (pp. 69–90). Baltimore: Paul Brookes.

Rice, M.,& Bode, J. (1993). GAPS ii the verb lexicon of children with specific language impairment. *First Language, 13*, 113–131.

Rice, M., & Kemper, S. (1984). *Child language and cognition: Contemporary issues*. Baltimore, MD: University Park Press.

Rice, M., Oetting, J. B., Marquis, J., Bode, J., & Pae, S. (1994). Frequency of input effects on word comprehension of children with specific language impairment. *Journal of Speech and Hearing Research, 37*, 106–121.

Rice, M., Wexler, K., & Cleave, P. L. (1995). Specific language impairment as a period of extended optional infinitive. *Journal of Speech and Hearing Research, 38*, 850–863.

Roberton, M. A. (1981). Motor development in learning disabled children. In J. Gottlieb & S. Strichart (Eds.), *Developmental theory and research in learning disabilities* (pp. 80–107). Baltimore, MD: University Park Press.

Rock, I. (1986). The description and analysis of object and event perception. In K. R. Boff, L. Kaufman, & J. P. Thomas (Eds.), *Handbook of perception and human performance. Vol. II: Cognitive processes and performance. Section VI: Perceptual Organization and Cognition* (pp. 33-1–33-71). New York: Wiley.

Rolfe-Zikman, S. (1987). Visual and haptic bimodal perception in infancy. In B. E. McKenzie & R. H. Day (Eds.), *Perceptual development in early infancy: Problems and issues* (pp. 199–219). Hillsdale, NJ: Lawrence Erlbaum Associates.

Rosner, J. (1981). Perceptual skills development in children with learning disabilities. In J. Gottlieb & S. Strichart (Eds.), *Developmental theory and research in learning disabilities* (pp. 108–129). Baltimore, MD: University Park Press.

Rourke, B. P. (1989). *Nonverbal learning disabilities: The syndrome and the model*. New York: Guilford Press.

Rowe, H. A. (1985). Preliminary considerations: Problem solving and intelligence. In H. A. Rowe, *Problem solving and intelligence* (pp. 1–35). Hillsdale, NJ: Lawrence Erlbaum Associates.

Rudel, R. G. (1985). The definition of dyslexia: language and motor deficits. In F. H. Duffy & N. Geschwind (Eds.), *Dyslexia: A neuroscientific approach to clinical evaluation* (pp. 33–54). Boston, MA: Little, Brown.

Rumsey, J. M., & Hamburger, S. D. (1990). Neuropsychological divergence of high-level autism and severe dyslexia. *Journal of Autism and Developmental Disorders, 20*, 155–168.

Rutter, M., & Schopler, E. (1987). Autism and pervasive developmental disorders: Concepts and diagnostic issues. *Journal of Autism and Developmental Disorders, 17*, 159–186.

Schiff, W., & Foulke E. (Eds.). (1982). *Tactual perception: A sourcebook*. New York: Cambridge University Press.

Scholl, H. M. (1981). Language disorders related to learning disabilities. In J. Gottlieb & S. Strichart (Eds.), *Developmental theory and research in learning disabilities* (pp. 130–168). Baltimore, MD: University Park Press.

Schwartz, R. (1988). Early action word acquisition in normal and language-impaired children. *Applied Psycholinguistics, 9*, 111–122.

Schwartz, R., Leonard, L., Messick, C., & Chapman, K. (1987). The acquisition of object names in children with specific language impairment: Action context and word extension. *Applied Psycholinguistics, 8*, 233–244.

Scruggs, T. E. (1988). Nature of learning disabilities. In K. A. Kovale (Ed.), *Learning disabilities: State of the art and practice* (pp. 22–43). Boston: Little, Brown.

Segalowitz, S. J. (1980). Piaget's Achilles' heel: a safe soft spot? *Human Development, 23*, 137–140.

Sevin, J., Matson, J. L., Coe, D., Love, S. R., Matese, M. J., & Benavidez, D. A. (1995). Empirically derived subtypes of pervasive developmental disorders: A cluster analytic study. *Journal of Autism and Developmental Disorders, 25*, 561–578.

Sherrington, C. S. (1951). *Man on his nature*. Cambridge, England: Cambridge University Press.

Shriberg, L. D., Aram, D., & Kwiatkowski, J. (1997a). Developmental apraxia of speech: I. Descriptive and theoretical perspectives. *Journal of Speech, Language and Hearing Research, 40*(2), 273–285.

Shriberg, L .D., Aram, D., & Kwiatkowski, J. (1997b). Developmental apraxia of speech: III. A subtype marked by inappropriate stress. *Journal of Speech, Language and Hearing Research, 40*(2), 313–337.

Sigman, M., Ungerer, J., Mundy, P., & Sherman, T. (1987). Cognition in autistic children. In D. J. Cohen & A. M. Donnellan (Eds.), *Handbook of autism and pervasive developmental disorders* (pp. 85–102). Silver Spring, MD: V. H. Winston.

Skinner, B. F. (1957). *Verbal behavior*. New York: Appleton-Century-Crofts.

Slackman, E. (1985). *The effect of event structure on young children's ability to learn an unfamiliar event*. Unpublished doctoral dissertation, City University of New York, New York City.

Slobin, D. (Ed.). (1985). *The cross-linguistic study of language acquisition*. Hillsdale, NJ: Lawrence Erlbaum Associates.

Smiley, P., & Huttenlocher, J. (1995). Conceptual development and the child's early words for events, objects and persons. In M. Tomasello & W. Merriman (Eds.), *Beyond the names for things: Young children's acquisition of verbs* (pp. 21–61). Hillsdale, NJ: Lawrence Erlbaum Associates.

Smith, H., & Bryson, C. (1994). Imitation and action in autism: A critical Review. *Psychological Bulletin, 116*, 259–273,

Snijders, J. T. (1977). *Snijders-Oomen Nichtverbale Intelligenztestreihe: S.O.N.* [Snijders-Oomen nonverbal intelligence test series: S.O.N.]. Groningen: Wolters-Noordhoff.

Stark, R., & Tallal, P. (1981a). Perceptual and motor deficits in language-impaired children. In R. Keith (Ed.), *Central auditory and language disorders in children* (pp. 121–144). Houston, TX: College Hill Press.

Stark, R., & Tallal, P. (1981b). Selection of children with specific language deficits. *Journal of Speech and Hearing Disorders, 46*, 114–122.

Stark, R., & Tallal, P. (1988). *Language, speech and reading disorders in children: Neuropsychological Studies.* Boston, MA: Little, Brown.

Sternberg, L., McNerney, C., & Pegnatore, L. (1985). Developing co-active imitative behaviors with profoundly mentally handicapped children. *Education and Training of the Mentally Retarded, 20,* 260–267.

Stockman, I. (1991, October). *Lexical biases in dynamic and static locative expressions.* Boston University Conference on Language and Language Development, Boston, MA.

Stockman, I. (1992). Another look at semantic relational categories and language impairment. *Journal of Communication Disorders, 25,* 175–200.

Stockman, I., & Vaughn-Cooke, F. (1992). Lexical elaboration in children's locative action constructions. *Child Development, 63,* 1104–1125.

Stone, R. K., May, J. E., Alvarez, W. F., & Ellman, G. (1989). Prevalence of dyskinesia and related movement disorders in a developmentally disabled population. *Journal of Mental Deficiency, 33,* 41–53.

Streri, A., & Pecheux, M.-G. (1986). Tactual habituation and discrimination form in infancy: A comparison with vision. *Child Development, 57,* 100–104.

Stuart, R. (1996). *The design of virtual environments.* New York: McGraw-Hill.

Sweeney, L. (1996, November). *Augmented sensory input in managing pervasive developmental disorders.* Annual meeting of the American Speech Language Hearing Association, Seattle, Washington.

Sweeney, L. A., & Levine, M. (1998, July). *Cognitive, language and behavioral outcomes following guided tactual interaction intervention.* Poster session presented at the 15th biennial meetings of the International Society for the Study of Behavioural Development (ISSBD), Berne, Switzerland.

Swisher, L, Plante, E., & Lowell, S. (1994). Nonlinguistic deficits of children with language disorders complicate the interpretation of their nonverbal IQ scores. *Language, Speech and Hearing Services in Schools, 25,* 235–240.

Tager-Flusberg, H. (1994). Dissociation in form and function in the acquisition of language by autistic children. In H. Tager-Flusberg (Ed.), *Constraints on language acquisition: Studies of atypical children* (pp. 175–194). Hillsdale, NJ: Lawrence Erlbaum Associates.

Tallal, P., & Merzenich, M. (1996, November). *New treatments for language-impaired children: Integrating basic and clinical research.* Annual meeting of the American Speech Language Hearing Association, Seattle, Washington.

Tallal, P., Miller, S. L., Bedi, G., Byma, G., Wang, X., Nagarajan, S. S., Schreiner, C., Jenkins, W. M., & Merzenich, M. M. (1996). Language comprehension in language-learning impaired children improved with acoustically modified speech. *Science, 271,* 81–84.

Tallal, P., & Piercy, M. (1973). Developmental aphasia: Impaired rate of nonverbal processing as a function of sensory modality. *Neuropsychologia, 11,* 389–398.

Tallal, P., Stark, R., Kallman, C., & Mellits, D. (1981). A re-examination of some nonverbal perceptual abilities of language-impaired and normal children as a function of age and sensory modality. *Journal of Speech and Hearing Research, 24,* 351–357.

Tallal, P., Stark, R., & Mellits, D. (1985). The relationship between auditory temporal analysis and receptive language development: Evidence from studies of developmental language disorder. *Neuropsychologia, 23,* 527–534.

Taylor, M. M., Lederman, S. J., & Gibson, R. H. (1973). Tactual perception of texture. In E. C. Carterette & M. P. Friedman (Eds.), *Handbook of perception* (Vol. 3, pp. 251–273). New York: Academic Press.

Thal, D., Marchman, V., Stiles, J., Aram, D., Trauner, D., Nass, R., & Bates, E. (1991). Early lexical development in children with focal brain injury. *Brain and Language, 40,* 491–527.

Thelen, E. (1989). Self-organization in developmental processes: Can systems approach work? In M. R. Gunnar & E. Thelen (Eds.), *Systems and development* (Vol. 22, pp. 77–119). The Minnesota Symposia on Child Psychology. Hillsdale, NJ: Lawrence Erlbaum Associates.

Thelen, E. (1995). Motor development: A new synthesis. *American Psychologist, 50*(2), 79–95.

Thelen, E., & Smith, L. (1994). *Dynamic systems approach to the development of cognition and action.* Cambridge, MA: MIT Press.

Thompson, R. A. (1971, July). *A comparison of the perceptual and motor abilities of learning disabled and normal students at ages eleven and twelve.* Unpublished master's thesis, Old Dominion University.

Thorndike, E. L. (1931). *Human learning.* New York/London: The Century.

Tolman, E. C. (1949). *Purposive behavior in animals and men.* Berkeley, CA: University of California Press.

Tomasello, M. (1992). *First verbs.* New York: Cambridge University Press.

Tomasello, M. (1995). Pragmatic contexts for early verb learning. In M. Tomasello & W. Merriman (Eds.), *Beyond the names of things: Young children's acquisition of verbs* (pp. 115–146). Mahwah, NJ: Lawrence Erlbaum Associates.

Tomasello, M., & Kruger, A. C. (1992). Joint attention on actions: Acquiring verbs in ostensive and non-ostensive contexts. *Journal of Child Language, 19*, 1–23.

Tomasello, M., & Merriman, E. (1995). *Beyond names for things: Young children's acquisition of verbs.* Hillsdale, NJ: Lawrence Erlbaum Associates.

Tomblin, B., & Buckwalter, P. (1994). Studies of genetics of specific language impairment. In R. Watkins & M. Rice (Eds.), *Specific language impairments in children* (pp. 17–34). Baltimore, MD: Paul Brookes.

Trares, M., & Stratthoff, S. (1998, July). *Improvement of nonverbal daily interaction in 2 brain-damaged adults following guided interaction intervention: a longitudinal study.* Poster session presented at the 15th biennial meetings of the Society for the Study of Behavioural Development (ISSBD), Berne, Switzerland.

Ulvund, S. E. (1989). *Cognitive development in infancy: A study with emphasis on physical environmental parameters.* Atlantic Highlands, NJ: Humanities Press International.

Vygotskii, L. S. (1962). *Thought and language.* Cambridge, MA: MIT Press.

Walker-Andrews, A., Haviland, J., Huffman, L., & Toci, L. (1994). Brief Report: Preferential looking in intermodal perception by children with autism. *Journal of Autism and Developmental Disorders, 24*, 99–107.

Wallach, G. P., & Libergott, J. W. (1984). Who shall be called "learning disabled": Some new directions. In G. P. Wallach & K. Butler (Eds.), *Language learning disabilities in school age children* (pp. 1–14). Baltimore, MD: Williams & Wilkins.

Waterhouse, L., Fein, D., & Modahl, C. (1996). Neurofunctional mechanisms in autism. *Psychological Review, 103*, 457–489.

Waterson, N. (1971). Child phonology: A prosodic view. *Journal of Linguistics, 7*, 179–211.

Watkins, R. (1994). Grammatical challenges for children with specific language impairment. In R. Watkins & M. Rice (Eds.), *Specific language impairments in children* (pp. 53–68). Baltimore, MD: Brookes

Watkins, R., Rice, M., & Moltz, C. (1993). Verb use by language impaired and normally developing children. *First Language, 13*, 133–143.

Watson, J. B. (1930). *Behaviorism.* New York: W. W. Norton.

Weismer, S. E. (1991). Hypothesis-testing abilities of language impaired children. *Journal of Speech and Hearing Research, 34*, 1329–1338.

Weismer, S. E., & Hesketh, L. J. (1996). Lexical learning by children with specific language impairment: Effects of linguistic input presented at varying speaking rates. *Journal of Speech and Hearing Research, 39*, 177–190.

Wickelgren, W. A. (1967). Exponential decay and independence from irrelevant associations in short-term recognition memory for serial order. *Journal of Experimental Psychology, 73*(2), 165–178.

Wilkinson, L. (1990). *SYSTAT: The system for statistics.* Evanston, IL: SYSTAT, Inc.

Winer, B. J. (1971). *Statistical principles in experimental design* (2nd ed.). New York: McGraw-Hill.

Wingfield, A. (1979). *Human learning and memory.* New York: Harper & Row.

Winitz, H. (1989). Auditory considerations. In N. Creaghead, P. Newman, & W. Secord (Eds.), *Assessment and remediation of articulatory and phonological disorders* (pp. 243–264). Columbus, OH: Merrill.

Withrow, F. (1968). Immediate memory span of deaf and normally hearing children. *Exceptional Children, 35,* 33–41.

Wolff, P. H., Gunnoe, C., & Cohen, C. (1985). Neuromotor maturation and psychological performance: A developmental study. *Developmental Medicine and Child Neurology, 27,* 344–354.

Wolff, P. H., Michel, G. F., Ovrut, M., & Drake, C. (1990). Rate and timing precision of motor coordination in developmental dyslexia. *Developmental Psychology, 26,* 349–359.

Wolfus, B., Moscovitch, M., & Kinsbourne, M. (1980). Subgroups of developmental language impairment. *Brain and Language, 10,* 152–171.

Zero to Three/National Center for Clinical Infants Programs (1994). *Disorders of relating and Communication* (pp. 40–45). Arlington, VA.

Author Index

Subject Index

A

Accommodation, 49-52, 182
Action, xxi, 4, 30, 34/35, 37, 39-41,
  55, 83, 100, 101, 104, 114, 139,
  152, 154, 174, 176/177, 193, 195,
  199, 201, 202, 207, 208, 210, 219,
  226, 227, 229, 232, 235, 236, 241,
  243, 273, 276, 277, 279-284
Anticipation
  see also Learning, 185, 188
Assimilation, 49-52, 115, 116, 123,
  126, 128, 132, 167, 182
Assumption, xiii, xiv, xviii, xxiii,
  xxv, 3-6, 44, 47, 53, 65, 70, 83, 85,
  104, 113, 136, 145, 164, 192, 195,
  197, 230, 231, 234, 248, 250
Attention, 36, 37, 42, 43, 49, 61, 114,
  166, 168, 183-186, 236, 240, 243
  attention deficit, xvii, 1, 33, 278
  attention span, 33/34, 157, 188
Auditory, xiv-xix, xxi, xxv, 6, 7, 9-
  11, 18-20, 22-24, 27, 29, 31, 32, 37,
  57, 69, 77, 141, 146-148, 157, 167,
  168, 171, 172, 178, 183, 189, 196,
  198, 202, 205, 206, 209, 211-213,
  221, 228, 231, 235, 236, 240, 245,
  249, 269-271, 275, 278, 283, 284
  auditory deficit, xvi-xviii, 6
  auditory deprivation, xviii, 19,
    21, 29, 68, 69, 141
  auditory discrimination, 43,
    212, 213
  auditory learning, 274
  auditory training, 271, 279
  deaf, xvi, xviii, 1, 18, 19, 30, 32,
    53, 116, 135, 190, 212, 269, 277,
    285

deafness, xiii, xviii, xxiii, 1, 269,
  274
Autism, 1, 32, 204, 205, 217, 219,
  222, 236, 245, 275
  autistic, xii, xiv, xvii, xx, 33, 36,
    157

B

Blind, 20-22, 29, 46, 47, 55, 58, 135,
  136, 141, 168, 172, 211, 273, 274,
  277, 279
  blindness, xiii, xviii, xxiii, 6, 19,
    21, 47, 210
Body tone, 173, 185, 188
Brain damage, 2, 3, 55, 59, 60, 135,
  147, 148, 153, 161, 162, 166, 171,
  172, 176, 182, 186, 187, 191-195
  head trauma, 154, 168

C

Cause-and-effect, xix, 61, 208, 210,
  214, 221, 223
Cognition, xiv, xv, xvi, xix, xx, 49,
  53, 109, 180, 197, 199, 201, 204,
  208, 223, 249, 250, 270, 273, 277-
  282
  cognitive, xi-xxii, xxiv, 3, 49, 53-
    55, 61-63, 71, 77, 81, 85, 87, 90-
    93, 97, 99, 100, 116, 125, 131,
    133, 139, 141-143, 146, 156, 157,
    164-166, 170, 171, 175, 194, 195,
    198, 203, 205, 215, 216, 224-226,
    231, 232, 234, 239, 240, 244,
    245, 247, 249, 250, 271, 272,
    274, 276, 277, 281, 283, 284